4/6

From Lady Burghclere

AUBREY DE VERE

Walter L.Colls, Ph. Sc.

Aubrey de Vere (Ætat. 20)

AUBREY DE VERE

A MEMOIR

BASED ON HIS UNPUBLISHED DIARIES
AND CORRESPONDENCE

BY

WILFRID WARD

AUTHOR OF 'W. G. WARD AND THE OXFORD MOVEMENT'
'THE LIFE AND TIMES OF CARDINAL WISEMAN'
'PROBLEMS AND PERSONS' ETC.

WITH TWO PHOTOGRAVURE PORTRAITS
AND OTHER ILLUSTRATIONS

SECOND IMPRESSION

LONGMANS, GREEN, AND CO.
39 PATERNOSTER ROW, LONDON
NEW YORK AND BOMBAY
1904

RIGHT HON. GEORGE WYNDHAM, M.P.

CHIEF SECRETARY FOR IRELAND

My dear Wyndham,

In asking to associate your name with this book, I had two persons to consider—Aubrey de Vere and yourself. To you I hoped that a record of the life and thought of an Irishman, who was a devoted patriot, a true poet, a thinker of great imaginative insight, —of one also whose personality was marked by spiritual beauty of the very highest order,—would be, alike from your tastes and your official position, of especial interest.

To Aubrey de Vere I felt that the association of your name with his would have been indeed welcome, had he lived to see the fulfilment, in the ideal you have aimed at in your own work for Ireland, of a dream which he cherished for forty years and more. That an English statesman should arise who should believe in the capacities and future of the Irish race, reverence their traditions, and, while treating them with understanding sympathy, should yet oppose with firmness the extreme courses into which, by imagination or resentment, Irishmen are at times betrayed—this was Aubrey de Vere's constant prayer and hope. He longed for it in 1846 when the sympathy of England for Ireland appeared to him so insufficient. He longed for it in 1886 when, in high quarters, that sympathy seemed to him to have become dangerous from its undiscriminating excess.

Perfect political ideals too often prove impracticable ; and, therefore, if I mention last what you have actually accomplished in grappling with a problem which so greatly exercised de Vere's mind—the Irish land question—I do so to accord it the place of honour. To have in this matter carried forward the poet's ideal—which you shared— to such important practical results, through all the difficulties which this rough world of fact presents, neither flinching from the immense detailed labour which the task involved, nor swerving from the great conception which had inspired your effort, is an achievement which would have called out all the gratitude of Aubrey de Vere's generous and thankful nature.

There still remains the question, which interested him so deeply, of providing university education for the majority of Irishmen. Should we live to see this problem solved, also by your efforts, I shall feel that the association of the name of the philosopher-poet, who for so many years dreamed and wrote of these things, with that of the statesman who should succeed in translating his dreams into facts, will have a singular fitness and complete justification.

Ever yours sincerely,

WILFRID WARD.

LOTUS, DORKING:
May 1904.

PREFACE

WHEN, as Mr. de Vere's literary executor under his will, I examined his papers with a view to publishing some of his prose remains, I found that practically nothing was written of the second volume of Recollections which he had planned. The letters and diaries, however, which he was revising with a view to their possible posthumous publication, at once struck me as in many cases suitable for this purpose, for they deal with matters of general interest, and include some graphic contemporary descriptions of great men. Contemporary letters convey a sense of actuality which Recollections do not always carry. The account (for example) given in 1845, of Alfred Tennyson smoking his pipe and 'crooning his magnificent Elegies' to intimate friends until one in the morning, will be to many more actual, than a retrospect, through glasses coloured by later events, and made when the 'In Memoriam' had long been written, and its author famous. Some of the letters and diaries give, moreover, a picture of daily intercourse with Wordsworth, of whom little was said in the Recollections.

But while such features of interest were probably what led Mr. de Vere himself to contemplate the publication of his letters, the present writer was yet more impressed by the picture they conveyed of their author himself—of a personality which for spiritual beauty, both of mind and of character, and for the completeness in it of the poetic temperament, must, I think, be allowed to be one of very rare interest.

The horror of self-advertisement and the shrinking from publicity which marked Mr. de Vere's character and formed part of its charm, led him deliberately to avoid making his published Recollections in any sense an Autobiography; and they are, so far, as Mr. Gosse says in the letter quoted by me in Chapter X., the play of 'Hamlet,' with 'the character of the Prince of Denmark omitted.'

Yet his personality was one which made a deep impression on those who were intimate with him. 'I have lived among poets a great deal, and have known greater poets than he is, but a more entire poet, one more a poet in his whole mind and temperament, I never knew or met with.' Thus wrote Sara Coleridge, the daughter of Samuel Taylor Coleridge, the intimate friend of Wordsworth and of the Southeys. Cardinal Newman once expressed to a friend an estimate of Aubrey de Vere very similar to Sara Coleridge's, and added that the power of self-expression displayed in his poetry (of parts of which the Cardinal was a great admirer) was not fully adequate to representing the beauty of the poet's mind.

The letters and diaries seem to me largely to supply these deficiencies in the Poems and the Recollections—adding much of self-expression, and throwing fresh light on some of the poems themselves. The present work is, then, in the first place an attempt at the exhibition of a very remarkable mind and character, as displayed in his intercourse and his correspondence with his friends. I have in my incidental selections from Aubrey de Vere's poetry had the same object in view ; and while poems acknowledged to be among his happiest are included among them, my principal aim has been to choose those which best help tő depict the poet himself.

The book is not, however, in the fullest sense a Biography. The limit of time prescribed by Mr. de Vere for its publication has made a full biography impossible. And I have not attempted to collect all his letters. I have drawn mainly on those which he had already collected himself, and was preparing for publication when he died. These supply, however, as I hope, sufficient material for a true picture of the man.

It will be to some readers an attraction, to others the reverse, that, as in the case of his beloved Dante, the poetry and philosophy of Christianity were the most absorbing subject of de Vere's imaginative meditation. The spirit breathed in the pictures of Giotto and Fra Angelico breathes in the letters and poems[1] of Aubrey de Vere. And to minimise this element would be to fail in depicting the central object of his life and thought. Yet, as in the case of his great hero and friend Cardinal Newman, the play of human nature was very graceful and varied in him ; and I have endeavoured in my selection of material to do justice to both sides of his temperament.

I must acknowledge in conclusion the kindness of many who have helped me—first and foremost of Mr. de Vere's niece, Mrs. Vere O'Brien, whose aid has been unfailing, and whose literary judgment, and keen appreciation of her uncle's work, have very greatly assisted me in my task of selection. To others of his relations who have supplied information or

[1] A selection of his religious poems, made by Lady Margaret Domvile, is being prepared for publication by the Catholic Truth Society.

reminiscences I must also express my indebtedness—to Mr. Vere O'Brien, Mrs. Monsell, Miss Agnes Spring Rice, Mrs. de Vere, Miss Ida Taylor, and to Miss Elinor Monsell, whose excellent picture of her great-uncle is reproduced in my book. To Mr. Edmund Gosse, and Miss Smith of Philadelphia, I owe valuable recollections of Aubrey de Vere. To Professor Eliot Norton, Mr. and Mrs. Wilfrid Meynell, Mrs. Coventry Patmore, Mr. Ellis Yarnall, Mr. Walter George Smith, Miss Arnold Forster, Mrs. Navarro, Baron von Hügel, and Mr. Ernest Coleridge, I am indebted for letters. To Mr. Alexander Carlyle, Father Neville, and other representatives of writers whose letters I have been allowed to print, I must also express my thanks, as also to M. l'Abbé L'Héritier, who has kindly allowed me to reproduce his two photographs of Curragh Chase.

I should add that all the extracts from Mr. de Vere's diary, and nearly all his letters here published, are now printed for the first time. I have, however, in a few instances, where my narrative required it, included letters which have already appeared in the Life of Sir William Rowan Hamilton, or in the Correspondence of Sir Henry Taylor.

W. W.

CONTENTS

LIST OF ILLUSTRATIONS

PHOTOGRAVURE PLATES

AUBREY DE VERE

CHAPTER I

EARLY YOUTH

1814–1837

AUBREY DE VERE was born at the family seat of the de Veres, Curragh, in the County of Limerick, on January 10, 1814. This beautiful place, successively during his own long lifetime the property of his grandfather, his father, and his two brothers, was practically his home for eighty-eight years. He lived in his ninth decade in the little room he had occupied as a child in the first decade of his life—looking out on the same spacious deer-park, watching its pleasure grounds develop year by year under his father's loving care, seeing from his window in later days the large stone cross beyond the lake, erected in memory of his dead father and mother and sisters. He read and wrote to the end in the library in which his father had read and written before him. Near his writing-table still hangs the portrait of the last Earl of Oxford, from whose grandfather the family was descended, and derived the name of de Vere.[1] The picture, with its historical associations, was well calculated to minister to the keen sense of the interest

---

[1] Aubrey Vere, second son of the sixteenth Earl of Oxford (born c. 1555), was the direct ancestor of the poet. This Aubrey Vere's daughter Jane married Mr. Henry Hunt of Gosfield, Essex, from whom was descended Sir Vere Hunt, of Curragh (now called Curragh Chase), the grandfather of the subject of this memoir. Aubrey Vere's grandson was the last Earl of Oxford, whose picture is in the library at Curragh.

B

—of the glory—of the past, which characterised the Irish
poet. Few men, perhaps, have ever realised more intensely
than Aubrey de Vere Goethe's lines :—

> Was ich besitze seh' ich wie im Weiten,
> Und was verschwand wird mir zu Wirklichkeiten [1]

This quality threw a special halo round the scenes of his early
life, of which, however, we only know the details supplied
to us in his published ' Recollections.'

Writing to a friend from Curragh as an elderly man—after
an interval of absence—he says ' It is to me haunted ground,
. . . it really seems to me a sort of enchantment. The
present becomes almost nothing—a mere vapour—and the
past becomes so distinct that I recognise the steps of the
departed as well as their voices. The most trivial incidents
rise up before me wherever I go ; and in every room of the
house and every walk of the garden or woods I see again the
old gestures, expressions of face, even accidents of dress
which no one could fancy could have lived in the memory
. . . the old jests are repeated, but with a strange mixture
of pathos and mirth.' His dead father and mother were,
he tells us, his intimate companions to the end, and his
brothers and sisters seemed to him ' once more as in the old
days of childhood and opening youth.' We gain from his
letters an impression not less keen than from Mrs. Craven's
' Récit d'une Sœur ' itself, of devoted family affection, and of
the constant living union of their writer with the beloved dead.

And the man who thus clung to the past, and held communion with the spirits of those who had gone before him—
to whom the past was an undying and unchanging fact—
seemed himself to be ever the same. As a boy he gained
before his time the powers of reflection and imagination
belonging to the maturer youth of a gifted man. And when

---

[1] ' What I possess I see as if afar, and that which has vanished turns to realities
for me.'

the present writer first knew him, as a man of threescore years, he had still the simplicity, the unspoilt keenness of enjoyment, the buoyant hopefulness, the trustfulness, the reverence for all that was great and good, which belong to a youth as yet untouched by the world, whose brightness is undimmed by the disappointments and disillusions of life In a letter written in middle age, he declares that he feels just as he felt at eighteen. And at sixty he appeared to his friends to be still unchanged. He was one of those of whom we are apt to think that they ought never to die.

Aubrey Thomas Hunt—as he was christened—was the third son of Mr. (afterwards Sir) Aubrey Hunt, and the grandson of Sir Vere Hunt of Curragh. The elder Aubrey was, like the younger, a poet—the author of some sonnets which won the appreciation of Wordsworth, and of the dramatic poem 'Mary Tudor.' In 1831, shortly after his accession to the baronetcy, he assumed by royal license the surname of de Vere in place of Hunt. The mother of the younger Aubrey was Miss Mary Spring Rice, a sister of the first Lord Monteagle.[1] Aubrey's two elder brothers, Vere and Stephen, successively inherited the baronetcy, and the younger of the two, who still survives, is a poet of considerable power.

Poeta nascitur. A native of the land of the imaginative Celts, and the son of a poet, his antecedents and surroundings were well suited to foster his inborn poetic temperament. The pleasures of imagination and the love of nature were very keen in him from his earliest years. As a boy of seven he was taken by his father to England, and the impression

[1] Thomas Spring Rice, first Lord Monteagle, sat in Parliament as member for Limerick from 1820 to 1832. He was in that year elected for Cambridge. In 1827 he was named Under-Secretary for State for the Home Department, and was Chancellor of the Exchequer in Lord Melbourne's administration from 1835 to 1839, in which year he was raised to the peerage. He died in 1866. A full-length portrait of Lord Monteagle as Chancellor of the Exchequer, painted by Eddis, hangs in the dining-room at Curragh Chase.

left on him by the beauties of Richmond in the course of a summer residence close to the 'Star and Garter,' was so vivid that its memory remained through life. He recalled especially the sunsets from its terrace and the 'long avenues and solemn groves of Ham House,' which he used to associate with ' a German fairy tale about a witch whose delight was to entice young lovers to her forest, then change them into birds, and hang them in the cages that lined the corridors of her palace prison.' In later life he used every year to visit religiously this scene of early memories.

Returning to Ireland in 1824, the family led a peaceful and regular life at Curragh. Young Aubrey was not sent to school, but read his Latin with a tutor—who, as the poet tells us, speedily pronounced him to be an idiot, and recommended him to cultivate his moral faculties, as his intellectual were non-existent. This opinion, however, underwent some modification as time went on. Nevertheless classics and mathematics evidently failed to arouse the lad's enthusiasm, and a subsequent tutor, Edward Johnstone, who introduced him to the beauties of Wordsworth's 'Vernal Ode,' was the first to tap the vein of the remarkable mental qualities of his pupil. Wordsworth, he tells us, exorcised the 'Byronic sulk' which a month's eager reading of Byron had wrought in him. Shelley, Keats, Landor, and Coleridge were also favourites. He became an enthusiastic and constant student of English poetry. His memory was retentive and his critical appreciation soon showed itself to be of a high order. His letters written at seventeen exhibit indeed a power and habit of analysis very unusual at so early an age. The home atmosphere was congenial to his literary tastes ; and a speech by Canning, Brougham, or Plunkett, or one of Sir Walter Scott's novels, or a work on travel or biography, was generally read to the assembled family in the evening.

The regular life at Curragh had few distractions, and literature appears to have been its chief incident. One event did stand out in his memory—namely the bonfires, which cele-brated Catholic emancipation in 1829. Young Aubrey joined in the national jubilation, climbing to the top of a pillar, on which he stood and waved his hat. Another incident—a yearly one—was the Christmas holiday visit to Adare Manor, the neighbouring home of the Dunravens. Apart from such very occasional distractions, these years were uneventful, and the boy's intensely keen perceptions and active mind were concentrated on nature and on literature. 'No change was desired by us,' he writes, 'and none came. The winds of early spring waved the long masses of daffodils till they made a confused though rapturous splendour in the lake close by, just as they had done the year before. . . . Each spring the blackbird gave us again his rough strong note. . . . Each year we watched the succession of flowers, and if the bluebell or the cowslip came a little before or after its proper time, we felt as much aggrieved as the child who misses the word he is accustomed to in the story heard a hundred times before.'

His occasional moods of intense imaginative pleasure—which in one of his letters he likened to the experiences of an opium-eater—are often visible in these boyish recollections ; and he tells us how his visits to a specially favourite spot—the 'cave walk,'—a deep hollow to which his father cut a path-way through the trees—gave him such joy, as he emerged from the cave into the balmy summer air, that he repeated the process over and over again, and 'felt as if life required nothing more for its satisfaction.'

Another trait which is apparent, and which was most characteristic of all, was his faculty of reverence. To-wards his father, above all, but also towards the men of genius, moral or intellectual, who influenced his life and thought, this feeling was almost unbounded. It was charac-teristic of his intense filial reverence that a single remark from his father transferred his allegiance from Byron to Wordsworth as being the first poet of the age. Wordsworth

became thenceforth his great hero. His readiness to admire
coupled with his acute powers of observation, gave him a
quality which may be described as the opposite to that of the
caricaturist. The caricaturist sees in everything primarily its
grotesque suggestions or associations ; and it is his gift to *see*
the grotesque most accurately, while he exaggerates its proportions. So too with Aubrey de Vere's sense of what was
most opposite to the ludicrous. He was equally removed
from the *nil admirari* of the *blasé* man of the world and from
the indiscriminate enthusiasm of the uneducated. He saw
with extraordinary keenness, and in most instances truly, the
distinctive genius intellectual or spiritual, of those minds
which especially appealed to him ; and he loved to think of
them as ideal embodiments of traits which in fact often
existed imperfectly and with considerable human alloy.

One object of his early admiration was the eminent Irish
Astronomer Royal, Sir William Rowan Hamilton, whose
acquaintance he made as a boy of seventeen, the astronomer
being ten years his senior. The earliest link between them
was Lord Dunraven's eldest son, young Lord Adare, who
knew Hamilton at Trinity College, Dublin. Adare writes to
Hamilton in 1831, describing a conversation with Aubrey de
Vere which had lasted from ten to one in the morning, and
speaks of him as ' very clever and metaphysical,' and as having
' a most beautiful, fine, open, countenance.' In the summer
of that year, the young poet and the astronomer met, and
a lifelong friendship was formed at first sight. De Vere has
thus described Hamilton :

' One's first impression was that he was a great embodied
intellect rather than a human being, Wordsworth wrote of
Coleridge as the " rapt one of the godlike forehead," but it
could not have been more marvellous than Hamilton's. The
moral expression of his countenance corresponded with the
intellectual . . . the nobility of his forehead, which alone
arrested one's attention, imparted a grandeur to a face not

otherwise remarkable. . . . Both at Adare and at Curragh Chase I used to sit up with him in his bedroom until near sunrise while he held such discourse as I suppose was the best compensation I could have had for never hearing that of Coleridge.'

Readers of Hamilton's biography will remember that the Irish astronomer became in these first years of their friendship attached to Aubrey's only surviving sister Ellen—an attachment which, in spite of the intellectual sympathy of Miss de Vere with her brother's friend, was not returned. Between Aubrey and his sister—who was married in 1834 to Mr. Robert O'Brien,[1] fourth son of Sir Edward O'Brien of Dromoland—there was ever the closest intimacy, which was fostered by similarity in talent and tastes : and the friendship with Hamilton, greatly cemented by his admiration for Aubrey's sister, continued unbroken after it became clear that his desire for a closer relationship could not be fulfilled.

It was under the influence of his new friend that Coleridge and Wordsworth fully established their empire over Aubrey de Vere, as in different ways prophets of great spiritual truths for their generation. Of the details of this influence on his life of thought more will be said shortly.

Those were days in which, to every thoughtful young man of a religious temperament, Coleridge especially was the great teacher of wisdom. Carlyle has borne testimony to this fact in his somewhat acrid and critical sketch [2] of the sage of Highgate. 'To the young and ardent mind, instinct with pious nobleness, yet driven to the grim deserts of Radicalism for a faith, his speculations had a charm, much more than literary, a charm almost religious and prophetic.' Highgate was already in the twenties a resort of frequent pilgrimage for

---

[1] The elder brother of Robert O'Brien inherited the Barony of Inchiquin, on the death in 1855 of the last Marquis of Thomond.

[2] In his *Life of John Sterling*.

Maurice and Sterling.   To Highgate repaired Arthur Hallam
in 1830 to sit at the sage's feet, and then told his friends
how

> Around him youths were gathered who did scan
> His countenance so grand, and drank
> The sweet sad tears of wisdom.

Coleridge died in 1834, and Aubrey de Vere never saw him.
But more than one of his friends came in personal contact
with the philosopher.   Hamilton, early in 1831, made a
pilgrimage to the shrine, and intensely eager was Aubrey to
learn the impressions of his friend.   These impressions were
quite equal to all anticipation.

You seem to have been completely satisfied with him
[Aubrey writes to his friend on May 20].   You ought to write a
poem entitled 'Coleridge visited,' and then let me see it.
Were the waters clear enough to let you see the weeds at
the bottom ?   Above all, while you stood on the bank could
you hear the inner voice from beneath the superficial eddies?
You know Tennyson's exquisite line, 'With an inner voice
the river ran.'   I think every great man has this under-current
of thought, peculiarly his own, continually flowing forward
with a grave and perfect harmony ; it is what characterises
him, what separates him from other great men ; it is a certain
tendency of his spirit which is often called his bias, or his
way of seeing things, although in truth a much more profound
principle.

What the boy was like at this time may be seen by reading
a few more extracts from those of his letters which have been
preserved.

A great literary critic—Richard Holt Hutton—used to
say that Aubrey de Vere would influence and help his
generation more by his critical studies of our great poets
than by anything else; for he had in a high degree the
often neglected faculty of analysing in relation to each
master the sources of poetic genius and achievement, and the
aims of the poet.   This habit Hutton always insisted on as the

indispensable preliminary to really accurate criticism in the sense of fault-finding; and it is to be seen already in Aubrey's early letters, written at seventeen and eighteen to his friend Hamilton, in which the distinctive qualities of Wordsworth, Shelley, and Keats, and the budding genius of Tennyson, are discussed.

His lifelong predilection for picturesque and romantic themes—the love of grandeur and of heroism which drew him to the Middle Ages—is apparent in such a letter as the following, written to the same correspondent on June 22, 1832 :—

I confess I do not admire Wordsworth's pedlars and spades and *id genus omne*. It is surely the duty of the poet to turn our thoughts and feelings from the difference of degree to the difference of kind ; from the splendours of rank to the splendours of mind ; from the voluptuousness of wealth to the emotions of the heart ; in a word, from circumstances to that which is ideal ; from that which is without us to that which is within ; from that which is visionary to that which is true— and thus poetry is philosophy ;—from that which is transitory to that which is permanent,—and thus poetry is religious ; but if the difference relates but to things external, I do not understand how the detail of low life is more interesting or poetical than those courtly gauds and barbaric splendours 'that show most bravely by torchlight.' If we agree in considering romantic and chivalrous poetry as inferior to the radiance that glorifies ; still I do not believe that it is easier to strip off the meanness and selfishness of low life from the great qualities of mind and heart, and from the supreme will struggling with difficulties, than it is to strip off the meanness and selfishness of high life. Are there not about equal pleasures and temptations in high and low life ? If then our poetry is to consist in exaggeration, are not the wilder passions and more rapid fluctuations of high life more suitable to poetry ? If, on the other hand, our poetry is to consist in stripping off all impertinent detail, is it not as easy to pull off the robes of the monarch as the 'waggoner's' frock of the peasant ?

Remarkably subtle in a youth of eighteen is the following analysis of the qualities needed by the reader for the appreciation of ideal drama—creative gifts which can hardly be common in an age of 'extended suffrage' in the reading world :—

I do not think that even if an ideal drama were written now it would be read ; we are so sunk in circumstance and habit that nothing can please us otherwise than selfishly, or interest us except through our sympathies. How inestimably superior in this respect are the Greek dramatists, particularly Sophocles, to all modern poets ! I think it requires a peculiar ardour of genius to give an individual interest to a generic character ; and it also requires an exertion of creative power in the reader to appreciate them. In this respect it seems to me that a reader of ideal poetry must differ from a reader of romantic ; instead of submitting his mind passively to impressions of beauty, it must be as thoroughly active as that of the poet himself : for a character which has been *conceived* by the author must also be conceived by the reader, if he would realise those few but radical traits, which have been thrown out to his imagination, or combining power in antithesis to the merely connecting instinct. While perusing this species of poetry, we are continually advancing in an intimate communion with our aspirations, and by an unconscious exercise of our creative energies renewing God's image within us.

Many will think that the boy's criticism on the modern reader of 1832 is far more true of the modern reader of the twentieth century—that the tendency to passive receptivity has increased and the habit of constructive effort has further diminished.

In October of the same year Aubrey went to Trinity College, Dublin. The following letter, written to Hamilton on the eve of going up, shows that the boy was father to the man in the unpracticalness of his view of his coming university course. Academic distinction as a path to success in life had little place in his thoughts. The intense inner life of reflection and the studies and intercourse which fed the flame were far more interesting to him :—

I assure you [he writes] you are very much mistaken if you think that my university preparations can ever be nearly as interesting to me as writing to you, and hearing from you —the last is the greatest pleasure I have. As for my university course, I really care very little about that at present. I should not be much gratified at getting a *few* premiums, and I have been so long engaged in studying English poetry and metaphysics, together with the more advanced classics, that I think the effort and sacrifice of time would not be at all repaid by the remote chance of getting high honours. . . . . I have a particular dislike to almost all the university course. I cannot bear the idea of reading over again ' Tityre tu patulæ ' or ' Jam satis terris.' I hate Juvenal, never could understand Persius, and indeed think very little of Latin poetry. It was an imitative, not a creative, art. People say what a poet Lucretius [would have been] if he had not been an Epicurean ! How could any great man be an Epicurean ? I am not devoid of ambition, I must confess ; but mine has taken another direction. I am extremely anxious at present to bring out a translation of Sophocles, and have just finished my version of the 'Antigone.' Will you let me send you a stanza of the last chorus in the Greek, for I have not made up my mind as to the meaning, and should be very much obliged to you for your assistance ? I was delighted with your last poem, not only for the poetry of it, but also for the spirit in which it was written. I cannot tell you how much obliged to you I should be if you would send me more of your poetry. I think I told you that I constantly read your poems with my Æolian harp in the window ; the unison of sound and song has often brought back scenes before my eyes with strange distinctness.

At Trinity Aubrey, under the influence of Hamilton, seems to have devoted himself with increased zest to the study of metaphysics, Kant and Coleridge being the special objects of his admiration. Benthamite or Coleridgian in those days—as

Mr. Mill has told us—was the alternative description of every thinking youth ; and Coleridge rapidly gained possession of very congenial soil in young Aubrey's mind. We find him asking Hamilton pertinent questions as to Kant's account of the Practical Reason as distinguished both from the Pure Reason and from the Understanding, and suggesting, with the lucidity and directness of an acute boy, and an Irish boy, that the Practical Reason is a 'particular form of mind or a mode of its acting *all together*, and under the influence of practical interests ;' a description which suggests more obviously the theory of Aubrey's later master, John Henry Newman, as to 'implicit reason' and the 'illative sense.'

In June 1834 his friend Adare visited Coleridge at Highgate, and Aubrey and Hamilton eagerly read his impressions of the visit. The philosopher had been ill for three months, and did not in the event live through the year. The general impression he made on Adare was most satisfying : 'such an eye, such animation and acuteness, so piercing,' he wrote. But the conversation was 'rambling.' Coleridge spoke of the Church, and said that religion had much alleviated the hours of pain. He talked, too, of Kant, and lamented that he was not better known. He spoke of his own forthcoming *magnum opus*. But the hand of sickness was on him ; and *disjecta membra* of his conversation, reverently retailed for reverent friends, seemed to make them realise that the great man still lived, but added little to their knowledge of him.

Wordsworth, Keats, and Shelley were much read by Aubrey in these years. Arthur Hallam's 'Remains' and Tennyson's poetry also came under review, and 'Philip van Artevelde' by Henry Taylor, afterwards his intimate friend, but then personally unknown to him, aroused his admiration.

In the long vacation he strove, like other young men, to make the home circle share some of his enthusiasms, especially his admiration for the works of Coleridge. The result of his efforts is given in the following letter, the concluding paragraph of which shows a very clear anticipation of an important point of later controversy between John Stuart Mill and Dr. McCosh.[1]

Curragh : March 24, 1835.

I have been introducing them all to Coleridge's works, and trying to make them like the 'Aids to Reflection,'[2] though not with entire success. Is it not singular that the ladies of the family should in most instances take very kindly to the said 'Aids,' while the men profess to find a great part of the work unintelligible, the rest of no value and practical importance; and the whole indemonstrable, as they say, and therefore worthless as philosophy? I was longing for you to come to my assistance in all my long discussions on the subject with them. Whether we were talking of the 'Aids' or 'The Friend,' the attack was always in this style: 'How is it proved? The speculative reason and moral sense are very fine things, but how do we know that they exist? How do you prove that the first is not Understanding and the last Expediency? for if this is not self-evident it must be proved; and if it can be, and has been disputed, it is not self-evident.' I used then to bring forward in support of first truths the forlorn hope of mathematical axioms—such as $1 + 1 = 2$, but the answer was still the same: 'You are begging the question. How do you prove that even these are not generalised from nature by an inductive process of the understanding?' or at other times 'mathematical axioms are nothing but *definitions*; if 4 means $2 + 2$, it is plain enough that $2 + 2$ makes 4.' Nothing that I could say got over this difficulty with them; and so, if you

[1] Dr. McCosh, Professor of Philosophy at Queen's College, Belfast, in his work *The Intuitions of the Mind* attacked J. S. Mill's theory that the truth of mathematical axioms is established by an induction from experience, their supposed 'necessary' character being due (according to Mill) to inseparable association of ideas. Mill replied to McCosh's argument in his *Examination of Sir William Hamilton's Philosophy*.

[2] He also introduced the book to some of his friends in the gay world and used to tell, with much humour, how one 'gay and fashionable person,' who was staying at Curragh, took it to her room at his suggestion, after breakfast, and brought it down again at luncheon with the remark that 'she had read it, thought it a very pleasant book—found nothing difficult in it.' When de Vere told this story to Hamilton, 'he laughed until he could no longer stand' (*Aubrey de Veres Recollections*, p. 43).

can give me any *demonstration* of some truth of moral or speculative science, or even that such science exists at all, I will go down into the battle again ; but, I confess, I do not see how such proof is possible, or even conceivable—it seems a looking for something to put under your foundation.   If this be so, is it not extraordinary that an individual in denying these truths should be able to deny his own nature?   Coleridge, I remember, gives a religious reason for man's being (as it were) enabled to deny his moral nature : but it seems also possible to deny our Speculative Nature, if we assert, and in perfect sincerity too, that the great first truths in arithmetic are merely abstracted by the Inductive Understanding, and that we only know that $2+2$ will *always* make 4 in the same way as we know that the sun will rise to-morrow.

In the same year (1835) he wrote a characteristic letter to Hamilton on the desecration wrought by the Dean of St. Patrick's in disinterring the remains of Swift and Stella for anatomical examination.   'We can hardly be astonished,' he writes, 'at the downfall of the Church when the venerating and meditative piety which built up the Church, that piety which " looks upon the dust of man with awe," is so far extinct among us as to allow of such things taking place.'

Whately was made Archbishop of Dublin in the early thirties, and a letter from Aubrey to his sister gives a graphic account of his impressions of the great logician :—

So you have been reading Whately's works—they are certainly very clever.   I was at a party at his Grace's last night; it consisted entirely of clergymen, and was amusing beyond measure.   The Archbishop lectured them, generally about practical matters, sometimes about doctrinal, in a style so characterised by originality, rapidity, and fearlessness, that the rest used now and then to stare at each other a little, and always to halt behind in a most lamentable manner.   Now and then some one would oppose him ; upon which the Archbishop would come down upon him in all the pride and power of Logic and Rhetoric, and roll him over as a greyhound rolls over the little dogs in play. He certainly possesses all the inferior faculties in a combination and perfection that is almost miraculous : whether he possesses the higher in any degree is a question which I should be afraid of deciding.

The high spirits and racy fun of the Irish boy are visible in a letter to Hamilton of July 10, 1837, the year in which he left college, in which he mentions incidentally that he has won the prize for a theological discourse,[1] and refers as a matter of course to Holy Orders as his future destination. I extract from it the following passage :—

I think we agreed at the Dargle that our pleasure was not to end with the day, but to revive every now and then in remembrance, besides being often repeated in reality. I can answer for the former part of our agreement. I cannot tell you how often and how pleasantly I have gone over those delightful scenes in imagination. It is very odd that it is not only the views and incidents which were most striking to us at the time that rise up again in memory, but little things of all sorts, which we did not remark at the time. I really think it is but a small proportion of the pleasure derived from such an expedition that we enjoy on the occasion. I would rather pass a whole week in the rain than lose the recollection of that day. Do you remember our dinner at the Waterfall—our chicken bone and glass of wine, our pæans to the torrent, and above all our gradual inebriation, produced, I believe, by the spray and mist, which had as powerful an effect on our spirits as if they had exhaled laughing gas instead of common air ? It was something like the excitement of your old greyhound ' Smoke ' at the river of Abbotstown. Do you know I can hardly look back upon a time of greater enjoyment than those ten days we passed together ? It is very seldom indeed that anything thrown so little back into the distance of imaginative memory affects me in the same sort of way.

Have you been lately at the Provost's beautiful villa

[1] He won the ' first Downes Premium ' for Theological Essay-writing in 1837.

'which the wild ocean breezes blow around'? I wish you would exhort him to build, instead of the unblessed thing which at present surmounts the hill, a Gothic cross, like that of Stourhead, or Waltham, or some of the others given in Britton's 'Antiquities.' You can find an excellent model in an engraving on the wall of our room in Kildare Street, and it could be made large enough to enshrine the present obelisk if it contains any relics, or is for other reasons too sacred to be destroyed. The building should be an oratory in the inside, with windows wonderfully dyed, 25 feet high, and 1½ broad. It should be surmounted by a great banner of episcopal purple—made of silk; or rather (for the sake of quiet and silence) of velvet : and thereupon should be emblazoned in gold the arms of the university. They should be broidered by his daughters working all night, with loud singing and other incantations. The old Bishop of Kildare should bless it and chant the Athanasian Creed over it. . . . . When all this is done, he must send for you and me, and Mr. Butler, and the children of the two Cathedral choirs ; and we will go up and eat strawberries and cream there, while the people think we are indulging in fasting and prayer ; and as soon as I am old enough to be in orders I will go and work false miracles there.[1]

[1] A letter of May 1838 to the same correspondent on Schiller's *Die Ideale* is interesting for a passage about Church discipline as a useful antidote to the subjectivity of an individualist spirituality, in which we may see the seeds of ideas which ultimately brought him to the Church of Rome :—

'*The Idea* is, besides its poetical value, of philosophical interest as illustrative of the state of high German mind. Such a "craving void left aching in the breast" as it describes must, I should suppose, be common in Germany in consequence of the degree in which spirituality exists there without a Church at once to develop, to organise, and to limit it, and to rectify it by that discipline of humility and hope, in the absence of which uncatholic spirituality is always either desponding or presumptuous. In my sonnets called the *Beatific Vision of the Earth* I had an analogous subject in my head, and my design was to show the manner in which Christianity, through its sacramental character (never of course understood where the Sacraments themselves are made light of) confirms to the outward world that Ideal character which otherwise fades with fading youth and secular experiences—confirms it with the advantage besides of stamping upon it the seal of reality.'

CHAPTER II

OXFORD, CAMBRIDGE, AND ROME

1838–1840

THE question of a profession became a practical one for young Aubrey when he left college. His father destined him for the Church, and, as we have seen, the son acquiesced. His own interest in theology and in religion was profound— even passionate. Yet we find his decision for years postponed. The absorption in literature and thought which made him indifferent to academic distinction at Trinity, seems to have made him equally unpractical in the sequel. He formed friendships—some of them very intimate—with the Cambridge friends of his elder brother and of his cousin Stephen Spring Rice—Tennyson, Monckton Milnes, Spedding, Brookfield and Dr. Whewell. He corresponded constantly with his cousin himself, on theology and Christian evidences —as he did also with William Hamilton.

Dr. Whewell urged him to take orders—giving the pregnant argument that a man without a profession wastes half his energies in forming his own groove, while the groove once fixed by a definite calling, all his powers are devoted to doing well the work before him. But for years Aubrey postponed the step. I say 'postponed,' for he refers to it still as possible in the later forties, within a few years of his joining the Church of Rome. In 1840 his friend Dr. John Jebb, nephew of the Bishop of Limerick of that name, and sometime Canon of Hereford, speaks of him in a letter, as on the

C

point of becoming a clergyman. Archdeacon Forster had already offered him a curacy. But nothing came of it. Aubrey refers in one of his own letters to his reluctance to undertake binding engagements. The pecuniary motive was one which would hardly affect his singularly unworldly nature. And I cannot but fancy that the ideal of himself as the poet chanting to his Æolian harp, singing like Wordsworth of inspiring and religious themes, was more congenial to him than the associations connected with the distinctly professional form of teaching religion, which was the alternative desired by his friends.

While his life was largely one of study, the picture of his social side presented by his diaries and correspondence is a singularly attractive one. It reminds the reader of his own description of Mrs. Augustus Craven at Holland House,— who looked 'so thoughtful among the giddy, so saintly among the worldly,' and who yet showed an inborn gift for appreciating and taking part in social life.

His intercourse was familiar, and for some weeks in the year constant, with some of the choicest spirits of the age, including Wordsworth, Carlyle, and Tennyson; and he seems to have had a kind of chemical affinity which attracted and assimilated all that was stimulating in general society, and at the same time remained untouched by the worldliness and pettiness which are found in any large group of human beings. This aspect of his career I reserve for my next chapter—which deals with the period at which the materials for its presentment are most abundant. The time I am now especially considering—from 1838 to 1840—was primarily occupied with the great theme which possessed the most thoughtful of that day—the religious revival which succeeded to the indifferentism of the eighteenth century, and to the irreligious philosophy which the pioneers of the French Revolution had made popular, and its issue had discredited.

Those were indeed years when religious interests were the

inspiring passion of great lives, lived in most widely different
surroundings. Newman, Arnold, Martineau, Maurice are only
a few instances in England alone of a phenomenon equally
visible in France and Germany. And Aubrey came under
the prevailing spell.

There was an interesting exchange of letters between
Aubrey de Vere and Hamilton in the fifties, in which the
latter suggested that there had been some love romance in
his friend's life. De Vere replied that his one romance had
consisted in his religious history, which had culminated in
his joining the Catholic Church. No true record of the man
can be given which does not present as the central interest
of his life this story, as truly the romance of his career as
the story told in the ' Apologia' was the romance of Cardinal
Newman's. Only half of his life can be known by those to
whom the halo of the Romantic movement, the nineteenth-
century Renaissance — too short-lived — of Christianity, is
invisible.

This religious history was largely determined in its
course by his reverence for great and good men, representing
widely different schools of thought. Yet he never suffered
the lessons he learnt from them to clash or to collide.
And none of his intellectual idols were ever shattered. From
boyhood he was a reader and disciple of his great countryman Edmund Burke. Very early Coleridge and Wordsworth
established their empire over his mind, as prophets of the
spiritual movement against Benthamism, radicalism, natural-
istic empiricism, and the false conception of progress formed by
an age which was intoxicated with the conquests of physical
science. Later on he was strongly influenced by F. D.
Maurice, and then he came under the potent sway of Newman.
Later still Rome appealed to him as the realisation of his
ideal of a Church which should keep in safe custody, and
administer according to the needs of man in each generation
the teaching of Christianity—which should preserve the

mysterious and life-giving truths for the spiritual polity, as
the civil constitution in Burke's eyes preserved the fundamental principles of secular order and well being. Yet Burke,
though respectful to the religion of his countrymen, and
appreciative of the ethical type it produced, considered the
theology of Rome to be intellectually effete. Coleridge
regarded Roman Catholics as idolaters. Maurice distrusted
the Newmanites, and detested the Church of Rome. Newman
in turn was the sworn foe of the latitudinarianism of which
Maurice was in practice the prophet. These collisions among
his heroes, however, did not affect de Vere. And to the end,
when Newman had donned the purple of the Roman Church,
Aubrey's pilgrimage to Edgbaston would be followed by a
visit to the grave of Coleridge and to the old home of
Wordsworth. Persisting from the first in reverent worship of
the greatest thoughts in each, he was untouched by their differences, and even by their mutual opposition. Partly perhaps this
signified an uncritical mind. But much more it was owing to
an exclusive sympathy with the deeper speculative thought
in each thinker, and an aloofness from the party contests to
which many of their differences were due. He saw that to
Coleridge the ideal Church was all in all; that to Maurice its
Catholicity was paramount; that the deeper philosophy in
Newman was based on ideas familiar to both the others. He
came by degrees to see in Rome the only existing Catholic
Church which was organically one.

Again, it was for the Church, as he always held, to dispense to the people the Christian symbols. Coleridge had
said : 'The doctrines of Rome are largely symbols of what is
true, but she treats them as idols.' De Vere accepted the
whole of this verdict, but considered Coleridge's 'idol' to be
synonymous with the symbol as popularly presented for the
apprehension of the uneducated.

The clash, the jar of theological conflict was abhorrent
to him. He loved great thoughts which stood beyond the

tangled jungle of controversy. He engaged in argument indeed at times, but he only entered the jungle to disentangle the great ideas from the petty sectarian differences. The Catholic Church, according to his final view of it, rose into an ethos above these quarrels. Her very peremptoriness meant in his eyes the banishment of petty disputes. She held high above contact with earth the spiritual truths taught in common by his earlier prophets, grasping, ' as with the talons of an eagle,' to use his own phrase, those central ideas of Christianity which elsewhere were often imperfectly realised, and which were in constant danger of being alloyed by the maxims and habits of an age which had lost the old reverence for the spiritual. Richard Hutton used to complain that Aubrey de Vere's Catholic Church was not the Roman Catholic Church which actually existed. If there was some truth in this criticism, it was a fresh instance of his power of viewing persons and institutions as the embodiments of the great ideas they inadequately realised. He viewed the Church as identical with the religion of its saints, and with the wisdom embodied in its polity, unalloyed in his imagination by the defects of its members and rulers.

He came in the end to be in England the Catholic poet of that Romantic movement which gave to Germany so many great thinkers and writers, from Stolberg and the Schlegels to La Motte Fouqué, the writer of romance, and Möhler, the theologian ; which gave to France Chateaubriand, De Maistre and their successors ; to Italy Manzoni ; to Spain Balmes and Donoso Cortes. But he reached his position, as I have indicated, by a path of his own. It was, as he saw it, a sunny path, marked out by converging rays of spiritual light. *Horas non numero nisi serenas* might have been the motto of his mental history. There was a spiritual light—in his view an unconscious reflection from the ever-living Church—in certain thoughts of Burke, of Wordsworth, of Coleridge, of Newman. This reflection marked out his onward road ; and

that road he followed. He found in the end that it led
him to Rome. In the solitude of his study, holding converse in the main with intimate intellectual friends, untouched by many of the real difficulties, but also by the
distracting pettinesses of the jarring world of fact, and by
the conflict of inferior and prejudiced minds, he serenely
followed his ideal path, until he found himself at the gates
of the Eternal City. In early days, indeed, Rome was to him
an object of mixed feelings—the home of ambitious priestcraft and of superstition, as well as of much true spirituality.
But these feelings seemed rather to fall off him than to be
overcome, as his inner thought and life moved on, and
Catholicism came in sight as its goal. In his way of regarding Rome, as in other things, the ideal and the beautiful so
filled him, that, much as little stars cease to be visible in
the light of the sun, so his earlier detailed criticisms ceased to
have any practical influence on him—even in cases where
they were still admitted speculatively, as corresponding to
earthly defects in a system which for him so largely realised
a heavenly ideal.

These influences must be here further particularised in the
order in which they affected him.

From his father he inherited conservative and High-Church
views. But while his conservatism was in no sense that of
custom or convention, while he had nothing in common with
the 'two-bottle orthodox,' neither was it simply reactionary—
a revolt from the excesses of the Revolution. It assumed
from the first, under Coleridge's influence, for which his
mind had been probably well prepared by the study of Burke,
a reflective and philosophic form. His starting point was the
realisation of the organic character, of society and of the
deepest social convictions. From Coleridge he learnt to view
religion, and especially Christianity, as the expression of the
universal mind of regenerate man—as something resting on
wider and deeper experiences than belong to the life of one

individual[1]—and as in some inadequate manner the partial reflection of the infinite mind of God.   Sectarianism, the outcome of self-confident private judgment, the attempt of the average individual man to construct a religion by means of his own defective dialectic, appeared to him in the highest degree unphilosophical.   The dialectic indeed of the wisest did not reach those deepest springs of conviction which racial experience and the intuitive reason had implanted in man.   The 'Reason,' in Coleridge's phrase, witnessed to truths which the 'Understanding' could not analyse.   Theological Liberalism, again, in the ordinary sense—the permission of latitude on the ground that all questions of dogma are simply beyond our ken, and that one opinion is as good as another —partook in his eyes of the same fault.   It substituted for the dogmatism of the sectarian not a wider purview, but an attitude of negation—the peace of dogmatic solitude.   Having assigned to dialectic a place which so small a fraction of the reasoning faculty could not sustain, liberalism treated its failures as proof of the incompetence of the reasoning faculty itself.   It therefore regarded as indifferent or beyond human apprehension truths which might well be held firmly by the universal consciousness of a Christian people, and by the Reason of man in its higher sense, though the root of these truths lay deeper in our common nature than any point which the dialectic of the individual could touch.

But an influence partly moral, partly intellectual, which is often inaccurately identified with theological liberalism, did act strongly on de Vere.   F. D. Maurice had learnt from Coleridge a veneration for the Church of England.   But, on the other hand, intercourse with the strenuous and acute minds of his contemporaries at Cambridge, had vividly brought home

---

[1] 'This belief in the collective mind of Christendom,' he writes a few years later, to Coleridge's daughter, 'which supersedes not individual intellectual exertion but private judgment, that is mere isolated exertion . . . was involved in the very idea of the Christian Church.'

to him the fact that men equally and intensely in earnest appear
to differ hopelessly in theological speculation. Benthamism
held men quite as earnest and able as those who accepted the
teaching of Coleridge. To suppose that opinions held with
passionate conviction, and with an insight which genius in
some cases seemed almost to guarantee as the genuine perception of truth, were simple falsehoods, appeared to Maurice
highly paradoxical. His solution was that each man saw a
part-truth; and that opposite convictions must often be
respected and borne with. To our limited minds such convictions appear contradictory; but to a higher mind they would
be seen to be but partial exhibitions from different points
of view of a larger truth which should comprehend and
develop them.

Hence Maurice's quarrel at once with the liberals and
with Rome. 'What sympathy,' wrote Maurice, 'could I
have with the liberal party which ... was ready to tolerate
all opinions in theology only because people could know
nothing about it?'[1] He desired not the triumph of
liberalism, but a truly 'Catholic' Church. He desired,
however, a Catholic Church which should be intellectually
comprehensive; while Rome was avowedly exclusive. But
also he believed that the varieties of opinion he would admit
into the Catholic Church, as he conceived it, were really
partial aspects of truth, witnessing to the power of the human
mind to have some share in a spiritual knowledge which is
above its grasp as a whole. Such varieties were not to him
as to the liberals equally tenable because the subject matter
was simply unknowable. They witnessed by their contradictions only to the immensity of the spiritual world, and to
the partial view of it attainable by the individual human mind.

De Vere was an assiduous reader of Maurice, whose acquaintance he made later on. The view I have indicated
profoundly influenced him, and imparted to his discussions

[1] See Maurice's *Life*, i. p. 183.

of religious subjects a comprehensiveness and candour, a sympathy for opponents, an utterly unsectarian spirit, which would else perhaps have been wanting. For his tenacious attachment to his own early traditions, and his sense of the shallowness of the ordinary liberalism, would not improbably have led to a far more uncompromising conservatism, in the absence of this fine distinction between the liberality which is a principle of progress towards a fuller vision of truth from opposite points, and the liberalism which decries the idea of dogma as superstitious or tyrannical. I may add that his close intercourse with Hamilton unquestionably told very strongly in the direction of recognition of underlying truth in views other than his own.

As the thirties of the past century waxed old, the words and thoughts of Newman and his followers naturally found their way to a mind so deeply thoughtful and religious as that of the Irish poet. And he found a more rigid and conservative principle than his own asserted by the Oxford School. But here again there was a distinction between Newman and the average Tractarian, as there had been between Maurice and the average liberal. Tractarianism was for the bulk of its adherents predominantly reactionary. Liberalism had meant license. The principles of the French Revolution had (they felt) destroyed much that made life beautiful, noble, high-principled. Theological liberalism was leading to a repetition of this bitter experience. 'Back to the Fathers' was therefore their cry. And men strove to live in the past; to bring back to the England of William and Victoria, a Catholic Church as Theodosius had known it. They became uncompromising, severe to opponents, intolerant to free thought. They shunned *a priori* speculation, and clung to history, and precedent and tradition.

Newman was not without a share in this attitude. But to the careful observer it was plain—and later events made it more evident to the world at large—that this uncompromising attitude by no means meant in him the denial of all truth to opinions of which he was practically intolerant. Before the movement began he had in his work on the Arians represented Christianity as the development and fulfilment of scattered half-truths in the old mythologies. Of the two attitudes apparent in the early Christian apologists in respect of the heathen—that which confined itself to breaking the idols, and that which looked in their creed for a worship of the 'unknown God'—he definitely assumed the second. He shunned free speculation on matters theological, not as intrinsically evil or worthless, but as apt to exceed the limits within which the human mind could deal with them successfully,[1] and as being consequently often sceptical in its practical tendency. He shunned its irresponsible indulgence. But he fully admitted the germs of truth in many varieties of earnest thought, even though the fostering of such varieties might be at the time disruptive. In some degree intolerant practically, as in the Hampden case, and in his opposition to the relaxation of tests, he was intellectually comprehensive. The meaning of the apparent paradox—of intolerance towards what might be largely true—became gradually clear. And to its solution De Vere also devoted himself in some letters of very high insight and interest.

The Church of Rome at this time appealed to Aubrey's imagination as a vast organisation embodying in the spiritual order the old imperial ideal of universal dominion. But it was, and long continued to be, in his eyes superstitious, tyrannical, and intellectually depraved by the over-great elaboration of its theological system. He called it a 'giant sect.' Its minute scholastic theology appeared to be an attempt on the part of self-sufficient man to define the mind of an infinite God. Such a theology appeared to be even rationalistic, for the Roman theologian seemed to Aubrey de Vere, as his mediæval precursor seemed to St. Bernard, to be

[1] See the historical note on Liberalism in *Apologia* (Appendix, p. 288).

spanning the gate of Heaven with his own small measuring
tape; to be striving to comprehend in his limited mind the
mind of God Himself. Its very coherence and completeness
was its condemnation, for apparent antinomy is a necessary
consequence of the attempt of the mind to deal with what is
above it.

Such in brief outline were the intellectual and spiritual
influences and thoughts which absorbed him during the years
following his college life.

In 1838-39 he paid three successive visits—to Oxford, to
Cambridge, and to Rome. And these three historic centres
of thought and religion seem to represent and group the
various ideas which had been forming themselves within him.
Oxford, which he visited in December 1838, represented
English Churchmanship with its roots in the past; Cambridge typified breadth of sympathy, love of science and
energy of thought—issuing in the variety of opinion which
Maurice hoped to weld into a new Church Catholic; and
Rome, amid all the corruptions with which De Vere credited
her, brought before his imagination the world-wide religious
polity which should voice the collective religious consciousness
of man.

The Oxford of 1838, indeed, represented at that time the
conservative churchmanship which was most congenial to
Aubrey. The lethargy of the 'High and Dry' was discarded
by the dominant school. More extreme developments had not
yet come. Tract 90 was not yet thought of. Newman,
Keble, and Pusey were still a triumvirate hardly divided in
council.[1] The religion of Andrewes and Laud seemed once
more to live in an even more spiritual form. Here was
Coleridge's ideal making itself realised; and Coleridge and
Wordsworth alike were held in honour.

[1] Yet the seeds of the division which became apparent in 1841 were sown in
the Introduction to Froude's *Remains*, published in 1838. Newman and Keble
here avowed their extreme dislike of the Reformers, while Pusey's attitude was less
hostile.

The fascination of spiritual genius—above all, of the genius of John Henry Newman,—the historical associations of the place, and the intense reverence for the past which marked the Oxford School, took, I think, a deeper hold on de Vere at the time than any feature in either of the other visits—to Cambridge or to Rome.

Cambridge, however, also interested him greatly. He went there in January 1839. The friends he made there appealed to him closely on the intellectual side. Probably his critical faculty, his love of our prose literature and of our great poets, met with a far more congenial response among these men than among the Tractarians. Some of his intimate friends had been educated at Cambridge—as Milnes, Tennyson, and Spedding, men who loved literature as he did himself. His cousin, Stephen Spring Rice, was a member of the well-known ' Apostles'' Club—so nicknamed from its membership of twelve—to which Tennyson, Maurice, and Sterling had given glory. Here all subjects were discussed with absolute freedom, equality being a fundamental rule ; [1] and religious questions were included.

But the prevailing ethos in religious enquiry at Cambridge was in Aubrey's eyes that of the philosopher rather than of the Father of the Church ; of Plato or Aristotle, and not of Ambrose or Augustine. The philosophy indeed was often not as spiritual as that of Plato. The trusted method was that of brilliant and ingenious exchange of ideas. He seems to have missed among the Cambridge group what he had learnt from Coleridge, the sense that the mind of man finds its true *organon* of discovery in such high matters, not by exercising the dialectic of the ' Understanding ' but by searching in the ' Reason ' for the footprints of a higher mind than its own. Such footprints, he held, are

---

[1] 'Within the society,' writes one of its members, ' there is no hierarchy of greatness ; all are friends. Those who have been contemporaries meet again as brothers.'

to be found—for the spirit of man is *naturaliter Christiana*. He wished for more reverent contemplation and less word-fencing and love of paradox than he found among the 'Apostles.' He was, I think, more ready to tolerate an occasional slowness or even dulness of mind, such as Oxford sometimes showed in those whose lives were fashioned by the deep and absorbing love of sacred traditions, than the clever irony of the Cambridge men, who seemed to him rather to adopt bits of Christianity in the spirit of the self-sufficient eclectic, than to strive for the renewal of the empire of revelation over the human heart. They were philosophers — more generally philosophers than the Oxford divines. But patient erudition, and reverent study, and a more active devotion to practical religion seem on the whole to have won the day with the deeply religious mind which came in contact with the two groups of men.

These impressions appear only by degrees in his correspondence, from which I proceed to make some extracts.

Of Newman and Oxford Aubrey had already heard in letters from Monckton Milnes. It was a sign of the times that such a mind as Milnes' caught the current influence of theology. Newman and the Newmanites had greatly impressed him when he visited Oxford by their earnestness and sincerity, and, intellectually, as grasping the idea of a Church polity—the great remedy for the anarchy of individualism. Still the Puseyites seemed to him *doctrinaires*, and deficient in a sense of the practicable. 'They want' (he writes) 'that wonderful combination of firmness and plasticity which distinguished Romanism—*she* never forgot that her foot was on earth though her head was in heaven.'

Of the two Oxford leaders—Pusey and Newman—Milnes sends the following impressions in 1838 :—

A fortnight ago I spent a week at Oxford to my great amusement, and perhaps instruction. I heard Pusey lecture on the mystical interpretation of Scripture—strangely, no

doubt, to the old drily orthodox walls, unintelligibly to
the greater part of his audience, but as seemed to me, in
a noble spirit of imaginative and learned devotion. On one
and the same Sunday I heard Hampden and Newman preach
—the former in the usual Evangelical method (of which I
have no doubt he will become a great light), the latter on the
building of churches, in a manner that a Bishop urging the
people to contribute to the ' Ostian Basilica ' in the time of
Theodosius might have envied and imitated. He is surely
a great man, and I sorrow that my plain judgment of things
as they are, will not permit me to hope for him any fair scope
for realising and formalising his high notions, any field of
action where his cause may be understood and followed. . .

When Aubrey himself reached Oxford in December 1838,
even the undergraduates were filled with the visions which
the great Oxford leader had conjured up in his sermons.
Aubrey's countryman, Archbishop Alexander, has described,
in lines too little known, the dreams which formed the topic
of their conversation in those memorable years :—

> Of forms they talked that rose, as if in joy,
>   Like magic isles from an enchanted foam ;
> They prophesied (no prophet like a boy)
>   Some fairer Oxford and some freer Rome.
>
> An Oxford of a more majestic growth ;
>   A Rome that sheds no blood, and makes no slave ;
> The perfect flower and quintessence of both,
>   More reverent science, faith by far more brave.
>
> Faith should have broader brow and bolder eye,
>   Science sing 'Angelus' at close of day ;
> Faith have more liberal and lucent sky,
>   And science end by learning how to pray.
>
> And ' Hail the hour,' they cried, ' when each high morn,
>   England, at one, shall stand at the Church gate,
> And vesper bells o'er all the land be borne,
>   And Newman mould the Church and Gladstone stamp
>   the State.'

The great man himself—to whom he had a letter of
introduction—called shortly after Aubrey's arrival, and he
has left in his ' Recollections ' a vivid word-picture of Newman

as he then was :—' Early in the evening a singularly graceful figure in cap and gown glided into the room.   The slight form and gracious address might have belonged either to a youthful ascetic of the middle ages, or to a graceful high-bred lady of our own days.   He was pale and thin almost to emaciation, swift of pace, but when not walking intensely still, with a voice sweet and pathetic, and so distinct that you could count each vowel and consonant in every word.   When touching on subjects which interested him much, he used gestures rapid and decisive, though not vehement. . . . As we parted I asked him why the cathedral bells rang so loudly at so late an hour.   " Only some young men keeping themselves warm," he answered.'

The visit to Oxford was immediately followed by the beginning of de Vere's lifelong friendship with Henry Taylor,[1] the author of ' Philip van Artevelde ; ' and the letter to his sister, in which some of his experiences at the University are recorded, gives also a picture of the first impression produced on him by his new acquaintance.   De Vere was staying at the time in Downing Street with his uncle, Lord Limerick, whose manner of speech on things political is conveyed in a few graphic strokes of the pen :—

Downing Street : Christmas Day, 1838.

. . . Lord Limerick is very well, and very much what I remembered him.   He generally keeps one eye shut, which makes the other one flash more fiercely while he abuses Whigs and Radicals of all sorts with a plentiful allowance of oaths. . . .

Oxford delighted me far beyond my expectations.   If I may judge by the kindness with which I was treated, it quite as well deserves to be called a city of courtesy as of learning. Newman is the most monkish-looking man I ever saw—very dignified, very ascetical, and so very humble and gentle in

---

[1] Afterwards Sir Henry Taylor, K.C.M.G.   In Sir Henry Taylor's *Autobiography* (Longmans) many particulars are to be found relative to his friendship with Aubrey de Vere.

manner that it would almost have the air with which the
Jesuits are reproached, if it were not accompanied by an
equally remarkable simplicity. Mr. Palmer, the author of the
'Origines Liturgicæ,' and other works of prodigious learning,
walked about showing me what is best worth knowing with
as much good nature as if I had been an old friend. When
I was going away he gave me a letter to Mr. Rose of Cambridge, now at Rome, and bade me farewell with a 'God bless
you' of primitive heartiness. I only wished I could have
stayed two months instead of two days. They pressed me
very much to return there some time or other, which I hope
to do. Maurice is a good deal known, but not much liked
by the High Churchmen. They say he is too much of a
Platonist, and has come by his orthodox doctrines rather
through *a priori* reasonings, than from either Biblical or
historical conclusions.

I will not attempt a description of those marvellous
chapels of Oxford. You must only imagine the most
exquisite combination of stone cut into lacework, and
enormous windows every single pane of which is blushing
'with blood of queens and kings.' I attended evening
service at Christ Church, and morning at St. Mary's, the
parish church, which Newman belongs to. It is about as
large as an Irish cathedral, and as rich as all of them put
together. Newman's reading is beautiful, a sort of melodious,
plaintive and rather quick half-chaunt. The prayers he says
kneeling on the steps toward the altar, only turning to the
people when he blesses them, as in the versicle 'The Lord be
with you,' 'And with thy spirit.' He looks like a very young
man made old by intense study—his forehead is very high,
but not very broad.

Those High Churchmen are not going to subscribe to the
monument for Cranmer, Ridley, and Latimer. I am sorry
for it, and when I told Mr. Palmer so, he said his feeling was
the same as mine. The day after I came here, I called on
Henry Taylor at the Colonial Office. He is very (I think
remarkably) handsome, and the most *stately* person I ever
saw. He talks very slowly and in a very measured manner.
There is, I confess, something almost formidable in the extreme

statue-like coldness and serenity of his manner. The conversation turned a great deal on Wordsworth, his character and life. Henry Taylor said that there was a great deal about him which at first seemed to indicate want of heart—the quiet manner, for instance, in which he takes misfortunes and bereavements. This, however, he says may be attributed to the extreme comprehensiveness of his nature, and the degree in which his peculiar style of poetry has accustomed him to idealise common life. On this subject H. T. said several things I thought very touching, notwithstanding the calm tone in which they were uttered, about the difference between Ideal and Practical affections.

I must not forget to tell you the news of Southey. Henry Taylor had been talking of him for a considerable time, and telling me that he had felt the death of his wife to a most deplorable degree, notwithstanding the state she had been in for four years. He then added, very quietly, 'he is going to be married.' The lady is his old friend, the poetess Caroline Bowles, who is fifty-three years old, and I believe a very estimable person. The fact is Southey must have some one to make tea for him, and his daughters will soon be all married. Still it is rather unpoetical. To make amends, I will tell you that he has for many years been engaged on a long poem, the longest he has written; and that it is likely to be published some time or other. Taylor is writing a play for the stage in which Dunstan is to figure. Tennyson has been writing a great deal of late, and, as his friends say, is much improved. I passed the evening on Friday with Stephen's friend Spedding,[1] who is a very intellectual and at the same time simple, kind-hearted man, and one not as much given to paradox as most of those Cambridge men are. He read us a long and very beautiful ballad of Tennyson's. On Saturday morning H. Taylor brought me to breakfast at Mr. Rogers', who treated us to the 'pleasures of memory' in the form of a great many good anecdotes and witticisms which, as it struck me, might have seen service. He has most beautiful pictures, and I wish you could see them.

---

[1] James Spedding, the biographer of Bacon.

From Cambridge he writes to his sister on January 8 :—

Cambridge : January 8, 1839.

I like what I have seen of the Apostles, though they are nearly the opposite of the grave and courteous Doctors of Oxford. They are full of 'Irony' and have a manner of playing with Theories and putting Thoughts into a fanciful combination and making them go through evolutions like troops at a review. It is very amusing, though Newman would say that the amusement was sometimes ' not less than profane.'

Did you ever observe an odd sort of personal feeling there is about a Card ? it makes one think of a person almost as much as his picture. I enclose you Newman's, which is also his autograph, and you may imagine he has just called to see you and ask when the baby will be fit to be— confirmed . . .

I saw Henry Taylor again, and sat with him for a long time—he was even more interesting to me than at first, but there really is something a little formidable in the extreme stateliness of his manner. He told me of his new drama, and spoke with great contrition of an abusive article he had once written on Landor for which Southey sent him a great scolding. You can find it, if you like, in the 'Quarterly Review' for 1824. I told him the 'Excursion,' 'Roderick,' and ' Philip von Artevelde ' were the three great poems of the age.

Of de Vere's wanderings in Switzerland and Italy, which began in the following March, he has left a full account in the 'Recollections.' His correspondence with his mother during their course gives the sense of the keenest enjoyment of nature and of the humours of the journey. He reached Rome in April, and it is interesting, in view of his subsequent history, to trace the various impressions, favourable and hostile, made by his first acquaintance with the Eternal City. The following letter is written to his mother immediately after his arrival :—

In perpetual quiet, Oxford I believe is the only city that resembles Rome ; but Oxford has one great advantage to compensate for its comparative smallness, in that extreme cleanliness, and an air of mutual courtesy and self-respect in which Rome is sadly deficient. All the Italian cities are desperately dirty, the necessary consequence of the character of the people, who seem to me both in their virtues and vices to resemble what you might expect from children grown up from six years old to man's estate in the course of a single spring. They are therefore superior to the English in the virtues of meekness and good humour, while they are inferior in the more manly qualities of justice, self-respect, and all the virtues indirectly connected with these. It seems to me a very great mistake to consider the Italians a very romantic people; to me, on the contrary, they appear particularly practical in their tendencies, though with much of imagination, and more of passion, besides.

The interest of the place evidently grew upon him. He became acquainted with Mr. Colyar, the kind friend and *cicerone* of so many English visitors to the city, and his acquaintance with persons and places quickly increased. Again to his mother he writes a little later :—

April : Lent.

. . . Rome is to me far the most interesting place I have ever been at. I am more surprised every day that it is not ten times as full of strangers as it is; for I should have thought that strangers from all parts of the world would have been continually flocking to Rome as a centre of universal interest. There is no refined taste which you cannot gratify here.

. . . The extraordinary number of churches gives Rome a monastic or collegiate character; and the extreme quiet of the streets is in harmony with this appearance. The greater number of those churches are, however, not fine on the outside; but the moment you enter them you are bewildered at the astonishing number of pictures and statues (the accumulation of centuries) with which they are adorned; you will discover something new in each as often as you visit it. Larger churches are often in immediate contact with monasteries, or the houses of the clergy, which extend their immense ranges on each side, the effect being sometimes not so much that of churches dedicated to Saints, as of the palaces in which the Saints actually keep a court, the nave and chancel forming only the presence chamber.

A day or two ago I went all over the College of the 'Propaganda' with Mr. Colyar. It was a strange sight, hall after hall devoted to the study of all languages, by boys of every nation, from China to South America, brought up there as missionaries. The boys are all supported by charity, and seem to be very happy. The library is immense and possesses very valuable MSS. . . . To-day we went up to the roof [of the Lateran Palace], which commands a most extensive view of Rome and one of the most extraordinary I suppose in the world. We looked over the top of an Egyptian obelisk which stands quite close to the Lateran, and beyond it we saw the enormous circle of the Coliseum. In a line with these, but at the opposite side of the city, rises the dome of St. Peter's, which seems to me as if it swelled beyond its usual size every evening as I see the sun setting behind it. Between these great landmarks the whole city lies with all its domes, pillars and ruins; and beyond them a labyrinth of immense red arches and remains of baths and aqueducts; beyond this extends the Campagna, one enormous plain, which looks as if it had been levelled by the ebbing of a deluge or the trampling of innumerable armies; and the whole picture is framed by a long graceful curve of violet-coloured mountains beginning with the Alban Hills, including the Sabine, and ending with Soracte. It is a view that one might look on every day, and never be tired.

He writes again, later in the same month :—

I have been passing my time delightfully here, every day making me acquainted with something new and interesting. It is not only pictures, statues and churches that you have to occupy you at Rome; there is no place in the world in which you meet with society so various and agreeable. Anyone who passes a year at Rome would meet a stranger combination of people worth knowing than he could encounter in ten years anywhere else. In the morning you are thrown in with a German Poet, in the day with an Armenian Patriarch, and at dinner with an English Fashionable. My difficulty is to keep out of society sufficiently to leave me as much time as I want for reading and seeing things. I have become acquainted with a great number of people, amongst others Lord Clifford, Dr. Wiseman, the Welds of Lulworth, the Princess Salmona, on whose marriage Milnes wrote the sonnet, and many others beside, as the Shrewsburys, who are extremely kind to me. Lord Shrewsbury drove me about the other day from monastery to monastery, bringing me all over them from top to bottom, and thus making me acquainted with them as I could not otherwise have been. We began with the great Jesuit establishment which was shown to us by a Father Esmond, a very eloquent man whom I heard preach a series of sermons. There is a remarkable union of grandeur with austerity in these buildings. You pass through galleries of which there seems no end, lighted by windows looking across the cloister over the golden roof of a glowing orange grove; further on you find a library of I suppose 50,000 vols., then a magnificent chapel hung round with pictures illustrating the history of the Order : and at last you are shown the cells, a strange contrast to all this grandeur, little low rooms with a chair, a bed, a shelf for books, and four bare walls. The most interesting part of the building is that which contains the rooms originally occupied by St. Ignatius Loyola. They are now changed into chapels, filled with relics, covered with pictures, or plated over with gold and silver as he left them, except the size and shape. Amongst the relics kept here are some interesting documents that belonged to St. Francis Xavier, and a number of little pictures on religious subjects, worked in coloured thread by the Indians converted by him. Those rooms belonged originally to the house of Ignatius, and round them as a shrine the rest of the convent has gradually been built. I can easily imagine people thus shut up becoming attached to their gardens in a degree that we know nothing of. We met a Jesuit every now and then as we walked round, and I remember being struck by a certain resemblance which they all bore to each other in their expression, particularly in an air of habitual humility and stillness diffused over their countenances, in strange contrast with a certain unsubdued haughtiness about the eyes; not a visionary pride, but as I thought one full of a practical, restless, unsatisfied imperiousness. We are going again to-morrow to see some more convents.

The other day I was present at a very gay scene, the marriage of Lady Mary Talbot to Prince Doria. The bride was looking particularly well and as happy as possible. Immediately after the ceremony, which was performed by Cardinal Giustiniani, the bride and bridegroom drove off to St. Peter's and returned thanks at the shrine, a custom usual here; on their return we sat down to a breakfast at which all the principal Roman families were present, and a few English. There was a chapel beautifully fitted up for the occasion in the Palace, a splendid display of gold plate in a gallery about 150 feet long, a great profusion of flowers, gay dresses and pretty women. . . .

Since then I was at a very different sort of marriage, that of a nun taking the veil. She was very young and very beautiful, and I thought the whole scene most affecting. The nun was very agitated on first coming into the church; she was afterwards quite calm and unembarrassed, though every one was looking at her as she sat alone near the altar in a white ball dress covered with jewels, and her long hair wreathed with pearls. She sat as still as a statue during the whole of a long sermon, in which the preacher represented her future life as a species of marriage, and gave her a great many exhortations as to the peculiar holiness in which she was to pass it. Then a number of prayers were recited by an old Cardinal so blind that he could hardly see his book, rubbing his eyes every moment as if he were weeping, and whose voice was so utterly wasted away with age that I could not understand one word. The nun continued kneeling the whole time, or rather lying against a great pile of cushions placed near the altar. At the end of each prayer a hymn was sung by the other sisters, who sat in a gallery concealed behind a curtain at the extremity of the church. During the music the nun used to smile occasionally and throughout the ceremony continued perfectly serene, though I thought rather absent than attentive, or attentive to her own thoughts more than to what was going on.

At last the old Cardinal put his hand on her head, selected a great tress of her hair and placed it between a pair of scissors. Unfortunately for him the tress was so thick, and his hand so weak, that he could hardly cut through it, and I am sure that some minutes must have passed before he succeeded in dividing it. He then placed it in her hand, and she threw it contemptuously into a basket, as if glad to get rid of all worldly vanities. Two old nuns, dressed in black, then came up with scissors, and, looking like the Fates, they cut off the rest of her hair, I thought with a very unnecessary particularity and closeness, and then took away one by one all her jewels and white robes, giving her in exchange for each some part of her conventual attire, until she was entirely covered with black. She herself assisted at this change apparently with the greatest energy, and a sort of joyful alacrity. After this the Cardinal presented her with a number of gifts in succession, a missal, a rosary, &c., and last of all a little figure representing the Infant Saviour; she kissed them each, and then gave it to the nuns who stood behind her. At last the Cardinal addressed her in a loud voice, telling her that her old name was departed from her for ever, and that a new one was given to her, 'Maria Seraphina.' He then pronounced a benediction, and she passed away and disappeared behind the altar. It was certainly one of the most interesting scenes I have ever witnessed.

I must not forget to tell you that I was delighted even beyond my expectations with the 'Miserere' in the Pope's Chapel. I heard it three times; it is, I think, the most exquisite music I ever heard; it is melancholy beyond all that I could have thought it possible to produce in sweet sounds, but at the same time so unearthly that you might fancy it the wailing of angels after their fall. The ceremonies of the Holy Week did not give me so much pleasure as I had expected, with the exception of the benediction from the balcony of St. Peter's. The whole population of Rome, and many from the neighbourhood, were collected within the embrace of the circular colonnades and in the court below ; and it was a grand thing to see the immense multitude bowing down, like a cornfield yielding to the breeze, as the Pope extended his arms in the shape of a cross and pronounced his benediction ' Urbi et Orbi.' I could never reconcile myself, however, to the fans of peacocks' feathers which are waved about wherever the ' Pontifex Maximus ' is carried.

I must not forget to tell you that I have been at some gardens lately as beautiful as those of Armida ; they belong to Prince Doria. I was often reminded by them of Tennyson's ' Recollections of the Arabian Nights,' particularly the line ' high-walled gardens green and old ' ; in some places the ilex trees are cut smooth as a hedge, and so look like great green walls, about forty feet high at each side of long dark alleys with fountains at the end.

The impressions left on Aubrey's mind by the visit to Rome are summed up in a remarkable letter written to his sister in the following month :—

Every day makes me find it more and more difficult to leave this wonderful place whose sources of interest are perfectly inexhaustible. There is a great deal of society which I enjoy very much, though with some degree of self-reproach for allowing any portion of my time to be taken up by it. Eliot Warburton was here for about three weeks, and is now at Naples. Here he gained golden opinions from all sorts of people by his wit and good nature, and there are a number of young ladies who regret him more than the ' cessation of miracles in the heretical communions ' which the Roman Catholics are perpetually throwing in our teeth. I was quite astonished at first by the entire belief in their own miracles which these over-credulous people really possess, and are quite willing to avow in this place, where the superstitions of their own Church are not kept in check as they are amongst us by the neighbourhood of Protestantism. A lady who was trying to convert me the other day mentioned as an incontestable fact the existence of a monk at present in Rome whose devotional raptures constantly lift him four feet from the ground, and keep him there suspended. Another gentleman assures me there is a monk here who sees all your thoughts, and Lord Shrewsbury asserts that all those things are so satisfactory in their proofs that no person of *common judgment* can doubt them. I wish all those persons who think the Roman religion has been changing its character with the advance of knowledge would come here and look around them ; they would soon confess that, though its policy changes as rapidly as Proteus himself, the principles of the Church of Rome are as invariably the same as the principles of pagan Rome, and that there is a very considerable resemblance between them, the ultimate object of each being a Universal Empire.

It is interesting to a person in Rome to observe the manner in which the character of the Power which rests on this spot as a centre is expressed and visibly represented by all the great objects with which you are surrounded. The really important remains of the pagan city are all characteristic ; they all refer to Power, Public Utility, and Universality. First you find the remains of roads perfectly straight, paved with rocks that no time can obliterate, and looking as if they were predestined to pierce through all regions, and afford a way for that people which neither respected anything national in others nor desired it for themselves, to pour themselves forth into all lands, ' conquering and to conquer.' Then you find still more stupendous works—enormous aqueducts winding in enormous curves till they are out of sight, and spanning valley and plain with bridges whose arches always vary in height according to the shape of the ground, themselves preserving the same invariable level. These aqueducts immediately suggest the idea of the world's great arteries through which all the tides of glory and wealth were poured into her heart. Then there is the Coliseum—an immense theatre where all creatures were brought from all regions to make sport beneath the eyes of the Roman people. In all these the prominent idea is Universality, as distinguished from Nationality—an actual centre and an imaginary circumference. In addition to these you find triumphal arches, that shape invented by the Romans as if to give to Form the

indestructibility of Matter itself; and triumphal pillars en-
circled with basreliefs which wind round and round, gradually
ascending as if aspiring to climb the ascent of Heaven itself.
These are the really important and characteristic Roman
ruins, and we find them all reflected in the universal preten-
sions, the anti-national tendencies, and unbounded ambition
of the Roman Church in its Papal character.

But you find equally strongly a Greek element in the
religion of this place. The Greek temples were in fact but
statue-galleries, because the religion of Greece was simply
the worship of the beautiful, and the moment you enter
one of the churches here, you perceive that, so far from
pictures and statues being a luxury, or simply of an orna-
mental character, they are absolutely essential to the religion
of this people such as it now is, viz. a religion as entirely
devoted to Art as Protestantism when left to itself becomes
devoted to merely scientific definitions. This artistic or
Grecian element of Romanism results more I think from
the character of the people than from the priestcraft of the
hierarchy. They might at least plead like Aaron that the
people demanded the golden calf, and that the amount of his
offence was simply that he had not the courage to oppose
them. However this may be, the fact is that all the high-
ways of religion are so beset with saints, martyrs and seraphic
doctors, that to get through them is as hard as to get into a
crowded theatre. Every day has its ceremony, every ceremony its legend, &c., so that one fancies that the Church is
afraid that the moment her 'long story' comes to an end, she
is to be strangled like the wife of the Commander of the Faithful. I am put in mind twenty times a day of the morning
salutation 'Pray sister, if you be not asleep, go on with that
delightful story, &c.' This second characteristic, which belongs
to the Church, not as it is Papal but as it is Southern, is represented in the Greek remains—the old statues and fragments
of temples.

After the great Greek and Roman ruins, you are more
struck by the Egyptian obelisks than anything else. There
is one opposite most of the great basilicas and at the end of
many streets. The first thing you see on entering Rome is

an obelisk.   Here you find the third great element of the Roman Church—Priestcraft, and no one who has not been in Italy
can imagine the extraordinary power and innumerable ramifica-
tions of this priestcraft, with its confessors, its purgatory, in-
dulgences, celibacy and monasteries, planted like the ' legions '
of old in every part of their empire, preserving under all circumstances and at all distances the same discipline and inflexible
obedience.   This Church contrives to stamp its own peculiar
character on everything and everyone its influence can reach.
From the humblest cottage hearth, to the haughtiest council
chamber, it makes its influence felt alike, and that influence
is to weaken every other tie of human life, domestic, social
or national, in order to make the ecclesiastical bond all in all
This priestly power is the most complete and complicated
imperium in imperio that ever was invented ; and might well
excite the envy of the old Egyptian flamens and augurs if
they could come to life again.   One has only to use one's
eyes while walking about Rome to see the visible representa-
tions of these three constituent elements of the Papal Church,
so far as it is distinguished from the Christian : first, the old
Roman element—the instinct of War and Law ; then the
Greek instinct of Art and Enjoyment—and, thirdly, Priestcraft
—the spiritual supremacy of the few and the servile condition
of the many, maintained by keeping the people always
ignorant and always amused.

These three elements, the most important forces of the
old world, are here concentrated, and were originally fused
together by a fourth element stronger than any, viz. Christianity.   And in proportion as Christian faith lost its first
fervour, these heterogeneous elements held in solution by it
began to assert themselves again in their proper and peculiar
characters.   There is one redeeming point about the system,
which is that it inculcates most strongly, though perhaps not
on very pure principles, the great virtue of Humility ; and
has thus preserved among the mass of the people a childlike
spirit of submission, to balance a childlike ignorance and
gregariousness, and more than childish weakness in resisting
impulses and passions.

I am afraid I have tired you with all this long discussion,

but whatever it may be worth as theology, it will enable you to form a very good idea of the physiognomic expression of this city and the manners of the people. You will perhaps think it a waste of time to devote much thought to polemics and politics in this place where pictures and antiquities might alone fill up all one's time, but I assure you it is not so easy to avoid doing so. Nothing can equal the zeal with which people of all sorts—Bishops, Jesuits, laymen, and even ladies—labour for the conversion of the heretics. It is of course very creditable to their sincerity and also (with their opinions) to their charity; but I wish they were not so successful as I fear they have been. I myself know five or six people who have lately been converted, and I fear there are many more likely to follow their example. When they wake from their illusion about a perfect Church they will be as much discomposed as Jacob was when he found that, instead of having married his Rachel, ' behold it was Leah.' There is a novel here which produces sad effects among the more enthusiastic people. It is called 'Geraldine,' and fascinates all the world by its mixture of Romanism and romance. The consequence is that half the young ladies are almost resolved to follow after Perfection in black and white raiment —they positively hunger for a forty days' fast, and aspire after the unknown joys of perpetual celibacy more devoutly than the good man of old desired to speak prose. . . .

Did I tell you that when I first met the Jebbs on the shore at Hastings, he began his salutation by calling out as I approached ' " I hear the roaring of the sea—Oriana"; remember you tell your sister these were the first words I addressed to you.' I went to Tivoli the other day and was enchanted with the Sibyl's Temple, the waterfalls and all the scenery of the place. I have also been to Adrian's villa, and mean to go soon to Frascati. Albano with its beautiful lake I shall see on my way to Naples, but have not yet determined when I go there. Pray write to me soon if you are strong enough, directing here. I need not tell you how anxious I am to hear of you. . . .

Ever your affectionate brother,
AUBREY DE VERE.

Ask Mamma to tell you a story about a Frenchman who admired the 'totality of the streets' at Paris, more than the side flaggings in London.   I never can walk out when the streets are crowded without thinking of it, and preferring practical to abstract philosophy—a Mayor and Alderman to a Pope and Cardinals.

The haunting dread of Roman domination, and yet a certain hidden spell of attraction, appear in some verses written by him at this time.   In one he depicts the following prophecy written in mystic characters on some old obelisk, that such a dominion is yet to come :—

> The Roman boast of universal Power,
> Scandal of crowns and hearths—the Grecian dream
> Of Beauty perfect in a finite mould—
> And sacerdotal Egypt's Priestcraft old—
> Three steps of one vast throne o'er earth supreme
> Shall these be yet.   Mankind, beware that hour.

His more abiding feeling is probably contained in the following sonnet—a deep feeling of the strength of Rome's claim, and yet an equally deep conviction that it was incompatible with the mental freedom which is our birthright :—

> Her beauty, and her venerable grace ;
> Her depth, her breadth, her cross-surmounted height ;
> Her planetary order, grave yet bright ;
> And all her hallowed claims of time and place.
> These call you loudly back to that embrace
> In which the world lay folded through the night
> Of ages, dazzled by no harsher light
> Than the meek halo round her reverend face.
> Nor is it shameful, having erred to mourn ;
> Nor, to a generous nature, hard to bend—
> Why, then, the earth with mad contention rend ?
> Why, boasting freedom, peace and safety scorn ?
> —Good friend, because to those the Truth makes free,
> Sacred as Law itself is lawful Liberty.[1]

[1] See *The Waldenses and other Poems*, p. 192 (Parker, Oxford, and Rivingtons, London ; 1842).

The religious ideals typified in his mind by the three cities—Oxford, Cambridge, and Rome—appear frequently in Aubrey's correspondence; and each contributed something to the conclusions he ultimately reached.

I will here select portions of the very full letters to his cousin Stephen Spring Rice, who represented the comparatively liberal views of Cambridge, written at the beginning of 1842. The correspondence is remarkable as being conducted on a plane of thought far higher than those of the contemporary theological wranglings which Aubrey used to describe as 'the plague of controversy.' Man is considered as placed in the world, eager to know his duty and his destiny, finding around him in a Christian land existing institutions which profess to tell him what he desires to learn. Are the existing Churches antiquated? Do they in some sense represent Divine truth? Can we combine a realisation of the outlook of modern criticism and science with adherence to them? Or must we construct a new Church? Or must we resign ourselves to ignorance of our destiny? These are the questions of lasting interest which occupy the thoughts of the writer. The treatment is throughout philosophical, and, apart from a few incidental applications, is as valuable now as when it was penned.

It is noteworthy that the Church of Rome is hardly considered explicitly in his investigations concerning a reasonable faith. So far as she is alluded to, she is dismissed as 'the giant sect'; as combining 'the spirit of a sect with the institutions of a Church.' On the other hand, underlying, the whole correspondence on de Vere's side is the conception, newly impressed on him by his visit to the Eternal City, of the 'Catholic Church' as a real world-wide polity, to which the Christian revelation had been from the first entrusted. The subsequent story of his mind was the history of this latent presupposition becoming more and more apparent, and of the growing conviction that only the Church which had preserved its union with the Apostolic See realised this indispensable condition. The *imperium* of Rome which had so greatly impressed him in 1839 was ultimately held by him to be co-ordinate with the only ecclesiastical polity which was at once historically the successor of the early Christian Church, and at the same time still world-wide and one. Thus the Church of Rome, from being in the intellectual sphere hardly worthy of notice, became in the end the indispensable foundation of the very line of thought to which she had at first seemed to be external.

At the time, however, of this correspondence his immediate concern was with the Church of his birth. What was the right attitude of a churchman in face on the one hand of the advance of secular knowledge of which Cambridge and the Liberals talked so much, and on the other of the all-dissolving free-thought which Oxford held up *in terrorem* as the necessary result of the modern spirit? Cambridge charged Oxford with identifying Christianity with the culture and superstitions of the fourth century. Oxford retorted that liberalism deified those tendencies of the eighteenth and nineteenth centuries which, if pressed to their logical con-clusions, were fatal to Christianity itself.

Aubrey de Vere accepts as his starting-point the desire of his Cambridge friends to 'hold all that is sound in Church principles,' but at the same time to 'keep themselves free from all conventionalities whether of the fourth or the nine-teenth century.' He desires to maintain Church principles 'in a manner as little as possible opposed to the spirit of the age.'[1] The problem before him is how to effect this—how to strip off the conventionalities of the fourth century without losing some of the substance of Christianity? how to resist the conventionalities of the nineteenth without resisting some of its vital and essential thought? Cambridge solved the difficulty by taking up the standpoint of the nineteenth-century philosopher and adopting what approved

[1] These are his words in a letter to Spring Rice, dated January 27, 1842.

itself from the fourth. Oxford took up the standpoint of
the fourth, and appeared to neglect the nineteenth. De Vere
regarded neither method as satisfactory. But he did see a
solution in their combination.

The Oxford reverence for tradition, though it was accompanied by a certain aloofness from the restless thought of
the modern age, could be the basis of a Christian philosophy,
while the Cambridge attitude could not. Cambridge treated
as the central standpoint the mind of the individual philosopher—which was judicially to appraise the evidence before
it. Oxford, in its concentration on the story of the Church,
became saturated with the sense of the continuous life of
something divine, outside the short-lived individual thinker.
It clung to the idea of an objective revelation, the part-
disclosure of the mind of God. That mind, symbolised by
the Church, was the normal standpoint whence religious
truth should be regarded. Oxford preserved the standpoint
of the Church by a hyper-conservatism in theology. It
regarded the mind of God and not of man as the centre of
theology, and so far was right. But it appeared in its dis-
paragement of later thought to discourage that present
activity of the theological mind which was necessary for the
constant stripping off of human accretions which each age
necessarily brings, when striving to make concrete and
practical the distant and intangible Divine truth. And here
the spirit of Cambridge came to the rescue—adjusting to
modern conditions a theology whose roots were in antiquity.

De Vere, in a racy and thoughtful letter to his Cambridge cousin, dated January 1841, attacks unreservedly the
self-centred philosophy of Cambridge—a spiritual Ptolemaic
system, which regards all things Divine as they appear from
the little planet of our subjective philosophy. He indicates—
though only slightly—the philosophy of development which
should meet the needs of new knowledge, thought and culture. The individualist philosopher makes the Christianity

of successive ages a series of dissolving views painted by
men : the enlightened Christian makes it the ever-growing
manifestation of permanent energising objective principles
which preserve an identical 'physiognomy' in the Christianity of all ages, while the concrete illustrative facts
accepted at each date must largely vary with human culture.

To begin with, he attacks the self-centred attitude and
the tone of philosophic irony current at Cambridge.

If anything (he writes) were to be done in the way of
vindicating Catholic principles, how is it to be done by you
and your set? I mean you Apostles or Apostolic men?
Are you not of Cambridge, out of which no prophet cometh ?
Are you not, one and all, utterly profane and unclean?
Are you not by profession scandalous, and by vocation good
for nothing? Are you not ironical persons? Is not your
creed that everything is everything else ? your practical code
to try everything and hold fast to that which is bad ? Your
devotional system to burn incense to a 'many-sided' kaleidoscope, and raise an altar to your own centre of gravity?
Further, do you not take up Church principles in the way of
private judgment? Are you not Catholic by way of being
original ? In a word, is not your very orthodoxy heterodox,
and your resolve, not to learn something from primitive
tradition, but to steal something—according to that text ' I
will run after him and *take somewhat of him* ' ? If you find
a page or two in the book of the Church that harmonises
with your philosophical reveries, you tear them out ; when
they suit you no more, you roll them up into a tobacco stopper.
Do you plead guilty to any part of this? If not, can you
say so much for your friends ? I distrust you Apostles much,
and the reason is your cynical Impudence, which you think
necessary to balance your Platonic Mysticism. It is reported,
and I partly believe it, that one of your order, a clergyman,
has written a treatise ' de usu et cultu sermonis ironici' in
creeds and prayers.

De Vere requires in the Church, on the contrary, something very serious and practical in its application of Divine

E

truth. The philosopher can easily show that Church dogma cannot solve all questions raised by the speculative intellect in man. But the common-sense conclusion is not to adopt the irony of the intellectualist, not to glory in exhibiting speculative puzzles, but to apply to the needs of man the practical outcome of such knowledge of things Divine as is given us, knowledge which is admittedly inadequate to the Reality, but is yet an important ray of light from an invisible sun. Theology must not, like an intellectual dilettante, take up now one intellectual theory, now another, but must pursue its task of guiding man, holding a consistent path, speaking simply and intelligibly, though such a course involves, like the procedure of any strong man of action—statesman or ruler—a refusal, even at the bidding of able critics, to make constant intellectual experiments in other directions than that of the course it has judged on the whole wisest, in the interests of the most fundamental truths.

It will not do (he writes) for the Cambridge men to take up Highchurchism in the spirit in which they took up Transcendentalism before—'Postquam nos Amaryllis habet, Galatea reliquit.' *Philosophy* is essentially contemplative—it sophisticates itself, and misses its vocation when it becomes practical, except indirectly ; influencing the goings on of the world impalpably as electricity acts upon vegetable growth. It is otherwise with the *Church*. She is at once heavenly and practical ; and as the Ideas of God are creative, and are intelligible to man only as constituting the *Laws* of the Universe, so the Abstractions of the Church must find access to her children in the shape of plain duties and objective doctrines. The Church does not, while on earth, herself know the thousandth part of the truth, or reveal to her sons one thousandth part of what she knows ; but when she speaks she must speak plainly—she is not double-tongued ; her eye is single and her speech simple.

Religion, then, cannot be exhaustively defined by man. It cannot on earth be completely reduced to system, because the full intellectual system corresponding to our faith can only be grasped by the mind of God. But, on the other hand, its gradual analysis must move on fixed principles ; it must be presented to man in certain definite outlines ; it must stand in majestic contrast to the kaleidoscope of human speculation, which is ever moving and suggesting to us a new pattern ; it must be a standing rebuke to subjectivity ; it must ever recall the reality and supremacy of what is deepest in human nature, which is apt in mere philosophic reverie to take its place, not as a fixed and certain ruling fact or law, but as only one of many possible phases of thought.

The desirable *via media* between the over-definition which means narrowness, and the arbitrary eclecticism which involves the risk of losing the essence of Christianity—between the excesses of Oxford or Rome and of Cambridge—is indicated in the following passage from the letter of which a portion has been already quoted :—

Logical definitions and compact systems (he writes) are quite inadmissible in theology. On the other hand, a plain unequivocal use of terms is necessary, and a general ' method ' is most desirable in teaching. This ' method ' is what is called the ' proportion of Faith,' without which religion may be so distorted as to be practically lost. In the spiritual part of religion, definitions are impossible for the same reason as in matters of pure Reason. To define is to limit ; and therefore cannot be applied to the Infinite. So again we can only systematise that of which we see the whole, or, at least, the more important parts of which we can compass and measure. When theologians do this, they take their stand as it were above religion, instead of below it. This is one error of almost all sects ; and of Rome that giant sect which so singularly unites the spirit of a sect with the institutions of a Church. . . .

If religion could be reduced to system, it would be the strongest argument against its Divine origin ; for while the works of man are systematic, the works of God are to us full of paradox. Thus we find the same impossibility in setting forth the limits of a child's obedience as we do that of a

Churchman's—and so in other instances. Casuists may be often puzzled by apparent contradictions in religion; but, practically, converse Truths and converse Duties, so far from destroying, support each other; and to simplify the matter by adopting such principles as suit us, and rejecting the rest, is utterly heretical. This is to cut off one half from our religion, and (as you say) to petrify the other into formalism.

Now let us look at the other side of the question. In every question of vital interest we must have clear thoughts and earnest feelings. Our duties above all must be plain. Such words as 'Faith' 'Mediator,' &c., cannot be defined; but we all know what they mean, and what course of action they prescribe to us. When we cannot explain our thoughts logically, we can by *description* and *illustration*; and, in this way, we are bound to do so. 'If the trumpet give an uncertain sound, who shall arm for the battle?' If we do not set forth our meaning, how can we know whether we have any? For the larger number of thoughts which float about in our brains are mere apparition and nonentities—they are inferences from false premises—inductions from a dream—distinctions between two things neither of which really exist or which belong to different categories—in fact, mere bubbles of fancy, coloured with the lights of the affections and prejudices, connected by some vague association, dissolving or changing every moment, and followed by a new succession more rapid than the generation of insects. Of all the thoughts at this moment going on, in the brains of men, not one in a thousand has anything that answers to it either in pure reason or the truth of things. What, then, if Religion, instead of holding forth a substance of Reality in the midst of this phantom dance, forgets her peculiar and positive function — watches the maniacs till she grows mad, catches the impulse and joins the rout? The history of heretical communions, the manifold and melancholy changes of sects from bad to worse, ought surely to be a warning.

For my part, I can see no hope of permanence except by holding up a fixed standard, such as the Creed. If we thought with the German philosophers that our religion were only the best phase which human thought has yet manifested—that all truth is relative—and all knowledge progressive—that Christianity might be called, like Wordsworth's 'Excursion,' 'part of the second part of a long and laborious poem in three parts,' then of course the less fixed are our words, the less trouble there is in changing them. If, on the other hand, the truth was committed to us once for all, we retain it in the Creed; and the Creed can itself be maintained only by plain and distinct unambiguous statements on the subjects controverted. . . . If it were not possible to be plain without being syllogistical, Christianity could not be a permanent thing in a world of change. So much as to the unambiguous use of words—in this I hope you will agree with me; and we shall not probably quarrel about system. We make religion a mere science or art, when we systematise it logically or rhetorically, making the Christian Faith take the mould and shape of our own brain. Yet this is precisely what everyone will do naturally if left to himself: and the only way to correct this evil tendency is to maintain that ' proportion of faith' which we find established in the Scripture, and preserved in the universal mind of the Church.

We cannot contemplate Christianity as a whole, but we can recognise its main Truths in the Scriptures interpreted by the Creeds: its great principles are still extant like the footsteps of Providence. These we can preserve impartially —we can denounce any novelty inconsistent with these, or calculated to alter the proportion of faith, to violate the analogy of doctrine, and give as it were a new physiognomic expression to Christianity. The more we contemplate Christianity in a catholic spirit, the more we shall find that this 'analogy' has a real existence; we shall daily discover more and more that it has great Principles, such as prove that a vast Spiritual System exists, though it is not for man to discover it. We know by calculation that the earth is round, though we cannot see its circle like that of a star. The Copernican system [in which our position is not central] has its laws as well as the Ptolemaic. Thus, it seems to me, that although we have no right to devise a religious system of our own, yet the only way of preventing every thinking man from falling into this very error is by adhering to a plain, permanent, unequivocal and methodical theology. The Church must remember that God has His system, and that her duty is to keep her face turned toward it; keeping the deposit of faith, and following those great common principles which, like parallel lines, point to one point, though that point is buried in infinity.

In a letter of the following month the controversy between Oxford and Cambridge was renewed. Some of the same lines of thought reappear, but on the whole the controversy in this second letter narrowed its issues. Spring Rice accused the Newmanites of a ' formality ' which was opposed to the life and the practicalness of religion—which substituted rites for deeds, traditionary superstition and over-definition for living thought. De Vere retorted that ' vagueness' was as much the enemy of a *practical* religion as ' formality,' that precision in expression, even though Cambridge might be right in pointing out that precise definitions are not co-extensive with the whole truth, was necessary for such clearness of thought as makes thought practical. Here the influence of Burke, as well as of Newman, was apparent. Superstition and theological definition are regarded by de Vere as the human setting of truths whose full and exact symmetry is above us. Prejudice is to de Vere, as to Burke, an inevitable element in our apprehension of truth if it is to be practical in man with his limited vision. To strip it wholly off is to blur the keen edge of practical perception and concrete motive. Thought is thereby dissipated into vagueness; and in place of grasping strongly one truth—a truth mixed with prejudice if you will—the mind touches loosely a vast number of considerations which it cannot grasp. The mental vision is paralysed by the largeness of the vista thus spread out before it.

This leads back again to the fundamental distinction between the functions of religion and of philosophy. Chris-

tianity gives in the first instance a *practical* view of life and
duty resting on presuppositions largely unanalysed. Philosophy undertakes the slow process of analysis. The former
offers us the tree of life, the latter of knowledge. But knowledge is not given to man on earth in any completeness. And,
again, a merely speculative philosophy which ignores that
deeper view of life and man, which Christianity presupposes
though it does not fully explain it, may (he argues) be simply
erroneous, as starting from first principles less deep than those
which Christianity implies. Philosophy itself must therefore
start from the deeper moral intuitions of the Christian era.

De Vere is careful to admit that revelation attains to no
complete definition on subjects touching the vast range of
thought with which philosophy is concerned. The precision
of revealed truth which suffices for action is no more exhaustive definition than the carpenter's precise practical
knowledge of his trade includes an exhaustive knowledge of
the chemical and mechanical properties of wood. Such
precision relates only to one aspect.

My object is to distinguish between ' definition' and
exactness, between ' system ' and methodical consistency, and
to assert that we must not declare war upon the principle of
precision, without which there can be no orthodoxy, but only
against the use of a false kind of precision, or a palpable
abuse of the right kind. . . . You say that ' Formality'
destroys the *practical* worth of our principles. I reply that
while this result follows from an excess of Formality, the
same consequence proceeds from Vagueness.

If indeed the vagueness, or the contradictions incident to
stages in a philosophical quest, are introduced into practical
religion, if the distinction between speculation on the Whole
and firm grasp of one aspect be neglected, the result is to
reduce religion to a nullity :—

It is not ' petrified ' but dissipated. It vanishes before
our eyes, to the unearthly music of ' harmonious opposites '—it

is polarised into a couple of vapours which lose no time in seeking their native clouds. We watch the Assumption of a great truth into the mystical heaven, and then—take our own way.

Oxford and Cambridge, then, Tractarians and the various shades of scientific thought and liberal theology, each represents a truth, and each witnesses to a danger. In the year 1841 Newmanism had become extreme and was dreaded as ' Popish.' Spring Rice consequently was disposed to advocate combination among his friends against a form of thought which he regarded as leading to tyranny and superstition. To this proposal, however, de Vere would not consent. Joint action among men is natural and useful. But he held that the Church supplied the only party bond which was lawful or desirable. And he had learnt from Maurice to regard her as the society which should include and assimilate different schools of thought, excesses being gradually reduced by healthy individual criticism and not by party action.

This unity in variety is the ideal. Men agreeing in principle but differing in detail, are by their mutually corrective discussions the normal instruments of advancing theological thought. The Church is conceived as avoiding alike the anarchy of philosophies which differ in first principles, and the cramping narrowness of a formal or sectarian interpretation of Christianity. It behoves all men to combine in observing its laws and doctrines, while they contribute their criticisms on individual excesses in theological opinion :—

The principle of ' No party ' [Aubrey continues] is not a mere rule or generalisation. It is a moral and religious duty, strongly opposed to our desires. . . . We wish to choose our companions, sphere of action, and mode of attaining our object. We therefore forget that a principle of combination has already been chosen for us, grounded not on peculiar fancies, but on our Catholic humanity—that each man has already his sphere of duty, and that he is to labour in faith, not by sight, leaving the result to God. If we can withstand this temptation, the result is Unity, Charity and Truth—if we try to win Unity, Charity or Peace, by combinations of our own, and devices of our own, the result will be discord, passion, and error, propagated in an infinite series. If the extreme men of Church principles have in any measure fallen into this snare, we should lament instead of imitating their error. Let those who disagree from them point out their errors ; but let each do so on his own grounds, and his own responsibility. Sympathy is one thing, combination another ; and even as to sympathy, I hope that the moderate Churchmen have many stronger grounds of sympathy connected with principles in which they agree with the Oxford men, than they could possibly have on the ground of their protest against their errors. This course has already been taken by Hook, Poole, Maurice and others, but the value of their several arguments would have been spoiled, if their witness had been sophisticated by a previous collusion, if they had agreed on a plan of attack, and endeavoured artificially to squeeze their own principles into an unnatural and unreal mutual resemblance.

I agree with you when you say that the errors of the Oxford men are the more to be feared because they tend in one direction. Such, however, must be the case always with reflective men—thus, all the errors of the Ultra-Protestants tend to Dissent and Infidelity. All this, however, makes no difference as to the mode of opposing them—the impropriety of forming a party against them.

I still persist in saying that the Tractarians (as they are called) have not passed the limits allowed by our Church, and therefore, that any public authoritative censure is of the nature of Persecution.

In principle, indeed, de Vere avows his agreement with the Oxford leader, John Henry Newman. Practical precision, coupled with the recognition of speculative mystery and paradox in Divine truth, is the true *via media.*

. . . Nature is full of paradoxes—so is the world of Grace. Nature, notwithstanding, is plain, sensible, unambiguous, decisive—so should the Church be.

De Vere sums up his position in the following remarkable passage :—

You say that I distrust the Cambridge Apostles because they connect philosophy with religion. I distrust them, however, quite as much for another cause. It is true that I suspect *their mode* of connecting science and Faith. If Philosophy does not say, like the Baptist, 'I am not He that should come,' 'I am not worthy,' &c., then we have a prophet 'coming in *his own name*,' and as such he will be received— but not by the Church. . . .

But I suspect the Apostles also, on Church matters, because of their *vagueness*. There is a way of holding Principles so as not to hold them. This is a modern discovery, and if it makes progress it will do more harm than utilitarianism itself. What they call 'harmonious opposites,' instead of mutually supporting each other (which is the case wherever there are two genuine converse propositions), neutralise each other. Just consider. Is there such a thing as orthodoxy? Is there such a duty as obedience? Now, abstract principles can neither constitute a ground for faith, nor give motive to action. Applied principles can, but to be applied they must become in a certain sense formal—nay, exclusive. Christ took a body—the Church has visible attributes. Spirit must submit to form, if it is to act on men. Formality can only be predicated in a bad sense when spirit is lost in form, instead of raising and quickening it. In Doctrine and in Ritual alike there must be form. We must believe in the doctrine of the Trinity—how? in any way, or as set forth in the two later Creeds? We must fast—when? in any way, or in particular modes and at stated periods? *What is not done at a definite time will be left undone. What may be believed in any sense will be unbelieved.*

In the meantime a Rubric or article remains 'to witness to a great idea.' Yes, but it witnesses also to a great neglect —to a great sin, and sin and idea are alike forgotten, in spite of its testimony. The office of religion is not fulfilled when she presents us with Ideas. She is to *realise* Ideas in Life and Social Polity ; thus only can she so much as *present* them to the poor and illiterate. Ideas correspond with Laws according to Plato. Philosophers treat of the former, the Church enforces the latter, and without precision she cannot enforce them. Thus the people perish and the Philosopher is presented with another great Idea—that of 'Instability' and 'Destruction.' The very Idea of Religion is lost through this excessive and undiscriminating dislike of System; for, observe the derivation of the word. Is not 'Religo' to *bind* again? and how can you bind except by Doctrines reduced to their orthodox form and Duties explained, applied and enforced. The light that lightens men must not be a magic lantern or Will-o'-the-Wisp—the city set on a hill must not be a castle in the air. St. Paul says the Church is to be listened to and obeyed; a German philosopher would put it into his pipe and smoke it . . . but the agreeable reveries he may thus be supplied with are not the gift which he was meant to enjoy through the Church. I have now put forward the reasons of that distrust which I feel for vague condemnations of formality in religion . . . and they may be summed up thus : Attacks on system are frequently urged in a manner so practically latitudinarian as to deprive Christian Truths of their specific force and substantive reality, and to make Discipline utterly impossible. If the Catholic Church is advocated in such a manner as this, it will be advocated in vain. Some persons, it is true, have a vocation to put forward merely its general Principles or Ideas, but these men ought surely not to quarrel with others, whose task it is to defend those principles logically, or develop them in detail.

Formality, I admit, is often abused by excess; and it is also abused in principle when System and Definition are substituted in place of method and precise specific illustrated and applied statements. When Formality is perverted in either of these two ways, then I think the consequences which you enlarge upon really follow—Petrifaction, Indifference, Infidelity. On this question I go all lengths with you; but to apply your doctrine we must first know, *when* these consequences may be expected; in other words, what is Formality?

That the use by the Church of a definite theological terminology is not formality, but is rather designed to enable us to apprehend the Reality by means of symbols, is maintained in the following very pertinent letter to Hamilton, written a little later :—

The terms of theology are not fanciful or arbitrary. They are symbols, not metaphors, not devised by man, but instituted by God, as all the visible Creation is, to give us the nearest notion we can form of the Invisible. The word 'Father' is symbolically applied to God ; but the man who does apply it and says 'our Father' knows more of God than if he sought a negative Spirituality by rejecting one of the aids given him to a positive Spirituality. The same may be said of the word 'Person,' and all the expressions used by the Scriptures or the Church to set forth its meaning by aid of analogies, founded on the symbolical relations of Nature to its Antitype, each of which points to some portion of the Truth, and all taken together to its centre. When we are children we 'think as a child,' and when we grow up we think as a man, and in each case we do well, for we think to more purpose than we could in any other manner. The child's thoughts are not erroneous ; but inadequate. So are the man's : but if he rejects such or such a view of Divine things because it has been shaped in a *human* mould, he refuses to think as a *man*, rejects something that was accorded him, and can do no more than intensify his gaze at some portion of Divine truth which is not the truth without some correlative thrown aside by him as childish, and which portion, if he examined it closely, would be found to admit a human element as with a peasant's notion of an angel (that of a gentleman with wings), which I believe to be much nearer the truth than the belief that angels and demons have no personal existence, but are only abstractions. Perhaps you will say that you see a certain vein of Scepticism mingled with my Catholicism when I say that I am in favour of Human views of Divine things, though I suspect that the Divine things are really very unlike them. However, you must remember that, according to my philosophy, Nature was made as it has been made on purpose to suggest a language in which, if we see spirit darkly, yet we do see it ; secondly, that I believe Humanity to have been made in the Image of God, and therefore to see Divine things *humanly* is to gaze at them in a mirror of God's making ; thirdly, that these ' Human views ' must be really Human, not fashioned by the eccentric fancies of individuals, and that the Church being the great Representative of renewed and reintegrated Humanity, the views which she has traditionally maintained are what I mean by Human views. The Church, which is, not metaphorically, but symbolically, the mother of us all, is extended over all places and times. Her Tradition excludes the fancies of particular places and times by its rule of Universality, while it unites the rays of intelligence flowing from all places and times. Her mind is therefore as one Human mind, such as Adam's might have been. It is perfect in shape and therefore reflects the truth without distortion. Its Faith is the one great Human-Divine Thought and the mind of Humanity, the Star of the Epiphany suspended in the firmament of Finite Intelligence—which will give us the best light we are capable of receiving, and last till the new heavens and new earth are made.

These thoughts absorbed Aubrey de Vere, and occupied a large space in his early poems. From them I here select one on the value of outward forms, sacramental or commemorative in bringing holy thoughts and cleansing the mind :—

> With solemn forms, benign solicitudes,
> (But each a sacramental type and pledge
> Of grace) the Church inweaves a sheltering nedge
> Around her garden vale in the wild woods ;
> Giving Heaven's calm to Nature's varying moods.
> She plants a cross on every pine-girt ledge,
> A chancel by each river's lilied edge,
> Where'er her Catholic dominion broods.
> Behold how two Infinities are mated,
> The Mighty and the Minute, by the control
> Of Love and Duty, linked with care sublime.
> On earth no spot, no fleeting point of time,
> Within our mind no thought, within our soul
> No feeling doth she leave unconsecrated.

CHAPTER III

RYDAL AND LONDON

1841–1846

DURING the years 1845–46 Aubrey de Vere kept a diary. They were years in which he associated much with his friends. They were years, too, of varied and in part painful interest. They witnessed his early intimacy with Wordsworth, the object of his life-long veneration, and with Tennyson, the poet friend of his later years. They saw the ripening of the great friendship of his life with Henry Taylor, who was now drawn closer to him by his marriage to Aubrey's cousin, Theodosia Alice Spring Rice.[1] These years witnessed, too, the crisis of the Oxford Movement and the conversion of Newman. The time in Ireland was critical. English statesmen had at last become alive to the injustice of refusing to give state aid towards the education of Catholic Irishmen. The Maynooth Grant was proposed and passed. Peel introduced his bill for establishing the Queen's Colleges, in which for the first time Catholics might receive University education on equal terms with their Protestant fellow-countrymen. Again 1846 saw the beginning of the great Irish famine which left an indelible impression on Aubrey de Vere. He and his brother Stephen devoted themselves heart and soul to measures of relief, and I cannot doubt that personal contact with the suffering poor, and the strenuous effort to aid his countrymen at that terrible crisis permanently deepened and strengthened the poet's nature.

[1] The ' Dofo ' of Aubrey's familiar letters.

But perhaps a deeper landmark still in his life-story was the loss in this year (1846) of his dearly loved father. Constant intercourse and similarity of tastes had made the bond between these two a specially close one. The story of the father's illness, which brought out, by the haunting dread of separation, the son's passionate love; the last months of tender intercourse ; the short-lived pang of relief when danger seemed past; the final catastrophe—in the end quite unexpected—these belong to the time at which the diary was kept, and give it a deep personal interest.

The earlier part of the diary, however, is chiefly valuable as giving, with the aid of contemporary correspondence, a very vivid picture of Aubrey's intercourse with his friends. And in this picture Wordsworth naturally claims our first atten tion.

De Vere first came to know the Bard of Rydal during a visit to London in 1841. In that year, too, he first met Sara Coleridge, the object of perhaps the most ideal friendship of his life. She was the daughter of Samuel Taylor Coleridge, and the widow of her cousin, Henry Nelson Coleridge. The following contemporary letter from Aubrey to his sister gives a graphic word-picture of the Bard, and records his first impressions of the woman whose friendship was so much to him while her life lasted :—

London : June 25, 1841.

My dearest Sister,—I found on opening my desk the beginning of a letter to you which ought to have reached you long ago. You must forgive my long delay in finishing the said epistle in consideration of the extreme difficulty one finds in commanding a quarter of an hour in this great Babel.

I have been seeing and hearing such a multitude of things since my arrival here that it is really difficult to know what to tell you about first. You will not quarrel, however, with my giving precedence to Wordsworth. I have been almost as much with him as if I had been living at his house. When he was with the Marshalls [1] they were not only constantly asking me to meet him, but also contrived in the kindest way to find a place for me in their different excursions. I need not say to you who know him that 'familiarity has not bred contempt' or even lessened the respect I had always felt for the old Druid. It is true I have discovered that he wears a coat and not singing robes—that he gets hot and dusty like other people, &c., and in this sense it is impossible to meet anyone without something being taken from the ideal, which is not only without faults, but is also, as you used to say, *denuded of impertinences.* This is necessarily true, but beyond this, Wordsworth is all that an admirer of his writings should expect. He strikes me as the kindest and most simple-hearted old man I know, and I did not think him less sublime for enquiring often after you, and saying that you were not a person to be forgotten. He talks in a manner very peculiar. As for duration, it is from the rising up of the sun to the going down of the same. As for quality, a sort of thinking aloud, a perpetual purring of satisfaction. He murmurs like a tree in the breeze ; as softly and as incessantly ; it seems as natural to him to talk as to breathe. He is by nature audible, as well as visible, and goes on thus uttering his being just as a fountain continues to flow, or a star to shine. In his discourse I was at first principally struck by the extraordinary purity of his language, and the absolute perfection of his sentences ; but by degrees I came to find a great charm in observing the exquisite balance of his mind, and the train of associations in which his thoughts followed each other. He does not put forward thoughts like those of Coleridge which astonished his hearers by their depth or vastness, but you gradually discover that there is a sort of inspiration in the mode in which his thoughts flow out of each other, and connect themselves with outward things. He is the voice and Nature the instrument ; and they always keep in perfect tune. We went together to Windsor, and you may imagine the interest with which I saw the old bard, so

[1] The daughter of Mr. William Marshall, M.P., of Hallsteads, Cumberland, married Thomas Charles Spring Rice, Aubrey de Vere's first cousin, whose sister became the wife of Mr. James Marshall.

thoroughly English in his feelings, looking upon those historical towers as old and grey as himself. We enjoyed all the pictures, wandered in the courts thinking of the Edwards and Harrys, and paced the terraces, looked forth over Eton and that glorious expanse of country beyond, and ended the day by hearing the full Cathedral service chaunted in St. George's Chapel, including the prayer for the 'Knights Companions of the Noble Order of the Garter,' and an anthem unusually fine, in compliment to Wordsworth. Amongst other subjects, we talked frequently on the Church. He is greatly interested about the Oxford Highchurchmen ; but says that he has not yet had time to study their writings sufficiently to come to a conclusion.

I like his wife also very much. She is as sweet-tempered as possible—single-hearted and full of a spirit of enjoyment and desire to make others enjoy themselves. His daughter I have met also—and she enquired much for you. She is just married to a person called Mr. Quillinan. They were in love with each other fifteen years before Wordsworth, who saw them always together, thought it possible. He was much vexed, because the lover is very poor, a holy Roman, and a person whom his family had taken up to console, on occasion of his first wife being burned to death. After some years more of patient waiting, however, [the poet] consented, and the bride seemed very happy. Wordsworth said once to me that he was very glad to have met a person who seemed so 'capable of appreciating his poetry' as I did. I thought the expression would amuse you. His entire simplicity often makes him say those things which are in truth as far removed from vanity as possible. I wish I could send you a list of even the subjects we have talked over, but this is impossible. He is in good spirits about politics—he says he does not wish to be called either Conservative or Reformer, but an 'improver.' He says that Landor is mad, adding that he himself heard him advising a lady not to teach her daughters to read much, but to be careful about their dancing and singing. He calls Mr. Sydney Smith a 'miserable old man.' He calls Miss Wyndham 'his little rose-bud.' He says that ladies ought to be very particular

F

about their dress, considering it as part of the fine arts. He says that he will publish a volume next year. He says that the 'Recluse' has never been written except a few passages—and probably never will. He says that the poem on the 'Individual Mind' consists of fifteen books, having been lately added to and quite perfected. He says also (and you must tell my father this, as I forgot it) that no copies are to be given of the sonnet he sent him, though he is quite at liberty to print it as a motto.

And now I must really say no more about him.

I have become acquainted with another person hardly less interesting to me—Coleridge's daughter Sara; the authoress of the 'Phantasmion.' She is a most singularly beautiful as well as attractive person—with great blue eyes, into which Coleridge looked down till he left there his own lustre, a brow that puts you in mind of the 'rapt one of the Godlike forehead,' and an air of intellect and sweetness the more interesting from being shadowed over with the languor of pain—her health is very indifferent. We have had some delightful conversations about poetry and art, and she seems always glad to talk of her father. I met her brother Derwent at her house yesterday.

Henry Taylor read me his new tragedy, which is finished, except the last act. I think it superior to 'Philip van Artevelde.' I cannot tell you easily how very much I have grown to like as well as admire him.

A little later Aubrey de Vere stayed with Miss Fenwick, Wordsworth's neighbour and dear friend, and saw the bard in his mountain home. De Vere's own tender friendship for Miss Fenwick also laid its foundations at this time. It was, he tells us, a case of 'friendship at first sight.' In 1842 he stayed in Wordsworth's own house—'the greatest honour,' he often declared, of his life. In the same year he published his first substantial volume—'The Waldenses and other Poems.' The longer poems in it are nearly forgotten, but it contained sonnets and lyrics which are still quoted in modern anthologies Even in this early volume the religious element is predominant. The Christian evidences—so often discussed by him with his friend Hamilton in the small hours of the morning—are a favourite theme in its pages. 'To those conversations,' he writes in the dedicatory letter to Hamilton, 'I owe much on many accounts, but I value them chiefly as associated with a friendship which will endure when the book has been forgotten, both by you and by your very affectionate friend—Aubrey de Vere.'

The volume was followed a year later by the 'Search after Proserpine and other Poems,' of which the title-poem won in later years the enthusiastic praise of Walter Savage Landor. Aubrey visited Miss Fenwick again in March 1845. In the lovely Lake country in which she lived were linked together all those associations in which he most delighted. It was connected in his mind not only with friendships which became ever more to him, but with the memory of his own father's early life, some years of which had been spent in the neighbourhood. Wordsworth's presence had gathered together men and women to whom the 'things of the mind' were all in all. In such an atmosphere Aubrey could not but feel that the thinker and the poet had a great—even the greatest—mission to mankind. Miss Fenwick's chief wish for Henry Taylor was that he should quit the Colonial Office, and make poetry the one object of his life. Wordsworth himself said to de Vere, a little later, that Frederick Faber [1] (whose poem 'Sir Launcelot' won his high praise) ought not to be a clergyman, as poetry should claim the whole man. Such views could not but have their effect on de Vere's own thoughts concerning his future, and deter him from any practical step towards realising his father's wish that he should take orders.

The following extracts from the diary enable us to live over again with him those interesting days from March 4 to March 10 :—

[1] Frederick William Faber, the well-known Oxford convert, afterwards Superior of the London Oratory.

March 5.— . . . . Called at Rydal Mount, found the old poet in great force and indignation about the railways—met Mr. Graves,[1] who read me a letter from Sir W. Hamilton. Wordsworth walked back with me to Miss Fenwick's. In the evening we met him again at the house of Mrs. Davy. The talk was of Miss Martineau and Mesmerism. Was introduced to Mrs. Arnold—a dark, eager, enthusiastic, vivid, interesting, and apparently strong-minded, woman. Miss Fenwick gave me an eyeglass which had belonged to Burke.

March 6.—Miss Fenwick and I called on Mrs. Arnold—felt on entering the grounds as if I had been familiar with them. Was struck by Dr. Arnold's portrait. Walked again with Wordsworth, who had slept the preceding night at Miss Fenwick's, as had Mrs. Wordsworth, who looks well, but is molested by her husband's worrying his nerves incessantly. . . . Got back somewhat late for dinner. Mrs. Arnold, her sister and daughter, dined here. In the evening I repeated Tennyson's 'You ask me why?' of which Mr. Wordsworth praised the manly diction.

March 7.—Walked again with Wordsworth, and admired the mountains, which were in some places covered with snow. That above Rydal was patched with spots of snow, and looked as if a flock of wild swans had been wrecked there on their way to the Poet. Wordsworth propounded a new reading of a passage in one of his Odes, on the conclusion of the war, which alteration I resisted successfully. Wordsworth's talk about poetry was deeply interesting. Nearly every one of his poems, he said, was founded on fact. His 'Tintern Abbey' was written at twenty-seven, and almost without correction. Mr. Quillinan dined with us; his conversation was very agreeable. After he went away I had a long chat with Miss Fenwick about Henry Taylor, and found her as anxious as myself that he should shake off his office. Prayers and bed, after reading a little of 'Sir Launcelot.'

March 8.—Had a long talk with Miss Fenwick, and found that, with respect to some sorrows as well as some joys, we

---

[1] The Rev. Robert Perceval Graves, then curate at Windermere, afterwards sub-dean of the Chapel Royal, Dublin, and the biographer of Sir William Rowan Hamilton.

were in singular sympathy. She spoke of her great desire
to see Mr. Wordsworth become a Catholic-minded man, and
pass his evening of life under the shadow of some cathedral.
Heard Mr. Wordsworth say—'I cannot raise myself to this
state of feeling. I feel and lament my own unworthiness,
but the feeling of penitence is lost in sympathy with the
virtues of others, or contemplation of our Saviour's character,
so that I seem to remember my own shortcomings no more.'
We took another walk. He proposed another alteration of
his Ode, with a view to rescue himself from a charge—
possible or impossible—of paganism. I resisted the innova-
tion; and we agreed that poetry ought to put forth great
truths, full-faced and singly, without trying to adjust the
balance between opposite truths. Miss Fenwick and I afterwards chatted alone. She is a woman of a large and noble
heart, with a peculiar spirit of self-sacrifice; and her imagination and feeling alike are as fresh as they could have been
at twenty. Hartley Coleridge dined with us, as did Mr.
Quillinan. They had a quarrel about Liberty before dinner,
Hartley Coleridge affirming that nothing but true religion or
500*l.* per annum would make any man loyal. After dinner
Hartley Coleridge read some poems of Wordsworth's aloud
with enthusiasm. He was much pleased at my remembering
his Sonnet on Adam. Put me in mind of Sir W. Hamilton,
Maurice, and his own father. He wandered about the room,
having as it were no hold of the ground, and supporting himself like a swimmer on extended arms. Every moment he
laid his hand on his round grey head—a strange, interesting,
forlorn being.

March 9.—Went with Miss Fenwick to the church at
Ambleside. Wordsworth stood with head leaning against the
corner, whenever the Psalms or Canticles were read, as if over-
powered or ashamed. I dined at Rydal . . . . he spoke much
about poetry. It was long, he said, before he had ventured
to hope himself a poet; from the beginning he felt his own
poetic vocation to be the expounding of the symbolic Bible
of nature. New thoughts, however deep, he said, were not
the staple of poetry, but old thoughts presented with immortal
freshness, and a kind of inspired felicity of diction. Words, he

said, in poetry were more than the mere garments of thought. Southey deficient in felicity and comprehension, Scott, and indeed all but the highest poets, wanting in truthfulness of poetic logic. He himself had owed his success much to his unwearied labour in perfecting each poem to the utmost. He made another attempt at altering his Ode, but again promised to give it up. I advised him to write on the subject of the logic of poetry, and give us more of his adaptations of Chaucer.

We went to evening prayers. I called on Hartley Coleridge, who was not at home, and walked to the shores of Grasmere lake, drank tea at Rydal Mount, and had a long talk with Miss Fenwick, who told me several instances of Wordsworth's strange vehemence and waywardness of temper. No degree of intimacy, she said, can diminish your reverence for him, though you would discover a small . . . man in the midst of the great and noble man—he has in fact two natures, though the better one prevails. Could not trust himself to write any but severe poetry. Wordsworth said that Sir W. Hamilton was the most remarkable man he had known except Coleridge. Coleridge had at one time taken to brandy drinking. He spoke with contempt of A. B.'s low ambition [to make money by his writing]. He himself, he said, had within the last seven years been making two hundred per annum by his poems.

March 10.—Spent another morning in interesting conversation with Miss Fenwick, and we bade each other adieu after an early dinner.

The end of March found Aubrey de Vere in London, staying, for the most part, at the house of his uncle, Lord Monteagle, in Brook Street. Wordsworth, too, had come up, and the Laureate was to present himself at the Queen's ball— which apparently in the event disappointed his expectations, for eminent recluses are apt to meet with disappointment in their intercourse with the great world. We find Aubrey de Vere associating in London with the Cambridge friends of his cousin Stephen Spring Rice—with Alfred Tennyson and James Spedding, whom Tennyson used to call

' the wisest man I have ever known ; ' with Edward Fitzgerald and Monckton Milnes; also with Dean Milman and Dr. Whewell; with Moxon, Tennyson's publisher ; with Brookfield, ' old Brooks ' of Tennyson's familiar poetic salutation, and with that interesting survival of a past generation, Rogers the poet. Tennyson was then writing his poem on ' The University of Women,' afterwards called the ' Princess,' and bit by bit advancing in the ' Elegies ' which became the ' In Memoriam.'

Wordsworth continues to be the central feature in the diary, and the intercourse which de Vere brought about between the old Laureate and his young successor has special interest. We obtain also from the diary, and from Aubrey's letters, an interesting contemporary picture of Tennyson as a young man—of his genius, so evident even then to the few who had eyes to see ; of his shyness, his ruggedness, his intense sensitiveness and occasional melancholy, and also of the largeness and geniality of his nature, and his wide sympathy with all that is human.

April 5.—Breakfasted tête-à-tête with Milnes, who seemed divided between literature and politics, and incommoded by a partial discovery of the necessity of earnestness for success.

. . . . .

April 17.—I called on Alfred Tennyson, and found him at first much out of spirits. He cheered up soon, and read me some beautiful Elegies, complaining much of some writer in ' Fraser's Magazine ' who had spoken of the ' foolish facility ' of Tennysonian poetry. I went to the House of Commons and heard a good speech from Sir G. Grey—went back to Tennyson, who ' crooned ' out his magnificent Elegies till one in the morning.

April 18.—Sat with Alfred Tennyson, who read MS. poetry to Tom Taylor and me. Walked with him to his lawyer's : came back and listened to the ' University of Women.' Had talk with him on various subjects, and walked with him to Moxon's. As I went away, he said he would willingly bargain for the reputation of Suckling or Lovelace, and alluded to ' the foolish facility of Tennysonian poetry.' Said he was dreadfully cut up by all he had gone through.

April 24.—Drank tea with Mr. Wordsworth at Moxon's. Mr. Wordsworth in great force—had borrowed Mr. Rogers' court dress, and Dr. Lang's sword for the Queen's Ball. Spoke against the Maynooth Grant, and said that what Ireland wanted was protection for life and property, reverence for labour, and the moral improvement of the people, especially in habits of self-respect, and regard for the comforts of life. He was very eloquent, and spoke of Coleridge's ' Celestial forehead and eyes.' A propos to Mr. Faber, he said that a poet should not be a clergyman, and that poetry demanded the whole man. I transmitted to Henry Taylor Moxon's invitation to breakfast.

April 25.—Breakfasted with Mr. Wordsworth at Moxon's. After breakfast Henry Taylor came in very well dressed, and looking very handsome. I was put in mind of my first breakfast with him at Mr. Rogers' . . . walked with A. B. to Lawrence's studio. I was much pleased by his portrait of myself as a poetic conception. Went to the House of Lords, and heard a speech from Lord Lansdowne, in favour of the Maynooth Grant, seated next me two smooth and meek, not unobservant Maynooth Professors. Moxon sent me Tennyson's portrait. Read Mr. Browning's comic poem on ' the Piper ' aloud. Called on Mr. Wordsworth, but did not find him at home—sat for a while by the cradle of the baby.

April 26.—Dined in Grosvenor Street [at the Whewells'], and went in the evening to Mr. Wordsworth. He seemed but indifferently pleased with the Queen's Ball.

April 27.—Went with Wordsworth, his cousin and Moxon to a magnificent Cathedral service.

April 28.—Breakfasted in Grosvenor Street, with Mr. Wordsworth. Wordsworth in great force : highly indignant with the Ancients for representing the nightingale as a sad bird, as well as attributing cowardice to the fox, ferocity to the wolf, &c. ; maintained that they had cruelly wronged Nature. Mentioned that Mr. Campbell had stolen his ' There is a change and I am poor,' of which he repeated the whole. Insisted on seeing Henry Taylor's child—took him in his arms

and kissed him. I asked him for a benediction, and he said
' to see a child in itself implies benediction, but I do not know
what more I can wish him, except that he should be a good
man.' Being asked whether he would wish him to be a Poet,
he replied ' not unless he was a great one.'

April 29.—Went to Spedding's rooms, and found Stephen
Spring Rice, Tennyson, Brookfield and Moxon—all very
jolly.

April 30.—Sat for an hour with Henry Taylor, making
strictures on ' Philip van Artevelde.'

May 4.—Brought Alfred Tennyson, murmuring sore, to
Hampstead, to see Mr. Wordsworth. Mr. W. improved upon
him. Rogers came, and there was an amusing scene in the
garden, Rogers insisting upon Wordsworth's naming a day
to dine with him, and Wordsworth stoutly exhibiting his
mountain lawlessness, stating that he would dine or not as it
happened, or as it suited his convenience, and saying that he
was sure he would find the best accommodation of every sort
at Mr. Rogers', whether Mr. Rogers was in the house or not.
Mr. Rogers at last replied : ' Well, you may as well tell me
at once to go to the Devil ; I can only say that my house, its
master, and everything in it are heartily at your service—
come when you will.'

May 7.—Asked Tennyson to dinner : we dined with
Stephen and A. B. We all made speeches on our health
being drunk, and were merry.

May 9.—Went with Wordsworth to buy spectacles, and
thence to Rogers—found Mrs. Davenport and another lady
with the octogenarian. We went to the Exhibition. Rogers
pointed out the artistic merit of some of the pictures, and
scoffed dreadfully at others. Wordsworth took up the theme
of such pictures as pleased him, and moralised on them.

Returned to tea, and received a letter from my mother.
Alfred Tennyson came in and smoked his pipe. He told us
with pleasure of his dinner with Wordsworth—was pleased
as well as amused by Wordsworth saying to him, ' Come,
brother bard, to dinner,' and taking his arm ; said that he
was ashamed of paying Mr. Wordsworth compliments, but
that he had at last, in the dark, said something about the

pleasure he had had from Mr. Wordsworth's writings, and that the old poet had taken his hand, and replied with some expressions equally kind and complimentary. Tennyson was evidently much pleased with the old man, and glad of having learned to know him.

May 10.—I went to Alfred Tennyson, who read me part of his 'University of Women,' and discussed poetry, denouncing exotics, and saying that a poem should reflect the time and place. Went with him to the British Museum, and with Mr. Hallam's help got to the room of the engravings, and saw a volume of Marc Antonio's prints from Raffaelle.

May 11.—Called on Tennyson. Spent three hours with him and Edward Fitzgerald, trying to persuade him to come to Hither Green. At last he agreed. We passed through Greenwich Park, and he was delighted with the view and pointed out all the rich effects of colour in the landscape. We had a merry dinner and a pleasant talk till 12.30, when we drove away in a fly. I got home after two, and spent a quarter of an hour knocking before I could get in.

The dramatic interest which Aubrey de Vere found in his comparatively short periods of social intercourse with his London acquaintance is visible in the diary. He had, indeed, a temperament the very reverse of that generally associated with the recluse, and probably gained more from a few months spent in London at long intervals, than the average *habitué* of society could attain in the course of years. His power of analysing social scenes and characters is illustrated by the following letter, which, though written a little later, belongs to the phase of his life which I am now describing, and therefore finds here its most suitable place. It was written to his friend Mrs. Edward Villiers, from the house of his uncle, Lord Monteagle, in Brook Street:—

We had a great dinner party here a day or two ago—it included Whewell, Hallam, Macaulay, and Milman, the first three such inordinate talkers by reputation that I was on the watch to see which would put the others down, as some great

stag in our park always puts the others down. Whewell I like
very much—he is a hearty, genial, honest man, with an
enormous physical force of intellect (if the phrase may be
admitted) which beats down all obstacles like the broad brow
of a bull. Macaulay is far from being ill-conditioned ; but
he is rather bluff and good-humoured than genial. His
mind is evidently a very *robust* one—it has also ardour
enough to fuse together into new combinations the mass
of strange and disorderly knowledge with which his great
memory litters him. It has also a self-confidence which
belongs to narrowness, and an utter inappreciation of all
matters which it cannot wield and twist about, but which
greatly increases his energy and apparent force ; but I could
observe in it no trace of originality, depth, breadth, elevation,
subtlety, comprehensiveness, spirituality—in one word, none
of the attributes of greatness. He is however a strong man,
and will do his day's work honestly, before his day is done.
I should think he despises falsehood, and likes, if not Truth,
at least the exhilaration of a hunt after Truth, or the animation of the battle for the cause of Truth.

Aubrey's sensitive, and in some sense fastidious,
temperament was, however, evidently irritated as well as
interested by the ' mighty talkers,' whom he characterises as
' overbearing, and loud, and discourteous.'

It is not [he goes on] that they intentionally violate the
rules of social propriety, but that they do not perceive any
except the most obvious and conventional. They seem to
have come out to make a display, and dash on with much
more eagerness than real self-possession, and with very
ungainly movements of mind. Even for women I think they
have little of reverence or kindliness, and in fact I like the
stiff English manner better. There was a young man there
of the name of Mr. Godley, who, whatever he may really
think of himself, certainly has no superficial vanity, and about
whom, fortunately, nobody makes a stir. I had half an hour's
conversation with him, and heard more of what was worth
remembering, mixed up with simple and cordial feeling, and

delivered in the tone of a gentleman, than from all the rest put together. I leave this in two or three days, and to say the truth am tired. I have still been sitting up very late. There is but one person in London for whom I would do this—but that one lives two miles off, which has occasioned me some long walks home at two o'clock on fine mornings, when I have generally found my fire out and my room very cold. Who is that person—a lady? Certainly, if, as old Coleridge said, every true Poet is inclusively woman, but not the worse man on that account—Alfred Tennyson. . . . He is the most interesting man I ever met except [Henry Taylor], so full of the humanities, so original, and yet so rich in sympathy for all that is natural.

Another group of friends recalled to Aubrey de Vere the interests which visits to Oxford had fostered. His cousins the Calverts—to whom the diary records several visits—were avowedly among the group whom the Oxford Movement had led towards Rome. The religious question was indeed very prominent in different forms, in the year 1845. The Maynooth Grant and the Queen's Colleges were, as I have already noted, first proposed in that year. The Oxford Movement had reached its crisis. Newman's series of 'Lives of the English Saints'—one of the best being 'St. Wilfrid' by Frederick Faber, author of 'Sir Launcelot'—had proved to be its high-water mark. The more moderate members of the party were known to disapprove of the attitude of Newman's intimates at Littlemore. W. G. Ward's 'Ideal of a Christian Church' had been condemned in February. Newman's secession to Rome was known to be coming.

These topics were to the front not only among clerical friends, but at such houses as those of the Gladstones, and the Lytteltons, where ecclesiastical interests were strong.

De Vere's attitude toward Rome was evidently at this time still decidedly hostile. He was sensitive to the sectarian spirit in some of the extreme High Churchmen—to the absence in them of that largeness of sympathy which he so greatly valued.

On the whole, he seems to have found the tender piety of Dr. Pusey, whom he knew personally, the most congenial exhibition of Tractarianism at that time. The diary thus continues :—

May 11.—Went to Margaret Street Chapel. Dr. Pusey, who officiated, was like a saint in tribulation, or one over whom some great calamity was impending.

May 12.—Dined with Mr. Richards[1]—Mr. Newman's conversion was openly spoken of. I saw a great deal of zeal, earnestness and Roman enthusiasm among the party, but nothing of largeness of mind, and fearless love of Truth. My impression was that such men could not appreciate Catholicity as distinguished from Romanism, and that they felt no loyalty to the Church of England. Surely, then, we may look for large defections. This however they denied, saying that Newman's change would not bring others over with him. It seems to me that the higher the Roman enthusiasm runs the less is there of internal seriousness and conscientiousness. Therefore it is that I expect a large revolt to Rome, the moment the High Church party is exposed to serious inconvenience.

May 13.—Dined with the Gladstones, met Lady Lyttelton and Lady Georgiana Fullerton, Captain and Mrs. Gladstone, Mr. and Mrs. Hamilton, &c. &c. I sat next Mr. Gladstone's sister-in-law, and liked her very much. She is very Irish— warm, natural, naïve and engaging—in singular contrast to the English ladies, who were handsome, dignified, and simple, but hard, and without chiaroscuro. Adare had much conversation with our host, and thought he meant to vote for the new [Queen's] Colleges.

May 14.—Called on Dr. Pusey. He looked ill, and seemed as if he had neither eaten nor slept for two days. He spoke cheerfully of the Church, but rather on Providential than on Philosophical grounds, and rather pressed my taking orders. He approached the subject of Newman three or four times, and glanced away again. At last he spoke of his change as certain, said it had been going on for these seven years, and would be avowed this year; said it would be a great crisis, and by far the greatest blow the cause had received. Seemed

[1] Mr. Upton Richards, of Margaret Street Chapel, the well-known Tractarian.

to fear that the example would be followed by many, though he said that the leaders, except Newman, stood firm ; said that the present movement went far beyond that of the Nonjurors, who held the doctrine of the 'Real Presence' imperfectly. He spoke hopefully of the Sisters of Mercy, and anticipated the springing up of other Conventual Institutions. Spoke of the growth of inward piety in many High Churchmen with confidence, said that he hoped the exertions of the Roman Catholics in England might be of use in gaining back Dissenters and Infidels ; observed on the greater boldness with which Churchmen were expressing themselves, without opposition, and referred to his own translations from Roman Catholic books. He praised much in Ward's book, though regretting the tone of it. Spoke with pleasure of Mr. Ward's numerous supporters, of the failure of the attack on Tract 90, and of Mr. Oakeley's probable acquittal. When I asked whether it would not be a dangerous decision, as proving that English Clergymen might be Romanists in doctrine, he drew a distinction between Popular Romanism and Essential Romanism ; said that Newman seemed called to some high providential part in the Church, and that the Church of England would not have him ; said that Newman had suffered much from the attacks made on him, and that last year he had been made ill by anxiety as to the course he ought to take. My impression was that Dr. Pusey was speaking with much conscientious reserve, and that he himself had drawn much nearer to Rome than of old.

May 15.—Read the Life of 'St. Wilfrid,' which seemed very far gone in Romanism ; sat an hour with Mrs. H. Coleridge, talking about poetry.

A few days later he writes :—

Went to Mr. Dodsworth's church, and heard a long sweet solemn sermon from Dr. Pusey.

One acquaintance which de Vere formed in 1845 in more general society was with Lord and Lady Ashburton, with whom he dined twice, meeting Carlyle the second time. Carlyle always interested and fascinated him. He regarded

him not as a philosopher, but as a prose-poet—a mixture of
prophet and cynic—' Diogenes-Samuel ' De Vere called him.
The journal records both occasions :—

May 18.—Dined with the Ashburtons—a party of eight
persons—sumptuous, but quiet and easy. My Lord shrewd
and active, finding out other people's opinions, and balancing
his own; the Lady clever, inquisitive, fond of amusement,
natural, and good-natured. [I met there some] London young
ladies, abounding in routine conversation, that might be that
of maid, wife, or widow—almost of man or woman—without
fancy or feeling, or any of that chiaroscuro of deportment
which invites us to penetrate more deeply into a world of
gladdening lights and half shadows; thoughts whose substance
is undraperied, whose colours are ungraduated, and whose
movements are rectilinear not curvilinear; opinions not easily
modified, though carelessly exchanged for their opposites—
and yet, under this hard, heartless, conventional manner,
symptoms of honesty, and possibly strong feelings. Returned,
and read some of Dr. Whewell's book on Morals.

May 28.—Wrote to Mamma, dined with the Ashburtons,
and met Mr. and Miss Lockhart, Mr. Carlyle and Lady Harriet
Baring—a dull, easy dinner. Lady Ashburton ill—Lady
Harriet hard, strong, reckless and honest. Carlyle inveighed
bitterly against Lord Brougham and ' oratory,' pronouncing
them both the merest shams. Went in the evening to the
Adares, and heard good singing—met Mrs. Gladstone, Lady
L. FitzGibbon, the Ladies Taylour, Lords Clare, Headfort,
and Bective; Milnes, E. Warburton, &c. &c.

De Vere stayed at the Grange later in the same year, and
repeated the visit several times later on. The following
account of the Carlyles, as they appeared to him at one of
these visits, will find its fitting place here. It is written to
Mrs. Edward Villiers :—

The Carlyles are here, and the Diogenes-Samuel denounces
all things as sharply as ever. To one who never heard him
before his talk must be striking ; but when one thinks that

all his time is spent in wielding Thor's hammer and trying to demolish the small fragments of Reverence and Truth that remain in embodied form, it is very sad. He certainly loves Truth and Justice, but our moral nature requires something more definite than an affection for abstract qualities. And even those loves are not altogether perfect. His love of Faith is a little ultra-Platonic, and he does not care what mountains or seas separate him from the object of his affections. Thus he will decry the most sacred and fundamental truths on hazard, and without taking the trouble to enquire whether they are true or not, merely to round one of those sentences to which, as a victim of phrases, he is subject. His love of justice has the opposite fault, and a good deal too much resembles the love of a wood-god for a fair and fleeting nymph. It is too flagrantly irreverent : and the sword of the Lord and of Cromwell, wielded by an unwashed and unsparing hand, is to cut every knot, civil or ecclesiastical, which Scotch intelligence is insufficient to disentangle. He interests me, but very painfully. It seems to me as if he had begun by believing what he now only repeats by heart, and once loved the virtues of which he continues to hate the opposite vices. I may do him injustice, but while he wages war on all that is not practical and ' veracious,' I can see little in him of genuine action, mental or physical, little of moral purpose, and little of honest search after actual truth on the most momentous of all subjects. Notwithstanding all this, I like listening to him better than to most people one meets in society. His expressions are pointed always, and often significant—his doctrines pungent, and I suppose that where every dish is insipid, the one you like best is that which has the sharpest sauce. His wife interests me too in her way. She seems sincere and severe, and has that proportion of still and quiet will which is always tragic, because one remembers against how many things in this world it will blunt itself, and how many of its victories will cost it dear, owing to the infirmities of the judgment associated with it.

The lady to whom this letter was written—Mrs. Edward Villiers, mother of the present Dowager Lady Lytton, and of

Mrs. Earle—begins to appear frequently at the point in the diary which I have now reached. Mrs. Villiers was the widow of Henry Taylor's great friend, Edward Ernest Villiers (brother of the fourth Earl of Clarendon), who had died at Nice, two years previously. Except Sara Coleridge, no friend corresponded with Aubrey de Vere more frequently, or aroused more of his sympathetic interest at this time, than Mrs. Villiers. But his intercourse with the two was different in kind—with the one almost exclusively intellectual and spiritual, with the other dwelling more on the lighter and brighter aspects of life. And while his deepest and most thoughtful letters are generally addressed to Mrs. Coleridge, the most racy are to Mrs. Villiers.

On June 9 he visits Mrs. Villiers at The Grove, near Watford, the residence of Lord Clarendon.

June 9.—Returned to town just in time to get to Grove Mill by an early train. Dofo and Mademoiselle drove with me to the Grove, where we found Mrs. E. Villiers and the children, arranging dinner along the floor in a little ruined temple—a very merry dinner, and great rapture on the part of the children. Dofo mounted a donkey, Mrs. E. Villiers and I walking beside for an hour. Mrs. E. V. and I drove to Watford and brought Henry Taylor home—a lively drive. Dofo and I walked in the garden conversing pleasantly till tea-time. Mrs. Villiers played and sang to the harp and pianoforte in the evening, and the baby was brought in to listen to the music, and to wish us good-night.

June 13.—Called on Adare, who mentioned that Dr. Hook had declared that the Church of Ireland must ever submit to change. Went to the House of Commons, and heard a pleasant row between a grand, fierce, blundering Irishman, and a sharp, bitter, adroit Englishman. Returned to Brook Street. Went out to Hampstead, and walked on the Heath, admiring the sublime effect of the lamps of London. Slept for ten hours at Jack Straw's Castle.

June 14.—Came back from Hampstead. We then went

G

to see Lord Egerton's pictures, a noble collection, including
three Raffaelles. Met Henry Taylor at the station, and drove
out with him to Grove Mill [Mrs. Villiers' own house]. At
Watford we met Mrs. E. Villiers, Dofo and Theresa. Drove
to Cassiobury [the country place of Lord Essex], from which
Mrs. E. Villiers and I walked home, discussing the duties of
an active life, and an alternative scheme proposed to me.

June 15.—I accompanied Mrs. E. Villiers and Theresa out
riding, my severe monitor advising me earnestly, but kindly,
to become manly, and accusing me of being effeminate. A
long and interesting, affectionate conversation, as we strolled
though the green lanes, and past the lairs of the young fawns.
Theresa implored me to find employment. A run before tea.
Round about in the twilight after tea. Music of the mirthful
sort. We sat on the sofa giving and taking advice.

The following letter to Mrs. Villiers, written at this time,
gives a very distinct picture both of the writer and of his correspondent :—

37 Brook Street : June 21, 1845.

Dear Mrs. Villiers,—Thank you very much for the lines
that accompanied the note which you enclosed. While
reading them I saw the sun flashing on your laurels, and
through them on your streams, and the heavy wreaths of
your honeysuckles, maintaining their ground against such
summer gusts as are able to make their way to your retreat.
Why do you accuse me of having troubled your children's
lessons ? If I idled you so that you could not attend to your
house accounts, it was very good for you to be idled ; and as
for your children, I showed you how to administer to them
that affliction of youth, the Latin grammar, and exhorted
them to great industry. Was not that doing good in my day
and generation ?

I left at Lord Clarendon's yesterday evening a parcel
for you containing the Review you had lent me, and which I
lost no time in reading, as I did not know whether you had
finished it. It contained also the profane volume of my
poetry which I was to send you. Do not be alarmed, for I
am very good-humoured and pleasant about my own verses,

neither expecting people to read them when they have them, nor to like them when they read them. Most of the poems in the volume are so light that I am half ashamed of sending them to you, my severe monitor (do you like the title?), but I have marked two of them which I should like you to read.

I was much interested by the critique on Goethe and Calderon. I knew by the pricking in my thumbs that I did not approve of it as I read, though what was the matter with the article I hardly understood till I had come to the last page. It would be very useful if every writer of equivocal doctrine were, with equal frankness, to let us see in his last page the ultimate drift and tendency of his principles.

I cannot subscribe to the doctrine that either the poet or the man should concern himself only with Relative, as distinguished from Absolute, Truths, that is to say with Truths that *seem* instead of Truths that *are*. The goal may be unattainable, but Faith is possible. It is by a star which we cannot reach that we steer our course. It is by the search after *Perfection* alone that we find what is worth having. Scepticism seems to me as poor and fruitless a habit in the Poet as in the Man; and the very clever article I have read is chiefly interesting as explaining, while it affects to vindicate, what has always seemed to me the insufficiency . . . of Goethe's poetry. . . . His works are deficient in that life and reality which can only belong to the products of a mind which has faith in absolute Truths, moral and spiritual, and which is capable even of a certain devotion to them, the condition, I believe, of apprehending them. Without this faith in immutable Truths independent of casual relations or the mere internal mechanism of the thinking mind, experience itself seems to me a thing impossible, however observant or practical we may be—because we have no fixed principle by which to collect and digest it, no bank against which the deposits of experience can accumulate. . . .

What can I have meant by heaping up all this philosophy upon you? I will take care not to get upon an abstract subject again, for when I begin I never can stop. How glad I am that you have this fine weather, and how much I hope that you are using it discreetly, abstaining from that rickety

horse, fasting from late hours, and rolling the children in the
hay until they are tired of it, and begin to look like red roses
turning white !

Aubrey de Vere himself enjoyed the fine weather from his
retreat at Hampstead Heath—where he seems at this time to
have often slept, coming into London in the daytime, or for
dinner, to see his friends :—

June 23.—Breakfasted at the Holly Bush (Hampstead)
and lunched on strawberries ; found out a hotel, the ' Hare and
Hounds,' at which we could live (with two rooms) for thirty
shillings per week.   Henry Taylor came to luncheon in Brook
Street.   I walked with him to his office, and wrote a letter there
to Mrs. H. Coleridge.   Dined at the Sterlings, where I met
Spedding, Brookfield, Baring, Lord Lyttelton, Lawrence,
Bloxam, &c.   Walked with Augustus Stafford O'Brien [1] and
T. Acland to the omnibus.   A. O'Brien told me Gladstone
and Acland had lost all influence.   Blew out my candle after
shutting ' Sir Launcelot,' and enjoyed the view of the great
city—a fire by night if a smoke by day—from my pillow.
June 25.—Was wakened at five by the rising sun.   Sat
by the open window admiring the morning, the great buildings
of London, and the separate leaves of the trees, articulated and
brought out in distinctness by the ' sun's discriminating touch.'
Breakfasted at Highgate—visited the tunnel.   Drove to Ken-
sington Gardens, where I read the new scenes in ' Queen Mary
Tudor ' ; came home, and discussed some alterations with my
father ; went to the Adares, and witnessed some mesmeric
performances of a very inconclusive character.   Drove out to
Mortlake, where I found Dofo and Mrs. R. Elliot.   Came
home on the roof of an omnibus.   Went with my mother and
uncle to the A. B.'s—a dull party.   Met Spedding, Milnes,
Bunsen, Milman, &c.

But at this time a shadow came over the merry London

---

[1] Augustus Stafford O'Brien, afterwards O'Brien Stafford, was a distant kins-
man of the O'Briens of Dromoland.   He was for some years M.P. for Blatherwick
in Northamptonshire.   He was a strong opponent of Peel in 1846, on the subject
of the Repeal of the Corn Laws, and was, later on, Secretary to the Admiralty.

life. His father arrived on June 19, and though the son describes him and his mother as both being well, he soon realised the seriousness of Sir Aubrey's condition. An operation was declared necessary, and Sir Benjamin Brodie was to perform it. The end of June and the month of July were largely absorbed by this anxiety, the society of Sara Coleridge being a valued solace.

June 27.—Sat with my father, who was as cheerful as if he had nothing to go through, and spoke of the pain as a thing of no moment, because forgotten when once over. Stayed in my room for half an hour after Brodie came, found my father in bed ; he said with perfect good humour that the operation, which was as painful as the successful ones, had failed in consequence of his not having been warned to keep quiet. All the evening he has had a good deal of uneasiness, which he bore with perfect sweetness of temper. We read ' Esther ' to him till eleven o'clock.

June 28.—My father had a bad night, and continued too uncomfortable to get up. . . . Finished 'Esther' and set to at ' Agincourt.' Wrote a letter to Mrs. Edward Villiers, and enclosed it with ' Sir Launcelot,' which I left at Lord Clarendon's.

June 29.—My father had a bad night, but was better in the morning. I went to Mr. Dodsworth's church, and heard Dr. Pusey preach a sermon like the reverie of a saint. Walked with Mrs. H. Coleridge to her door, and was sorry to find that she had been ill and sleepless. We went on reading ' Agincourt.' . . .

July 2.—Read some of Ruskin to my father, who enjoyed it much.

July 4.—My father much as before, and as patient as ever ; we went on reading Ruskin, who seemed to make out his case in favour of the modern landscape-painter.

July 9.—I sat with Mrs. H. Coleridge, and read in the evening with deep interest, the copy of ' Waldenses ' which she had marked.

July 14.—Found my father in low spirits. At two, Brodie, and I went to my room. We passed half an hour in great

suspense, and then Brodie came out, saying that the operation
had been successful.   We found my father suffering a good
deal, but cheerful and relieved.

July 17.—My father better and cheerful.   Read Cooper's
'Afloat and Ashore' till luncheon.   Wrote some sonnets in Sara
Coleridge's copy of the 'Waldenses' and paid her a long visit.
She pleaded guilty to being a 'Pious Rationalist.'   We discussed theology, and then went to poetry.   She told me that
Edith Southey, Dora Wordsworth and herself were the heroines
of Wordsworth's 'Trias.'   She was shocked at my placing that
poem in the first class of Mr. Wordsworth's poetry.   I carried
my book home again, and was promised the marked copy of
the 'Proserpine.'   Called on Lord Clare and the Wyndhams,
Charles and Stephen [Spring Rice] rather discomposed at my
not having dined at the Sterlings'.   Caught a Camden Town
omnibus, and walked out from thence to Hampstead.   Wrote
more notes in my book.

July 22.—My father much as usual, but wearied and out
of spirits.   We read to him Dana's 'Three Years before the
Mast.'   The Whewells lunched with us.   I received my
'Proserpine' (from Mrs. Coleridge) a second time with more
annotations, some very sad, some mirthful, all familiar and
interesting ; also some pretty verses and a pleasant letter.
Went in the evening to the opera with the Whewells and
heard 'Lucrezia Borgia.'

July 23.—Breakfasted with the Milmans, and met old
Rogers, who was cross but pleasant ; and said that Henry
Taylor could do anything in poetry, and that he could 'take
pains.'

July 24.—My father suffered much, but was in good spirits.
I read to him till five o'clock, and then brought 'Mary Tudor'
to Mrs. H. Coleridge.   While sitting with her, a note was
brought in announcing the death of Derwent Coleridge's
infant—the old lady was much shaken and agitated, exclaimed 'O my poor children !' and burst into tears.   Her
daughter wept also, and I took my leave.

Some passages in the diary for this month tell of intercourse
with Alfred Tennyson—who was in these years already en-

gaged to marry Miss Emily Sellwood, an engagement which
was prolonged for many years, until the poet's success should
bring him an assured income.

July 1.—Driving in from Hampstead I met Alfred
Tennyson, who was little pleased to see me, and seemed
living in a mysterious sort of way on the Hampstead Road,
bathing and learning Persian.

July 14.—Went out to Hampstead with a copy of the
'Waldenses.' Called on Alfred Tennyson, who railed against
the whole system of society, and said he was miserable.

July 16.—Found my father rather less well. On my way
in, paid a visit to Tennyson, who seemed much out of spirits,
and said that he could no longer bear to be knocked about
the world, and that he must marry and find love and peace
or die. He was very angry about a very favourable review
of him. Said that he could not stand the chattering and
conceit of clever men, or the worry of society, or the meanness
of tuft-hunters, or the trouble of poverty, or the labour of a
place, or the preying of the heart on itself. . . . He complained much about growing old, and said he cared nothing
for fame, and that his life was all thrown away for want of a
competence and retirement. Said that no one had been so
much harassed by anxiety and trouble as himself. I told
him he wanted occupation, a wife, and orthodox principles,
which he took well.

The end of July and the first half of August saw a
measure of intercourse with friends ; but a background of
anxiety remained :—

July 25.—Found my father better, though after a bad
night. We went to the Queen's Pavilion, Stephen Spring
Rice and Ellen being of the party. Thought the affair
childish and petty, but admired the view of the gardens and
lake. . . . Wrote to Mrs. H. Coleridge enquiring for her
mother, and enclosing Miss Woodroffe's volume. Heard
from her in return. Received also a note from Mrs. E. Villiers,
asking me to Grove Mill for Sunday. . . . The Whewells
dined with us, and were very pleasant.

July 26.—Wrote to Mrs. E. Villiers, lamenting my not being able to go to her. Read 'Lucy Harding' to my father. Dined with the Whewells in Grosvenor Street, meeting only Miss Mary Cayley—a very pleasant evening, Dr. Whewell very agreeable.

July 28.—Received a mocking note from Mrs. E. Villiers. My father not well. Reading aloud as usual. Wrote notes in the 'Proserpine.' . . . The Whewells dined with us. I heard from Mrs. Colyar a whole budget of Roman news. We had a large dinner, including the Whewells, Bishop of Norwich, Dr. Holland, Eddis (the painter), Sir R. Ferguson, A. Helps, &c.—a pleasant evening.

August 1.—Sat for a while with Mrs. H. N. Coleridge, but could not get her to praise 'Mary Tudor.' At last her mother fairly turned me out.

August 4.—Breakfasted at old Rogers' with my uncle and Lord Northampton—the old man animated, but somewhat profane.

My father better than usual and in good spirits. I wrote a long letter to Mrs. E. Villiers, in answer to a very sad one from her. Read 'Mercedes' to my father.

August 6.—Called on Mrs. H. N. Coleridge, and sat with the old lady, listening to her stories of old times. She told me of a gentleman who had proposed for her daughter (Sara) at thirteen. Said that when she and her cousins played on the lawn, people used to look at them out of the bedroom windows, wondering at the beauty of the group. Mentioned that her husband was not twenty-three when they married; that Mr. Hazlitt used to worry them with his visits, that Mr. de Quincey used to say to Coleridge, 'I should be so much obliged if you would speak a little more near the level of my comprehension;' that she used to ask her husband, 'Man, do you really understand yourself?' that her daughter had received 130*l.* for a translation she made as a child; that all her daughter's admirers had died early, so that whichever of them she had married, she would equally have been a widow; that her attachment to her husband had begun when she was nineteen, and had gone on till they married at twenty-five, in spite of opposition of friends; that the marriage was a very happy one, and that she had wonderfully refined and elevated her husband—yet that for three years she had suffered so much from the spine and nerves, that she was always weeping and wishing to die ; that ' Phantasmion ' had been written in bed, and that she used to write little poems on cards for her children.

The old lady spoke also a great deal about Mr. Southey, whom she had known from childhood, and about her sons. In fact, her garrulity was more interesting to me than Macaulay's conversation could have been.

August 7.—My father less well than usual, and depressed. I sat with Tennyson for an hour, during which time he read me an account of Laura Bridgman. When he came to her recognition of her mother, he threw the book over to me, and said, ' Read it for yourself, it makes me cry.'

August 10.—My father better. Bought Mrs. Calcutt's illustrations of Giotto's Chapel at Padua, and gave it to him I procured Kugler's Handbook of Painting.

August 12.—Called on Mrs. H. N. Coleridge, and sat nearly two hours with her discussing theology. She gave me a book of poetry for children written by herself, the volume to be transmitted to Ellen. Opposed the ordinary doctrines with regard to Angels and Daemons.

August 14.—Found Mrs. E. Villiers at luncheon, gay and attractive. . . .

August 15.—Called on Mr. Richards [1] at the British Museum. He seemed fagged and anxious. He expressed great horror at ' Hawkestone,' and said that Dr. Pusey felt as he did, and that the breach between Sewell and the rest of the High Churchmen was widening daily. Spoke as if he thought that, unless the Bishops showed them some sympathy, a large defection like that of the Nonjurors would take place : seemed also to anticipate many secessions to Rome, among them Ward and Oakeley.

August 16.—Called on Mrs. H. N. Coleridge and found her mother very unwell. Mr. John Coleridge,[2] son of the Judge, came in, and mentioned that Ward had written a letter saying

[1] Mr. Upton Richards.
[2] The late Lord Coleridge, Lord Chief Justice of England.

that he would join Rome after a month's deliberation, also that Newman's ways were as mysterious as ever, and that they were adding to the buildings at Littlemore. . . .

August 19.—Brodie performed another operation, which he hoped might be the last. My father was better than usual after it, but in the evening was feverish and depressed.

The hope was not verified, but at last, ten days later, the operation was repeated, and all seemed to promise well, for the great surgeon ' pronounced it final and my father cured. Great joy on all hands, in which the servants heartily joined.'

August 29.—After Mamma's return from her drive, I called on Sara Coleridge, whom I found sitting with her nephew, John Coleridge, who got into a somewhat hot, sharp argument with her, and asserted that the whole of the High Church party would go over to Rome. We had much pleasant conversation, amongst other things about Wordsworth's ' Waggoner ' and the ' Trias.' She spoke of her past life, lamented her little twins, and told me how they had been brought to her bedside in their coffins ; said that, not having any little children growing up made her look with such sorrow on Edith's growth. . . . A merry dinner at home. My father in excellent spirits. I read ' Redgauntlet ' in the evening.

August 28.—My father's birthday, and a very happy one to him and all of us. My father came down to the drawing-room and thence to the parlour, where we all dined together, the first time for two months. We began reading ' Sybil.' Spedding came and sat with me for two hours.

August 30.—On leaving breakfast we found that my father had already come downstairs to the drawing-room, and was resolved on taking a walk. He, Mamma, and I set out and walked in Grosvenor Square, Hyde Park, for an hour. After luncheon we went to Westminster Hall, and were particularly pleased with one of the cartoons by Maclise. I paid a visit to Mrs. H. N. Coleridge, and promised to read the ' Waggoner ' again. Charles Spring Rice sang to us in the evening, and after that we went on reading ' Sybil.'

August 31.—Went to Mr. Dodsworth's church, and heard

a very beautiful sermon from Dr. Pusey. After dinner we went on with ' Sybil,' stopping now and then to abuse the book.

September 4.—Found Spedding at the breakfast-table. He came with us to Hampton Court. At the station we met Lady Glentworth. We passed a very delightful day roaming about the old Palace and the garden.

September 5.—I called on H. Taylor, who brought me out with him to Mortlake. Spedding joined us after tea, and we had a pleasant, brilliant, genial evening—nothing could be more satisfactory.

September 6.—We passed a pleasant morning, H. Taylor admonishing me to undertake some considerable work in prose, an exhortation in which Spedding joined. We three drove home together on the top of an omnibus.

Aubrey de Vere's intercourse with Sara Coleridge was now very frequent, and we gain from the diary, as from their later letters, the impression of a friendship between them, very unusual in its exhibition of an affection and sympathy, so spiritual and intellectual, that the thought of a closer relationship seems never to have dawned on either :—

September 2.—Walked into Regent's Park and met Mrs. H. N. Coleridge, not far from the lake by which we had walked not two years ago ; walked together, and sat down ; she was pale, tired and sad ; she said that her evening rambles were a relief to her, after she had long been trying to keep up her spirits among her children. . . . I left her at her own door, and found [our own party] at dinner. In the evening Charles went to Spedding, and we read ' The Prevision of Lady Evelyn' aloud. Wrote to Mrs. H. N. Coleridge, asking her to come to the Houses of Parliament with us.

September 3.—Drove to Chester Place for Sara Coleridge and returned with her. She liked my father's new pictures, and half approved of the busts. We roamed about the Houses of Parliament for an hour, and admired them immensely. She looked pale, but was often lively, and rallied me upon being so sanguine, and always living in the ' potential

world.' She said that I would end by becoming a Romanist,
but added that she did not quite mean that. After luncheon
we four walked to Westmacott's [1] house, in the hope of seeing
the statue of Byron, but it was packed up. We drove home
with her to Chester Place, called on Lady Glentworth, saw
the great houses in the Victoria Road. On our return I
received a note from Mrs. E. Villiers, mentioning that her
journey was postponed, in consequence of her mother's illness.
I wrote to Mrs. E. Villiers, and went to bed after one o'clock.
Sara Coleridge spoke very affectingly, during our drive from
Chester Place, of her desolate position. . . . 'Time,' I said,
' will do something for you.' ' It will,' she replied, 'if I grow
more religious.'

September 6.—After luncheon we drove with Sara Coleridge
to the Zoological Gardens. My father and mother were lost
for some time, but turned up at last.

Mrs. H. N. Coleridge advised me to get into some active
way of life, saying at the same time that it was very presumptuous of her to do so. Horatio came to me in the
evening, and we went to the Coliseum—the cavern struck
me as admirable.

September 7, *Sunday.*—I went to church at Mr. Dodsworth's ; walked home with Mrs. H. N. Coleridge. We walked
in the Park also, and sat down ; Edith, who was very winning, and Herbert, being with us. Mrs. H. N. Coleridge
enlarged on her views with regard to the absence of all bodily
form in a future state, and mentioned that from the time she
first saw a dead body, she had learned to disconnect it from
her idea of a personality, and that she nowhere felt less near
her departed friends than when visiting their tombs. We
went to the evening service at Westminster Abbey, and were
much pleased with the music and building.

September 10.—Went to see Mrs. H. N. Coleridge and
brought her some flowers—almost dead. We talked about
poetry, and I offered her a volume on Keats, in exchange for
her father's poems, which she agreed to. In the evening, my
father spoke of going on Saturday to Boulogne.

----

[1] Sir Richard Westmacott, R.A., Professor of Sculpture at the Royal
Academy, and a pupil of Canova.

September 11.—Heard at luncheon from my father that he had bought a picture of the Rembrandt School,[1] and another after Correggio ; went to see the latter, and was greatly pleased with its luminous hilarity. I called on H. Taylor at the office, and made him promise to come back to Brook Street in the evening. He arrived just at the same moment as the Correggio. We looked at it all the evening, and he admired and enjoyed it, though he maintained that the child's neck was dislocated. . . . I lay on the sofa marking Keats.

September 12.—Drove with my father to get his passport ; paid a visit to Mrs. H. N. Coleridge, who came down with a sort of timid intrepidity, holding in her hand Edith's portrait of herself, and her own notes on Wordsworth, which she gave to me. We discussed some of them, and I gave her the Keats and bade her adieu.

September 13.—Wrote in Mrs. H. N. C.'s album, as my father, Mamma and Henry Taylor had done, and sent it back to her with Thomas a Kempis' ' Imitation.'

On September 13 Aubrey de Vere went abroad with his father and mother, going to Paris and visiting the cathedrals of Abbeville, Amiens and Beauvais on the way, and returning by St. Ouen and Dieppe. The diary is resumed on his return. During his absence old Mrs. Coleridge passed away. Aubrey only learnt the news on reaching London :—

October 4.—We reached London at four. I went to Mrs. Coleridge's and was shocked to hear from her maid that the old lady had died the Wednesday before last. The maid was crying, and said that her mistress was very low and unwell.

We three dined tête à tête. I found a parcel waiting for me enclosing an acceptance of my article on ' Philip van Artevelde,' and a copy of it in print, fifty-two pages long.

October 4.—After breakfast I put into the post the letter of condolence I had written the preceding evening to Mrs. H. N. Coleridge. Went to Mrs. H. N. C. After sitting for some

[1] Now in the drawing-room at Curragh Chase.

minutes nearly in the dark, except for two faint candles, the door opened, and she came in. She sat down on the sofa, looked very pale, nervous and tearful. She spoke much of her mother, but smiled more than once before I went away. Her eyes looked brighter than ever, and I never found her more interesting or gentle. Carried home the volume of her father's poems.

Stephen Spring Rice and Horatio at dinner, which was a very cheerful one. Went in the evening to Mortlake, found Dofo looking very young and fresh and happy, and H. Taylor reading my article to her. We passed a pleasant hour before they went to bed. After reading through my article, which turned out to be tolerably correct in its printing, I read some papers enclosed by Mrs. H. N. Coleridge, principally poetry or criticism, but including some very kind sisterly counsel The volume of her father's poems seemed also much enriched by her notes.

October 5, *Mortlake.*—Little Freddy Elliot came to wake me. After breakfast went with him and Dofo to church. H. Taylor came in at the second service, and we three again partook of the Sacrament together. I thought so much of poor Mrs. H. N. Coleridge, that she seemed to be among us as Mrs. E. Villiers was the last time. After our return Spedding came in. We had a pleasant dinner.

October 7.—Called on Mrs. H. N. Coleridge, and found her in better spirits. She was reading the 'Christian Remembrancer' with Keats and Thomas a Kempis, on the sofa, which I thought a bad selection. We had a great deal of interesting conversation.

October 10.—Finished my letter to Mrs. E. Villiers, and corrected the second series of my own Sonnets. H. Taylor, Dofo and I walked to the omnibus, and he and I drove into town together. I found a summons from Lady Ashburton, also a letter from Sara Coleridge. It enclosed a very powerful and able critique on the 'Laodamia.' It was in other respects deeply touching as regards her own bereavement, and to me full of sisterly friendliness and gentle trustingness in my sympathy. Her opinions on the subject of the Resurrection seemed the same as before, and it seemed to me that

there was a something wanting to her in her religious views—
an over-spirituality and want of substance. I wrote (in a
new fashion) my name in the volume of Keats. How much
I wish that this most interesting and remarkable being were
strong, and happy, and at peace !

October 11.—I went down to the Grange—hired a phaeton
at the Station, drove along a lane, and through three miles of
wood before the lights of the house glimmered between the
boughs—dressed for dinner, and found the family, including
Lady Bath, sitting in the dark, waiting for dinner. Was very
kindly received : a pleasant dinner, and cheerful evening.

The three days' visit was pleasant but uneventful. The
beauties of the place were duly admired, the conversation
was agreeable, and Aubrey particularly enjoyed the last
evening, passed in telling ghost stories.

October 14.—Walked with Lady Ashburton till 12.30,
when I went away—got to town early enough to call on Mrs.
H. N. Coleridge. She spoke a good deal about her husband's
last illness, and wept much ; at last Edith came in, which put
an end to our conversation ; and I went away at nearly eight
o'clock. Went out to Mortlake.

October 15.—Breakfasted with Dofo, and chatted with
her about ' my ladies.' Walked with her to Kew, and to the
little court in which she dispenses charities. . . .

I drove into town and visited Mrs. H. N. Coleridge. She
was livelier than usual, and spoke of her early Keswick days
—her friendship with Edith Southey, and said she wished I
had seen her at eighteen. Afterwards the conversation grew
sadder, and she spoke of her uncle, her father and his early
friends. We bade each other an affectionate farewell, and she
gave me her translation of the Life of Bayard.

October 17.—Breakfasted with Charles, and drove to Euston
Square and on by railway to Leeds.

Found Mary [Mrs. James Marshall, *née* Spring Rice] well
and very affectionate. She gave me a good supper, and
after discussing her new church, I got to bed, having written

to Mrs. H. N. Coleridge, enclosing my sonnet to her. Read of Mr. Newman's change.

Four days later Aubrey de Vere bade farewell to London, after a six months' stay there. He travelled north, and after a brief visit to the Marshalls near Penrith, joined his father and mother at Ambleside, on a visit to Miss Fenwick. This was a time he loved to look back upon. 'My father spent there,' he tells us, 'the happiest weeks of his later life. His childhood was with him again. He seemed to have forgotten nothing in that neighbourhood.' It was the last time of peaceful familiar intercourse between father and son, amid surroundings which appealed so powerfully to both. And it was unclouded, for the elder Aubrey seemed for the time to have regained health and strength.

The diary records the daily occupations—visits to the Arnolds and to the tombs of Wordsworth's two children, near which the poet himself was to be laid—and gives a sadly interesting glimpse of two persons,—Dorothy Wordsworth, now nearly an octogenarian, and for years robbed by illness of her brilliant gifts, and Hartley Coleridge, of whom it has been truly said that one failing sufficed to make void the promise of genius. On October 24 we read :—

After luncheon [my father], mamma, and I drove to the Grasmere and Rydal. Old Miss Wordsworth in her scarlet cloak repeated a poem to us.

On the following day :—

Hartley Coleridge came in after dinner. He read us two beautiful poems (one on his sister's bereavement), tried to write a sonnet to the Picture, and was very delightful just before going away. My father and mother very much and sadly, though kindly, impressed by him.

On the 27th Sir Aubrey and Lady de Vere took leave of Miss Fenwick, and started for Ireland.

CURRAGH CHASE, ADARE—THE HOUSE FROM THE LAKE.

VIEW FROM A BALCONY AT CURRAGH CHASE, ADARE.

CHAPTER IV

THE IRISH FAMINE

1846–1848

AUBREY DE VERE remained a few days with Miss Fenwick after his parents had returned home, and then proceeded to Scotland. Harriet Martineau and Hartley Coleridge dined with them on October 29. Coleridge 'never exchanged a word with Miss Martineau. . . . but read his father's poetry as well as his own drama of "Prometheus."'

On the 31st he records 'a long coze about Miss Fenwick's past life, and my future career,' and a visit from the Arnolds.

On November 1 he bade adieu to Miss Fenwick, and went to the Marshalls at Patterdale. Thence he proceeded northwards, on the 4th driving to Penrith, and taking the Carlisle mail as far as Douglas Mills. He drove next day to Glasgow, which struck him as a 'combination of Liverpool and Manchester, with something of ancient associations.' He enjoyed the dry Scotch humour of a chance acquaintance of that evening, 'an amusing fat man, at once farmer and manufacturer, who informed us that the true way of fattening cattle was to put out their eyes—they had then only just to feed, with nothing to trouble them.'

The next three weeks were spent in wandering about Scotland, reading the while Burns, Scott, and Wordsworth's 'Highland Girl'—of whom Aubrey vainly strove to find the original. Loch Lomond and Loch Katrine delighted him ; but he was faithful in his allegiance to Cumberland, and preferred the English lakes to the Scotch. Stirling Castle and the

H

neighbouring church of the Grey Friars, where James VI. was crowned, aroused historic memories. So did Edinburgh, which he reached on the 23rd. Here he visited the Roman Catholic church, and heard a sermon on the Oxford conversions.

He read the list of 'verts in the 'Tablet' that week, received an alarmist letter on the subject from Mr. Richards on the 7th, and adds in his diary : 'Spent the evening in Politico-theological meditations of a not sombre sort.'

On the 9th he dined with Lord Jeffrey, of 'Edinburgh Review' fame, meeting a large and pleasant party, and sitting 'next to a young and handsome authoress, a Puseyite.'

Next day he made the acquaintance of Professor Wilson, known as Christopher North, the 'rusty fusty Christopher' of Tennyson's *jeu d'esprit* :—

December 10.—Went to Blackwood's, and then made acquaintance with Professor Wilson, a strong, hale, elderly man, with a face full of wild energy, and long locks. He spoke with affectionate reverence of Wordsworth, and with the warmest interest and indulgence about Hartley Coleridge. Read Burns in the evening, and wrote to Miss Fenwick.

December 11.—Went to the college, and heard a lecture from Professor Wilson, in support of a modified Utilitarianism —it was delivered with a sort of pompous energy disproportioned to the occasion, and apparently unreal. Here and there it inclined to paradox, but it contained striking things, especially a sentence on the depth and spiritual import of happiness.

December 12.—Had a talk with Professor Wilson, at Blackwood's, respecting his lecture. Dined at Sir John McNeill's. . . . Invited Mr. Wilson to Curragh. He gave me an account of several tours which he had made in Ireland, and seemed to have been much pleased, both with the people and the country. Went in the evening to Lord Jeffrey's.

On the 16th Aubrey left for the South, stopped at Melrose, visited Abbotsford and the grave of Sir Walter Scott. He went to Carlisle and Penrith three days later, sat in Southey's place in Keswick Church, on Sunday the 21st, staying at the house of the Myers' family—a name familiar to readers of the Lives of the Lake poets—and visited Southey's home on the following day. On the morrow they all dined at Greta Bank with the family of his and Tennyson's friend James Spedding.

On Christmas eve he found himself again with Miss Fenwick :—

December 24.—Bade adieu to my kind friends. Drove on the coach to Ambleside ; found Miss Fenwick established in a very little house close to the church, and very well. Passed the evening talking over Church matters. Miss Fenwick perfectly fixed in loyalty to our own Church. She alluded to a certain degree of reserve on the part of the Patriarch since she had expressed her views on some matters, and thought him less accessible.

Four days were passed in this happy spot, and the great bard was seen daily :—

December 26.—Found Mr. Crabb Robinson at breakfast with Miss Fenwick. He sat with us a long time, talking very agreeably, chiefly about Goethe ; told us a story of Alfred Tennyson who on being asked by Rogers what he thought of Mrs. A. B., who had just left her place next Tennyson at dinner, replied that he felt as if a serpent had just dropped off. Mr. Wordsworth came in, and passed some hours with us. He was looking well and hale, and spoke with anima-tion of Burns' poetry, but with qualified approval—of Scott's with contempt. Passed the evening in religious converse with Miss Fenwick.

December 27.—Miss Fenwick and I drove to the Arnolds, leaving, at the turn to Rydal, Mr. Wordsworth, who had break-fasted with us. . . . Dined at Rydal, where we met Mr. Moxon, and Mr. C. Robinson.

December 28, *Sunday.*—Went to church, and found Miss Arnold in the pew. Mr. Arnold dined with us. Mr. Words-worth came in the evening, and was as interesting as ever.

December 29.—Miss Fenwick's cold rather worse. Mr. Wordsworth paid us a visit. . . . I bade good-bye to him and to Miss Fenwick at two o'clock, and drove under the pelting rain to Lancaster, whence I got on by rail to Coventry at two A.M.

A flying visit to London on his way home gave him an opportunity of a talk with Sara Coleridge :—

January 1.—Called on Mrs. Henry N. Coleridge, and sat four hours with her. . . .
A very affectionate and pleasant interview, mixed up with theological discussions. Returned to Mortlake late, in the fly with H. Taylor and Dofo, after drinking tea in Brook Street, where were the Poles and W. Marshall.

Two days later he journeyed to Ireland, according to the conditions of the journey in 1846 :—

January 3.—Took a ticket for Liverpool, changed it for one for Chester. Got on thence on the mail to St. Asaph at midnight.
January 4, *Sunday.*—The day beautiful. Drove on to Bangor, admired the coast road immensely. Dined and got on to Holyhead. Sailed in the packet, admired and disliked the waves swelling in the moonlight.
January 5.—Went at eight o'clock on shore. Got into Dublin, breakfasted at the Hibernian Hotel. Called on Todd Lloyd, McCulloch and Mr. Anster. Dined at the Fellows' table. Thought Anster more agreeable than anyone I had met in England. Left the party with sorrow. Drove on the mail as far as Kildare, and [got] wet.

Only a few days after his return home, while he was revelling in renewed intercourse with his loved father, reading with him and revising poetry, came the distant rumbling of one of those social storms from which Ireland is never long free. The potato famine had begun. Misery and want were the consequence. Outrages followed, and on January 21 came the news that four baronies were proclaimed under what was then, as now, called a 'Coercion' Act. Sir Aubrey from the first strove to allay the public agitation. But the temper of the people was aroused. The following entries tell their own story :—

February 21 *to March* 14.—The gentlemen of the Grand Jury refused my father's proposals . . . and also refused to apply for an addition to the representation of Ireland. The Coercion Bill excited people's minds very much. Stephen was vehemently opposed to it as tyrannical. My father opposed to the clause imposing the support of the additional police on the disturbed districts. I read Kane's 'Industrial Resources of Ireland,' and was much struck by the field for enterprise and prosperity there disclosed. When will the Irish learn to help themselves ?

Sir David Roche and Mr. Lyons fired at while driving home from the Assizes. G. Fosberry's steward also fired at. The Arthurs came over to us. The same evening after their return, three shots were fired into the house.

March 18.—Read part of Berkeley's 'Querist'; remarkable how applicable that work is to the present time, the reason being that the character of the Irish has so much to say to the condition of the country. Stephen greatly incensed at the Coercion Bill, and inclined to take extreme courses. Music in the evening. I finished the copying out of my poem on Rome.

The agitation, however, was not yet, as it became later, acute and constant. Aubrey de Vere still spent most of his time with his books, or in conversation, or in writing letters to Miss Fenwick, Mrs. Villiers, Henry Taylor, and Mrs. Coleridge. The following letter to Sara Coleridge, written shortly after his arrival in Ireland, over and above its intrinsic interest, supplies an important landmark in the progress of his mind :

Curragh Chase : February 12, 1846.

My dear Friend,— . . . I wish you would persuade your friend, Miss Barrett, to write with as much grace and refinement as ever, and not talk about 'garrulous God-Innocence,' and such extravagant, over-strained things, which are as

objectionable as great unfeminine strides, and abrupt movements. I wish she had less ambition, or rather more and of
a nobler sort, that of writing like a woman of genius—as she
is—not like a man. Genius may be either masculine or
feminine, and each is most perfect in its own way. But she
is injured by taking men models, instead of fancying how
Sappho and the poetesses of old wrote, or else what a
woman's poetry would be if thoroughly genial—the expression of genius in a feminine mould, and singing its inspirations with that female voice, which is a different instrument
from a man's voice. I meant a great deal by those verses
on Female Poetry, but unluckily my skill is chiefly to 'hide
the matter.' Do you take up the subject, for you are in no
danger of falling into the fault which I wage war on therein.

Pray go on writing and send me more. I have written
to Rivington telling him to send you a copy of my poems
for your sister. I am very glad that she likes them ; but she
does not say enough about Henry Taylor's. Let her read
the last often, and she will discover that they are graven upon
marble—not written upon pink paper, pleasantly perfumed
now in rose water, now (which is worse) in incense. Do not
forget to send me your father's autograph. I am glad to
hear that the 'English Review' has the sense to praise him,
in spite of theological differences.

By the way, I am very glad to hear of your brother
Derwent's stall at St. Paul's. He will, I have little doubt, rise
high in our Church, and I look to him for much. He has
already done much for the Church, at St. Mark's. I am glad
to hear that the Bishops are going to vote for the repeal of
the Corn Laws. It will be the popular course, and if 'aught
could teach us aught,' they ought to have learned by this
time the meaning of the text 'put not your trust in princes.'

. . . I think this measure raises Peel immensely as a
statesman, and will hand him down honourably to posterity.
It has quite turned my thoughts to Politics, and I should
almost like the speculation of going into Parliament as an
honest politician. But then I suppose everyone begins with
such aspirations, and I should soon become as dishonest as
my neighbours. How great a mistake to think it easy to be

honest! It is easy to be honest enough not to be hanged. To be *really* honest means to subdue one's party spirit, one's vanity, one's prepossessions, ideals—stating things fairly, not humouring your argument—doing justice to your enemies, whether you are stronger than they or not; making confessions whether you can afford it or not; refusing unmerited praise; looking painful truths in the face, and not merely seeing 'the utmost part of them'; knowing what one means, and knowing when one has no meaning, and shaking off one's plausibilities, and fifty-five things which men see with pleasure, and which the angels see through, as we see through a transparent Dragon Fly, in a solar microscope. You will say if one could learn to be honest in this outrageous sort, one would find a fair field anywhere—as for instance in Theology, at the Bar, &c.—and that is true. In the meantime it is much easier to get the crowning virtues of humanity than those foundation virtues which, being out of sight, are apt to be out of mind too.

I do not quarrel with you for all you say about Sewell. He is my *philosophical* friend, and one takes attacks on such philosophically; but I am very unkind to say this, for I am very grateful to him (as an Irishman) about St. Columba, and I have a great liking for him, and he was very kind to me at Oxford, some years since. I have also a high opinion of him. He is an enthusiastic, self-forgetting philosopher, whether one likes his philosophy or not, living in a few great ideas, always thinking of the public good, and cherishing a vision, artistic, metaphysical and religious, of an ideal of Society yet to be realised.

. . . . What a religious flame all the world is in now! On my way lately to Ireland, I found myself in a railway carriage with a very dashing young man, who was arguing at a great rate with a simple-minded companion, whom he seemed resolved to convert within the hour to Unitarianism. One of his arguments was that the Unitarian doctrine is that which most does honour to our Lord, ' for,' said he, ' if you make him to be God, where is the difficulty of being good, and what credit does he deserve?' I like much better to listen than speak, except where I like the party speaking, and should have said nothing on this occasion, but that the gentle companion of this dashing theologian had but little to say for himself. Accordingly I quoted the verse 'God so loved the world,' &c., to which after some rumination he replied that 'the Devil could quote Scripture for his own purposes.' So Miss Burdett Coutts is giving 30,000*l.* to build a new church. These are the signs that give us hopes for the age. But Mr. E. Coleridge's giving up his drawings is a far nobler thing.

I have been reading Newman's book[1] with attention. The theory is an interesting theological exhortation, and a brilliant imagination plays on the cloud palace. I have found out, however, some tremendous sophisms in such parts of the argument as needed to be strong. I must not launch out on this subject. It is dangerous to be dishonest on Theological subjects, and difficult to be thoroughly honest on subjects that really interest one. Newman's book is not wholly honest (though the man is), how then should my remarks on it be fair? unless I had much time to make them so. Besides I am writing down my thoughts in a book which I keep by me, and will show it to you some time or other if you like it. His argument does not seem to me to shake the true Catholic doctrine at all—hardly to touch it. That unlucky phrase *via media*, only politically applicable to our Church, is working against us, and prevents us from seeing that Catholicism occupies the whole ground both of Protestantism and Romanism, and reconciles whatever each holds of *positive* Doctrine. I wish you would make Maurice write an essay on Newman's book. I agree with him more than anyone else, but have thought always that he lacked precision, and hardly recognised the fact that the Church is not an Idea, but rather the living Law represented by that Idea. Newman's distinction between Principles and Doctrines seems to throw a light on what I have found or fancied deficient in Maurice. The latter is strong in Principles, but shrinks from Doctrines, and cannot see why people should ask him 'yes or no' on specific questions.

I read Milton nearly every day—about one page—for we sometimes lose our power of appreciation after a very

---

[1] The *Essay on the Development of Christian Doctrine.*

short time. After all I must say that he is better as a builder than as an architect. I deny all analogy between his poetry and York Minster, and hold by the comparison to St. Peter's. As a builder he is supreme. It is curious to examine his first two sonnets, and see how inferior they are in point of structure to his later sonnets. They are comparatively weakly, made out with cramps, joinings on, and grammatical afterthoughts. That on Cromwell is one arch of 'adamant eterne' which even an elephantine critic might put his foot on without shaking it. He is sublimest of the sublime. There —that is all I am going to say of him.

The worst line in Wordsworth is that in which he calls our great Mahometan Poet 'Holiest of Men.' I thought for a long time that he meant *himself*, and as such admired the line as a piece of poetical parrhesia. What a *low* conception of the Supreme Being, that of making him a Theologian! I would rather he called him a 'cloud-compeller' than made him a wielder of theological clouds, which evidently rise from the swamps of our fallen humanity when Apollo chooses to play with it. Dante's conception of God was a thousand times loftier and purer. Just observe the feeling of the *Infinite* which belongs to the last few lines of his poem—the one great Christian Poem. Advancing from height to height in eminence of beatific vision he last comes within sight of the Mystery of the Trinity. Then he said, the *Mind* stopped and staggered, but the *Will* rolled forward still, like that Wheel on which Heaven and all the Stars revolve. Milton's conception of woman was Eastern, and was wholly without spirituality, tenderness, or chivalry. The highest thing about him was his conception of man, the being 'for contemplation and for valour formed.'

My quotation about 'indulgent Heaven' was from Mr. Southey's grand ode on the death of the Princess Charlotte, one of the first-class lyrics in our language. How did you happen to forget it? I have been reading your Father's poems lately and admire them more than ever. I covered a sheet of paper with remarks on the latent merits of his 'Æolian Harp,' and 'Fears in Solitude,' and the numberless qualities that make up those poems ; but the moment we go deeply into these things the matter is endless—true poetry is infinite. O! for five such volumes! Since the days of Orpheus there never was such philosophic poetry as he might have given us if his 'bark' had not been blown away from 'the Fortunate Islands of the Muses.' . . .

Adieu, my dear friend,
Affectionately yours,
AUBREY DE VERE.

Aubrey's daily life during these months is represented in the following entry in his diary :—

March 26 *to April* 8.—The usual routine. Up at seven—read (principally Montesquieu) till breakfast. Revised poetry during the earlier part of the day. Walked with Vere to the plantation, and discussed politics. Read Carlyle's 'Past and Present,' and much approved of his grim jeering at Mammonism and Dilettantism. Received a letter from H. Taylor, mentioning that he had finished his first Act and begun an Ode. Parish meetings about the distress and quantities of work laid out. Adare and W. Monsell[1] paid us a visit, and the former gave a bad account of Church matters in England. Heard from Mrs. H. Coleridge, who sent me some lines on Crashaw. Received yesterday a letter from Harriet Thompson, mentioning that she and her husband were going to join the Church of Rome. Her letter written in a serious tone and in an amiable spirit.

Summer brought the wish to see his London friends once more. His father, though complaining at times of slight indisposition, seemed practically well again. The record of his London visit in the diary leaves the impression of special gaiety, and of enjoyment without a cloud of anxiety. I subjoin a few typical extracts :—

May 26 *to June* 19.—Sailed by the three o'clock packet—a very smooth passage—walked up and down the deck with

[1] William Monsell of Tervoe, the neighbour and intimate friend of the de Veres. Mr. Monsell long represented the county of Limerick in Parliament, was Postmaster-General in 1871, and was in 1873 created Lord Emly.

a man whom I sat next to at the entrance examination at the University. Got to town by railroad at one o'clock, found Lady Monteagle, Janet and Matilda. Called on Mrs. H. N. Coleridge. I sat a long time with her—thought her looking much as last year. Went the next day to Mortlake, found H. Taylor and Dofo looking very well, and in excellent spirits —the baby much improved. Captain Elliot, Mrs. E. and Freddy came. I was much struck by his great energy and redundancy. They took me back in their carriage. A small family party at dinner. W. Marshall and his wife came in the evening.

Went about leaving cards and ordering clothes. Called in the evening on Lady Limerick. Drank tea with Caroline Russell. Went afterwards to Mrs. Calvert and Fanny, with whom I found Edmond Calvert, a young engineer.

Paid more visits. Found the Ashburtons at home, who asked me to visit them near Ryde. Drank tea with the Adares. We had some very good music and much conversation about St. Columba. Adare much disgusted at the state of things in our Church.

Wrote letters (Saturday). Called on Fanny Calvert, who explained her state of mind to be that logically she was convinced that the Church of Rome was the true and only Church ; but that there was much in it that shocked her moral sense, and in the meantime that her feelings inclined her to remain with the Church of England and Mr. Richards, though she had no longer the pleasure she had once had in Margaret Chapel, and in fact did not feel as if the Sacraments were in our Communion anything more than emblems and memorials. Lady Strong came in, and took luncheon with us—a merry party. She praised her daughters to me with affectionate exultation, and made me walk with her to see Kate. We met her in the street, and she struck me as a very beautiful, frank, and engaging person—a grown-up child. I roamed about the Park in great health and spirits, visited Mrs. Gurney-Barclay, with whom I found Mrs. Wrightson. Visited Mr. Brookfield, whom I found preparing for a journey to Italy. Went to the Opera with Horatio.

Tuesday.—Breakfasted with the Adares, met the Bishop

of Oxford, Mr. Manning and Mr. Godley.   Mr. Manning the
most ecclesiastical man I have seen.   The Bishop a little
round, mercurial, plausible man, with great energy and great
ability—somewhat sly perhaps by nature, but not apparently
from interested motives.   We talked on the Irish Church, and
arrived at no conclusion but that it was an anomaly, and that
no one knew either what could or what would be done with
it.   The two divines seemed to have no objection on
principle, either to abolish the Establishment or endow
Romanism ; but the Bishop said that as the Establishment
existed, he thought it ought to be maintained, whatever was
done as to Romanism.   On this subject it is quite plain that
High Churchmen are completely at sea.   Called on Macready
with a letter from Serjeant Talfourd—found him very agreeable and courteous—he promised to read ' Mary Tudor ' and
report on it, though he said that there was no theatre in
which to bring out a play worthily.

Aubrey writes thus to his father of the visit to Macready :—

Ladon House, Mortlake : June 24, '46.

My dear Father,—. . . I called on Macready in the course
of the day, and found him an extremely agreeable and well-
informed person.   He spoke with great enthusiasm and also,
as I thought, discernment on dramatic literature, but at the
same time in the most desponding way of the present state
of the stage, and indeed as if he were himself about to retire
from it.   He said that there is really no theatre at present at
which a work of high dramatic claims can be worthily brought
out.   Nothing is thought of but music and pantomime, and
the small company which has been scraped together at the
Princess's Theatre is already dispersed, or going to be dispersed
again and (as he seemed to think) not likely to reassemble.
This was not very encouraging, but he asked many questions
about your play, and ended by expressing a desire to read it
at all events, and promising to give his opinion as to its
fitness for the stage.   He spoke so much as if he had himself
done with the stage, that I suppose there is little chance of
his taking the play himself, but I have no doubt from the
cordiality and friendliness of his manner that he will do

whatever can be done in the way of advice, and in the way of furnishing letters of introduction to managers, he himself no longer possessing the management of a theatre. . .

I met Moxon, who immediately enquired what you were going to do about publishing. I mentioned what your intentions were, and he advised me first to make Macready's acquaintance, and if nothing came of that, to make acquaintance with Mr. Webster, the Manager of the Princess's Theatre. The only other theatre I believe, in which the legitimate drama is acted is Sadler's Wells—a rather out of the way place, I suppose, but still I think it would be worth while to speak to the managers of both these theatres, and if they are encouraging in their expressions, to give them an opportunity of perusing your play. I had a very long and agreeable conversation with Macready, who said many things which will interest you to hear, though they are too long to be written. Amongst other things he said, as I have heard you remark also, that there was no greater mistake than that of imagining that a play was the less adapted to stage purposes because it contained eminently poetical passages. No passages, he said, tell more on an audience than poetical, provided only that the poetry be dramatic in its character, and introduced appositely. Shakespeare, he said, was as wonderful in his knowledge of stage effect as in everything else, and all the alterations in his text made by managers have been for the worse. The post is just going out now, so I have not time for more. I sent the MS. to him yesterday evening, and then came here, where I had the pleasure of finding all well. H. Taylor is most anxious to read your play again. I hope I shall have a good account of your health in my next accounts from Curragh.

With best love to all, ever, my dear Father,
Your affectionate Son,
AUBREY DE VERE.

The diary continues :—

Friday.—Stephen came . . . told us of the division against Government, and discussed politics, anticipating a junction (ultimately) of the Moderate Whigs with the Peel party. In the evening Stephen produced his Sonnet, which we all liked very much. There was a long discussion on my way of life. I spoke of a political career. H. Taylor replied that I was probably not fit for it, and Stephen that it was hardly fit for me, as a poor man. H. Taylor urged some literary task upon me, by way of discipline.

July 2.—H. Taylor and I went to breakfast with Mr. Rogers, and met Mr. Macready and Captain Lyons—much pleasant conversation, but the old man seemed a little less vigorous than he used. H. Taylor liked Macready and asked him out on Sunday. I called on Mr. Richards, who seemed much worn, and had grown very grey. He said that more conversions must be looked for, and spoke with severe disapprobation of the conduct of the converts to Romanism, especially Mr. Oakeley. He mentioned a new Institution at Harrow for the purpose of training choristers, at which Dr. Pusey and Mr. Keble (both of them as firm as ever—the latter had not read Newman's book) had preached. He spoke also of a great Monastery, which the Jesuits were going to set up in Wales, and said they would ' convert the Principality.' He spoke in despair of the Irish Church—of the English he said we must go on ' hoping against hope.' From him and F. Calvert, I heard that there were great efforts now being made in our Church to revive conventual institutions, Confession, &c., but he confessed that the Catholic movement had received a decided check from the conversions.

At the beginning of July, his happy London life was abruptly terminated by the news that his father was dangerously ill :—

July 3.—I came into town, intending to call on Macready. Found in Brook Street a note from Vere stating that my father had passed the afternoon of the preceding Tuesday in excruciating pain ; that the Griffins were much alarmed, and that they were about to send for Dr. Crampton. I returned to Mortlake for my things—bade adieu to Dofo and H. Taylor, who drove me as far as Hammersmith, and set off by the mail-train at 9 P.M. At 5.30 we arrived in Liverpool—got on board, and slept till near twelve. We reached Kingstown by 5 P.M.

All the bay of Dublin was illuminated by the brightest sun, and enlivened by innumerable pleasure boats. The ships hung out all their flags in honour of the Regatta. The scene was one of the softest and loveliest gaiety, and I could not but feel strongly as though it were an omen of good. I called on Crampton—he was out—on Mrs. Heron—she was out also. Walked towards the Post Office, when crossing towards the bank I saw her and her daughter Mary. The sorrow in their faces came home to me like an arrow, and their words confirmed this impression. She told me that Crampton had said on his return, that he only wondered that he had been sent for, so hopeless was the case.

Aubrey took the mail that day for Limerick, and drove on to Adare, passing ' all the time on my knees in prayer.'

July 4.—Met the coachman close to the Adare gate, with the pony carriage. He was pale and weeping, and warned me to make haste. Edmond met us on the approach, and spoke as if there were no time to lose. From Normoiles we ran all the way home. Anna came to me in the drawing-room. I ran upstairs and found all the family standing, kneeling or sitting about the room. They told me to go on—the moment my dear father saw me, he raised himself up, threw his arms round me and exclaimed in quite a strong voice ' O my dear Aubrey, do I see you again ? I am so happy.' Then, ' What hope do you give me of Horatio ? ' I said, ' I hope he may come to-night,' and he answered nothing, but sighed.

My poor mother sat at the foot of the bed, now weeping piteously, now quietly looking at him. His face was very dark, and he moaned constantly, though, as he told Stephen, more from distress than pain. Mary Lucy [1] leaned over his pillow ministering to him with a devoted tenderness. Ellen sat at the foot of the bed, her countenance entirely composed, and her eyes never moving from him. When she spoke she was also perfectly serene ; and said once or twice ' How shall we ever do without him !'

---

[1] His eldest brother's wife.

Robert and Louisa were in the room. Dr. G. was on the bed by him, weeping, when I came in. The servants were outside the door, which was open. After a time Vere came to the foot of the bed, knelt down, and, everyone else kneeling, read some of the prayers out of the Service for the Visitation of the Sick. My father used to repeat ' Amen ' at the end of each prayer, and the second versicle in the 'Gloria Patri.' Vere then gave me the book, and I read several prayers aloud.

My father still had great strength and moved restlessly in his bed. My mother always moved so that she could see him. While suffering much he laid his hand on his heart, and M. L. heard him say, ' All is peace and quietness here.' She heard him also say to my mother several times, ' Why do you cry ? ' About an hour after I came, he began to sink fast, and his sufferings seemed less. . . . For the next hour he lay pretty quiet, half sitting, half reclining, but with a sort of loud sigh that accompanied every respiration.

For the last half hour he seemed to have no pain. Vere and Stephen were kneeling on the sofa at the foot of his bed, as was I generally. Anna and Edmond came in. John was sent for ; but could not bring himself to come inside the room. Hickey and Kingsley were close to the bed. Vere again took up the Prayer Book, and read the Lord's Prayer, the Creed, &c. &c., all kneeling. The last words my father was heard to murmur were ' Father, Father,' evidently in prayer. For a considerable time no one moved or shed a tear—all sat watching him in profound silence. Once Vere rose and pressed the cross on his Prayer Book on my Father's forehead. Gradually his respirations came at longer intervals and with less and less sound. My mother lay aslant on the bed, her face close to his shoulder—her eyes shut, and she looked at him no more. He lay perfectly quiet—his hands lying across his body—his eyes slowly moving under his low-hung eyelids. When he drew the last breath (July 5, 1846, about 2.15 P.M.) no one knew—so peaceful was his end. For several minutes we stood round gazing at him, but silent. At last my mother raised herself on her elbow, but not high enough to see his face, and then sank back again. Once more she lifted herself, and looked steadily in his face. She

then said in a clear distinct voice, ' Is—it—all—over ? '
Dr. G. advanced, and after a moment bowed sorrow-
fully in answer. Some one was then bending forward, as if
to touch him, or close his eyes. My mother again half raised
herself, and waved her hand in a calm but authoritative way,
putting all aside—her head again sank back on the pillow.
After a time she raised herself enough to place her left
hand on his—gradually her hand rose and lay a moment
on his breast; a little after it touched his chin. Then it
mounted to the brow, and descended first on one lid, then
on the other, closing them both. She then looked fixedly
at the face for a time—kissed his hand, his breast and
his brow. . . . Almost immediately she fainted, and they
carried her [into another] room, and laid her on the bed.
After a few minutes she revived—threw her arms wide, and
exclaimed in a low wail, ' Oh—is it possible, can it indeed
be all over ? ' . . . . Ellen, whom I had supported along, was
placed on the sofa in Vere's room ; she was quite calm and
occasionally wept.

It was a strange thing that during that awful death scene,
though our souls were wholly fixed on him, yet the outward
senses could take note of outward things. The windows were
open, and the countless trees which he so loved, as they waved
in the sunshine, and murmured in his dying ears, seemed at
once to sigh as if for sorrow, and to whisper of comfort. To
me it seemed as if half my nature was frozen, and the other
half awakened to an intense and tranquil life. During the
latter part of the time, however, my abiding feeling was : God
is here in the midst of us ; as surely as He is personally
present in Heaven, He is present here in this room. If
' wherever two or three are gathered Christ is in the midst of
them,' how much more is He among us now ! No doubt, the
angels who look on us now, contemplate this as the true and
just solution of the problem of human life. They see here a
family gathered around its dying head. He is but rehearsing
for us the part which each will soon have to play. A few
years will pass, so many hours, and each of us will be lying as
he is now lying there. Each of us will at that moment remember this scene, and feel and know that he was himself

I

born but to go through it in his own person. There was much of awe ; but Death seemed to have lost its terrors as we knelt in the immediate presence of Death. After a little time I came back to the room, where I found Vere, Stephen and one or two of the maid-servants. His face was profoundly calm, and wore also an expression of severe, but deep and secret happiness, as if some mystery which had perplexed him long was at last laid bare. Every one went out of the room for awhile. I continued to sit by the bedside. I kissed the brow—there was something very remarkable in the loftiness and grandeur that it had assumed, the lower part of the face being worn somewhat thin, and the forehead lying smooth, white and unwrinkled, with all its noble developments.

July 6.—In the night I sat up (the room as before being full of humble mourners, poor men and women of the place) till the coffin was brought up, and I cut off some of his hair. Stephen remained to see him transferred to it. I waited in the hall on the stairs. When I returned, there was still the same noble expression of countenance, the very features and proportions of the face being apparently cast in a nobler mould. The hands were exposed—those hands that had so carefully abstained from evil deeds looked whiter and more innocently beautiful than ever after death. They were cold, but soft. I lay in the great chair by the coffin till nine o'clock, sometimes dozing. I could see the cold grey dawn brightening upon the tops of the sighing trees, and at intervals hear the whispering of Hickey, with Hogan, my grandmother's maid, who had raised a piteous lament on seeing him first.

July 7.—I looked on the face so noble and serene in death. Vere said, 'In that brow I see his whole character—reverence—imagination—honour.' Kingsley then drew the hood over the face. This was the saddest moment of all. It was as though some strange eclipse had taken place in a moment. The lid was then closed down.

They buried him on July 9, and the succeeding days were passed by the family in recalling details of the illness, and of their father's life. The diary contains, on July 10, Aubrey's own impressions of his father's character :—

His singular purity was the more remarkable as he had not only the example of his young companions to lead him astray, but also that of those he most respected. . . . His utter repugnance to all sorts of profligacy was not more striking than his complete tolerance for all who had been betrayed into the courses which he denounced.

There was in him such singleness of character, that, believing entirely what he believed, the slightest intimations of duty, once admitted, were to him as laws. Thus, the habit of copying, when learning to write, the formula ' jest not with holy things ' had preserved him all his life from an irreverent use of Scripture, &c. He was wholly true and guileless in word and deed, seeking no private ends, and taking no advantage of any man—any one who conversed with him saw all that was passing within him. He was just, at the same time that he was generous, and possessed so chivalrous an elevation of mind as communicated a noble dignity not only to his outward bearing but to all his thoughts and feelings. He was indeed the Soul of Honour, and his chivalrous disposition showed itself in everything, in his reverence for kings, for priests, for women —towards whom he always looked with a mixture of tenderness and respect—for children, for all who were aggrieved or oppressed, for all things that were pure, lovely, or of good report.

The only mode in which anything that could be called in any sense worldliness showed itself in him was in the extraordinary zeal with which he applied himself to the making of a great place, and adorning it. In this design two parts of his nature met and worked together, his love of the beautiful, and his reverence for the ancestral and hereditary principle. Though he had much family pride, he was personally humble as a child. He had no confidence in anything that he wrote if disapproved by others ; the humblest praise elated him ; and there was something most touching in the childlike simplicity with which he appealed to your sympathies. It was this extreme distrust of his own powers which prevented him from achieving that high place in the literature of our day, to which they undoubtedly would have raised him, if fully developed and disciplined—at least if judgment, imagination, a large heart, a noble spirit, pure taste and a pure vigorous style, entitle a poet to permanent fame. His heart was so tender a one that no woman ever was more care- ful not to give pain, more solicitous about the sufferings of others, or regardful of their feelings, and even of their weaknesses —yet when bodily trials came upon him he bore them with a manliness that surprised his physicians. He never shrank from them in anticipation, and when his spirits were worn out by long-continued suffering, though he sighed from weariness, and perhaps with a childlike demand for sympathy, he never complained ; and his gratitude was unbounded for attentions which he would have felt as nothing, if called to bestow them on another. His religious convictions were deep and gravely practical ; and the expression of them not only unostentatious but unexaggerated—in this respect as in others, he realised his own apothegm, ' A man should be ever better than he seems.' They were his first through the docility of faith. They were subsequently confirmed by conscientious study. They were not only firmly based, but fresh and youthful, appealing to his heart, and giving him consolation in the time of bereavement and on the bed of death—and as his life advanced his religious principles deepened. Never had they shown themselves so strongly in the form of active charity as during the last two months of his life, which were spent in constant exertions to relieve the poor from the afflicting distress of the season though during all that time he was constantly oppressed by an illness which weighed heavily both on his body and his spirits. One of the last things he said to me was ' I cannot build [stables] this year for I must build those two cottages, and I think it is somewhat better to build for men than for horses.'

July 11 *to August* 20.—I passed several days reading over and arranging my father's correspondence with my mother— strange and deep was the interest of thus having nearly the whole of my father's life passed, as it were, in review before me. It gave, I think, a deeper feeling of tenderness, though not of filial tenderness ; and was accompanied by a feeling of the transience of all things in this world, such as I had never realised before—seeing those whom we have been accustomed to think of as old, or at least venerable, acting as the young, and regarding others as we had always regarded them, makes the very ground on which we stand seem to stream away beneath our feet, and flit past us like a river.

Some of the thoughts which crowded within him are given in the sonnets, written during these days, to his father's memory:—

I

At times I lift mine eyes unto ' the Hills
Whence my salvation cometh '—aye and higher—
And, the mind kindling with the heart's desire,
Mount to that realm nor blight nor shadow chills :
With concourse of bright forms that region thrills :
I see the Lost One midmost in the choir,
From heaven to heaven on wings that ne'er can tire
I soar ; and God Himself my spirit fills.
If that high rapture lasted need were none
For aid beside, nor any meaner light,
Nothing henceforth to seek and nought to shun :
But my soul staggers at its noonday height
And stretching forth blind hands, a shape undone
Drops back into the gulfs of mortal night.

II

Then learn I that the Fancy's saintliest flight
Gives or a fleeting, or a false relief ;
And fold my hands and say, ' Let grief be grief,
Let winter winter be, and blight be blight ! '
O Thou all-wise, all-just, and infinite !
Whate'er the good we clasped, the least, the chief,
Was Thine, not ours, and held by us in fief ;
Thy Will consummate in my will's despite !
' Blessed the Dead : ' and they, they too, are blest
Who, dead to earth, in full submission find,
Buried in God's high Will, their Maker's rest :
Kneeling, the blood-drops from their Saviour's feet,
Their brows affusing, make their Passion sweet ;
And in His sepulchre they sleep enshrined.

August 6, 1846.

August brought another death at Curragh Chase. The wife of a dependent of the family died after childbirth. Aubrey had been godfather and his mother godmother to the

child. The mother lingered for five days, and died on the
25th, the de Veres being assiduous visitors at the bedside.
The mysteries of life and death took—as may be seen from
the diary—a deepening hold on the poet.

Aubrey de Vere now devoted himself heart and soul to
the work of the Relief Committees. It had been his father's
absorbing task during the last weeks of his life, and this gave
additional sacredness to what was in any case a duty. We
find the work energetically resumed in September. Providence seemed to have given him the active and purposeful
life which his friends desired for him, without his selecting
a definite profession. A letter to his friend, Mrs. Villiers,
on October 6, describes the effect on himself, both of his
father's death, and of his labours for his unfortunate countrymen. After repeating the narrative of events already given
in the diary, he thus continues :—

You wish to know what my feelings have been. For
several days after our bereavement, I think that we felt our
loss less than you would have anticipated, knowing our
affection. Death is at first felt to be what it really is—a
spiritual mystery—too marvellous and deep a thing to be
contemplated with selfish feelings. We seem almost to die
with him who is dead, and only to move about here by a
sort of charmed life, which is to break in a moment like our
other delusions. After some time, Life comes back with its
cares and its duties, and there is then much more bitterness
in our sorrow—the wound is colder and sorer. We have,
however, had many consolations besides those religious ones
which are all in all. One of these is the distinctness with
which we can now contemplate the noble character of him
who is gone. While they are yet with us, we hardly know
those who are nearest to us—we think of them in their
relations to ourselves, not as they actually are. I have found
that all I have been thinking of my father's character is
exactly what the others have been thinking, and the remembrance of such a character is a possession that cannot be
taken away. How much I wish that you had known him

well ! . . . [But] indeed, very few could have known him—he was too humble to develop one half of the large and various powers which he possessed, and those only who were constantly with him can know how to interpret aright the few hints which he has left behind, of what he might have done. If a nature magnanimous and elevated, exquisitely tender and absolutely pure, be worthy of reverence, his was worthy of it ; and we who have such a character to contemplate and remember are less to be pitied than many who never were bereft.

Another great consolation which we possess is the degree in which we endeavour to realise all that he would have wished, or that he intended. A week after his death my eldest brother, who I think was more shaken, if not more grieved, than any of us, said 'We must remember everything that he ever intended doing in this place, and treasure up every hint that he dropt from time to time ; while we carry his designs into execution, we may be able to think that the picture he had shaped to himself is gradually being realised, and that every new Spring makes it more like what he had imagined.'

We have always 'dwelt in unity' in this family, and this circumstance cannot but mitigate the blow in a great degree. On the other hand, there are some circumstances that aggravate our loss. I cannot help feeling with much pain that I might have been more to him than I was—not that I have ever been less dutiful or devoted to him, I suppose, than the average of sons, but, taking into account what he was, I ought to have been much more to him. If he had been spared to us one other year, or if one year ago we had known how soon we were to lose him, we might, it seems to me now, have been drawn so much more near him. It would have been to him no shock to know that he was to die at the end of a year. He would have removed his thoughts wholly from earthly things, and thought only of the next world, and of doing good to others while yet time remained. Must we not have been all the better for such communion if it had been granted ? But what God has appointed is no doubt for the best. We cannot tell how much bodily suffering he might

have had to go through. I dreamed not long ago that he
was still among us, but that he was again attacked by the
complaint from which he had suffered so much during the last
few years, and so great was my pain, that it was a relief to
wake and remember that he was now beyond all touch of
mortal trouble. I think of him constantly, but often think
myself unfeeling for not grieving more, and I do think that
he would have grieved more if he had lost one of us.

There are, however, I trust, other reasons beside my
hardness, for my not being more cast down than I am. Life
has never seemed to me much of a reality—now it seems
more than ever a dream. The lapse of time, and the speed
with which life streams from under our feet, has become as
pleasant a thought to me as it used to be a painful one. We
are going to build a mausoleum in this place (it was one of
his wishes that he should repose in the midst of the scenes he
had so tenderly loved, and adorned with such a careful affection), and I can [dwell] with pleasure on the thought of the
time when we shall all rest together within it. Now more
than ever it seems to me of less importance to get on well in
the world, than to get well out of it.

If I were to fall into any ambitious or worldly schemes,
I know that my regret for him who is gone would become
more sore in proportion as it became secularised. At the same
time the circumstances of this year have forced me to become
very active, and activity mixed with uncertainty gives a
strange sort of impulse to one's nature. I do not know
whether, in your southern Paradise, you have heard of our
Irish famine. It is, however, such as was probably never
known before. In the course of one month we saw nearly
the whole food of the great mass of the country melt like
snow before our eyes. All over the country, works are being
set on foot to enable the poor people to buy Indian meal—
works which are calculated to cost about ten millions. My
ears are sometimes dinned for a day together by the
wrangling of people at Relief Committees, or Road Sessions,
and I assure you I have learned how to make use of my eyes
also. I was out from after breakfast till nine o'clock at night,
a few days ago, making a census of the people in want of

food, and many a strange spectacle I saw while engaged on this occupation. In this part of the country there is little *except want* to contend with ; but some of the scenes which I have witnessed in wilder parts of the country are desolate indeed. In one day I have sat within nearly eighty mud hovels, without windows or chimneys—the roof so low that you could not (in some cases) stand upright, and within and around a mass of squalidness and filth. Many a trait of native goodness, or even refinement, I have noticed in such an abode—many a countenance I have marked traced with the characters of goodness, long endurance, and piety, though seen dimly through a veil not only of pallor and smoke, but one worn by the blasts and rain of many an adverse year. And in the midst of these horrors I have seen such strange gleams of humour, and heard many a sad tale told with a gay indifference.

I told you just now that life seems to me a lighter and more fleeting thing than ever ; and yet no less true is it, that I have never before been half so deeply impressed with the duty of doing what in us lies to lighten its load to the thousands who surround us, and whom, directly or indirectly, we may benefit, if only we take the trouble of going among them, sympathising with them, and understanding them. I am sure that the poor are on the whole the best. In all those homes of misery I never heard an impatient murmur. When the poor people are congregated in masses, they are more inflammable, and seem to set each other on fire, like the branches of a dried-up tree rubbed together by the wind. We have had a good many rows in the cities. Indeed, they say that Lord Stuart de Decies, one of the most popular men in Ireland, only saved his life by the swiftness of his horses, and the timely arrival of a troop of cavalry ; but, considering the amount of distress, the people have behaved admirably hitherto. I am at present leading as active a life as you, or Henry Taylor, could desire, and the more active I become among the real trials of life, the more do I rejoice that I am not confined within the conventional bands of a narrow money-making profession, pursued with the cant of duty, but in the spirit of trade. Heaven forbid that all professional men should labour in so low a spirit ; but, on the other hand, pray believe that a person need not remain a dreamer all his life, though he does not take up a professional sphere of activity. Now, have you had enough of me, and do you repent your charge that I did not tell you anything of myself?

Aubrey and his friends regarded as unsatisfactory the unproductive works which the Government instituted during the early part of the famine, for the employment and relief of the destitute. The old and infirm could not profit by them. Half the cost was charged upon Irish land ; and yet the labour was avowedly unproductive, and did nothing towards developing the resources of the country. The de Veres regarded it as an instance of the thoughtless way in which even kindness to Ireland was administered by the English, and the blunders of those charged with carrying out the programme confirmed this view. It was therefore proposed to substitute the distribution of Indian meal for the destitute—whereby twice the number could be relieved at the same cost as that of the unproductive works—and to secure the adoption of Mr. Labouchere's suggestion, that productive labour should be organised in accordance with the real needs of each locality.

Aubrey's labours for these ends were eventually successful ; but some idea of the difficulties of the time, and of the want of organisation among a people by nature unpractical, may be given by citing almost at haphazard some entries in the diary :

October 8.—Walked with Stephen to Pallas, where we met Vere, who had walked from Mount Trenchard. Our meeting of the Relief Committee was a perfect Babel, no one seeming to have the power of understanding anyone else, or of making himself understood. I found it impossible to ascertain the simple fact of how much Indian corn was necessary for the support of a family, and no one seemed to consider this an enquiry of any importance. One member of the Relief Committee said that a labouring man required two pounds per day, another that one pound was sufficient. Two of the leading members got into a personal altercation, after which all parties were at cross purposes. Every one talked at the same time—no one listened, and in the various propositions shot in at the spur of the moment, there seemed no reference to any general principle, and no reference to exact facts. Half from diffidence, half from indolence or preoccupation, the principal person there took hardly any part in the deliberations ; and there was no attempt to manage the disputants by a little tact. The meeting at last just before breaking up voted that depôts of Indian meal should be procured, and referred the mode of its sale, the question of the Destitute, and the collection of contributions, to an adjourned meeting five days distant. I was impressed with the conviction that—

1. People cannot really deliberate in public.

2. An agreement must always be virtually arrived at behind the scenes.

3. Great temper and tact are quite as requisite as wisdom, to effect public good.

4. A person of dignity and suavity is needed as an amalgam at such meetings, in order to make the rest work together.

5. Petty jealousies determine the gravest questions.

6. When the public are present in numbers each speaker virtually addresses the public, or represents their views instead of simply speaking his mind.

7. When tired out, men will vote anything, to have done with the matter, and will prefer a vague or equivocal vote, or one that postpones the decision.

8. A meeting has the best chance of working well if practically governed by a single individual, who will thus feel his responsibility, and be at the trouble of ascertaining what he would be at.

October 23.—Vere and I drove in the pony carriage to the Relief Meeting. Captain Dill was assailed by a mob of infuriated country gentlemen, but prevailed over them at last by a mixture of firmness and gentleness. He came home and dined and slept at Curragh. We liked him much. He mentioned that in the North, the great factories gave out large quantities of thread to be spun by hand looms, and that on some estates 400 such were employed in one house.

October 28.—We went to the Presentment Sessions at Pallas — my uncle chairman. After much ado it was discovered that the meeting was called by mistake—by another mistake the Engineers fancied that the railroad was not to be sanctioned by the Board of Works, and so did not press it. Accordingly the meeting was adjourned without doing anything. My uncle returned with us to Curragh.

October 29.—Vere, my uncle and I drove to Newcastle. There was a meeting at Lord Devon's at which, for the first time, the gentlemen of the county had a little private consultation, and agreed to avail themselves of the ' Reproductive Works.' Prince George of Cambridge lunched with us, and was very courteous and agreeable.

November 3.—Corrected two proof sheets of ' Mary Tudor ' and sent them to Pickering. Attended the Relief Committee at Holly Park. Much trouble from the people crowding in, in spite of us. At last Father Foley laid about him with vehemence, and in a practical way, and shoved them out by main force. I drew up a number of presentments for the tenants to put in to-morrow.

November 4.—Went to the Presentment Sessions and did nothing—the meeting had been summoned by a mistake on the part of the Government, founded on a tricky suggestion of Lord A. B.'s. He sat back in the corner, apparently as ignorant as any one as to the cause of our meeting.

November 5.—Tried as much as I could to soften William Monsell's indignation against the Government, and abate Augustus O'Brien's voluntary misery. Neither of them chose to be consoled. On our way home we called at Elm Park.

November 27.—We drove to the Sessions at Shanagolden. W. Smith O'Brien[1] made a speech, trying to dissuade the meeting from acting under Mr. Labouchere's letter. After we disposed of some Electoral Divisions a mob assailed the court-house, which the police defended. W. O'Brien and Father Cleary kept speechifying to the people outside the window

---

[1] William Smith O'Brien, leader of the Young Ireland party, and M.P. for Limerick County, was the second son of Sir Edward O'Brien of Dromoland.

while we got on with the business within. At last the mob came in with W. O'Brien, who made three or four ineffectual attempts to introduce the subject of double tickets, my uncle insisting on going on with the business before us. By an exertion of great address, coolness and perseverance, my uncle got all the business done in a satisfactory way, and wound up the day with an eloquent and efficient speech to the people. W. O'Brien made another attempt to get a pledge from the officers of the Board of Works, that the issue of tickets should be on a larger scale. Mr. Owens refused to give it. On coming out he was furiously set on by the mob, but saved by Mr. Liston and Stephen. There was a strong tussle for a quarter of an hour between the police and the mob. We got off by the back way. My uncle made several speeches to the people in the streets, and was well received. He acted with great vigour and manliness, and prevented the soldiers from being called out. Mr. Owens after all was cheered as he got off. Pat O'Brien, being himself in a great fright, had got into a dishonest passion with the Board of Works, and put wind into the heads of the people. The row in the street somewhat formidable. S. E. Collis much frightened. On reaching home we found that Milnes had arrived.

December 3.—Vere and I went to Pallas. We resolved upon revising our books without delay, and removing tickets from those who were not entitled to them. Music in the evening. Stephen Collis prophesying nothing but woes, Vere, Stephen and my uncle all of the same way of thinking. Everyone desponding, and most people looking pale, thin and careworn. A certain proportion of the gentry of the country likely to lose their wits if these troubles go on increasing ; half of them have lost their heads and the hearts of many fail. Certainly the time is a critical one. Nothing can right matters except we can get the labour of the country back into the hands of individual employers. The work of individuals cannot be done by public bodies. Labour, without the true bonds that unite employer and labourer, degrades and pauperises the labouring class and disorganises society. The problem of Government is how, in this emergency, to help the proprietors to help themselves, without helping them so much

as to render them dependent and therefore insignificant. The
more they are stimulated and compelled to help themselves,
the better they will be for such discipline, and the more able
to cope with the times, provided the weight thrown on them
is not more than they can bear. It is now that we experience
the baleful effects of the profuse habits of our proprietors ;
living beyond their means and burthened by debt, they are
reduced to a mean condition, compelled alternately to beg
and to bully, and unable to perform their duties to their
dependents and their country. Prodigality is dishonest.
One of the chief dangers of the time is that of insubordination.
The gentry are too few and scattered for the emergency, the
inferior gentry are easily frightened, and the Relief Committees in many cases allow themselves to be bullied. If
once the people are allowed to feel that they can carry
matters by intimidation, the framework of society collapses,
and anarchy becomes the order of the day. The difficulty is
not so much that the storm is heavy, but that the ropes and
timbers are half rotten, and will not bear much strain. In
every place the great bulk of the gentry can at best do nothing
but follow the lead, and those who lead have too much thrown
on them for their health. Vere said to me the other day,
' I often think that it is well for my father that he is removed
from the trouble of the time.' My uncle [Lord Monteagle] is
quite worn out at present, but particularly affectionate and
grateful for attention. Before leaving Mount Trenchard he
said : ' I once knew a gentleman who was popular in this
country—his name was Thomas Spring Rice.'

The horrors of that winter left an indelible impression on
Aubrey's imagination ; and he has given us a graphic picture—
in his poem entitled ' A Year of Sorrow '—of the pitiless
season, and of the death from cold and starvation which
would overtake the peasants in the dead of night :—

> Fall snow and cease not ! Flake by flake
> The decent winding sheet compose ;
> Thy task is just and pious ; make
> An end of blasphemies and woes.

Fall, flake by flake ! by thee alone
Last friend the sleeping-draught is given ;
Kind nurse by thee the couch is strewn,
The couch whose covering is from Heaven.

Descend, and clasp the mountain's crest ;
Inherit plain and valley deep ;
This night on thy maternal breast,
A vanquished nation dies in sleep.

Lo ! from the starry Temple Gates
Death rides, and bears the flag of peace :
The combatants he separates ;
He bids the wrath of ages cease.

Fall snow ! in stillness fall like dew,
On church's roof and cedar's fan ;
And mould thyself on pine and yew,
And on the awful face of man.

On quaking moor and mountain moss,
With eyes upstaring at the sky ;
And arms extended like a cross,
The long-expectant sufferers lie.

Bend o'er them, white-robed acolyte !
Put forth thine hand from cloud and mist ;
And minister the last sad Rite,
Where altar there is none, nor priest.

The state of things a few months later, and something of
the nature of Aubrey's own work for the people may be
gathered from the following letter to Henry Taylor :—

Curragh Chase : May 31, 1847.

My dear Henry,— . . . . If you wanted me to have a
little practical training in the course of my life, you have had
your wish. 'Let Euclid rest and Archimedes pause' has
been the only line of poetry which I have allowed myself to
ruminate in my walks ; and as for learning to 'measure life
betimes' I am sure I have taken its measure as carefully as if
I were a tailor going to make a suit of clothes for it. In the

first place we have had our 'Relief' business, which has
worked such persons as chose to take the labouring oar about
as hard as a clerk in an office.   So far, then, I have fulfilled
your desire and become a man of public business (a desire,
by the way, which I think you shook off).   In the second
place, we have set up all sorts of industrial employment
for the women of the neighbourhood, which have of course
entailed no end of trouble in the management, as well as
perplexity in the disposal of manufactures which nobody
wanted.   Thus you see Mrs. Edward's prescription for me
has been adopted with my wonted docility, and I have
become a manufacturer.   In the third place, since the new
system of relief has been introduced, and the people have
been idle, the country has been cumbered with vast mobs
shifting about hither and thither like tides and counter-tides—
and I have been obliged to set up as a field preacher; for
wherever I walked or rode I was sure to meet multitudes of
people who assured me that they were going to demolish
some mill, or carry off some gentleman's cattle, an intimation
which naturally provokes a rejoinder.   In the fourth place, the
bad passions of the people have got [so far] loose during this
period of misrule, this saturnalia of misery, that conspiracies
without end have been hatched all over the country; and if
I could transform myself into a Fouché, that sublime thief-
catcher, it would give me something to do to watch and
counteract those with which I have some concern.

Whatever else is to be learned in this stormy period, there
is one of your favourite virtues which the state of things round
us has no direct tendency to teach, and that is straightforward
dealing. If I were to mention to one informant what I heard
from another, the first would probably be shot before evening,
and the second before the next morning; and I should go
without information in future.   There is one man from whom
I have derived much information, and whom I have done all
that I can to protect from conspiracies formed against him,
who is himself so much of a conspirator that to my certain
knowledge *he was himself the man who got up a party by
which his own house was attacked the other night and his
servant boy beaten.*   This was a stroke of policy, as he

considered it, to throw suspicion on a rival. The end of his mining and countermining will probably be that both he and his rival will be killed before the end of the year.

The other day an armed party did us the honour of paying us a visit. They met me and demanded that a steward should be dismissed, a proposal which I politely declined. Since then I have found out that the friends of the said steward had got up a similar party of their own for the purpose of removing another man ; and that it was only the condemnation of this scheme by a third party which prevented its having taken place.

There is much that is ludicrous in the state of things, which is fortunate—we could never get on in Ireland if there were not a great deal to laugh at as well as a great tendency to laugh. For instance, the White Boys have formed themselves into two parties, like Young and Old Ireland. The young White Boys attacked three farmers' houses close to this place, and carried off arms from each. One of these farmers was popular in the country, and the old White Boys (who called themselves the 'right boys') were so indignant that the next night they paid a visit to the young White Boys, and gave them a most unmerciful beating—desiring them at the same time to bring back the guns. This was done accordingly in open day, and without any disguise. The parties are well known, and the incident is a common topic of conversation among the people ; but as for getting information for the purpose of prosecution, you might as well advertise a reward for the discovery and conviction of the principal fleas which bit you on some particular night when you were lodging at Numero Cinquanta, Chiaia, Napoli. Just before the works were stopped, the men on one of the roads brought their own steward prisoner before the priest of the parish (they would have been above going before a magistrate), stating that he was so afraid of them that he would certainly run away, which would be counted as an outrage on their part, and occasion the suspension of the works. The Priest, a very clever man and a great friend of mine, revolved the matter in his mind for a minute, drew out from

K

them by cross-examination that four of them had without the knowledge of the rest made the man swear to decamp, commanded the steward to break his oath forthwith, and directed the crowd to find out the men who had threatened to kill him, and give them a good beating. His advice was taken as a command, and everything went on quietly afterwards.

Aubrey de Vere seems to have fairly astonished his friends by the energy and practical ability he displayed at this crisis. The dreamy poet was transformed into the man of action. A little later Henry Taylor saw him in London, whither he had come to give evidence before the Parliamentary Committee on Colonisation. Writing to Miss Fenwick in July, Taylor gives the following further particulars of his friend's work :—

Aubrey has gone through strange adventures, and has become a most active man of business and a most efficient mob orator. In one instance the troops came to attack a mob of several thousands, and, finding that they were in Aubrey's hands, who had stopped them and was making a speech from the top of a wall, the officer in command very wisely took away the troops, and Aubrey brought [the mob] to reason, and persuaded them to give up their enterprise and disperse. He looks very thin, but not unwell, and is and has been in good health and spirits. His spirits have never failed him, and he says that if he were not to take things lightly it would be impossible to do what is to be done in Ireland at this time. In his neighbourhood they are spared the horrors of any absolutely mortal amount of famine, but they have much riot and disorder to resist. One parley he had to hold with eight muskets and pistols pointed at him, not, he says, with any desire to shoot him, but in order to prevent his advancing so near to the parties as to be able to identify them. It was not safe to advance, therefore, and at the same time he felt that it was more dangerous to retire, for a bold front is the first requisite for safety with such people. His invariable self-possession is a valuable quality in such circumstances as he has been placed in ; and he understands the people thoroughly, and has almost always succeeded, either in obtaining their confidence in himself or destroying their confidence in their leaders. The people who pointed their guns at him ended by professing great respect for him and his family, but a determination to kill the steward, which was what they had come about, Aubrey having given them a point-blank refusal of their demand for his dismissal.

At the beginning of 1848 Aubrey de Vere published his book on 'English Misrule and Irish Misdeeds,' which attracted considerable attention. It was written in a spirit of sympathy for his fellow-countrymen, which aroused the hostile criticism of some of his English friends. He distinguished the 'good England' from the 'bad England,' and maintained that there had ever existed a harsh and unsympathetic attitude among the majority of Englishmen, which was largely responsible for those very faults of character in the Irish which were so much criticised. He urged the development of Irish Agriculture and of systematic emigration. Lord John Manners [1] wrote to him in February his opinion that this 'most remarkable and stirring book . . . is the most valuable contribution to our Irish political literature since the days of Burke' ; and indeed the book recalls Burke's own writings, in its union of the judicial tone with keen sympathy for the Irish people. Lord Clarendon, on the other hand, writes that he ' can't bear its tone,' though it is able, and 'at times very eloquent.' Why, he asks, does he not develop the theme of 'two Irelands,' as well as 'two Englands'—the North 'industrious and thriving,' ' the West and South indolent and pauperised, both having been exposed to the same laws'? The book is—he sums up— 'an energetic but injudicious appeal, deserving to be much admired and severely handled.'

---

[1] Now Duke of Rutland.

The estimates of the book by Mill and Carlyle have special interest. Mill writes thus :—

India House : February 3, 1848.

My dear Sir,—I am ashamed not to have sooner acknowledged your kind present of your book on Ireland, especially as I read it immediately on receiving it. Anything you write on Ireland must be well worth attending to, as no one can doubt who has read your Evidence before Lord Monteagle's Committee [1]—to say nothing of anything else. No one can sympathise more than I do in the feeling which pervades your book, that England is not entitled to throw the first stone at Ireland, being, so far as that expression can be used of a nation, guilty of all the guilt as well as of all the suffering and folly of Ireland. I have always strenuously urged the same doctrine in all I have ever written or said about Irish affairs, which is not a little in quantity at least. I agree too in most of the opinions you express, except that I look much more than you do to reclamation of waste lands and alteration of landed tenures, and less to emigration as a remedy. Perhaps also I should not let off the generality of Irish landlords quite so easily as you do, though there are among them not a few of the most meritorious landlords (probably) upon earth.

Very truly yours,
J. S. MILL.

Carlyle's view was less sympathetic to the author and his nation :—

Chelsea : February 5, 1848.

Dear Mr. de Vere,—You did not come to see me ; but how can I severely reprimand you when you are otherwise so kind? Let me hope I shall be luckier next time you come across to us.

Many thanks for the Book ; which indeed is a gift I was much gratified with. I have read the eloquent performance with attention : part of it Milnes had already read aloud to us at Alverstoke, multifarious running-commentary ac-

---

[1] Probably the Parliamentary Committee of 1847 on Colonisation. See p. 130.

companying him. Indisputably enough it is eloquent; has a chivalrous noble tone in it, which anywhere, and especially as coming from Ireland, it does us good to hear. For the rest, you anticipate rightly, I find much to dissent from; but, what is better news, there is also no passage, or hardly any, in the Book in which I do not find much to agree with. Yes, beyond doubt, there is good in Ireland that we know not; if Ireland consisted all of Hill-of-Tara meetings, of O'Connell balderdash, and rusty pistol shots and Machale letters, Ireland could not cohere at all; its pot, very languidly simmering of late, would long since have ceased to boil altogether. On the other hand, and this is my fundamental all-pervading objection, it seems to me of no use, when one has fallen into misfortune, to blame one's enemies, one's friends, one's government; or indeed any creature or entity whatever, till once one has thoroughly blamed (and amended) one's own poor self. Alas, my friend, the Government of Ireland, Saxon Government, with its bloody hoof, &c. &c., is precisely what the governments of other nations, and considerable provinces are and always were—the concentrated *Practical Likeness* of the Nation itself;—natural to the Nation, as its own face is, as the hair of its own head, growing up out of the whole being and structure of it, rooted in its very heart, nourished by the inmost drop of its blood. For no Nation, I do believe, will or can long wear an adscititious face (a *mask*), or submit to a tar *wig*; no, it acquires such face and hair as *it* can grow, and therewith walk abroad. Men, and Nations, do indeed fall among thieves, and are sadly maltreated and trampled out of shape; but a man, you will find, is generally responsible for his own face, and a Nation, I venture to assert, is always so. Let it not blame its government. The court of the Universe will hear no such plea from any Nation; let it, if insufferably ugly, say, 'I have deserved to be so.' There is no hope otherwise, I believe, for any Nation or man. These you call cruel sayings, and turn a deaf, scornful ear to them; but perhaps you will not always do so. Depend upon it, there is sincerity in these sayings too;—and much would it please me if a patriotic heart, of such insight and sense of truth as yours, offering an example to all such hearts, would look earnestly on that side of the question, and exhaust what of truth is in it. We will not despair under the given omens.[1]

Alas, alas, what England wants and Ireland only a small degree *more*, is that we should know, among our multitudinous populations, the units that are men and *free*, and the millions that by Nature's own verdict are and remain *slaves*,—whom it is the cruellest injustice to call or treat by any other name, the whole universe standing ready to *contradict*, and nullify with costs, all treatment of that kind.

Yours very faithfully,
T. CARLYLE.

From other letters on Aubrey's book written by critics of weight, I select three :—

Sir James Stephen to Aubrey de Vere

Torquay : January 20, 1848.

My dear Mr. de Vere,—It is very pleasant to receive a book from you, though on the saddest of all secular subjects ; because the book says, as plainly as need be,—'He who wrote me bears you in kindly remembrance.' If the book would go on in an equally agreeable strain I would master it all before sunset, short as the days are. But it makes my heart heavy to think on your text ; and I am, from mere self-indulgence, half reluctant to listen to your discourse. Within and without, lamentation and mourning and woe are written on all books about Ireland. I have passed my life in a chaos of offensive colonial controversies. I would not return to them for the wealth of the Rothschilds. But Irish contro-

---

[1] In the following year Carlyle visited Ireland and wrote to Aubrey in the these characteristic terms :

'The crops are beautiful beyond precedent, the weather beautiful and bright— and far and wide, waves once more in boundless breadth the fatal potato ; as yet quite luxuriant, but which all people are regarding as their Knell of Doom. The reasonablest men I talk with, not to speak of poor wretched serfs and savages, miscalled free citizens, seem to consider the potato their one dream of salvation. If the potato will revive, we live ; if it die, what can we also do but die ? More grievous stupor and stolidity I never witnessed on as wide a scale before. It seems to me the sufferings of this people will be great before they learn their lesson. Learn it, however, they must ; continue on upper earth *without* learning it they cannot, let the potato do its best.'

versies are as much worse, as (according to Burke's image) a single wild cat in one's chamber is more terrible than all the lions who are roving in Mauritania. You are not a Celt, but a naturalised Norman or Saxon ; and therefore to you I hazard the confession of my faith, that the real cause of the calamities of Ireland is the want, not the excess, of the belligerent character and qualities among the Celtic race. Every people on the face of the earth have been oppressed by their stronger neighbours ; and all people have sunk under that oppression into a degraded and servile state ; those only excepted who have had the heart to fight it out, trusting to God, and trusting to each other. If the Irish had resisted your ancestors half as gallantly as my ancestors, the Scotch, wrestled against Plantagenets, Tudors, and Stuarts, England would have become just, humane and liberal, in the only way in which nations ever acquire those virtues ;—that is by being well beaten into them. At the present moment, when the two islands are making war on each other with the pen instead of the sword, I cannot but think that the Irish are still showing the same deficiency in the art of war. The calm bitterness of the ' Times ' is ten times more effective for its dismal purpose than are all the rhetorical paroxysms of the Irish agitators, clerical or laic. I rejoice that, without the abandonment of any duty, I am free to avert my thoughts from the spectacle and from the prospects before us. I rejoice still more that you are fixing your eyes steadily on both. You have youth, which has long since taken leave of me ; and many talents to which I never had the slightest pretension, even when I was young ; with leisure, which never visited me till now when I can no longer employ it in the public service. May God guide, sustain, and help you in the strenuous use of those opportunities for mitigating the very wretchedest condition into which any nation, within the precincts of the civilised world, has ever yet been brought, since the subversion of the Roman Empire.

Dearly as I shall have to pay for my freedom, I am perfectly satisfied to have made the purchase. I believe that I have become quite well again, saving some inaptitude for intellectual labour, and saving the ill effects of having had my eyes opened to the existence within me of morbid tendencies, which did me little harm until I was taught to stand in awe of them. But, so far as my experience of three months carries me, I should say that your abdication is a very pleasant thing; and that to live without either task or task-master is necessary if one would learn to live to any purpose.

Ever yours,

JAS. STEPHEN.

The Comte de Montalembert to Aubrey de Vere

. . . I cannot refrain from expressing to you the very great satisfaction I have experienced in going through with great attention this valuable volume. I thought till now that you were *but* a poet—this *but* I do not mean to be in any wise disrespectful, as I feel for poetry the deep veneration which is generally felt for *forbidden fruit*, never having been able myself to commit anything like a verse, not even in Latin. But I had no idea you were such an excellent *pro-sateur* (as we say in French), and such an ardent politician. In my younger days I have read much about Ireland, but I do not remember ever having met with such a masterly picture of your country's rights, and of her unparalleled wrongs. Your style is most racy and spirited; but what I still more admire is the lucidity and impartiality of your judgment. A mind so completely freed from all national or religious prejudice I have scarcely ever found, particularly amongst Anglo-Saxon or Anglo-Norman authors. The fundamental idea of your plea, which seems to be that of two different *Englands* constantly in contradiction with each other, is, in my opinion, the best explanation that can be given of all that we liberal Catholics find to admire and to deplore in the British Nation.

W. Smith O'Brien to Aubrey de Vere

London: February 19, 1848.

My dear Aubrey,—I shall gladly talk over the points suggested in your letter when next we meet. At the same time

I do not feel it necessary to argue with you. You cannot stop where you are. Assuming your data, your sympathies, your convictions, I feel assured that you must end by becoming a Repealer—I will not say a separatist. You will find yourself disappointed in all your expectations from better England, and the enthusiastic affection which you bear to your native land—your identification with her interests, your jealousy for the maintenance of her honour—will necessarily lead you to the conviction, that her welfare and her fame can never be protected except by her own sons, armed with power to manage their own affairs, and if necessary to defend themselves from every aggression. I wish much that I could urge as a motive for a hearty avowal of this conviction the consideration that you would in the struggle find yourself enlisted in a band comprising all that is noble and generous in the land. Alas I must admit that such is not the character of a great majority of the present professed advocates of Repeal. Many of them are doubtless jobbers without character, who traffic upon the honest enthusiasm of the people and inflame their worst passions, for the purpose of promoting under the name of Repeal their own selfish ends. But why is this so? It is because the gentry, those who ought to be the ἄριστοι, the genuine aristocracy (for I acknowledge no other title to the name than that of being foremost in danger, foremost in every great and noble effort) shrink from the position of being leaders of the Irish people—some from abject fear, some from sybarite selfishness, some from habitual subserviency to the power, for whom during centuries they have acted as a garrison in our island.

Who leads the Repeal of the Union between Sicily and Naples? The nobles. Has Ireland less cause to complain than Sicily? Who maintains the independence of Hungary against the despotism of Austria? The nobles—i.e. the gentry. Who, rashly perhaps, but with chivalrous magnanimity, ventured to raise the banner of Poland (see Mrs. Elliot's song) against the colossal tyranny of Russia?—the nobles.

Where and what are the nobles of Ireland?—a class despised abroad and hated at home; and this occurs amongst a people of all others the most easily won to the support of aristocratic influences—amongst a people all whose prepossessions and sympathies are favourable, instead of being adverse, to the prerogatives of Birth and Station. Meditate on these things, and consider whether you would not employ your time more profitably in battling for Irish Freedom in and out of Parliament, and in making that Freedom when attained available for the happiness of the Irish people by labours in an Irish Parliament, rather than in dreaming a vision of Future Repentance and Restitution on the part of England—a vision which,

> Like the circle bounding earth and skies,
> Allures from far, yet as you follow flies.

It provokes me to see so much talent and genuine feeling thrown away. Until I read your last work I did not know that you were capable of executing many things which you still hesitate to undertake. That book has convinced me that a *mission* has been appointed to you. Gird yourself boldly and nobly to the accomplishment of that task—and begin it by exchanging *Self Reliance* for Reliance upon a brave and noble-minded people whose only fault has been that they have been too confiding, and have therefore been duped and misled —exchange, I say, for a noble reliance upon your own countrymen that tutored sentiment of dependence upon England which none knows better how to excuse, but which none more deeply regrets than

Your affectionate friend,

WILLIAM O'BRIEN.

William Monsell sums up, in a letter to Aubrey, the general verdict of the educated public in England on his book :—

76 Eaton Square : February 19, 1848.

My dear Aubrey,— . . . . All who have read the book admire its great ability. Some, as for instance Mr. Wakefield, who wrote the statistical history of Ireland in 1812, and takes the greatest interest in our affairs, declare it to be the best book ever written on Ireland. But the majority found fault with the tone—Mr. Cornewall Lewis regretted the tone very much. He said that if a few words had been altered, the book would have done a great deal of good. This gives you an honest account of the amount of the success of the book.

As to my own opinion, I must find an idle hour to write it to you at length. For the present I limit my criticism to this :—I think the style in many parts more suited to a pamphlet than a book, and I should have liked it better if it had been shorter—shorter perhaps, or longer, but if longer in a different style. I sincerely think that the book shows the greatest knowledge of Ireland, and the greatest ability, and that the sooner the writer of it writes again, the better for himself and for his country. But what tone he should take in writing I do not know. Tell truth, they say, and shame the devil ; but you can't shame the English—they despise us so heartily. . . . I must except English Roman Catholics from this charge. They do sympathise with us very much. You saw what the 'Rambler' said about you. I believe there is only one remedy. Let it be your theme. Let the Irish Protestants move into England, and the English Roman Catholics into Ireland, only don't put Lord Shrewsbury (who was enquiring for you) into Machale's Diocese.

Kindest regards to all,
W. MONSELL.

The active life of the past two years, and the general recognition of his ability as a political writer and thinker, naturally brought the idea of public life more definitely before Aubrey de Vere. And his decision against it in these circumstances was clearly final. It is given in a letter to Henry Taylor :—

Curragh Chase : February 21, 1848.

My dear Henry,—The rain of letters, you see, still goes on. I write now to tell you that I agree with nearly all that you say as to my being in Parliament. You give me the several items of the account, but do not yourself sum up ; so I conclude that if you heard to-morrow that I was in Parliament you would be, like myself, rather glad, and a good deal sorry. First—what you say about pecuniary matters is doubtless true. I should be living above my due scale of expense ;

and nothing is to me more odious than having to stuff a carpet bag with more than it will hold. As for office coming to my aid, I could not build much on that. My poverty would make me, I suppose, in some slight degree less inclined to accept or retain office than I should otherwise be. It would also, I suppose, with this gross and money-making generation, detract from my political 'respectability.'

As to my not being able to pull with others, I could do that if I chose. On my relief committee I was an element of peace and used to keep people together. There was a very stormy man upon it who never could achieve a single quarrel with me; and when I knew he would oppose some important measure if brought forward by me, I used to make him bring it forward himself. At the same time parties are very distasteful to me ; and I should assert my independence except where joint action was pretty obviously necessary.

As for soliloquising in the House, I do not think I should do that. If a matter is practical, I take to it heartily and rather passionately, if I cannot pass it by. My book may be pooh-poohed as soliloquising; but depend on it that is not its fault. It *offends* on account of the faults of those who are offended, and it is comparatively *uninfluential* on account of its own faults : but it is *ad rem*. I do not think that either my speeches or political writings would be musings in the air, though I doubt either being popular. At the same time remember, I could never be discourteous to individuals. I should have some respect even for Mr. Hume, because he is a man ; but there is nothing for which I feel so little respect as for the public. In the first place, the Public has no Personality, and is therefore no more than it seems. In the second place, there is no proportion between the real worth and power of the public, and its imaginary greatness. One may respect weakness as well as strength, but when some foolish, weak thing struts about, swinging a censer under its own nose, and receiving tribute from hundreds, who can respect that ? I should be more respectful to honourable members than to the public, in my writing.

If I went into Parliament, I should do so in the spirit of work, and not shrink from drudgery. I should study hard and labour, and give myself up to the thing until I found it of no use, when I would give it up. Whether all this labour would turn out any good I hardly know. You are quite right in saying that my studies have been of a character the opposite of those which would avail me in Parliament.

Aubrey spent some weeks after the appearance of his book under his friend's roof at Mortlake, and he writes Miss Fenwick a graphic word-picture of the Taylor household, which gives the reader an equally distinct impression of himself as a devoted friend :—

Mortlake : January 14, 1848.

My dear Miss Fenwick,— . . . . Henry has been in excellent spirits almost the whole time. Now and then, for an hour or two, when in an uncomfortable state of body, his spirits have also been depressed ; but generally he has been very happy, and begirt as he now is with children, he seems to me much more strongly built up in happiness than he used to be. It is most interesting to me to observe how the parental feeling has by degrees risen up within him. At first he seemed hardly to know what to do with his boy, and held him as if he were a piece of china that might break, or a kitten that might scratch, but this last time I have observed that he is quite a father. In the course of time I prophesy that he will be quite as fond of his little girl as of the boy (for the daughters of Eve have always found favour in his sight), but at present, as you know, he greatly prefers his ' man child.' I can now quite understand your feelings towards that little boy. He has been in the habit of waking me every morning ; and but for his ministrations, I fear that, after somewhat sleepless nights, I should have been even later than I have been in the mornings. But it was a great amusement to me to perceive the working of that instinct of courtesy within him, which you described to me, and which made it difficult for him to go away without having some special engagement to plead, or unavoidable cause of absence. Sometimes it appeared that his ' top ' was waiting for him in his ' other nursery '—at other times his ' wass ' (watch) warned him that breakfast was ready. Dofo says that he is fonder of his other godfather; but I have some hopes that she says this only to provoke my love by jealousy. At all events, I have given him a little book of Scripture pictures which may, by degrees, sink into that mysterious thing, a child's inner life; and I think that the bon-bons which he has been eating, and which have lasted very long in spite of his infantine liberality, in consequence of his being contented with one *little* cup full at a time, cannot but lay a solid foundation for a rational friendship between us in after days. Dofo has been quite well of late, and very happy in the midst of her serene and well-managed household. I can hardly tell you how delightful and strange it seems to me to contrast this household (with all its added blessings) with the happy but childless household in Blandford Square.[1] What a joy would it not have been could I have seen in vision what I have now seen in reality, during some of the less happy hours of our happy travels—could I, on some evenings when he went to bed tired and unwell after a week in which he had seemed to advance, have seen him surrounded with all the blessings which he now enjoys. I do not repine at his imperfect health, because it is not good for us to have everything about us quite prosperous. He has almost everything within and without to make a wise man happy, and though no one is less likely to be carried off his feet by a tide of prosperity, yet it is doubtless good for him to have a little wholesome bitter in the cup. He turns his blessings, it is true, to the best account, and receives them in a religious spirit; but we may feed on the sweets of religion itself, until our stomachs are no longer fit for its strong meat. . . .

Amongst my other pleasures here Henry's two new books have been a very great delight to me. I like to see him thus full of his literary activities; and as he has had the strength of mind to discard the prospects which to some would have been dazzling, of official rank and emolument, I draw good auguries from this wise abstinence, as to his having leisure in future for those poetical works which will be remembered, when the petty distinctions of the day are

[1] Where the Taylors had lived until 1844.

resolved into their native dust. You should have seen the
zeal and energy with which, while my proof sheets were
pouring in upon me, he devoted himself to the task of helping
to correct them. If, instead of an ephemeral book on an
ephemeral subject, the work had been something 'adamantine
and eternal,' in poetry or philosophy, he could not have been
more anxious to remove blemishes from it. I was delighted
to hear him yesterday speculating on writing an Epic Poem,
and devoting five years to it. The 'Eve of the Conquest'
proves that he has the faculty, and a narrative poem would
take less out of him than tragedies. If he writes a first-rate
Comedy, and narrative poem, he will be the greatest poet
since Milton, except Mr. Wordsworth, who, on the whole, is,
I think, the great poetical exponent of the England of the
nineteenth Century. May his tread be ever firm and his
countenance catch new brightness, as he continues to 'step
westward.'

Your affectionate friend,
AUBREY DE VERE.

CHAPTER V

1848-1850

THE loss of his father, and the sad experiences connected with the Irish famine, deepened if possible the hold of religion on Aubrey's mind. And these events came with the final parting from youth, and entrance on mature manhood—for he was now in his thirty-fifth year. He had already written down the thoughts which must at this time have come back with intensified meaning :—

> Sad is our youth, for it is ever going,
>   Crumbling away beneath our very feet ;
> Sad is our life, for it is ever flowing,
>   In current unperceived because so fleet.
> Sad are our hopes, for they were sweet in sowing,
>   But tares self-sown have overtopped the wheat :
> Sad are our joys, for they were sweet in blowing ;
>   And still—O still—their dying breath is sweet.
> And sweet is youth, although it hath bereft us
>   Of that which made our childhood sweeter still.
> And sweet is middle life, for it hath left us
>   A nearer good to cure an older ill :
> And sweet are all things when we learn to prize them,
>   Not for their sake, but His who grants them or denies
>   them.

The public events of the early forties had, as we have seen, placed vividly before Aubrey's imagination those religious controversies which were then absorbing so many thinking minds. The Oxford Movement had been at the acute stage of its development for four years after the publication of Tract 90. Then had followed Newman's secession in 1845, the collapse of the Tractarian party, and the change of communion on the part of so many of Newman's followers. During his father's illness Aubrey had read the ' Essay on the Development of Christian Doctrine,' and though he at first declared that volume to be ' as full of fallacies as the sea is of fish,' before he finished it he found portions of his own deeper philosophy of faith underlying theological disputations which were to a great extent distasteful to him. He records also in the same year how both his brothers were already feeling dissatisfied with the form of religion in which they had been brought up—how his brother Stephen refrained from taking the Sacrament with the others when his father was at the point of death ; how his brother Vere, deploring the disuse of extreme unction for the dying, had said bitterly ' Our Church forsakes her children on their deathbeds.'

Though it was fairly evident, however, in 1848, which way his own mind was moving, he still preserved a vague sense that Rome was superstitious, and a fear that the light which so greatly attracted him would singe his wings if he got too near it. We find him in this year writing to his friends of the various interests which absorbed him—the Roman question cropping up ever and anon.

A pilgrimage to Coleridge's grave, in the summer, a visit of Alfred Tennyson to Curragh, and his own visit to the Grange in September 1848, were occasions of the following letters to Mrs. Edward Villiers :—

June (?) 1848.

I have been on a pilgrimage to the tomb of that grand old mystical bard and seer, Coleridge, a man to whom I give more of love and admiration than I generally squander on writers, and whose works have had more influence on the formation of my own opinions than those of any one else. Not having any other paper at hand, I copied the inscription upon his monumental tablet into the last page of your book. And for this I believe that I owe you no apology, as it will interest you as it did me.

It is not out of place in that very popish, though very

L

beautiful book,[1] and, notwithstanding all that you say of my Puseyism, I assure you that I did not leave the grave of Coleridge, without an earnest desire that the Church which he loved, and the land which his genius had adorned might never again be given over to the superstitions which he—I will not say *despised* (the word should have no place on sacred subjects),—but which he saw through and condemned, though he revered the profound principles which they symbolised, and the deep cravings of human nature which they coarsely satisfied.

Curragh Chase.

Alfred Tennyson is very little restive, and I hope I shall make this visit pleasant to him. I wonder why he came, and whether he is fond of me. I fear not much so. Yesterday when I looked up at dinner, and saw him sitting between my sister-in-law and her sister, in this remote land, strange to him, I felt all at once such an affection for him as made his noble face look very dim and misty. He has, indeed, a most noble countenance—so full of power, passion and intellect—so strong, dark and impressive. I find I am growing very much attached to him. He is as simple as a child, and not less interesting for his infirmities. He is all in favour of marriage, and indeed will not be right till he has some one to love him exclusively. He was delighted with Mary Lucy's singing last night—well he might be, but I feared he would not. He is to breakfast alone, and sit alone half the day, musing and writing poetry. I have also other designs on him which I will explain to you hereafter. . . . Now that there is a confidence between us, I shall have a great deal to say to you, but I am afraid you will find me an egotist. How much I wish you were here! Why do you not pay Lord C. a visit, and then go to see Killarney, taking this place by the way? I would go with you. You would enjoy yourself much here. If you came while Tennyson is here, you would delight in him and do him so much good. Who is that handsome Mr. Jenkinson? I do not care about him, but still I do not think you can be as well anywhere else

[1] *The Imitation of Christ.*

as with Miss Fenwick, till you are settled at Mortlake or Grove Mill.

Mrs. Villiers' keen curiosity about Alfred Tennyson provokes in another letter an expression of humorous jealousy :—

So you 'want' to see your old friend, and are 'dying' to see a new one. Now do you not think I have some right to be indignant with you, or at least jealous of Tennyson? However, I forgive you, because you draw such a pleasant, cheerful picture of your drawing-room, your red geraniums and sparkling fire, fanned by gusts of 'soft high wind' from the conservatory. The picture brought you very vividly before me, and made you look very gay and happy, which is what I like.

The Grange : September 1848.

Charles Buller is here, and has been talking in a manner so Roman Catholic this morning, that if his actions were to follow his opinions, he would soon add another to the fold of the infallible Church. In spite, however, of his expressed opinions, Liberty works in his heart like the milk of a forgotten mother, so that instead of moving on with the decorous sacrificial procession, a lamb among the lambs, he stands like the goat in the old bas-relief :

> Stubborn goats that eye the mountain tops
> Askance ; and riot with reluctant horn.

If he thinks what he says, his only protection consists in caring for none of these things ; and if he and Carlyle are to be taken as representing two of the main tendencies of public opinion, then let my Lord Legate, the Archbishop of Westminster, draw out of his pocket his diploma for restoring the Hierarchy, 'stoop to conquer,' and pull on his scarlet stockings without more ado. Did you know that Dr. Wiseman is secretly Archbishop of Westminster, Primate of England, and that he has only to lift up his hand, open his commission, and appoint twenty-six bishops in England when he pleases? Now, then, I suppose you conclude that I am moving with accelerated speed toward that great Luminary,

L 2

the centre of the whole *mécanique céleste* of my ecclesiastical aspirations. I cannot, however, see by what sort of logic you arrive at any such conclusion, and I would contradict still more vehemently, only that I am provoked by your saying that if I ever join the Roman Catholic Church you will discard me as a friend.

There is a young lady here who is very fond of poetry, but will never be the cause of poetry in others; and there is another young lady with a neck as white as this paper and a face and bust which remind you of what may be called the characteristic expression of Reynolds' female portraits, but the moment she gets up and walks, she walks out of any heart that may have given her a temporary resting place.

In a letter of December 8, to the same friend, he gets nearer to the centre of his attraction to Catholicism—as having preserved that unearthly spiritual atmosphere, which the mediæval world expressed in its ethical ideals and in its art, and which the modern world had so completely lost. He still professes to admit that it is partly lost, too, in modern Romanism—a profession which was gradually discarded. With occasional penstrokes which suggest a Catholic Carlyle, he describes the pictures of the Saints, by Perugino, Pinturicchio and Fra Angelico. And the contrast drawn at the end of the letter, between the ideals of true progress in the fourteenth century and in the nineteenth, thrown out though it is in sentences marked by racy fun and paradox, is a very remarkable revelation of his own deeper sympathies— which were, as his friend Hamilton used to say, from the very first, those of a Catholic :—

[The pictured saints] look as if they lamented because of the fate of the Asian Churches, or the recapture of Jerusalem by the Saracens, or as if the last dirge heard at Rama were still echoing in their ear. And yet in the midst of all this sorrow, you trace in their countenances a mystical joy no less— the blessing promised to those who mourn. They look down into a Lily (young virgin or rocky anchorite), as if they had an inner eye which saw in it an Eden fountain of eternal purity and peace, and seem already to breathe a divine air and hear the still rustle of angelic wings. I do not know what *your* Perugino is like; but this I know, that I can never gaze on a really good picture by an early master of the ascetic school, Fra Angelico for instance, without seeing as plainly as the sun at noonday, that whatever his errors may have been, he had either discovered or inherited an ideal of holiness, of moral beauty, and of that Divine Humanity which I suppose constitutes the Christian character, which has never revealed itself in northern regions or modern times to the spectacled Muse of Biblical Criticism, who forsakes the temple and the wilderness alike, for the Synagogue and the market place. I do not say how the fact is to be accounted for—whether it was that the theology of the Middle Ages, with all its faults, had some sustaining and sublime qualities, which have been evaporated from ours during the process of threshing out and winnowing which it has gone through—or whether the heart of man was stronger, and his imagination higher, then than now. But the fact is a fact, and we can gain nothing by turning from it.

The glory of the old pictures did not come from superior skill of hand, but from a better head and heart: the Ideal of the fourteenth and fifteenth centuries transcended ours, and the Saints of Perugino, Pinturicchio, and a host of almost *nameless* painters (men who stood on a high level, but had probably individually no extraordinary genius), exceed in dignity, sweetness, purity, strength, pathos, elevation, sublimity, in all that belongs to the human, and all that belongs to the Divine type of character, what we can now conceive, or even what we can generally admire, almost as much as human beings exceed the brute creation. I do not mean to say that men were all right in old times, much less that it was Romanism that made them so. On the contrary, this noble ideal is *now* as much lost in Romish Italy as in Protestant England. All that I mean is that, whatever their errors or corruptions may have been, we have wandered far away from the spiritually beautiful and true—the proof of which is that we have not lost the manual skill of the painter, but that we have lost the great human Ideal, and that many of our accomplished artists and amateurs look upon men as they might look on them with the eye of a dog, neither seeing nor creating more than belongs to the animal life, and the milliner's consecration thereof.

Just sit down before your Perugino and look on it, not as a picture, but as a poem, or simply as an expression of human thought, addressed some three hundred years ago to human sympathies ; and then ask yourself what it has been saying all this time.   What would the forms delineated say, if they could speak ?   What would be the sound of their voices ? how would they move ?   I assure you that when, in my ' Ode to Italy,' I spoke of Raphael's Saints as

> moving slowly
> With steps that *lead* the Elysian measures

I but feebly intimated my habitual sense of the Divinity which ' doth hedge them in,' and that soft Supernatural which belongs to them, and only does not make itself universally acknowledged because it is too perfect to be obtrusive.   Whenever I let an old picture reason with me, its voice, though as sweet as that ' music of the spheres ' (which was said to remain unheard by men merely because its harmony included no admixture of discord, or *noise*), always leaves me sad.   It is not given to reproving or denouncing ; but it makes me say, ' Certainly we moderns have gone very far astray.'   Measured by our own standard, of course we are advancing ; but I suspect that the pleasant south wind of self-approval, and the ' Spirit of the Age ' have been drifting us into very Boreal regions.   Those Saints have been singing psalms to us, praying like a-Kempis, expounding great ideas like Augustine, chaunting that antiphon amid the flames of martyrdom like St. Laurence,—' this Fire is no Fire at all, and all things *grow plain* in this Light ! '   And our amateurs have stood by talking about ' chiaroscuro,' while our well-dressed ladies have said, ' I really should like a copy of that sweet Carlo Dolce.'   Certainly if an angel lived amongst us we should think we had done a great deal when we had offered him a pinch of snuff, asked him to dinner, and said ' he is not a bad fellow, and *I* really do not think him dull.'

The fact is we have grown a little dog-like—that is our foible. We are always questing about for something, and poking our nose into everything to discover whether it is good to eat. We are grown very hard, yet apparently not very brave—we are coarse, yet effeminate. . . . We are secular. It is certain that we believe in *this world*, though we have heard of, and do not disbelieve in another; whereas it is plain enough that St. Agnes believes in another world, is *already in it*, looks on this world as the visionary thing. . . . Moreover I fear we are not humble. After all, how can we be? Dogs are not humble. If we lived in a world of wonders and signs, we should be as little self-sufficient as those Apostles who have just found the Virgin's tomb, filled with roses, or those wedding guests who 'taste the water which was made wine.' Our life, however, *is* as wondrous, as miraculous as theirs.

Kings and Priests are to us magistrates and schoolmasters a little over-paid, and women are but females. Why should they not have seats in Parliament? Even God is announced to us as a sublime mechanician and true philanthropist. Well, if Mr. Babbage and Mr. Wilberforce could be united in one man, that would not be so very wonderful. Also we do not seem very contrite. Those tender spirits have evidently dropped many a tear

of sweet remorse
And pious awe that feared to have offended.

Well, *we* take things easy—no penance—and if repentance, repentance in purple and fine linen. Sackcloth would be ostentatious—ashes self-righteous—besides a contrite nature is a loving nature, and in us self-love has murdered love. Again, we look on offences chiefly as against society, or against our own dignity—if they were regarded as against God, then indeed there would [be] an element of the Infinite about them : but then we should want a real God, not a Babbage-Wilberforce God—a maker and mender and regulator of world-watches. Neither do I see amongst us that awe, or hope, or health, which looks out from those old pictures. And most of all I miss that harmony, which not only obviously reigns among those sacred human beings, but also plainly unites the various faculties of each in a beautiful subordination—a Hierarchy descending from the spiritual through the moral and intellectual to an animal nature, which, so subordinated, is ministrant only,—is lost, merged, has no separate consciousness, is as blind to itself as our first parents were to evil, before their eyes were opened, and their vision of God dimmed. With us it is different. Society with us is more like the squeeze at a theatre than a 'goodly company' trooping to church, and the internal being of each man is in as much confusion as a hive from which the queen bee has been stolen. The fact is our men are unmajestic, our women (except a few) unwomanly, and our children a reproach to us from the degree in which they remind us of the brightness, the spontaneity, yet docility, the free dependence, the Faith, Hope and Love, the healthful joy in life, and happy contentedness to die, which we have lost.

It looks as if we had been broken up, and were forming again upon a distinctly new and lower type; for not only we are not like what we see in those pictures, but we have no such Ideal, and see in it nothing to desire. We too are advancing, but perhaps not in the right direction, and if so the faster, the worse. It seems doubtful whether we should be as good as these pictured men—who began by reasoning with me, and have ended by wrestling with me,—even if we could realise our Ideal, and then hire a Perugino of our own making to make us immortal, or at least paint a portrait of us to hang up in our domestic chapel, the dining-room. I doubt whether I should prefer our state to theirs, although we had achieved our Ideal—although every man was rich and respectable, no 'operative' married while there was a chance of his children reducing his beer and bacon to bread and milk ; although the Police regulations were perfect ;—although there were a Bedlam and a penitentiary in every village, and not a beggar's rag to be detected by the most sharp-nosed cur that ever barked before a new-painted railing; although kings were paid like clerks, the Upper House made to work 'by the piece' ; the nobles sent the way of the priests ; women changed into Females and sent to parliament, the pulpit, the counting-house, and of course, the market ;—although war had become economically impossible, and peace of hearth (that degrading lethargy) unimaginable ;—although the whole English nation had been changed into one great joint-stock company, and the whole of the Irish smothered by mistake in their national poor-house, like the seventy emigrants who were smothered the other day on board their ship, because the captain was a little too strict in his abstract notions of order, and less exact than he would have been in his own case, about trivial details relating to the number of men who *can* be supported by a given quantity of air ; although Property and Communism had shaken hands ; although Capital reigned supreme ; although every man were *Independent* ! ! ! although newspapers flew upon wings ; although every one knew everything except how to revere, to love, to obey and to be silent ; although every disease had its cure, and there were an insurance office which provided for every heart sorrow ; although wit was sold by the bottle and virtue by the dose ; although England had become one town, and the country remained but as parks in it ; although streets moved on railways like trains, and night had been finally abolished ; although all the blacks had been set free, and all the whites had sold themselves into bondage ; although (finally) the dominion of trade were universal and the social treadmill certain to revolve for ever and ever ;—still I say that this ideal state would not be as good as that which Perugino thought of, or rather as lay in his mind without his [distinct] consciousness.

Was there ever such a rhapsody ? However, it is all true ; and when I get upon a subject, I cannot get off again. I had been looking at your new gallery in imagination, and so ran on in reverie, as if I were in the Borghese gallery—which I suppose those blockheads [1] will burn. I was at first very angry with Pio Nono for giving in, instead of letting his palace be sacked, and thought his expression about avoiding the effusion of blood poor enough, as if they had made a quaker Pope by mistake ; but I see what he is at—his two short notes to the Ambassadors and his Minister are admirable from the things that they do *not* say. The Italian is ' molto astuto,' and he will

---

[1] Pius IX., it will not be forgotten, was at this time forced to leave Rome, which was in the hands of the revolutionists.

not go back to Rome till they have cut their own throats long enough to cool their ardour. I could almost wish the Republican cause successful in Rome, that the secular and ecclesiastical powers might be separated. I suppose the 'Standard' will propose that the living vacated by Baptist Noel should be given to the Pope, on his signing the Thirty-nine Articles in the non-natural sense in which every one signs them, except the Bishop of London.

A little later Aubrey's growing sense of the substantial identity between the Roman ideals and the mediæval evidently betrayed itself, and in writing to a friend, he speaks of Mrs. Villiers as 'annoyed by my Roman tendencies,' and welcomes the deterrent effect on himself of her influence as a useful antidote to the events of the day, which were leading so many to the Roman Communion. He alludes also to the 'evils of precipitancy, and the gravity of any step taken.'

Aubrey seems, early in 1849, to have spent some time alone at Mortlake, whence he writes to Miss Fenwick on January 24 :—

My lonely life agrees excellently with my health and spirits, and in other respects is still more desirable. On my spirits it always acts as wine seems to do on that of others. Occasionally, however, it is broken by a visit from Carlyle or Alfred Tennyson. The latter was here two days ago. He is more full than ever of King Arthur, and promises to *print* at least his exquisite Elegies, and let his friends have a few copies. What do you think of my being at a wedding last week? Our good little tutor's, Mr. Johnstone's. He wrote to me a few days before, telling me the news, and asking me to be at the Church of Hampton at 10.30. There I went accordingly, and acted as his bridesman, signing his papers, &c. Indeed, in the confusion, I was rather nearly married myself in his place ; but it turned out very well in the end. He tells me he has educated the young lady for himself, and that she is still in her teens. She is good looking and pleasant in manner. . . .

The illness of Wordsworth, and his death in the summer of 1850, went deeply to Aubrey's heart. The devoted Miss Fenwick was under the poet's roof when the end came. The following letters to her give de Vere's feelings at the time, and in the succeeding months, when he read for the first time the dead poet's ' Prelude,' and visited his old house at Rydal Mount. The first is written from the home of Henry Taylor :—

Mortlake : April 9, 1850.

. . . May it be long before this country has to mourn the loss of perhaps the greatest man that now remains to her, and may his removal, whether it be soon or late, be in peace. How many has he not confirmed in peace ! How many has he not taught to look for rest above the agitations of this lower sphere ! If but a small portion of that elevated rest which he in his generation has given to myriads, through the wise and dutiful exercise of his nobler faculties, might but be restored to him again, how beautiful and glorious his decline would be ! He has had but few illnesses ; and if it should please God to raise him up again from his present bed of sickness, and plant his feet but once more on the heath of his native hills, we may hope that that illness will be for his spiritual health. . . . What a trying time this must have been for Mrs. Wordsworth, and for you hardly less so ! I wish very much you could be here now.

This sunny household is in one of its sunniest moods. Henry Taylor is in his very best health and spirits, Dofo in fair health, and the children well and good. I can hardly tell you how much pleased I am with my godson. He not only abounds in beauty and in ability but, what is much better, there seems to me an indescribable air of nobleness and moral rectitude about him. He takes very resolute views of things, and I like to fancy that he may be in some respects like what Henry was at his age. He sat with me all this morning, and read to me a great deal (among other things a great deal of the Catechism, though he is not learning it yet), and I could scarcely believe that he has been almost wholly self-instructed. When he came to the passage about renouncing the ' pomps

of this wicked world' he stopped, and asserted that the world
was not wicked, but corrected his rash judgment, on remembering that there were gipsies on the Common.

Grove Mill : June 10, 1850.

. . . How glad I should be if I could know that matters
are equally well with you and your friend, in that long-happy
and ever-venerable house which is now your abode ! It would
be needless to tell you what my feelings were (and how many
must have felt the same) when the news came at last that that
was a bereft home. The expectation of such an event does
not prevent the blow being felt when it comes, and many who
never saw him who is gone to his rest, must have felt as if they
had lost a friend, or more than a friend, when they heard that
England had lost her greatest man. He had done his work,
however. Perhaps no other poet has ever as completely done
what was given him to do, and surely few have ever drunk so
deeply of all that is best and deepest in our human lot. I have
heard that Mrs. Wordsworth bears this short separation well.
I should have expected it ; and it is better that she should
be for a time deprived of him than that he should have been
deprived of her. May strength, and peace, and light be given
to her, ever more and more, as the semblances of this earth
give way to more assured and more glorious realities.

Ladon House, Mortlake : August 13, 1850.

. . . As you will probably have expected, the philosophical
and the personal interest of the ' Prelude ' has come most home
to me during my first perusal of it. . . . I seemed to see the
poet as he passed through the various stages of his progress.
His own vision of Milton at Cambridge is hardly more vivid
than that which he unconsciously leaves of himself; but how
different are the two visions—the latter carrying with him
amid grove and aisle a mountain freedom and a forest wild-
ness, as of a creature newly caught and never wholly tamed.
Each of the great poets, though for very different reasons,
evidently felt himself but imperfectly at home within the
cloistral pale. One of the most beautiful parts of the
' Prelude ' struck me as that detailing the poet's life at Cambridge, and the effect of Nature upon him after he had left it.

On the whole, however, the last book is that which I admire most. The poetry of this work appears to me to be more equally diffused over it than over the 'Excursion.' It has fewer eminences ; but the tableland is on a higher level. This at least was my first impression. What my second may be I cannot say. It is on a repeated perusal that beauties of detail come out most vividly, and I promise myself many a perusal of it. . . . How touching and how deeply interesting is the profound affection for Coleridge by which the whole poem is animated ! It seems to have been such an affection as inspired Tennyson's 'In Memoriam.' Are you not greatly pleased by that book ? It does not seem to me to have yet worked its way to its legitimate *conclusion* ; but it is surely a profound and noble poem.

Aubrey went to the Lake country in September, to see the desolate home :—

. . . I had great satisfaction in seeing Mrs. Wordsworth again [he writes to Miss Fenwick from Keswick, on September 28]. She struck me as looking well—light and agile as ever, and not otherwise than cheerful. Afterwards I spent a long time in wandering about the little lawn, and all the haunts which had been so long frequented by the great and good man departed. I saw again everything that I had seen in former years—the terraces made by his own hands—the little field which he had bought, in the hope of bequeathing it to his daughter—the pool in which the gold and silver fishes had been set at liberty, and the rifted old oak above it. The garden was rich with autumnal flowers, and as I walked along the paths, by which he had led me of old, his favourite points of view gleamed forth again through the mist, as the sunbeams worked their way through drifting showers. I saw his old sister [1] as she was drawn about in her chair before the door, but she did not observe the stranger. His faithful James was cleaning the walks, and had no difficulty in recognising 'Miss Fenwick's friend,' though he forgot my name. He told me many things of his old master that interested me much.

[1] Dorothy Wordsworth.

June 1850 had witnessed two important events in the life of Aubrey's friend, Alfred Tennyson—the publication of ' In Memoriam,' and the marriage of its author.

Spedding, who was here the other day [Aubrey writes to his mother], gives an excellent account of Mrs. Tennyson, saying that she is very good, sensible, and anxious to make her husband write poetry. She is thirty-seven years old, and has much beauty, and they are happy together. . . .

Not long after the marriage, Tennyson went with his bride to Coniston, to stay at the house of Aubrey's cousins, the Marshalls. From Coniston Aubrey himself writes in October—again to Miss Fenwick—a letter in which Tennyson divides his interest with the dead bard :—

Coniston : October 14, 1850.

My dear Miss Fenwick,—I had wished to write to you again and give you an account of some of your Ambleside friends. Various engagements, especially those connected with the Tennysons, have, however, prevented my making an expedition to Windermere and Rydal as yet. After I have made it, you must let me write to you again. In the meantime I must send you a few lines, if only because I can never be in this mountain land without feeling as if I were with you, or very near you, and it seems unnatural to sit in the same room with a friend, and never say a word. Besides I am sure you will be glad to hear of my mother, particularly when I can send you a good account of her. She is both in good health, and on the whole in good spirits. . . . Mary [1] is exceedingly affectionate to her and full of the most considerate kindness. She has been extremely pleasant, and useful too, to the Tennysons, who like her very much. By the way, you will be glad to hear that the Poet's wife is a very interesting woman—kindly, affectionate . . . and, above all, deeply and simply religious. Her great and constant desire is to make her husband more religious, or at least to conduce, as far as she may, to his growth in the spiritual life. In this she will

[1] Mrs. James Marshall.

doubtless succeed, for piety like hers is infectious, especially where there is an atmosphere of affection to serve as a conducting medium. Indeed I already observe a great improvement in Alfred. His nature is a religious one, and he is remarkably free from vanity and sciolism. Such a nature gravitates towards Christianity, especially when it is in harmony with itself.

In proportion as the humanities are developed in a character, there is a foundation for that religion which is the complement of the humanities ; and Alfred has always been, to an extraordinary degree, human. He has been surrounded, however, from his youth up, by young men, many of them with high aspirations, who believe no more in Christianity than in the Feudal System, and this no doubt has been a great hindrance to one with his strong sympathies. It is but of late years that I have been at all aware of the immense extent to which infidelity or scepticism prevails among the educated classes, especially the more thoughtful among them, in this country. In Ireland we are steeped to the eyes (and a little higher perhaps) in false doctrine, heresy and schism ; but infidelity hardly exists among us—rich or poor. I have never before had half so much pleasure in Alfred's society. He is far happier than I ever saw him before ; and his ' wrath against the world ' is proportionately mitigated. He has an unbounded respect for his wife, as well as a strong affection, which has been growing stronger ever since his marriage. That marriage was obviously, equally creditable to his judgment and his heart, and it will, I doubt not, be attended by a blessing.

They have left us to-day ; but, in true poetic fashion, they know not whither they are going. They think they may form one household with his mother and sisters ; in this case they would want a good-sized house, and seem disposed to try again near Mortlake or Kew. He and Henry might be mutually of much use to each other. She thinks always of what is *good for him* ; and is anxious that he should cultivate those who might confirm him in all things wise and healthful. She seems to have a great distaste for ' High Church ' opinions, and a great horror of Rome. We did not discuss

these matters much . . . indeed, only just enough to let her
see that my views were different. It seems very undesirable
that he should get into any region of controversies on such
subjects.

Your affectionate friend,

AUBREY DE VERE.

Aubrey de Vere to Miss Fenwick

Coniston: October 20, 1850.

Lord and Lady Monteagle left this yesterday, and my
mother and I accompanied them as far as Ambleside, and
paid some visits in its neighbourhood. My mother did not
see Mrs. Wordsworth, unluckily, as Lady Monteagle and I,
who preceded her in the other carriage, found that Mrs.
Wordsworth was suffering from an attack of rheumatism or
lumbago, and thought it would be better for her not to receive
another party of visitors that day. She was not otherwise
than cheerful, notwithstanding the inconvenience of such an
attack, and her manner had all that sweetness and kindness
which impart such a touching interest to her in her old age.
She spoke much of you, and did not forget to enquire after
my sister, whom she saw but on one occasion, and that many
years ago. Her son William's wife was with her, and seemed
to me a very interesting . . . person. Mrs. Arnold tells me it
is beautiful to see her little child with Mrs. Wordsworth. The
infant seemed at once to recognise her grandmother's claims
on her affections, and *took to her* in a very remarkable way.
After leaving Ambleside we went to Mrs. Fletcher's. As we
were at luncheon, Mrs. Arnold came in with her daughter,
Mrs. Forster, who was looking very well. . . . Her husband
we found there, and of course we made his acquaintance.
Though a *wet* Quaker, I thought his manner somewhat *dry*,
and I can imagine that if we were to have a great deal of
conversation, we should find several subjects on which our
sympathies were very 'imperfect.' However, I must say
nothing against him, as I hear that he was one of the Quaker
band which so liberally and sedulously assisted the Irish, in
the famine. Mr. Angus Fletcher was of the party, and I liked

him. . . . Mrs. Forster spoke . . . of some institution with which Mr. Maurice has lately connected himself, founded on what is called 'Christian Socialism.' It is an attempt to produce combinations of workmen, by means of which the 'selfish principle of competition' is to be excluded, and great Industrial works [are to be] carried on upon principles of mutual love and aid alone. The scheme sounds to me visionary ; but the experiment, like all that is going on now, will cast some light, by its success or failure, on political and religious philosophy.

I need not say with how deep an interest I looked on the grave of the great poet. It will be a place of pilgrimage in future times. And yet I think that of his daughter touches me more. Her life seemed to have been less completed.

In the following letters, persons and things theological are ever coming to the front, amid the lighter topics suggested by his daily life, and intercourse with his friends. The Gorham Judgment, which had asserted so decisively the supremacy of the Privy Council over the Church of England in matters of doctrine, made a great impression on Aubrey de Vere, as it did upon Manning, Hope-Scott, Gladstone and T. W. Allies. The second wave of conversions to Rome came five years after the movement of 1845. The agitation in the same year (1850), on occasion of the 'Papal Aggression,' witnessed in an unmistakable form to the anti-Catholic animus of the country : and a view of the Church of England as Catholic in her doctrine, appeared to be contradicted by the logic of facts. Several of Aubrey's own friends—his two brothers, and such men as William Monsell and Manning— were going, or gone, to the Communion of the Holy See.

Aubrey de Vere to Lady de Vere

Ladon House : August 14, 1850.

I returned here on Monday evening, after passing three or four delightful days with Archdeacon Manning. How I wish you knew him, or could even see him ! He is the most spiritual, and at the same time the most ecclesiastical looking

ɪ

man I ever met. You would think that a saint of old had
stepped out of a picture by Raphael, or Perugino. His
manners are not less interesting, including a marvellous
union of grace, decisiveness, and sanctity. His hopes for the
Church are not apparently very high. He has, however, put
forth (as a sort of forlorn hope) a manifesto, in the shape of
a document signed by himself, Dr. Mill, and Archdeacon
Wilberforce, stating that the Royal Supremacy extends only
over temporal things and spiritual things in their temporal
accidents, and that it has no place whatever either in matters
of doctrine or discipline, and can be allowed none consistently
with the character of the Church as constituted by Christ.
This paper is now sent to every clergyman in England, and to
laymen connected with the Universities; and the question is
how many will have courage to sign it.

. . . I have promised my beautiful friend Virginia[1]—the
Virginia of the ode—to be present at her marriage, which
may perhaps be delayed so as to interfere with my plans, but
is expected to take place at the end of September or early in
October.

Aubrey de Vere to the Hon. Mrs. Edward Villiers

Curragh Chase, Adare: January 10, 1851.

. . . This is my birthday. May I celebrate it by passing
a little time with you? I want to know a great deal about
you. Therefore give me an account of your day as well as
of your health, and tell me whether the donkey that you ride
is black, brown, or grey, and whether the girl that guides
it is fat or thin, that I may fancy that I see you. I thought
I should have been at Nice long before now; but various
delays arose, and at last Archdeacon Manning, who was
travelling with me (I almost fear not so much in order to
see you as to see Rome) gave up the expedition. By that

---

[1] Miss Virginia Pattle, now Countess of Somers. Aubrey was also acquainted
with her three sisters, Mrs. Cameron, Mrs. Prinsep and Mrs. Dalrymple, who
are referred to in some of his letters as the 'fair sisterhood.' They were the
daughters of a Bengal civil servant, and the eldest, Mrs. Cameron, was for
many years Aubrey's intimate friend. Some account of this remarkable woman
is to be found in Sir Henry Taylor's *Autobiography* (Longmans).

time it was late, and I had got deep into theological reading, and my people wished me to pass the winter with them, and I thought it would be better to go to Italy in good time next autumn. Accordingly I have deferred doing so till then. I am encompassed with folio barriers of our old Divines; but I make a bound over them as easily as if they were a cactus fence, in order to join you at the other side.

You must long since have received a letter from me, saying that I expected to be with you before Christmas. You could not answer it, not knowing where to direct. How stupid of me not to have begged of you to write on the chance of my being still at home! Most welcome would your letter have been wherever it had overtaken me. Yes, though it had found me with you. Perhaps you might have given me or poor Ireland a terrible scolding the same morning; and then doubtless the letter would have seemed kind by comparison, breathing a southern climate, and an odour of orange groves. If it were not for the theological studies which so engross me at this most interesting and critical period, I would certainly go to Nice for some time this spring, though I went no further. But if I were near you, I doubt whether, even if I could take my books with me, I should study much. I almost fear I should like a stroll with you in the lanes better than the finest passages from the Fathers. Shall I send you one of them? No: for you would believe I had forged it. You English-women of the nineteenth Century, you have no faith. Even your most affectionate friends seem to you Jesuits. In the mean time Mrs. Allies, Mrs. Henry Wilberforce and others actually join the great mother, even before their husbands, drawing them after them. Are not they, then, female Jesuits? Pray do not say so of all converts (except in the good sense), for never were conversions so frequent as now. Nearly every newspaper mentions the name of some Anglican clergyman who has just seceded, and the lawyers are keeping them in countenance. Mr. Bowyer, Serjeant Bellasis, James Hope and Mr. Baddeley (names among the most eminent at the Bar) are gone or going. Dodsworth is gone. Manning is supposed to be just on the move. How would his secession affect the

FitzClarences? Would they go with him, as the Feildings and Camdens have preceded him? All this follows the Gorham Decision, and the 'no popery' row, and is just what I expected. When a Church is swallowed and spit up again by the State, it looks so ugly that people can hardly believe it to be the real thing, though the Lord Chancellor and the Bishop of London vouch for it.

But no theology!

This is a beautiful day—so warm and soft, that I believe a Jew would love his enemy, so a Christian may be expected to love his friend. How I wish you were here or I were there. I could forgive you anything, even your being so provoking as to give me nothing to forgive. But we have no flowers and you doubtless have many; and that is unjust. What pleasant airs must blow about you! What [radiant]¹ lights must rest on the brakes, and flash on the blue sea! I dare say you often go to the shore to see it. Are you living in the Maison Nicolas, and how does the good man get on with his wife? And is his old mother living? I should like also to know something of our little abode under the shadow of St. Rosalie, and of the good woman to whom it belongs. I think I will go often to Nice in the winter. Do you hear from Henry Taylor often? He has just lost his old father, and his mother is expected to follow very soon. . . . How does Ernest get on? As for the twins, I expect them to come back from that inspiring climate as tall as young poplars. Mr. Watts stayed with us about five weeks, and left golden opinions, and very affectionate regards behind him. He is a most interesting man.² By the way he seems to take much interest in you, and half intended to go to Nice to see you. . . . Do write to me soon, and write at length. Tell me a great

---

¹ The letter is torn here.

² The visit of G. F. Watts is also referred to in a letter to Miss Fenwick :—
'. . . . Mr. Watts, who came over to pay us a visit, was of our party, and won golden opinions from all—especially the children, with whom he was never tired of playing. He is a most interesting person, full of deep feelings, and high aspirations. If art were generally cultivated in so noble a spirit, it would do more to fulfil its great vocation as one of the "honourable women" who accompany their mistress, Religion, in her progress, through the world.' Mr. Watts left a record of his visit—a charcoal drawing of Dante and Beatrice—on the walls of the staircase at Curragh, the faded remains of which are still visible.

deal about yourself. How I wish I were sure you were in
good health and spirits! There are few of whom I think so
often—fewer still of whom I think as affectionately. I go
over again many talks and rambles we have had together, and
none of our quarrels, in which I hardly believe. When shall
you return to Grove Mill, and will you ask me there? I
hope your young blue-eyed friend Emma is well. My
accounts from Miss Fenwick are indifferent. Write to her.
It will do her good, but write to me too. God bless you.

Your affectionate
AUBREY DE VERE.

In his letters to Miss Fenwick, written in the previous
November and December of 1850, the religious element is
more prominent than in those to Mrs. Villiers. One specially
noteworthy point is the suggestion, which he afterwards
developed, that the new vista opened out by modern Biblical
criticism could be reconciled with Christianity only by a
Church which is regarded as the guardian and interpreter
of the Bible—whose office it must be to reinterpret portions
of it, in the light at once of revelation, and of the results of
critical research :—

Your letter, and the two volumes of the Southey Correspondence [he writes] reached me safely the morning that
my mother and I left Curragh to come hither. I can wish
no better than that these two volumes may interest me
as much as the previous volumes have done. There is no
one whose personal character seems to come out so clearly
in his letters as that of Southey, and well does it bear the
light thus cast upon it. The domestic fireside, and the
cloister of literature are brought before us in every page.
It does provoke me to hear people talk of Southey as if they
contemplated him from a height, and could make allowance
for this and that. This disease, which I venture to call by a
newly invented name, that of the 'sophism of an imaginary
elevation,' seems to me to infect people every day more and
more. Persecution having ceased, people seem to take refuge

in a quiet habit of *despising* those from whom they differ.   It is also a convenient mode of shielding oneself from the force of opinion, with which one cannot cope in argument.   It is thus that poor Carlyle fancies that he looks down on all the forms of Christianity from some supposed height—probably in the moon—deciding that this doctrine was suited to one time, and another tolerable at another time.

It is plain to me that the form which Infidelity is now most disposed to take is that of a good-humoured super-ciliousness, which is the more dangerous because it is too impalpable to be easily met by argument.   As for the views of the Bible taken up so generally in this country, which has so long boasted of its peculiar respect for, and almost exclusive possession of, the Holy Scriptures, they seem to me utterly inconsistent with the maintenance of anything worthy to be called Revealed Religion—except indeed they happen to be united with a belief in the Church as some-thing capable of interpreting what would, on modern principles of Biblical criticism, be a mass of confusion.   However, I have no doubt that all the confusion now going on is over-ruled by the providence of God, and that the truth will more and more be made manifest in proportion as it is assailed.

97 Upper Ebury Street, Eaton Square.

My dear Miss Fenwick,—. . . There are some questions of great interest, religious I mean, which I should so like to talk over with you, though I fear I could not hope that we should take the same view of them.   My studies during the winter, and my discussions with my friend Jebb,[1] have not tended to reassure me with respect to the position of the Church of England, as settled by the Reformation, and as *elucidated* by late events.   That in many respects the English Reformation was overruled by a special Providence, especially as regards the Prayer-book, I am as strongly convinced as any Anglican ; but such a position would of course be quite consistent with a belief that, in the *same sense*, Providence overrules *recent events*, such as Puseyism, and the considerable accession of strength which the Roman Catholic Church has met with in this land.

[1] Dr John Jebb, Canon of Hereford.

I have no doubt that the Anglo-Catholic school (for I fear it is but a school) has had, and probably still has, a high mission. Indeed I do not doubt that the Establishment, considered merely as such, exercises a most *indispensable* religious office in this land, both as a great instrument for the diffusion of Christianity, and as the main support of morals and social order. But at the same time, I seem to perceive every day with more clearness, that something more is necessary . . . —that a more authoritative Dogmatic Standard is necessary, as well as a surer guarantee for the 'Sacramental System,' and for Ecclesiastical Freedom. The sixteenth Century endeavoured to retain the *doctrinal* and the *moral* portions of Christianity, discarding its immemorial Ecclesiastical constitution. The nineteenth Century has found that experiment a failure, and would fain retain the moral part of Christianity alone, discarding both the doctrinal and the Ecclesiastical. That enterprise I look on as more hopeless still, as indeed must be every effort to separate what God has joined. I thus find myself daily more disposed to regard the Roman System as the complete type and permanent form of Christianity, that form in which it will be able to do battle at once with the world and with heresy, and above all with that vast inroad of infidelity which I regard as certain and not distant.

I have not arrived at *convictions*, and feel the utmost distrust of *myself*, rather than of the many arguments which seem to me to converge towards one point, but still I am most deeply impressed with the fact that so many of the Roman doctrines, when studied in Roman books, and not looked at with an unfavourable eye, appear very different from what they seem when dislocated from their context and crammed for inspection by no friendly hand, into some part of the Protestant system. Neither can I help observing that the ordinary *prejudices of the world* against Rome are just what might have been expected if her claims were true, and if yet her ministers were not secured from corruption, and her means of grace from abuse. They are in the main the prejudices which branded the early Christian Church as a conspiracy against social order, governments, nay

humanity itself—as a system of magic and incantation, as
maintained by a mixture of fanaticism and imposture, and as
inconsistent with good morals and good sense. The Church,
which we at least admit still to produce saints, seems to me
the only Church against which *such* charges are brought, by a
world which looks on it as a *great Reality*, and as one which
it (the world) cannot manage. However, I must not go on
writing Theology to you. With my own views still imperfect
I should be sorry to influence those of others, and from my
friends I wish but for sympathy and their prayers. I do not
wish you, however, to be ignorant of the movements of my
mind.

> Believe me, dear Miss Fenwick,
>> Affectionately yours,
>>> AUBREY DE VERE.

The concluding words of the following letter show that the
spell of Catholicism had now seized him in earnest—the spell
of a religion 'which changes not in a world of change, and on
whose impassive brow are written Strength and Peace.' The
letter was written from the house of his old friend, Dr. Jebb,
Canon of Hereford and nephew of Bishop Jebb of Limerick,
to Sara Coleridge :—

Peterstow, Ross, Herefordshire : April 10, 1851.

I came here to see a very old friend, a man of 'High
Church' principles, but at the same time 'sound.' I hope
you know what that word means, since, *as I do not*, I
cannot explain it. However, he is as much opposed to
Rome even as you are, though he would certainly condemn
you to the flames for wishing that the fable of the Nag's
Head Consecration had been a truth. When the fagots
began to blaze, however, he would snatch you from them,
bring you home to tea, adjure you to hate Rome in
England, to respect it on the Continent, to believe all that
'all the old Divines' believed, and also all that was held
by the ancient Church, during the time of the first four
Councils, before Circe had changed 'pious antiquity' into the
'superstitious middle ages,' together with several other acts

and omissions which would severely tax you as well as me. He has a library of 10,000 splendidly bound and well-chosen folios and quartos. If they could *all* begin to argue with the wonted fury of Theologians, I suppose our *senses* would convince us that the clamour was Babel. Why do not our *minds* tell us that if our private judgment has to fight its way through them, an intellectual Babel is likely to be the result, and that the Church must be a living voice, not a Library?

. . . . Pray, is it true that Manning has 'joined Rome'? If so, how many has he taken with him? Here we never see a newspaper. The great ecclesiastical 'Eviction' seems going on pretty fast. The Bishops have brought out their address in the form of an Indulgence, dispensing with the *law* of the Rubric where it exceeds the *usage*, and making chaos the measure of creation. Poor men, just as they began to rest, the Queen writes to tell them to do something a little more practical in the way of solving the insolvable problem. The fact is that the High Church party must, in the opinion of statesmen, be got rid of—'*Christianos ad leones.*' Last year, the demand was only that the *Gideonites* should have the benefit of the latitude of the Church, which is neither High nor Low, but Broad. This year the High Church school are to be deprived of the latitude. Who does not see what this means; and was ever a 'no popery' nation so bent on serving the Pope? They *must* go on—their fate is driving them. In the meantime I 'lift up mine eyes to the hills,' and see something based on earth but irradiated from Heaven, which changes not in a world of change, and on whose impassive brow are written Strength and Peace.

May finds him at Mortlake with the Taylors, whence he writes to his sister, Mrs. Robert O'Brien—mainly on the subject which was now absorbing him. To meet Ravignan, Döllinger and Manning together was a memorable chance :—

Mortlake : May 15, 1851.

My dearest Sister,—I was able yesterday to give your collar to Mrs. Cameron, who had just returned from Paris,

whither she went to meet her husband, on his return from
Ceylon. She was delighted with it, and doubly delighted at
having it from you, as she begged me to tell you with her
best thanks. Both she and the rest of the fair sisterhood
have heard so often of you that they fancy they know you,
and always enquire about you and your children.

I cannot tell you how glad I am to think of your being
at Curragh again, and of your children running about our old
garden and wood walks. How I wish I could be in two
places at a time! There are some things here of such interest
that I would not readily miss what perhaps may not soon be
procurable again. The other morning, for instance, breakfasting with W. Monsell, I met three of the most distinguished
Theologians of three nations, whose conversation, as you may
imagine, was such as is seldom heard. They were Manning,
De Ravignan and Dr. Döllinger. The mode in which the
three countries were represented by these three minds was
extraordinary—the depth of the German, the scientific
precision of the Frenchman, and the grave vigour of the
Englishman. Among other things they discussed the religious prospects of Europe. Döllinger took a sanguine view
of them, De Ravignan rather a gloomy one, but all three
agreed that the world would eventually be polarised into two
great sections, the Roman and the Infidel, and that all the
intermediate theories were used up, and worn out. How far
this may be true I know not, but certainly I am every day
more struck by the great difference which I observe between
the Protestants and Roman Catholics with whom I converse.
The former seem so vague in their faith, and so shifting in
their arguments; the latter always seem to me to hold all
the great truths of the three Creeds as in Eagle-talons.
Whatever may be the character of their *peculiar* tenets, the
great *common* Dogmas of the Faith seem to me secure with
them only. This circumstance I own increases my reverence
for Rome daily. . . . I cannot doubt that to all who desire the
truth, and keep themselves free from prejudices, all the truth
necessary for them will be revealed, and in the meantime I
do not feel as if any difference of view on these matters could
produce any estrangement among those long and deeply

attached to each other, and certain of each other's religious sincerity. It is those who care least about religion that are most subject to religious jealousies and animosities. Pray write to me soon, and tell me a great deal of news—especially how you and my mother are. Tell me, too, whether you would like the ' Paradiso.'

Ever your affectionate brother,

AUBREY DE VERE.

But even at this time of preoccupation with religious problems, the cult of the great departed bard was not forgotten, and before the end of the month Aubrey made his pilgrimage to Rydal Mount. He writes thus to Miss Fenwick :—

The Island, Keswick : August 29, 1851.

Though you hear so frequently from Mrs. Wordsworth, you will not be sorry to hear the impression she made on those who had not seen her for nearly a year. My mother and I agreed that there was no change to be detected in her appearance. She looks as well and moves about as lightly as ever. She complains that her eyes do not serve her as well, however, and uses them chiefly in knitting woollen stockings. To my great surprise she presented me with half a dozen pair, which I received with great gratitude. I do not know how I am to trample under my feet what has been worked by her hands. If, however, my feet should avoid all 'evil ways,' they will best show their sense of the honour thus unexpectedly done them. They were intended to enable me to tread the evil ways of the mountains with the less injury. . . . I can hardly tell you the interest which I felt in again wandering about those grounds, which I did, though it was a wet day, and the rain trickled down from the trees above the terrace walks, and saturated the hollyhocks that leaned upon the raspberry bushes. Everything seemed as it used to be ; and everywhere the voice of him who is seen there no more, seemed to follow me like the murmur of the pines. He will be more associated with the regions among which he dwelt than any other poet has ever been; and the pilgrims who visit the tomb in Grasmere, and the laurel bowers of Rydal will have a reward, as well as an inducement, which few such votaries have. I shall not be at rest till I have written something, in the way of critical illustration, on his poetry; though after all, it is not worth while, since it is with the heart that even poetic faiths are entertained, and no guide is necessary from the eye to the heart. I shall try to see Mrs. Wordsworth again. She is all that one could wish for, even in Wordsworth's widow.

Aubrey de Vere to Lady de Vere

37 South Street, Park Lane : October 21, 1851.

I called twice on Mrs. Wordsworth on my way to Windermere, having sent my things on by coach. Not finding her at home at first, I walked to the two Rydalian waterfalls—which the old poet had first shown me—accompanied by his faithful James, who spoke all the time of his master. On my return I met the venerable lady walking up the hill [coming back] from her walk, and sat with her half an hour. She enquired much after you. I then went to the Arnolds, who asked me to stay to tea. The evening was a delightful one. I have always had a particular liking for Mrs. Arnold; and her two younger daughters (the only ones with her) are remarkably pleasing girls, fresh, frank, earnest and engaging. We had great discussions about the more difficult poems of ' In Memoriam,' as to the meaning of which we generally came to an agreement. Mrs. Arnold told me that she meant to drive over to Keswick some day soon, returning in the evening. I said I was sure Catherine would be more obliged if she would stay the night, and recommended that she should write and propose to do so. This, however, she said was impossible, and probably it would be the more difficult as she has no carriage. Notwithstanding, like other impossibilities, I dare say it could be effected if Catherine wished it. I went away at a late hour, finding the night so dark, that for some time I had to feel my way with my umbrella. Gradually it grew a little lighter, and I had a pleasant walk to Windermere, whence I came on the next day, arriving at 10.30 yesterday. I went to breakfast with Archdeacon Wilberforce, who has since gone to the marriage of the Bishop of Oxford's daughter. I shall probably travel to Rome with Manning; but am not sure whether I shall wait for him in London or at Paris. Mrs. Coleridge looks certainly weaker than when I saw her last. Her daughter, however, does not speak very despondingly.

CHAPTER VI

'NACH ROM'

1850–1852

THE 'spell' of Catholicism had now, as I have said, seized upon Aubrey in earnest. His complete absorption in this crisis of his life recalls the picture set before us in Newman's 'Apologia' and in 'Loss and Gain.' The letters immediately preceding and succeeding his actual reception into the Communion of Rome are very unusual specimens of this class of literature, and reveal a coherent philosophy of religion, the outcome largely of the thoughts contained in his correspondence of ten years earlier, with Stephen Spring Rice.

The chief outstanding points, which appear in his letters to Sara Coleridge, are the following :—

With Samuel Taylor Coleridge, Aubrey regarded the 'understanding' of man, and its processes of argument, as inadequate to reach even those fundamental religious truths —Theism and Immortality—of which Christianity is the complement and development. The infidel movement which he saw around him, which touched his own thought, and made him tremble lest his belief in Christianity might be shaken, must (he held) be counteracted by a different faculty—by the higher Reason, including the intuitive spiritual perceptions.

But, again, such perceptions may be in the individual weak and vacillating. They may seem at times to give, in Tennyson's phrase, not 'light,' but only 'idle gleams.' They are, however, reinforced, and made steady and distinct by the Church, which voices the ' universal reason of the regenerate race.' The Church, too, represents the wisdom embodied in the consistent action of her saints, whereby the apprehension of spiritual truth gains the force and edge, which distinguish deep practical conviction from the process of striking the balance of speculation. And she makes concrete in symbolical rites and dogmas the revelation of Christ Himself; while her liturgy preserves the meditations of the saints of old. What may seem in the individual consciousness an uncertain impression of the reality of the spiritual world, is thus exhibited and interpreted by the Church as a share, however partial, in the persisting and fruitful belief of the Christians of all ages and places. And such corporate belief is in reality the partial manifestation of the persistent action of the Holy Spirit in the Church. This objective confirmation of individual religious instincts redeems them from the reproach of mere 'enthusiasm,' indulged in as an escape from 'scepticism.'

So far he stands almost where Coleridge had brought him. But the further step which his mind took, under pressure of recent events and further observation, was that membership of the Catholic Church, thus conceived as organically one, as the preserver of revelation and tradition, could have no existence in communities where schism had bred a different attitude of mind and heart to that of the early Christian disciples. The attitude of faith which reverently clings to the Church as a repository of spiritual knowledge above the reach of the unaided individual mind, was opposite to the attitude of 'private judgment.' The disintegrating effect of 'private judgment' had in reality broken up the ancient Catholic Church. That Church still survived only in the Roman Catholic Communion, which, retaining the ancient ideal, had sought, as a security against anarchy, a yet closer uniformity and unity than that of primitive times. Thus, just as St. Paul urged the Athenians to identify the God of the Christians with the deity they had ignorantly worshipped.

de Vere came to identify the Church in union with the Apostolic See with that Catholic Church which he had with Coleridge long acknowledged as the normal means of preserving among the mass of men faith in the invisible world.

Here he parted company once for all with Stephen Spring Rice.   Both of them had bitterly lamented the Gorham judgment, as allowing the vagaries of private judgment, under the ægis of the civil power, to prevail in the Church of England over the immemorial belief of the Catholic Church.   But for his cousin the result was that Church principles seemed unrealisable ; for Aubrey they were realised elsewhere.   ' We probably differ in this respect' (Aubrey wrote to his cousin) 'viz. that you see no refuge in case of the worst : whereas the effect of a year's meditation and reading with me, as well as of the reflections of fifteen or twenty years, during which theology has been its chief subject of thought, has been that I see " a great ship lift her shining sides " near our crazy little bark.'

The spectacle of the concrete united Church which he saw when he ' raised his eyes to the mountains,' was to him in his new state of mind so overpowering, when contrasted with the discordance of the English ecclesiastical atmosphere—its discords having in them no principle of resolution—that many of the old objections to the Church of Rome appeared simply to be forgotten, through the small proportion they bore to those luminous outlines of her organic structure which appeared to be the concrete realisation of his deepest principles.   And the degree to which other objections were found, on closer examination, to be based on English prejudice and misapprehension, helped to confirm him in this attitude.   I do not find that his early objections to the over-great definiteness of scholastic theology were ever explicitly answered.   And his own theological thought was wide, persuasive in form, based on deep and broad principles.   But the facts of the time, and a further study of Roman theology,

seem to have reversed his earlier sense of the relative proportions of the different elements in the Roman Catholic
system. He no longer took the excessive definition, incident
to mediæval and modern theology, to be the essential feature
of Roman Catholicism. He found *underlying* Catholic theology and practice a profound philosophical system—*unconscious*, as he expressly says, but really energising. And this
system was the concrete and practical exhibition of principles
which in Coleridge had been abstract theory. Rome actually
did what England could not do—she realised the idea of *one*
Church, having its roots in the earliest Christian tradition,
which had ever jealously guarded and taught, with an un-
faltering utterance that gave edge to belief, the primary
Christian truths. These truths the unregenerate reason is
unequal to firmly grasping, but the regenerate reason of
each Christian can apprehend and hold fast to them under
the influence of the deeper and fuller wisdom of that body
which claims to voice the highest universal reason of the race.
The faith of the individual enables him to participate in the
wisdom of the whole Church.

So long as the Catholic Church had been in his eyes identified with minute points of controversy with Protestantism,
and with detailed theological arguments incident to this controversy, it had been to some extent distasteful to him. He
did not indeed undervalue the importance of some of these
points. The cultus of the Saints appealed to him strongly.
He rejoiced, again, to find Leibnitz arguing that transub-
stantiation was consistent with sound philosophy. But the
root of his attraction to Catholicism lay deeper. The Church,
if identified *merely* with her distinctive dogmas themselves, was
apparently but one of the many sects at war with one another.
But he came to consider this point of view, in which he had
been educated, to be misleading. It was part of the provin-
cialism of English controversialists, who had failed to apprehend the fundamental *idea* of the Church, in their quarrels

N

with certain aspects of her theology. When he came to view the Church as the normal guardian of Christianity, of those very truths which were the life of Protestant Christianity itself, although the theory of Protestantism could not preserve them permanently, his earlier attitude was reversed. Many controversial positions in the Catholic theology of the time, to which he had formerly taken exception, were now seen to be incidental outworks, raised according to the requirements of the hour, to stave off sectarian division, or to protect great principles—outworks perhaps unsightly in themselves, intelligible and admissible only if understood in reference to the whole scheme. And one great proof of their necessity lay in this—that the Reformed religion, which laughed at them, was ever more acceptable to infidels and secularists than Rome was. The reproach of Christianity, its opposition to the natural man, was preserved by Rome, and lost elsewhere.

The following letters illustrate the course of his mind in the year preceding his actual change of communion :—

To Mrs. H. N. Coleridge

January 1850.

I fear that I may but have worried you by the rough notes which I sent you, relative to some of the positions on the Roman Catholic controversy, which I have grown to believe substantially sound, and of paramount importance, partly as supplemental to, partly corrective of, other positions which we continue to hold in common. *I* entirely believe the principles I allude to to be consistent with all I have so long prized in your father's philosophy. I cannot guess whether, had he lived to this day, he could ever have come to think so. That would have depended partly on those personal associations, early habits of thought, and other *non-essential* opinions, which constitute the 'hay and stubble' that necessarily gather round the intellectual, as well as spiritual being of each of us. It would have depended also (on the hypothesis that my estimate of that philosophy which really underlies the Roman Theology is not a Delusion) on his having, or not having, been led by chance or providence to contemplate the Roman Catholic system from a new point of view, though but for a day, and tentatively.

Be this as it may, he did a glorious work ; and apparently no teacher is allowed to do more than his own special work. If I am right, and if he had carried out his Philosophy in the direction it seems to me *probably* capable of taking, he would have been the Augustine of the modern Church, as he is the Plato of English Philosophy. It is wonderful, however, how connected with their own time are the views of men, even the most above their time, and most frequently opposed to it. It probably never occurred to Alexander Knox (though a somewhat advanced Puseyite, at a time when to be so required both courage and originality) to ask himself the question whether the claims of Rome might possibly be true. '*It is not to be thought of*' is the argument all-persuasive, for good or evil, with most of us, though, as time changes, and the scene shifts, we apply it to different things. The question he probably asked himself was how Rome came to unite so much of good and evil, how its genesis might be accounted for on philosophical grounds, without abandoning Church principles— how we might manage to love Fénelon, revere Bossuet, learn theology from Pascal, and devotion from Thomas a-Kempis, without ceasing to believe (with a catena of venerable men who must otherwise have admitted that the Reformation was carried out in a schismatical manner), that the cultus of the saints and the Blessed Virgin Mary is idolatry, or at least idolatrous. The belief *he* arrived at on such subjects, I have no doubt, required much more ability than it requires to see the simple truth, viz. that such an estimate of the cultus of the saints, and of the Mass, is but the result of a false theological *perspective*, itself occasioned by the suburban and out of the way spot in which (owing to the events of the last three centuries and the practical corruptions of the Church before the Reformation) we first woke to religious consciousness, and had to lay the foundations of our theories. . . . The truth is that our views are mysteriously limited by circumstances both spiritual and social ; that at the same time the use which genius can make of the materials at its hand is all but unlimited ; and that in all cases we live in a wonderful system of compensations.

All this is but a long-winded way of vindicating a belief which seems paradoxical, viz. that the Philosophy based on a special belief in the Reason as distinguished from the Under-standing, will eventually find itself in alliance not only with what it now deems to be *exclusively* Faith, but with a Faith which, *beside* spiritual intuition, includes humbler qualities, which not only acknowledges but practically educates a more child-like docility, which recognises something spiritual in external authority, as complemental to internal perception, and which can, without credulity, believe things which it now deems superstitious, and, owing to such belief, can cherish with a stronger faith, more ardent love, and firmer hope, truths which it already recognises as spiritual truths. That any external authority can *produce* faith is an absurdity which no Roman Catholic would maintain. Faith is the gift of God ; Grace is given to us, like time, moment by moment ; the only question is as to the conditions under which it is given, and when given is so exercised as to perform all its right functions, and go on daily increasing. Personal action is not only the mode, but the *only* mode of intercourse with God ; it is with our own eye that we see, whether we use glasses or reject them. But *personal* action and *private* judgment are surely wholly different things. I do not think that it is *sin* in us which prevents us from seeing clearly and certainly all the essential truths of Christianity by the aid of private judgment, but the impossibility of 'making bricks' rightly without straw.

You know, however, how little I think myself qualified to dogmatise on such matters, especially while I am but a learner. There is but one thing which I would implore those whom I most love, which is, not by any act or habit of will to change opinion into certainty in favour of either side, and to remember that there *may be* a House of Faith and Love, and an Eden of Hope close beside them, which they have not entered ; but in which they may find one day what they sometimes feel the need of, and find also the perfection of all they desire.

To Hamilton he writes on January 24, 1850 :—

The separated religious bodies are always regarded
with comparative indulgence by mere *men of the world* and
by *infidels*. The latter will often tell you (as they have told
me) that, assuming the truth of the Bible, and the reality of a
supernatural order, the Roman Catholic Church is the only
logical result of it, the only form of Revelation which can
even be *conceived of as being* authentic. Notwithstanding,
they solemnly adjure one not to become a Catholic, whatever
one does. Practically they infinitely prefer all forms of
Protestantism. And why? Partly because Protestantism,
as they say, has 'got its face turned to the right direction,'
and ever moves in that direction, when it does not fall asleep ;
but principally because Protestantism, in making a *Concordat*
with the World has lost so much of authentic Christianity
(ever a very *unmistakeable* thing, and one sure to enkindle
hatred or fear where it does not enkindle love) that it has lost
its *reproach*.

John Henry Newman and his brother Francis were at the
time conspicuous instances of the opposite directions in which
thinking minds were moving, and they are compared and
contrasted in the following letter of November 11, 1850, to
Sara Coleridge. We see in this letter, again, as in one of his
earlier letters to Miss Fenwick, the first lines traced which our
own day has seen further produced—of a view of the Catholic
Church as the only milieu in which Biblical criticism can be
frankly pursued without destruction to Christian faith : for the
living Church can supplement and reinterpret the Bible, in
accordance with newly discovered facts.

You compared, I remember, the two Newmans in a former
letter. The two brothers are marvellous types of the opposite
spirits of the age, and remind one of the text 'one shall be
taken,' &c. They resemble each other in the logical faculty
and in courage ; but in J. Newman the logical faculty works
in subordination to faith and the spiritual mind : and

the heroic courage does not cast away humility and reverence. These circumstances seem to me wholly overlooked by those who find a sceptical tendency in J. Newman. His understanding alone is eminently sceptical because it is an eminently powerful one, and the understanding *alone* can but prove all things and hold fast to none; but he never allows his understanding alone to master him. He uses it as an instrument in conjunction with others, and uses it with the freedom of one who knows he is not its slave.

As a fact, I know that Newman is wholly free from temptations toward infidelity; that he anticipates an unprecedented outburst of infidelity all over the world;—that to withstand it he deems his especial vocation, and that he is quite annoyed at having to spend any time on Anglicanism. There is, as you say, occasionally an iron hardness in J. Newman; but in him, as in Dante, there is also an exquisite and surpassing sweetness, which makes me regard the hardness as but that tribute of strength and hardihood which accompanies the heroic mind. His brother seems to me the worse half of John Newman cut off from the better. *Breadth* of mind may not be Newman's peculiar excellence, but that is only one form of greatness out of many. The only part of his mind which I do not like is that which comes out in his vein of irony. I must say I thought his lectures full of matter, though of course they apply chiefly to the Anglo-Catholic phase of the controversy.

I have been reading lately some books on Biblical criticism which profess ' German principles ' in a mitigated form. How far they are German I cannot say, but it is clear to me that on such principles the Bible could be no *Revelation*, relatively to the human mind, and that it presents to us no Revealed Religion. I cannot see what other development such principles could have except unbelief or indefinite scepticism, *unless indeed they happened to be conjoined with a strong belief in a Church as something supplemental to the Bible, and capable at once of interpreting its meaning and supplying its deficiencies.*

But I must stop, for it is time to dress for dinner. We

return to Curragh in a few days. My mother sends you her love. Adieu and God bless you.

Ever your affectionate friend,
AUBREY DE VERE.

Aubrey's elder brother Stephen had joined the Roman Catholic Church not long after their father's death. The change was not due primarily to intellectual causes. He was dissatisfied with the Church of his birth. He was deeply impressed with the goodness of the Irish Catholic peasantry to whom he devoted his life. He came after some years of indecision to share their creed. Aubrey refers to this event in writing to Sara Coleridge :—

Curragh Chase: February 17, 1851.

My dear Friend,—I must not go on putting off writing until I have time to write a letter, or I shall have to go on a great deal too long without knowing how you are. Pray write, and tell me how your health has been of late, and how your spirits are. If you have such weather as we have here you must be often tempted to ' Primrose Hill.' How pleasant those half-rural fields between you and Hampstead are ! I hope it is not being very cockney to be fond of them. Years and years ago, when we were but children, I remember my brothers and I walked to Primrose Hill with my father ; and he told us that if he were very rich he would build a great Temple on it, and make it a ' Palace of Art.' It is strange how closely my earliest remembrances of him correspond with my latest. Had he not been very humble, and rather proud, and large in sympathies, and hedged round with occupations, the world would have known much of him. As it is, he gave it but the exuberances of a few months scattered over his life. I am glad you knew him.

I send you my brother's pamphlet. If you do not like it, you need not be afraid of telling me so, for I think it so sound in logic, sense and temper, that nothing can put me out of conceit with it. It is the first thing he ever wrote, but apparently composition comes easily to him, as he wrote it within a few days, in the broken intervals of his charities—feeding the hungry, teaching the young, and nursing the dying, only brought into his house to die. You are aware, I believe, that he became a Roman Catholic some years ago. He never read a line of the High Church writers, saying that their books were all patchwork, and that he could smell Romanism in them, a mile off. He read very little, but mused, and prayed, and said that it was his *reflections* and *observations* that converted him. Some people attributed it to the prayers of the poor.[1]

I am going on with our old Divines. I must not, however, get on Theology, or there will be no end of it. You are quite right when you say that our estimate of either side in this controversy depends very much on the prepossession with which we take it up. *Prejudice* we *may* guard against, but some *a priori idea* we must have, which doubtless ' half creates ' the harmony which it sees. I used to have great philosophic objections or antipathies to Rome. Now that I read of Roman tenets in Roman books, I am amazed at the vastness of that philosophy which lurks, *unconsciously*, in the most prac-tical and only historical form of Christianity.

Your affectionate friend,
AUBREY DE VERE.

Aubrey de Vere to Mrs. H. N. Coleridge

Curragh Chase : February 27, 1851.

Pray let me hear from you soon. You seem to think me nearer to Rome than I could say of myself that I am. All I can say is that, whenever I submit myself to her, if I do so,

---

[1] Of his brother Stephen, Aubrey writes as follows in later years : ' From his early youth Stephen's life has been one of labour for Ireland. He has saved sons of hers from the gallows -laboured in their schools—abstained from wine for twenty years that he might encourage temperance among the poor, brought dying men into his house that they might have more comfort in death, pleaded their cause in public and private life, and during thirty years he has reduced the rental of the property by about a fourth below what would have been considered the fair value. You know of his going out to America as a steerage passenger (I think it was then a six weeks' voyage) that he might speak as a witness respecting the sufferings of Emigrants. He has always been a Liberal as he is now ; and (unlike me) he approved of Gladstone's recent Land Act, having himself recom-mended nearly the same thing to the Government in 1870.' Sir Stephen de Vere is also a poet of no small merit, as witness his translations of Horace's odes.

it will be in the conviction, not that she is the *better* Church, but that she is *the* Church, that with her Christianity is indissolubly united, and that through her alone it can make its great stand in the latter day against Infidelity and Heathenism. It may sound paradoxical, but is true, that, if I believed all this, and therefore left the Church of England, I should still, not only wish well to the latter as the noblest institution in the land, but continue to attribute to it all that is attributed by most of its sons, perhaps all that is claimed by itself. I have loved her well and long ; but cannot love her blindly.

Aubrey de Vere to the Same

Derwent Island, Keswick : September 29, 1851.

My dear Friend,—Though I hope very soon to see you, I must write a line just to ask you how you have been of late, and to tell you how you have been my companion (though in imagination only, unluckily), while I have been moving about in those scenes which used to be so familiar to you. I have always had an odd habit of seeing what does not exist, to compensate perhaps for the converse one of not observing often what lies before me, and I have constantly met the inmates of Greta Hall in my rambles by the side of the river, which still flows on as brightly as when they snatched at the weeds in its stream. How long the name of ' Southey ' will cast a halo of its own over those hills ; how many a student of English poetry will walk up and down Friar's Crag with a volume of ' Kehama ' or ' Roderick ' in his hand !

A few days ago I was asked to read his lines on Lodore to a large party of visitors here ; and I am sure that the laughter with which they were greeted must have been as merry as that in which the Laureate first joined. He has left a most interesting legacy to this spot which sheltered him so long, in Miss Southey. I have seen a good deal of her, and have a great liking for her, as has my mother also. She is so simple and natural, as well as agreeable, and there is so much that is touching in her position. At present she has a whole family of little children to take care of, which makes her own 'uncared for' position more striking, though I hope it rather enriches her solitude than adds a burthen to it.   They are particularly nice children, with amiable attractive manners, and looks at once frank and modest, such as make children look as if they were on good terms with their Guardian Angels.   Two of them, indeed, are very pretty. Your old aunt interests me also, especially when she speaks of old times, or when she speaks of you.   She speaks much of Greta Hall.   That old household, once so happy, is now scattered : but it is a blessing to know that that eye which watched every member of it from birth, without looking aside for one moment, keeps the same unwearied watch of love and wisdom still, allotting to each what is best—whatever may *seem* best in this temporal cloud.   There is surely no thought more wonderful than that of the Divine Sympathy which counts

The beatings of the solitary heart,

and loves each as if there were no other creature in creation.

I am sending you a volume of poetry of which I only know that it is one of great genius, and by an unknown author.

I sometimes speculate as to what is to become of all the poetic genius in the world if the public should cease to read poetry.   I suppose it must find some other mould in which to shape itself.   At present the public can only afford to keep one poet (Tennyson), and even H. Taylor's late volumes have hardly sold.   I should like to see a *cheap* edition of your Father's minor poems, omitting the 'juvenilia.'

I have been much occupied of late by a book in five good-sized volumes called 'Théologie Affective.'   It is a com-pendium of Thomas Aquinas' 'Summa,' interspersed with moral and spiritual applications.   It was published a couple of centuries ago by a French theologian, and has been recently re-edited.   It is to me profoundly interesting to see the whole scheme of Roman Catholic Theology thus presented together.   One part casts light on another, and doctrines which taken separately seem defective or wrong, when taken conjointly seem complemental to each other. . . .

What impresses me most, however, is the principle, which we have talked of once or twice, though we have never had time to discuss it, viz. that for the certainty of *Faith* two things are necessary, *i.e.* the recognition (internally) of a spiritual sense, and the corroboration (externally) of an authority not speaking from within, but from *above*, whose credentials appear *probable* to the moral Reason, and which presents such an *object* to Faith that, if its claims be true, we may, by Faith, recognise it as coming from God with a certain belief, bow before it as God's Prophet, as the early Christians bowed before the Apostles, and thus put a seal upon merely individual convictions which no external authority, indeed, could render credible if they were opposed to the Spiritual Mind, but of which we could never be sure that they did belong to the Spiritual Mind, if they were the result only of internal balances and individual opinions.

I cannot help feeling that, while the *two-fold Witness* gives us an *opportunity of* exercising *Faith rationally*, and not merely *enthusiastically*, or *arbitrarily*, and therefore gives us the *possibility* of spiritual *certainty*, the internal witness alone must leave us hovering between scepticism and enthusiasm. The reason that it is not so felt generally I take to be this, viz. that in every separate mind, as in England at large, there are really *two* religions, more or less consistent with each other, the traditional and the consciously acquired ; and in each case the faith learned at a mother's knee is that which gives substance to what we seem to owe to our personal researches. Little Freddy Elliot used to complain to Dofo ' I seem to myself at church to be singing like a little Angel ; but when the rest of the people stop, I feel as if I were only making a small hissing sound.' Not less unsatisfactory would be our belief in our own religious opinions, if they were not corroborated by the remaining faith of childhood, and the general assent of the Christian body, both of which rest on the Ecclesiastical, not the Protestant principle. There is no *via media*. The appeal from Scripture to *antiquity* is but an appeal from oneself *au naturel* to oneself with a wig on. The question is whether all such tests are to be *applied* by the individual, or by the Church. If the former, then learning

can but multiply the means of one who had already means
enough, but lacked the power of using them.   If the latter,
then in submitting to the Church we do not sacrifice our
reason, but gain access to the *Reason of the Race*; we do not
put out the eye, but use the telescope; we do not discard our
personality, but burst through our isolation; we rise by
humility and submission, to the one and universal *Point of
View*, as the evil Angels fell by Pride into the prison of
darkness.

All this assumes of course two things—(1) that the
Church is a permanently Representative Body, (2) that it is
really God's Prophet, just as Peter or Paul was.   I am not
determining this, but remarking that it is only in proportion
as we approximate practically to this hypothesis that *the
certainty* of Faith becomes a possibility, in other words that
we can have a Religion as distinguished from a Philosophy
only, supposing Theological Truth to have a place in Religion.
The most clear-sighted minds are beginning to see more and
more that Protestantism means Rationalism.   Now this is a
confession that Protestantism finds itself driven upon a course
which its great early Doctors would have reprobated as fatal.
The nineteenth Century has (as it strikes me) only the choice
between going on to a *new Reformation*, or reconsidering that
of the sixteenth Century.   For my part I will only say that
that principle of Ecclesiastical authority which, except in
heretical bodies, was never shaken till the great ' barring out '
of the sixteenth Century (for there cannot surely be a greater
mistake than to think that men were ' Bible Christians ' in the
first ages), seems to me the only principle consistent with a
sound religious philosophy, and the belief in a permanent
Christendom.   Every day, too, I see more reason to think,
on *independent grounds*, that, deceived by a few traditional
misconceptions, and inheriting a position originally unsound
and daily developing its unsoundness (in which our ancestors,
after a few convulsive movements, found themselves caught
as in a trap), we are utterly *out* in our estimate of Rome, seeing
everything through a false medium, looking at the wrong
side of the tapestry, catching therefore at the ends of threads,
and taking in nothing as a whole.

Of course I do not mean that I am certain of all this. Whenever I am even morally certain, I must act on my convictions; but I feel as if I were daily approximating to that conclusion. I am also very far from being insensible to the degree in which my secession from the Church of England would cause regret to some of my friends. Still, however, as one's first duty to God and oneself is to act on the truth, so far as we know it, so our first duty to our friends, and the highest service we can do them, is to witness to the truth by action, since words are a weak witness. What I wish for them as for myself, now, is that we should meditate on these subjects with that *profound humility* which alone befits a Creature, and could possibly win for us the Grace necessary if we have the prejudices of centuries to discard.

But few know the subtlety of *pride*, and I fear it pervades almost the substance of our Souls. The love of truth is seldom humble enough to be quite pure; and purity is that which sees God. I trust, however, that neither I, nor those who are dear to me, will be left to ourselves in this matter. Adieu, God bless you.

Affectionately yours,
AUBREY DE VERE.

On the thought underlying the last paragraphs of this letter—of the spiritual insight which can only be gained by the childlike humility of faith—he had already written some memorable lines :—

> Ye who would build the Churches of the Lord,
> See that ye make the western portals low,
> Let no one enter who disdains to bow.
> High truths profanely gazed at, unadored,
> Will be abused at first, at last abhorred :
> And many a learned, many a lofty brow
> Hath rested pillowed on a humbler vow
> Than keen logicians notice or record.
> O stainless peace of blest humility !
> Of all who fain would enter, few alas
> Catch the true meaning of that kind sad eye :
> While thou, God's portress stationed at the door,
> Dost stretch thy cross so near the marble floor
> That children only without bending pass.

To his sister, Mrs. R. O'Brien, he writes in October, when
the change of communion had become a practical certainty :—

37 South Street, Park Lane : October 20, 1851.

Is Harriet getting up her spirits again ?   William Spring
Rice took such a liking to her.   How does Grace's farm get
on ? and do the little girls go on galloping the carriage horses
over the stone walls, in the way that surprised Watts so
much ?   I have not seen any of the fair sisterhood yet [1]
(Watts' ' Holy Family,' as H. T. calls them ;) and indeed all
my spare time is taken up in that gravest of all matters,
Theology. . . . I will not go into controversy, which I know
you would rather avoid ; but I will add that I feel more
plainly every day what I have long felt, viz. that conversion
to Rome can never, so far as the *converts* go, produce the
least estrangement.   They simply feel enriched ; and hold
more fully all that they had ever held in common with their
friends, except a few negative points.   I have very little
doubt now as to the end of all my meditations ; but no one is
quite certain till he has fixed a day.   The one great thing
which I look to is the advance in the spiritual life.

Aubrey's earnestness in the course his thoughts and
conscience were taking was put to a very severe test.   To
few men were friendships or family affections so absorbing.
Yet now that he was daily approaching to a change of communion, it became clear that he must give deep pain to some
of those dearest to him, perhaps in some cases risk estrangement.   The deeply intimate spiritual friendship with Sara
Coleridge was in less danger than his friendship with Mrs.
Villiers—whose point of view was less philosophical, and who
could enter less into the thoughts which affected him.   But
in the case of all those who were nearest and dearest he knew
that he must give pain.   Not one of his most intimate friends
even tended to follow him.   Besides the two of whom I
have just spoken, his mother and sister, Henry Taylor, Sir

---

[1] The Miss Pattles.

William Hamilton and Miss Fenwick were all quite unable to sympathise in the course he meant to take. He had to go on his way alone. 'Je mourrai seul' was Newman's motto in 1845 ; and with Aubrey de Vere also it was this rending of the bonds of human affection which gave a painful and dramatic interest to his course during these months, as he followed the guiding star of conscience, feeling intensely inevitable estrangements, the pain of which, however, never made him flinch or swerve from his path.

There is a ring of true pathos in the following letter to Mrs. Villiers, written when he had definitely told her of his coming step :—

37 South Street, Park Lane : October 25, 1851.

' Stay where you are and do not trouble me ' does not sound like you. ' You have the privileges of an acquaintance ' sounds still less like you. If the friends whom I have loved most deeply and most steadily choose to cast me off, they may do so ; but they must do so wholly. I shall in that case have learned one lesson more (I have learned several of late years), and I shall form no more friendships. I should have been true to them under all circumstances. If they act thus, they act heartlessly, though probably not without remorse of heart ; unjustly, because they punish where there has been no offence ; irreligiously, because they violate the law of Love. They act also from prejudice and passion, though they may imagine that they act from principle ; and they show that the doctrine of private judgment and religious freedom was, with them at least, but a name. Alas, they show something more. What is the meaning of the statement that the great fundamental truths of *Christianity*, e.g. the Trinity, the Incarnation, the Atonement, the love of Christ and the Fellowship of the Spirit—that these things are all in all to us, if friends who hold those doctrines as strongly as ever, and as they think, far more strongly—friends who read their Bible as devoutly as ever, and endeavour more strictly to realise its Divine Commands —become to us as enemies or as aliens, because, believing all that we do, they believe more also? It is a delusion. It is not 'war, war, between us for ever,' or for a day. If to cry 'peace, where there is no peace' be an evil, how much greater an evil must it be to cry 'war where there is no war'? Churches will have their controversies for the next three centuries as for the last; and consistent Protestants will say that unity of belief is but servile uniformity, and that religious thought and feeling are promoted by discussion. Be it so; but let us be consistent. While Churches carry on their controversies, individuals on both sides, if they have the true love of God, and the grace of Faith, hold in common the great fundamental truths, the support of the *individual*, spiritual life.

I passed yesterday evening in earnest and delightful religious intercourse with a friend who is as strong a Protestant as you, and knows as well what my opinions are. We spoke of all that is most sacred in Christianity, all that is most hallowing in life, and precious in death. Yet there was no word, direct or indirect, of controversy, no endeavour on the part of either to alter the peculiar opinions of the other. But I appeal to our own past experience. You say, and with the deepest truth, that we have for years had religious communion and intercourse. Yes, but that intercourse was wholly on the basis of a common *Christianity*. We both knew that we did not belong to the same school of Theology. Puseyites have long been assured that their characteristic principles were *essentially* the same as those of the Roman Catholic Church, and that there *only* they could be eventually realised. The latter truth they could not see; the former they in a large measure admitted; but in the meantime there was ample ground for Christian sympathy (though not the most perfect and absolute) between the really religious of both schools. It will be so still with the really religious, and with those who have really been friends. False friends and factious controversialists alone will find themselves separated. The excitement of the present moment will subside; but Christian, and human, love will both abide; and heated opponents will find that no new thing has come upon the earth.

Dearest Mrs. Edward, let us have no more controversy. I have *not* sought it, though I cannot decline it ; and you are not the only one of my friends who has first introduced discussion (from the kindest and best motives, I know) and then assured me, *and others*, that I could speak of nothing but polemics. There is at present a feverish excitement on all subjects that border on Theology. I have been accused of theological meanings because I alluded to the civil government of the Papal, nay of the Neapolitan territory ; and I have found that I unwittingly hurt the feelings of a friend because I could not acquiesce in the charge that Rome would, if she could, burn all Protestants. My letter to you [1] would not be thought controversial by anyone accustomed to theological studies. I wished to say a few words in defence of a great man assailed by a great mob. . . . The rest of my letter was but one solemn and affectionate entreaty, which, if dying, I would leave as my bequest to all my friends, an entreaty that, whether or not they may ever deem it wise to make such enquiries as I have made, they should at least leave themselves free, and not bind themselves over by an act of will, to think always what they think now, whatever new lights Providence may throw upon the little stage on which we move for a moment.

That is not controversy, nor am I one who acts with indirect aims. There is an adage ' give a dog a *bad name* and hang him.' I dare say many may say to me ' We should not mind the Roman Catholic ; but we hate the factious proselytiser, and scorn the insidious Jesuit, who talks of Michael Angelo to make us in love with Madonnas, and of King Alfred to insinuate that trial by jury was enacted in popish times ; besides it is a duty to take care of the children and servants. Begone. We love you as well as ever. Be warmed, and be clothed, but begone. What you might have received from us is laid as "a gift on the altar" of Private Judgment. Dear Christian Brother, Fanatic, Idolater, Adversary, Old Friend, Adieu.'

Hereafter (if no new Protestant light should reveal itself to me) you will feel and know, what in your present,

---

[1] A letter written a few days earlier in defence of Newman's then recent lectures at the Birmingham Corn Exchange on ' The Present Position of Catholics.'

traditional estimate of Rome, you cannot even imagine, namely that as to *Christian* sympathies we are not divided. You will know too that, although I cannot but think you lose much that might elevate the lower part of your nature, and realise the loftiest of your early aspirations, I am yet very far from wishing to obtrude my views on you, lest I should do harm not good, shake old convictions, and not implant new, increase your responsibilities, and not increase your Faith. In the meantime, let us avoid controversy by keeping off even the borderland of theological topics. The world of thought and feeling is wide, and the Heaven of a common Christianity bends over all. I do not think that you 'have heard all I have to say.' I have a good deal to say, which I shall probably say one day in print. You spoke from the kindest motives, and I am most grateful to you for this as for every act of friendship. Believe me that, though I cannot look on myself as an apostate, or even as an infidel, as a renegade, as either an idolater or 'idolatrous,' as a denier of the Bible, a voluntary slave, an enemy of my country, a foe to civilisation, a deserter of my friends, or a 'curser of my fathers'— all of which titles have been given me by old friends who are equally positive with regard to the genuineness of their Faith and of their charity—though in fact I do not look on myself as a malefactor, still I am very far from thinking well of myself, and am not without my share of anxieties. In many things I can and do sympathise most warmly with my friends. They have reason to be pained, though not offended ; nor could they be expected to understand theological necessities which *for them* do not exist. With their religious feelings how is it possible that I should not sympathise, I who have held (and believe that I hold still) all that is positive, spiritual, and really Scriptural in their principles, though I have ceased to hold the traditions and associations which have clung to those principles since the Reformation, in this land? I know how sacred such associations must seem, how sacred they *are* at a particular stage of our progress. Most deeply do I feel the preciousness of those religious associations which connect your present views with the memory of your husband. Such associations and such remembrances are to be found in every sect, and in every Church. They constitute therefore no argument. But they are most holy, most precious, most near to the soul's health, and the heart's life. May such recollections be ever near you, like ministering angels. May they bring you peace from the wells of the past, and health from the springs of Eden. I also have such; and I shall not leave them behind me. That which was indeed the consolation of dying friends, the central faith, fixed like the centre of the world, that which in the cleansing fires of Penitence and Pain burned brighter, when all else burned away, that is what I retain; that is what I aspire more intensely and consistently to realise; that it is which, if realised, will constitute daily a closer bond between me and those I have lost; yes, and between me and those who may abandon me. We do not lose the Dead, when we learn first, with the early Christians, to pray for them the prayer of Faith.

I cannot say how deeply I sympathise with you when you speak so humbly and gratefully of all the blessings that surround you, 'the Bible, the means of Grace, holy books, pious friends, God's beautiful world.' If, indeed, you lack nothing but that which alone, as you say, you miss, a some-thing *within* to correspond with all those gifts, may that inner Grace be more and more amply conceded to you. If you lack also 'one thing' external, that too God will supply if you use what He has given. You do well to 'call no man good.' You do well to revere the Bible, and make it the rule of your Faith as far as you can comprehend what did not come from man, and is vaster than man. Make it also the rule of your life; and remember that the blessed 'liberty of the Gospel' means that Spiritual Freedom which belongs to those who serve God as closely as they may in the bond of the Spirit, and the Body of Christ. Advance ever in Faith, Hope and Charity; I both believe and hope that you will, and you will advance not less in strength and peace. Judge not, that you be not judged; but continue for those who love you, and whom you think in error, the benefit of at least an occasional prayer.

God bless you. Yours ever affectionately,

AUBREY DE VERE.

Pray write me a line, if only a line, to say how your health is now. To-morrow, you know, there will be no post.

The correspondence with Mrs. Villiers slackened for a time. Feeling was probably too acute on both sides for its continuance. But to Mrs. Coleridge Aubrey continued to write frequently, with knowledge of her disagreement, but with the appeal which a singularly large and masculine, as well as sympathetic, intellect prompted. He evidently felt strongly that the thoughts they had in common were far deeper than those which divided them. It was the view of the Roman Catholic Church as sectarian, as identified *only* with the special beliefs or practices which the Reformers rejected, which made the points of difference seem to his friend so significant. To him the Catholic beliefs and practices were ministrative to and protective of Christianity itself. In his eyes the Church was before all things, as we have seen, the *guardian* of those very fundamental beliefs which he and his friend held in common, which needed such guardianship if they were to be preserved for mankind at large.

Early in November, in company with Henry Edward Manning, Aubrey travelled to Paris *en route* for Rome. When bidding good-bye to his friends, Miss Arnold and her sister Mrs. Cropper, at Fox How, he said : ' I am going to Rome '—and then, after a pause, added, smiling, and with some hesitation—' I mean *geographically*.'

On November 9 he writes as follows to Mrs. Coleridge :—

Paris : November 9, 1851.

My dear Friend,—You see that I do not lose much time in writing to you. There is no one of whom I have been thinking so often since I left the grey shores of England ; and assuredly I shall see nothing on my journey which can give me half as much pleasure as I should feel if I received a letter from you, giving an improved account of your health, or saying that you were, either in mind or body, as I could wish you. I fear from the tone of several letters that you are very much out of spirits. I cannot wonder at it. You are, indeed, sorely tried. But God is most with us when His hand lies heaviest on us ; and it is then chiefly that He endeavours to draw us to Himself. Could we but yield to that gentle violence and be with Him indeed, how soon should we find ourselves in the very centre of spiritual peace, whatever outward troubles or anxieties might surround us ! Pray write to me, directing Poste Restante, Rome, and tell me how you are. Indeed I should wish to hear, if it were only that I might be assured that you were not wearied or annoyed by that long disquisition which I wrote to you, during my last days in London. . . . You will naturally ask why I have not already acted on such strong opinions. Till lately I have been waiting to avoid the chance of intellectual illusion, and to try my opinions in every way that they can be tried by me. For some time, however, I have felt as strong an intellectual conviction, as I imagine to be possible, on such subjects, previous to action. Every part of my nature seems alike to confirm those views, except the lowest part of it, which clings to lawless liberty instead of seeking spiritual freedom, and recoils from that examination into all the worst details of a life, and that confession of them, which precedes submission. . . .

I much hope, however, that obedience to what I deem the divine will, will bring me the divine blessing ; and in no other form can I so much wish for that blessing as in the gifts of contrition and love. Had we but these gifts, our errors would fall from us like a mist, and the Spirit of Life would uplift us, and make all things plain. I feel as if all the evil of my past life were hung like a stone round my neck, and all but prevented me from looking up. Every glance which I can cast upwards informs me of the same great truths. In their coherence they are to me, not only credible, but certain. Taken separately, and seen from my point of view, I feel that, although up to the present time I believe them (knowing them to be but one Truth), I yet could hardly expect to retain the power of belief, if I were to trifle with the Grace accorded as well as

with the Providence which has helped me thus far in many
special and undeserved ways.   I cannot tell you how intensely
I feel that I relinquish *nothing*, except what, indeed, it is
hard to abandon, my own lawless will.   All personal agency
and intellectual freedom, I feel certain will be mine in a
fuller and more real sense than they have been; for the
reason of an individual must, if its work be genuine, concur
with the reason of the race.

Good-bye and God bless you.   I must not add any news,
or my letter will swell to a volume.   When I write next you
shall have an account of my journey.   You are remembered in
my prayers every day.   I would wish much to be so in yours.

Ever affectionately yours,

AUBREY DE VERE.

I think I shall part company with my companions at
Marseilles, as they go on by sea, and I want to see Nice and
the Corniche road again.

There is much force in Newman's Lectures of this year.

From Paris Aubrey de Vere and Manning proceeded to
Avignon.   In this city, where the Popes had once sojourned
for the best part of a century, the final determination was taken.
On the morning of November 15, in the Archbishop's chapel,
Aubrey de Vere was received into the Catholic Church.   He
writes on that day to Mrs. Coleridge :—

Avignon : November 15, 1851.

My dear Friend,—After my letter to you from Paris, it
will be no surprise to you to learn that I was this morning
received into what I believe to be that one Catholic and
Apostolic Church confessed in the Creed, and commissioned
from on high by God Himself.   For some time my convictions had been far clearer than those which we require
for action in matters of secular concern, nay, had been as
clear as I believe to be possible previous to action, on matters
which admit of no absolute and scientific demonstration
because they belong to the supernatural region of Faith.
Such convictions involve duties, and that which we believe we

are bound to confess. Such convictions, if they be true, come to us also, by Grace and through God's Providence ; and His gifts, if not used, will be withdrawn. In this belief I have acted. May He accept the act as one of obedience to Him, and may He bestow on me those spiritual gifts of which obedience is the Gate, especially humility, contrition and love.

Such submission I regard as an act of obedience ; and yet hardly of self-sacrifice. I firmly believe that in submitting to that authority on which Christ has set His seal, I but exchange a lawless freedom for a ' glorious Liberty.' Reason also tells me, after many deliberations, and a life, in the main, of thought, that though personal action and personal responsibility must ever be ours, it is yet our very highest Reason to merge what is merely individually ours in the universal Reason of the regenerate race, and such I believe the mind of the Church to be, guided as it is 'into all truth,' by the Spirit bestowed on it at Pentecost. Reason, in itself, is a ' light that *shineth* in darkness, and the darkness comprehended it not.' But Reason Incarnate *is come into* the World ; and this Wisdom, I believe, speaks to us through the Spirit and the Church. To contemplate Reason in this personal way and allow Him to speak to us as little children, seems to me the highest act of reason.

Good-bye and God bless you, my dear friend, and guide you aright in all things. Pray for me that I may not abuse the means of Grace which I believe to be now mine.

Ever your affectionate friend,

AUBREY DE VERE.

To Miss Fenwick

Leghorn : November 28, 1851.

My dear Miss Fenwick,—It is so very painful to write what will give pain to those who are dear to us, that, although I believe our last conversation hardly left you in doubt as to the step I should take, it is yet not without a great effort that I write to tell you that that step has been now taken. It was at Avignon, on my way hither, that my convictions with respect to the claims of the Roman Catholic Church seemed to me to reach such a degree of certainty and moral urgency as left me no choice, as a conscientious man, desirous of being sincere with himself and with others, and of obeying the will of God, so far as it had pleased God to reveal it to him. There, accordingly, I made my submission as I trust to God, in submitting to what I believe to be the authority which He has Himself set up upon earth.

I had not intended to write to you, dear Miss Fenwick, till I had arrived at Rome and received my first Communion. However, I have been delayed by various occurrences on the road, and do not wish to defer writing longer, for I would rather you heard of what must be the great crisis of my life, from myself, than indirectly through others. I will write again when I have had a little more experience. Hitherto I have felt a deep and tranquil satisfaction in the course which I have adopted, though comparatively little of that more enthusiastic and rapturous delight which I have heard many converts speak of. My course has not been adopted in any enthusiastic state of mind or imagination, but most truly

> Through no disturbance of my soul.

There is one thing of which I feel quite certain, dear Miss Fenwick, and that is that no religious change can, in the smallest degree, separate me from my friends. I only hope that it may as little deprive me of their affections and sympathies. I have never thought so often of them as since that change took place ; and of few have I thought so often as of you. How I wish I knew that you were pretty well. Adieu for the present, dear Miss Fenwick, and may God be with you and bear with you every trial it pleases Him to cast upon you, for His greater glory now and your spiritual good for ever.

Ever affectionately yours,
AUBREY DE VERE.

The following letter from Mrs. Arthur Martineau to her sister-in-law, Mrs. Robert O'Brien, helps us to realise the sense of regret and separation, the inability to comprehend the course he had taken, which gave something of tragedy to

the acquisition of what Aubrey de Vere ever described as
the greatest blessing of his life :—

December 4.

I have thought constantly of you and of what you
were thinking and feeling for some days. I cannot but
feel deep grief and sorrow about this last blow, though I
have known how it *must* be for some time. Ever since
my visit to Keswick I have given up all hope, and in truth
think it must be better to be settled in one's faith any way,
than to go on as I heard poor dear Aubrey had been
doing—avoiding Church, but wholly engrossed with controversy, deriving no benefit from our Church or its ordinances,
and having as yet no other fixed guide. I heard more from
James Spedding and Miss —— than from Catherine, and
could not but feel that it would never do to go on as he was.
He talked and thought of nothing else—but still it was not
with any repose or certainty. So if he writes now as if he
had attained to that, and so had made great gain, you must
consider that he had not attempted for a long time past to find
that rest with us—he had not used our gifts of grace—rather
he had slighted and despised them. God grant he may not
have taken a false step, and gained a dangerous repose. We
cannot throw off our individual responsibilities on any priest,
though I see how it is that those who persuade themselves
they can may gain for a time by it. Oh! for the happy
past. I can think of nothing but Curragh and its walks and
talks, and your days and years of happy heavenly intercourse
with that fine mind. It is a great, great trial, but no doubt
there is some great good which we cannot see now—spite of
it all I feel more and more deeply impressed with the idea
that the system of Romanism is tottering to decay ; it cannot
stand. Nations who have had it longest are weary of it, and
yearn for the bright sunshine of God's presence unobscured by
man's complicated machinery. Italy seems to heave under
the burden of the priesthood, and even our own blind devoted
Isle of Saints sees a light springing up in the darkness from
the simple beautiful words of the long hidden Scriptures, and
its rulers dare not bind on its chains lest they should be
rudely snapped for ever.

Nearly a month after the great step was taken Aubrey writes himself to his sister :—

Rome : December 10, 1851.

My dearest Sister,—I am sure I need not say how constantly I have thought of you ever since I took finally a step which will to few have been so deeply interesting, and which, I fear, must have given you pain, prepared for it as you were, and free as you are from all narrow-minded bigotry on the subject of the Roman Catholic Church. I considered that in writing to my mother on the subject I was writing to you also, as I begged of her to forward my note from Avignon to you ; and I preferred to write to you, directly after I had become fully a Catholic, i.e. after I had made my general Confession and received the Holy Communion. I have done so within the last few days, and I lose no time in assuring you that in proportion as I become more and more initiated, and learn to understand the moral and spiritual bearings of what, while a student merely, I could but investigate on intellectual and logical grounds, in the same proportion does my satisfaction increase and become elevated into what I trust may be no transient gladness.

I feel as if I had at last been permitted to grasp the *Reality* of those things, the mere projected shadows of which had beckoned me forward all my life to a better land. Many parts of the Bible also, especially the Gospels, which before had but little significance to me, have come out in new and deeper meanings, and in fact I seem to myself to have exchanged what, by comparison, was but a religious *philosophy* and sacred *literature*, for a Religion. I could say infinitely more as to details, especially as to what I deem the wonderful practical benefits of confession, but I wish to avoid all controversy, even in indirect forms, and indeed all discussion, except where it is invited and therefore is seasonable. I mention only what is most immediately personal to myself, knowing how anxious you will be to know how I have found in practice what I had but known, before trial, in speculation. Nothing, I know, can console you more for my adoption of principles which you cannot see as I do, than the fact that in their working they not only give me entire satisfaction, but afford me, I am quite certain, means of Grace from which I was before excluded, and *of which, if I should prove worthy, I have little more personally to desire.* I hope you will also bear in mind, if you continue to regret my course, that with the views which I had finally and absolutely taken up as to the present position of the Church of England (as illustrated by recent events), a great change was *to me* become inevitable; and that if I had not discovered that my principles were realised in the Roman Catholic Church, I must have fallen into some of those forms of Latitudinarianism, the direction of which is more easily seen than the end. Of one thing above all I must assure you, viz. that, as I had expected, not the smallest alienation in religious sympathy is produced by a change which abandons no substantive belief I have ever held, but on the contrary retains the whole of it, and adds to it what seems at once its consummation and its crown. . . . Pray write to me, and tell me all the little events that take place in your little circle, and still more all you have been thinking and feeling of late. How is Lady O'B.? better I earnestly hope. Was the Dowager Lady O'B. much incensed when she heard of my change? How does Grace's farm get on? Tell her I wish I could drive with her to see it in her pony carriage. She will have the prayers of the poor with her all her life, and they are next to the ministry of angels. I want also to know of Anne and Harriet and poor Kate, who I trust improves. Is Robert less worked than he was, and how does Aubrey get on? Our old friend Mary Phillips and her husband are here. She is just as she was, speaks much of you and sends you her love. The Camdens, who are here, are very kind to me and I like them much. I went with them to see the Coliseum yesterday by moonlight. Mr. Bennet passed some time here, but is now gone away with Sir John Harrington. He is very 'popish' I hear, though still in a state of doubt and suspense, as well as great anxiety. Mrs. Alfred Montgomery, whom I met at Avignon, says she will cling to the ship till the 'last plank.' Adieu, and God bless you, my dearest sister.

With best love to all about you,
Ever your affectionate brother,
AUBREY DE VERE.

To Mrs. H. N. Coleridge

Rome : Feb. 20, 1852.

. . . . Do not imagine for a moment that a convert to
Roman Catholicism loses any portion of sympathy with his old
friends. I find exactly the contrary to be the case. Rome
itself is half thrown away upon me from the degree in which
my thoughts revert to those whom I most value, and my
affection for whom seems to make newer friends of little
interest. . . .

From what Catholicism has taught me of Christianity, and
from what confession (that most misapprehended of all things)
has taught me of my own heart, and especially of the power
of pride in its *latent* forms, I do not think that I could have
continued a Christian had I not become a Roman Catholic,
though I dare say I should have given the name of Christianity
to whatever new heresy, or new version of an old one, I
preferred to the ' Faith once for all delivered.' As for others,
though I should think I was trifling with them cruelly in
affecting to give them an 'absolution' or an 'indulgence'
which is not mine to give, or in withholding any truth to which
my personal experience can witness, yet assuredly I am not
tempted to think worse of others for denying themselves the
aids which Catholics possess, than of myself for turning them
to such little account. It is not old affection only that makes
me wish that others could know but for one week what
Catholicism really *is*, but also a belief that in many cases they
would so realise it in *life* as well as in *mind*, as to glorify God
truly, and benefit His Family upon Earth. If, for instance,
Carlyle were a Catholic, to what a height would not spiritual
elevation rise, built upon a basis so strong as his moral
sincerity and probity, pierced through, and rendered adamantine by faith divine, and enriched with those charities and
aspirations which can no more find adequate nourishment in a
Protestant soil than cedars can grow upon coral reefs. How
soon would all who know him shake off at least the prejudice
that Roman Catholicism is in some way connected with
weakness or want of integrity. . . .

And you, if you were a Catholic, how soon you would

convince people that Catholicism casts no fetter on the mind, though it furnishes the laws as well as the ideas through which mental energies reach results, and arduous thought attains an exceeding great reward. One of the things which I saw most clearly even before I was a Catholic was that, as a Protestant I could never, though I meditated for a lifetime, rise above the very first problem of Revelation, and that after years of labour, the question would be still one respecting the foundation of an edifice which might have been half-built, and the answer would probably be a doubt. Could you but know, my dear friend, the complete freedom of thought which a Catholic attached to speculative matters possesses and the utterly *negative* character of that freedom which alone he has abandoned ! However, I will not run the risk of wearying you on the subject. . .

Aubrey de Vere stayed in Rome for some months. He had a difficulty in finding suitable apartments. At last some one suggested that a young English ecclesiastic had an excellent sitting-room near the Piazza della Minerva, and would perhaps share it with a compatriot. Aubrey wrote to the address indicated, and knocked at the door of the young man's room. The ' Avanti ' which followed told him that the owner was within. He entered and (as he has more than once told the present writer) stood transfixed by the beauty of the English boy of twenty-two, saying to himself ' Good Heavens ! if you are like that, what must your sister be ! ' The boy was Herbert Vaughan, the future Cardinal Archbishop of Westminster. The two men made their compact, and became fellow-lodgers, and thenceforth fast friends.

Friends, in sympathy with the great object of life they continued to be, but they were very dissimilar. The Cardinal once told me that the affectionate Irishman, who wrote constantly to his mother and sister, and talked daily with lingering love of his Irish home, could not understand—could scarcely believe in—the phase of ' ascetic detachment ' in the Englishman, which made him at this time speak of family ties

as of no interest to him. At last Aubrey became convinced by
further intimacy that Vaughan had given an accurate account
of his sentiments. ' I really believe,' said the poet in exas-
peration, ' that if some one told you that your father, mother
and brothers had been burnt to death in the next room, you
would simply ring for the servant to clear away the ashes.'

Of the friendship with Vaughan, and of a memorable event—
the first audience with Pius IX.—Aubrey writes to his mother
in the course of the following letter dated February 28 :—

I was presented the other day to the Pope. He was very
kind and paternal in his manner, and so entirely natural and
genial that no one ever feels the least embarrassment in his
presence. He asked me a good many questions, among others
what kind of poetry I wrote, and recommended me particularly
to write hymns in honour of the Blessed Virgin and the
Saints. He is rather fat, very strong, and takes a great deal
of exercise. His life is one of extreme labour. Every
Catholic priest, and he among the number, is obliged to
devote about three hours a day to devotion. The countless
questions referred to him (the Pope) take up all the rest of
the day. On all political questions he is completely and
entirely free from all *anxiety*, come what may. He has the
most absolute reliance on Providence, and probably if led out
to execution, would feel confident that the cause of Religion
and the Church would gain much more by his death than his
life. Whenever he has to decide anything of importance he
goes up to a little chapel above his bedroom, and remains
in prayer before the Blessed Sacrament for some time. He
then takes his course, and puts the matter out of his head.
He is generally believed to be a man of almost saintly piety :
and after all his sufferings his face quite beams with an
expression of happiness and peace, as well as of kindliness.
    . . . . One of [the Papal Chamberlains], Monsignor de
Mérode, has had a curious history. He is the eldest son of
one of the greatest and most ancient families in Belgium.
He entered the army, where he remained for some years, a
highly distinguished personage. On one occasion somebody

quarrelled with him and challenged him to a duel. Monsignor de Mérode refused to fight, having religious scruples. He said, however, that he knew that in so doing he destroyed his prospects and forfeited his reputation. Accordingly he threw up his commission in the Belgian army, and joined that of France, entering a regiment just ordered to Algiers. In Algeria he performed prodigies of courage, serving on forlorn hopes, &c. &c., and returned covered with honours and decorations. He then abandoned the army, became a Priest, and has already the reputation of being a saint.

During the siege of Rome he returned again to the scenes though not the labours of his youth, consoling the wounded on the ramparts, and administering the sacraments to the dying, while the balls were flying round him in all directions. I heard him preach his first sermon during the octave of the Epiphany. He showed me the other day a little chapel at the Vatican which constitutes a portion of his apartments, and is far less known than it deserves to be. The walls and groined roof are covered all over by paintings from the hand of old Fra Angelico da Fiesole. The subjects are the lives of St. Stephen and St. Laurence, and of the treatment one need only say that it is worthy of the master. His works always seem to me the summer moonlight of painting, as Perugino's and Francia's appear to have drunk up its sunset glories ; and the same *celestial* expression which we remarked in those faces of his the morning that we visited Lord Ward's collection, looks forth, on a larger scale, and with less of an evanescent gleam, from those pictures in the little mystic chapel. I could not help thinking that the man who said Mass there every morning at six o'clock had caught from the faces which surrounded him a portion of their luminous stillness. It is not very uncommon in Italy to see that peculiar expression, utterly unknown in the North ;—in monasteries especially one remarks it, and so learns that the old painters painted what they saw, not merely what they imagined. If you should chance to meet Mr. Anderdon (Manning's nephew), who has just left this for England, you will observe something of it, especially in an eye which has at once an unsleeping and a never-troubled expression. I am as well as possible, and

so are my eyes. Lent here is not at all severe, and I shall
not have more to do than in other years as to fasting. . . .
I will write to Miss Fenwick, as you suggest, in a day or
two. Poor thing, how much of suffering she has always had !
but doubtless it has brought and will bring its blessing. I
hear pretty often from Mrs. Coleridge, and but seldom from
Mrs E. Villiers, whose sister, Lady Blomfield, is here, and
whom I like very much. I see a good deal of the Lindsays,
the Camdens, the Feildings, and meet Italian society at
the Doria and Borghese Palaces, but keep as quiet as I can
and read a good deal. . . .

I like my companion in my lodgings better every day. I
must have mentioned him to you ; he is a Mr. Vaughan, the
eldest son of one of the great old Catholic families of England.
He renounces prospects as brilliant as almost any man in
England can command, to be a priest in some out-of-the-way
village in Wales, and seems as happy as the day is long at his
studies and devotions. He is very handsome and refined, and
as innocent as a child. He sits up half the night reading
Thomas Aquinas, and tells me the next morning that he has
been dreaming that people had been burning him alive and
that it had given him no pain. . . . I mentioned to you, I
think, having heard odes recited in forty-eight languages
on the Feast of Epiphany. Here there is not much news.
Every now and then a new convert falls in, and I hear that six
or seven are to be received in a few days. . . . What does
Sir R. Bourke tell you of the Jebbs and Percevals ? I suppose
they are a little angry with me.

De Vere seems to have brooded much at this time over
the thought of the Church with Rome as its centre, as the de-
pository of that accumulation of Christian life and meditation
to which the Saints and ' doctors of the Church ' have contributed in the course of her history, which serves as the
capital from which each Catholic draws, just as each partner
in a great commercial business trades upon the capital of
the whole. This thought often reappears, and it led him
to compare and contrast the genius of London—the great

centre of material commerce—with that of Rome, the centre of spiritual combination.

He had written on this subject a little earlier to Sara Coleridge :—

Man is invested with certain attributes, in the natural order, which enable him to engage in commerce. The consequence is, that each individual finds himself, and at a comparatively small cost, possessed of the products of the remotest climates. In this lower sense he 'inherits the earth,' on the twofold condition of exercising his own faculties with honest industry, and also of remaining obedient to the laws of human society. But whether he rejects or accepts what might thus be his, the advantages offered to him result from certain essential laws of society and energies of human nature, which exist independently of him, and of their own special results, and which are involved in the idea of humanity developed into civilisation. An analogous process takes place in the supernatural order. As isolated individuals, or barbarous tribes are organised into the unity of nations and of civil society, and as from that union each unit becomes an inheritor of what belongs to the whole, so also all nations, nay, humanity itself, as renewed and reintegrated in the mould of the second Adam, have become invested with a finer unity, and reappear in the form of the Church, universal at once and one.

In that archetypal and perfect form of society are found the chief characteristics that belonged to the lower forms of society, *but with a proportionate elevation*. In the supernatural, as in the natural order, combination produces power. The combination of natural energies produces commercial wealth, and that of natural faculties produces *probable* knowledge as the ordinary guide of life.

Combination in the supernatural order of society, which is founded not on the Creation but the Incarnation, is that which receives the august name of the 'Communion of Saints.' From that fountain flow the treasures of celestial riches, love, prayer, sacraments ; and for that reason we gain thence that certain and Divine knowledge which comes by faith, not sense,

P

and which is our guide in the heavenly life. Through the
Communion of Saints, all things belonging to the supernatural
order are *in common* among Christians. Their knowledge
must therefore, by necessity, be likewise a common knowledge,
emanating from the Holy Spirit, who is the mind of the
Church, and passing through the Church, of whom He is the
living bond, to the individual. . . .

Its knowledge has illuminated him from his childhood up
and imparted to him the Christian faith long before he was
able to judge or decide for himself. A mirror of Divine truth
had thus been created in the world; a mirror in which all
lesser mirrors had been melted down, that they might put on
a nobler unity, and in which all individual aberrations had been
corrected. A mind had thus been created, such as the mind of
unfallen man might have been; a mind world-wide, in which
the prejudices and limitations of individual minds, as
modified by race, climate, or local accident, had no place.

The parallel and contrast between the accumulated spiritual
capital of the Church, and the commercial wealth of ancient
Rome or modern England is touched on in the course of a
letter to his mother :—

Rome : April 24, 1852.

I shall leave Rome probably in ten days or a fortnight,
proceed to Florence by Perugia; and after a little boating
on the Italian lakes return to England by Switzerland. I
suppose that about the beginning of June I shall be in
London again. Are you likely to be there then? I can
hardly tell you with what joy I look forward to the prospect
of our meeting again. . . .

As, during former visits, I had devoted myself chiefly to
the Arts and Antiquities, so, on this occasion, I have given
myself chiefly to the churches, monasteries, and other religious
institutions. As in the world there are many men, so in Rome
there are many Romes; and there can hardly be a greater
blunder than that committed by those who pass their days
poring over pagan antiquities in that region which is
pre-eminently the city of the living, not of the dead. The

description of pagan Rome given in the 'Paradise Regained' might in some measure illustrate the intense Life in the great metropolis of Christendom, if one substitutes Divine things for human, a spiritual kingdom for a material, and processions to shrines, or the arrival of pilgrims for senatorial pomps and the trains of ambassadors on the Appian way. The moment one dips beneath the surface, and acquires that key through which alone such things receive an interpretation, what strikes one in Rome is that its whole structure is one stupendous living Reality, based on the Reality of spiritual things, and energising in the centre of them much as London goes on energising in the centre of that great world of commerce, physical prosperity and secular ability which it so forcibly represents. Rome and England, while in one sense the most extreme opposites of each other, are also in another singularly the counterparts of each other, each having its Empire on which the 'sun never sets,' each being in earnest in its special sphere, each finding it difficult even to understand the other, and each feeble where the other is strong. . . . . Only imagine people reporting in England that Manning has been found so heretical that he has been put in prison, as also that he has gone mad, and had his head shaved—the good man being for many years bald. The English are leaving this every day for Naples or the north, and those that remain are enjoying themselves daily more and more as the Spring advances and covers the vast spaces within the ruins with a floral growth that hides the bones of the great extinct animal that rolled himself about here till he had shaped a bed for the Church. I have been reading a good deal of late, among other things Ranke's 'Lives of the Popes,' and an interesting work by Donoso Cortes, in which he maintains that the world has but two alternatives, a real Christianity or Communism.

Aubrey de Vere did not in the event leave Rome in May as he had proposed, but lingered on until June, writing still to his friends concerning his new life and surroundings.

Perhaps the best summary of his final impressions of

Rome is given in a letter to Sara Coleridge. We find in
its course that Rome realised for him the central thought
which had driven him to her communion : namely, that to
preserve the spiritual life of Christianity is her distinct
mission, the object both historically and actually of her
liturgy, her art, her theology. Theological controversy had
ever been but a necessary means to an end—often a dis-
agreeable means. Living in Rome, he feels the Catholic
life to be so independent of theological treatises as to bring
home to him afresh the fact that even the greatest of them
give but the science, and not the reality of religion, which
exists in the living Church apart from its science, just as
flowers exist independently of books on botany :—

Rome : 1852.

I find the pursuits native to Rome so profoundly interesting that I have not much time for society. I am no longer
driven on Theology by the fear that if I do not keep my
watch in time, and steer by the stars, I may drift whither I
know not, and hear only that sad voice . . . which I always
expected to hear, although (curiously enough) Scepticism had
looked at me only, never laid her hand on me, while still [I
was] occupying a region which I perceived, with daily increasing
light, not to belong to the region of Faith. Scepticism must,
however, have found me in time. . . . I do therefore think
that, relatively to myself and my own prospects at least,
my change ought to give pleasure, not pain, to all who have
my interests at heart.

You will be glad to know how far Rome satisfies me. I
can hardly tell you how entirely it does so. . . . I should
probably have been a Catholic years ago if I had not been, in
some sort, a poet, and had a poetical predilection for the vague
in thought, and the vagabond in life. Such dispositions are not
quickly shaken off, and even after my reception, I was more
annoyed (as a matter of taste) by seeing these Southerns spit-
ting in church, than I was gratified by the marble of the
temples and the incense cloud. But in all substantial things

I have had a grave and solid satisfaction from the first; moral, intellectual and spiritual, and that satisfaction has been progressively deepening the more I have seen, thought and felt. The Roman Catholic Church is so very much more than I had expected to find it, and that, while a Protestant, I ever imagined that a Church could be. It is so distinct from, and so raised above, the very highest of its precious possessions. Abounding for instance in books, it is so wholly distinct from a 'literature' that millions might pass their lives (even among the intelligent) with hardly a remembrance that it has more than a few devotional books, the Bible, and the decrees of the Councils.

It is equally independent of Science. If all the Schoolmen and the Fathers vanished in a moment, a Catholic feels that the sacred processes of the Church, her inner and outer life, would go on just as before, even as Nature would carry on her glorious works of mercy and power, though all the books of natural philosophy should be burned.

It is so equally with Art. The poorest village or mountain church in which there is an Altar, and the Blessed Sacrament, makes a Catholic feel a diviner presence than I as a Protestant ever felt in Cathedrals—that diviner presence which bears the same relation to Christianity and the Incarnate Word that the sentiment expressed by Gray's celebrated lines 'Presentiorem perspicimus Deum' &c., bears to Natural Religion. And yet I feel daily more that the Church while independent of all except the truth and the Grace of God, can alone draw their true meaning and power from adventitious things. I *feel* daily also, that Catholicism is *really* a service of *freedom*, compared with which every other system founded on Revelation *must be* either a narrow despotism, or possess only the liberty of anarchy. . . . The degree in which it distinguishes between the functions of head and heart, and at the same time enlarges the sphere of each, fills me with ever new surprise; as does, yet more indeed, the marvellous instinct as well as habit with which it combines a thorough, genial, hearty and consistent belief in the Supernatural with an unerring common sense. Without the former *Religion* can exist but in name;

without the latter nothing is sound, good or permanent. But to combine the two is what no separated body can ever do. The Supernatural becomes enthusiasm and the judicious falls into the flats of secularity.[1]

[1] In the Appendix (p. 411) will be found extracts from other letters to Sara Coleridge, filling in some further details in the philosophy of faith to which Aubrey attained at this time.

CHAPTER VII

THE NEOPHYTE

1852–1856

AUBREY DE VERE found himself in England again in the summer of 1852. To join the Church of Rome in those days meant, for nearly all, years of estrangement from old friends. And we have seen that in some instances Aubrey's own case formed no exception to the rule. But his singular sweetness of character, together with the large view he took throughout of the true genius of Catholicism, kept most of his old friendships unimpaired. His own conviction that he only held more firmly, and with a wider outlook, the Christian beliefs which he still shared with his old friends, was so deep that he felt in no way estranged from them. For some years we find him striving with gentle persuasion to make others see as he did. But by degrees, the inevitable difference between mind and mind, and the existence, in prepossession and mental conformation, of invisible and irremovable barriers to agreement, forced themselves even on his sanguine nature. His most constant correspondents after his conversion were still old friends who remained Anglicans—Sara Coleridge and Miss Fenwick up to the time of their death,[1] Henry Taylor, Sir William Hamilton, his beloved sister and mother. And in their case he himself characteristically ascribed to his own faults, his failure to win them to what was to his eyes so beautiful, and so evidently a fuller realisation of Christianity.

[1] Sara Coleridge died in 1852, Miss Fenwick in 1856.

In other cases he attributed his failure to the narrowness and bigotry which English Protestants had inherited.

A meeting which must have been very interesting took place between him and Robert Browning in Florence, on his way back from Rome. Conversation on the problems of religion was prolonged to the small hours of the morning. The great poet's sympathetic insight carried him far ; and the glow of the 'newness of life'—of the dawn of spiritual daylight which Aubrey found in his membership of the historic Church, was recognised by Browning. 'I was much interested,' he wrote to Aubrey, 'by the hours you gave me on that last evening of yours in Florence, and grateful too, and *not* "tired." The sense of the spiritual, the exercise of the soul's instinct, the attitude of the life towards the Truth and the Love, are always interesting to me. *I am never tired of sunrises.* That I believe you to be mistaken in much, is obvious ; but you think worse of the act of mistaking than I do—which is obvious too—and so it is true (though a paradox) that I differ less from you than you differ from me. In spite of which, you were very patient, and at the same time loyal with me, for which I thank you entirely.'

Other correspondents were less sympathetic on the subject, and he found his own charge against Protestantism, of narrowness and the persecuting spirit, retorted against his new religion. It was not to Catholicism as Aubrey understood and interpreted it that the following trenchant letter from Sir James Stephen was truly applicable. The view of 'Roman' intolerance gently indicated by Browning in the letter quoted above, was very frankly insisted on by the acute critic, whose well-known admiration for Hildebrand meant no sympathy with Rome :—

My dear Mr. de Vere,—As I read the Paper which you have had the goodness to communicate to me, I said to my-self 'Come, I will annotate this for the behoof of the writer.' So, with my scanty time, and a very bad pen, I put down one remark after another, till I became convinced that what I was writing (even if legible) would be of no use, and that to complete my proposed review of your review, would be fatal to the completion of a certain Anti-Auguste-Comte lecture which I had on hand. Shall I throw my fragment into the fire, or forward it to you? The former would be the wiser, and perhaps the more courteous method; the latter the more sincere, or rather the more open and direct, so I prefer and adopt it.

If I had no other reason for dreading your present choice, it would be reason enough for me that it would place me in the frightful predicament of finding myself, even in this present life, surrounded with — dare I write it? — the damned. Kindred, friends, fellow-countrymen, the Leightons, the George Herberts, the Granville Sharps, the Wilberforces, the Howards of former times, all in hopeless endless perdition— the companions with whom I have taken counsel, and walked in the House of God as friends, all perishing—all smitten with the Anathemas of your Church, which the Omnipotent is to carry into execution! If this is Christianity, commend me to any form of Fetishism rather. Being what and as I am, I, on the contrary, have the consolation and the delight of believing that you, and such as you, are travelling Heavenwards by a circular and ill-chosen path, as it seems to me, but yet under the guidance of the Good Shepherd, in the love of Him and in the imitation of Him.

That my aspect of the world is pleasanter than yours, does not of course prove, or tend to prove, that it is the more accurate. But it proves that the arguments which should induce me to become your fellow-traveller ought to be irresistible. For if you and your co-religionists be right, this world is such a place that no honest man could, I think, join in the thanksgiving, in which you once joined, for our creation in it. The Philosophy of Candide, at the end of all his troubles and speculations, which was condensed into the maxim 'Let us grow our cabbages,' would be the only Philosophy in which I could take refuge, if you could make a convert of me.

It is with a genuine admiration of the gifts which God has

bestowed on you, with a sincere delight in the use you have made of them, with much regard for you personally, without any real doubt that I am safe in my ecclesiastical dissent from you, and with exceedingly little leisure in which to express or explain all these feelings, that I subscribe myself,

Ever yours,

JAMES STEPHEN.

With Henry Taylor, too, Aubrey crossed swords in theological controversy. But his letters were no more effectual in persuasion in that quarter than were the discussions with Browning or Stephen.

From the correspondence with Miss Fenwick we obtain some pictures of Aubrey in the first years of his new life. The glamour with which he ever invested the objects of his reverence now surrounded especially the Catholics whom he met. In August he visited the Vaughans at Courtfield. In September he stayed with his old friend William Monsell, now a Catholic, at Tervoe, and there met Father Faber, erstwhile poet, admired of Wordsworth, well known to Miss Fenwick herself, and now like Aubrey a convert to Rome—a neophyte in his first fervour. The visits are described to Miss Fenwick in the following letters :—

August 23, 1852.

. . . . The other day I went fifty miles off to make acquaintance with the family of a young man, Herbert Vaughan, with whom I lived much at Rome, and who had given up a 'great position' in his county and all this world calls happiness to be a poor despised priest in the more heathen districts of Wales. I have seldom seen such simply-noble, generous, devout, and humble people. The beautiful mother of *twelve* children cannot feel satisfied unless her six sons all become priests, and the six daughters nuns, though this would cause the extinction of one more of those old Catholic English families which for centuries have held their ground in stormier days than these. Almost within sight was the house of my old friend Jebb, who, while dissuading me from Rome last

year, had yet confessed that, if he had lived at the time of
the Reformation, nothing would have induced him to join the
Innovators. . . .

You can imagine how strange it must have seemed to me
to reflect that while I was so warmly received by perfect
strangers, I should have created nothing but annoyance and
embarrassment at the house of an old friend, who wrote to my
brother, on his change, to say that friendship must now be at
an end.   Yet he is a particularly kind-hearted person, steady
and strong in his nature, as well as constant, and attached to
justice.   Such are the effects of prejudice ; and prejudice
finds aliment even in the nobler part of our nature, though it
is rooted in the lower and darker.   Friends find it hard not
to resent changes of this sort as a personal wrong, while
nothing is farther from the fact than that, in such changes, they
were forgotten *even for a moment.*

Curragh Chase, Adare : October 1, 1852.

Most deeply do I lament every aggravation of bodily
suffering or diminution of comfort with which you are tried.
How difficult it is for us to realise the idea that every single
throb of pain or touch of pleasure with which we are visited
comes to us specially and entirely from the Will of Him who
is infinite Goodness ! nay, that He who wears our flesh in
heaven, deifying the very garb of His mortal sufferings, loves
each of us singly with a love a thousand times surpassing that
which all the Saints have ever felt or can ever feel for Him
or for each other !   This theme was touched with thrilling
power the other day by Father Faber, in a sermon preached
at Limerick.   'Who has not felt,' he said, 'in periods of the
most prolonged and intense suffering, the very finger of Omni-
potence touch him, as it were, in a moment ?   Who has not
felt himself, when patience itself seemed all but exhausted,
drawn into sudden and mysterious contact with God Himself—while a peace was diffused over his anguish which made
him almost fear its removal ? '

A deep pathos was imparted to this passage by the
circumstance that his own sufferings, which make him look
fifteen years older than he is, are so intense that when his

headache is on him he can hardly speak or move. He is now better, however, and though his ill-health has been much increased by his unremitting labours, he has at least the consolation of knowing that those labours have brought forth fruit a hundredfold in the sanctification of multitudes who, but for him, would hardly have known that there is a God. I passed almost a week with him in the house of my friend, W. Monsell, and I often felt during that time that I could not be easy till I had written you an account of your old friend, in whom you have, I know, never ceased to take an interest. . . . I can safely assure you that seldom in my life have I been so deeply impressed by any one as by Faber. I could hardly name to you another who (so far as I may attempt to judge of such high matters) appears to live so entirely in and for God. In that one thought he seems to live and breathe. There is a something almost tremendous in the earnestness, and, at the same time, simplicity, of his religious sense. . . . In his manner there is at the same time an unguarded, and almost childlike, frankness and simplicity which make his whole being transparent to you. Not a trace do I find now of the faults chiefly attributed to him in early youth, such as affectation, insincerity, or triviality. These may once have been faults of his; but if so never has a man more completely triumphed over the lower part of his nature.

He still sometimes talks in a manner that some people would call *vain*; but this I think proceeds only from the simplicity, geniality, and love of sympathy that belong to him; nor do I think that even on those occasions the charge could be more justly made against him than against Wordsworth, who, whatever he may have appeared to unfriendly critics, was full of a deep humility. What makes me think this is that he is quite as apt to allude to his own failures as to his successes; and that he speaks with much more zeal of the successes of others than of his own. When he speaks on Religion, it is with an eloquence, fervour, and impressiveness I have never known equalled. When other subjects, such as poetry, art, nature, &c., are introduced, you soon see how deeply he appreciated multitudes of things which he sacrificed for the 'one thing needful.' Whatever he may once have been, he is now by nothing more marked than by simplicity, *masculine strength*, and spiritual power. . . . How far I am a competent judge of course I cannot say ; but I thought it might interest you to hear what my impressions were respecting him after not a little of intercourse. I must not forget to say that he spoke with great affection of you, and expressed a great desire to see you again.

A very touching interchange of letters with Miss Fenwick, in which the tender and almost womanly sympathy of Aubrey stands out, came in the following year, when advancing age continued to bring illness and suffering to his old friend :—

June 27, 1853.

My dear Aubrey de Vere,—Though I have been silent so long, yet I have never ceased to remember you, and that with love ; but it has pleased our Heavenly Father to afflict me with many sufferings, and these have made me very helpless, and except a few scrawly lines to Henry Taylor, or on necessary business, I have written to no one, except a line now and then to dear Mrs. Wordsworth, who has been stopped by those around her from coming to see me once more—in this world ; but for the last two or three weeks I have been taken out of bed, and put in a position more fit for work. I am better in some respects, but my malady has made me a wreck. I may linger a little longer, and my kind physician would persuade me that I am still able to be taken to the Uplands, and he would himself accompany me—but the sun must shine very brightly when I entertain the thought that such a remove is possible. I would not bring a cloud on that happy home, and all the suffering and trouble connected with the final scene—but—till July is over I will not give up all idea of it. I cannot read, dear Aubrey, for my sight is weakened—and my hand soon tires of holding a book. I must live upon what I know ; if more is needful more will be given me—would that the Heavenly Manna may not be bestowed in vain on me !

My very dear love to Lady de Vere. I think lovingly of

your sister too, and tell her so. How much I have in my heart to say to you, but this I can only say now, that I am

Your loving friend,

I. FENWICK.

Mount Trenchard, Foynes: July 4, 1853.

My dear Miss Fenwick,—It is long since a letter has given me so much pleasure as I derived from receiving one from you once more. It was a greater one still because I had not ventured to hope for one. I know how difficult for you it must be to write, and very grateful I am to you for having made such an exertion. I am grateful also that you were able to give an account of your health, much as there is still to be wished for, or rather much as there is which we cannot help wishing for, well as we know that everything that comes to you is sent from Him who 'counts the beatings of the solitary heart,' who has heard every sigh we have breathed since we came into the world, compared with whose Human Sympathy that of our dearest friend is but coldness and harshness;—who is never more near to us than when He seems to stay away from us for a time, as He *seemed* to stay away from the sick bed of Lazarus, though such was His love and sympathy that He wept with the mourners but a few minutes before He raised him up.

I very much hope, dear Miss Fenwick, that you will be able to go to the H. Taylor's, and that you will not let yourself be discouraged from doing so. It will be to you another gleam of such sunshine as belongs to this lower world. To them it will be a great joy, and may be a blessing to an extent we know not. Life and the throng of life, when they are full and strong, are a sort of madness within us and around us. It is hard, in the glare, to see heavenly things, or to hear, in the tumult, the harmonies of a higher world. When we are with the sick, and with those whose sojourn below is well nigh over, we are placed, as it were, nearer to the gates of that higher world, and it is easier for faith to hold communion with what is within. I say this with reference to a passage in your letter in which you express an apprehension lest any increase of illness on your part, should such occur, might be a burthen to them. I am convinced that under all circumstances alike, a visit from you would be equally a blessing to them, and that it would leave behind remembrances by which their new home would be made more to them ever after.

Your affectionate friend,

A. DE VERE.

Two further letters to the same correspondent chronicle interesting visits—one to the family of Ambrose Lisle Phillipps at Grace Dieu in Leicestershire, the other to the Tennysons in the Isle of Wight. Grace Dieu combined for Aubrey the glamour which old association cast over everything connected with Wordsworth, with the special charm which the neophyte found in a Catholic household and in the proximity of a Cistercian Monastery. Wordsworth had loved the neighbourhood in his early life, and had sung of Grace Dieu. The house of Beaumont—the collaborator with the Elizabethan dramatist Fletcher—was hard by. Aubrey writes of his visit as follows :—

Grace Dieu Manor : October 25, 1853.

My dear Miss Fenwick,—I really cannot help writing you a few lines to tell you of the great pleasure I have had in treading again Wordsworthian ground. This place, you will remember, is celebrated in the Coleorton Inscriptions, occupying as it does the

> craggy bound
> Rugged and high of Charnwood's forest ground,

and constituting the chief feature in the view from Coleorton. I went over to Coleorton the other day, and wandered about among its groves and grassy slopes, and found and read its inscriptions. Three of them have been put up, and will in future days make that place classic ground. The fourth apparently never was put up ; but the Beaumonts have a fifth which was never published, and which they intend to have engraven on a marble tablet. I did not see it, in consequence of Sir George being out. The limetree avenue has fulfilled the poet's command, and formed an aisle, which will in good time be as stately a one as that at Cambridge. The 'winter garden' is a *lovely* thing, made out of an old quarry. The ground is exquisitely shaped, and all its slopes are turned to the very best account by a poetic skill which seems there to have exerted itself as happily as in shaping the lovely lines in which it is celebrated. It is planted with cedars, pines, juniper, cypress, and other evergreens, and must look even more striking and genial in the winter than now. But in all seasons alike its

> perennial bowers and murmuring pines
> Are gracious as the music and the bloom,
> And all the mighty ravishment of Spring.

It would be difficult for me to say with what delight I looked on these memorials of genius and friendship. It seemed to bring back the days when the great poet [Wordsworth], then in the prime of life, walked with his painter friend along those terraces. One of the inscriptions might more properly still be placed here, relating as it does almost exclusively to this spot. Here is the stream beside which

> Francis Beaumont strayed, a careless child,

and here too are

> The ivied ruins of forlorn Grace Dieu,
> Erst a religious house, which day and night
> With hymns resounded and the chaunted Rite.

The stream is as bright as when Beaumont sketched it, and as musical as when Wordsworth and Fletcher's associate sang beside it. The 'chaunted rite' is again revived and returns its antiphonal response to the same hymns which St. Benedict sang in the fifth, and St. Bernard in the thirteenth Century; for in the most craggy and picturesque part of Charnwood Forest, about two miles hence, a new Cistercian Abbey has reared its head, the church of which will, in a couple of years more, exceed that of Tintern in size. By the way, it will interest you to hear that the Abbot of it told me yesterday that his first inclination to the monastic life had arisen from his reading those lines in the ' Excursion '

> The life where Hope and Memory are one,
> Earth quiet and unchanged ; the human soul
> Consistent in self-rule ; and heaven revealed
> To meditation in that quietness.

They rise at two hours after midnight to sing the Divine Office, just as before the ' chasing storm '

> Shook the tenants out into the fields,
> Like wild beasts without home ;

and whatever time is not spent in psalmody, vigil and meditation, is spent in manual labour ; and accordingly already

> The sylvan waste retires
> And airy harvests crown the upland lea.

Could he see that pile and the work it does, Wordsworth could not but rejoice, both as a Patriot and as a Poet, but most of all as a Christian : for in it he would see God glorified, the poor aided, and the venerable strength of ' plain old times' not merely invoked, but evoked to sustain the weakness of these feeble and garrulous days.

Now I must say adieu ; but I could not be thus again with Wordsworth without wishing to be with you also. Love to all about you, and kindest remembrances to Mrs. Wordsworth, whenever you write to her. I have rejoiced much in your being together again.

Ever affectionately yours,

A. DE VERE.

Aubrey soon discovered to his joy that Wordsworth had visited the Monastery before his death. In the course of a letter to his sister two days later he writes :—

I have been interrupted by the arrival of Lady Beaumont She is very beautiful, young and winning ; but only think— *not* an admirer of Wordsworth. However, she has promised to read certain poems of his, of which I am to send her a list ; so that she may be converted still.

Think of the pleasure with which I heard that Wordsworth had visited the great new Cistercian monastery which has lately been built among the healthy hills. He must have heard the 'Chaunted Rite' resounding through the dark aisles in the very same harmonies as in the time of St. Bernard, and, centuries earlier, of St. Benedict. I have no doubt he was delighted with all he saw; and gave it at least a poetical, if not a theological, blessing. . . . Wordsworth's portrait is hung up on their walls. The Monastery is a stone from the sixteenth century, working its way up through the gravel road of the days which have Macadam for their father. I could write for ever if I were to describe it. . . .

The people here are the most delightful people you can conceive. You would think it a lovely image of a Christian household. There is choral service in the chapel morning and evening, the younger children dressed in red soutanes and acting as acolytes, until displaced by a still younger batch. There are already twelve children. You would delight in this house, and feel nothing in it to make you uncomfortable. Ambrose Phillipps is called by some of his friends 'a tremendous *Puseyite.*' The fact is that he is a great lover of theirs and of all their doings, and a great believer that the whole Church of England is some time or other to come back *as a body.* The consequence of this is that, though 1,500 people in this neighbourhood have become Roman Catholics, he is less anxious to make converts than any religious Roman Catholic I ever met in my life. He and his wife are overflowing with charity and hopefulness, and seem to believe that all parties are trying to do right, and will be sure to be guided some day into union.

. . . . How happy I shall be whenever we are together again! It is true as you say that the pleasure is not an unalloyed one. When any topics are excluded there is of course a certain feeling of discomfort as the result. This has been the case also in my relations with Dofo. In other cases it seems to me that as much has been gained in the way of religious sympathies, &c. as has been lost.

However, we must trust that all will be for the best. One thing is certain, that whoever desires wholly to do God's will need fear no lack of Divine guidance, support and aid.

A letter to Miss Fenwick in the following year, written from Swainston, the house of Tennyson's friend and neighbour, Sir John Simeon, refers to a visit to Tennyson in his new house in the Isle of Wight :—

Swainston, Newport, September 24, 1854.

My dear Miss Fenwick,—. . . . I can hardly help thinking that the delicious sea breezes of Freshwater would be of use to you. There is to me something quite inspiring, in a bodily sense, in the smell of the sea. I passed some ten days there with the Tennysons ; and it was a real pleasure to me to be under their roof. Certainly A. Tennyson has been very greatly blessed in his marriage ; and he deserved it ; for he seems to have been guided by the highest motives, and to have followed the true wisdom of the heart, in his choice. He is much happier and proportionately less morbid than he used to be ; and in all respects improved. I never saw anyone richer in the humanities than he is, or more full of that cordiality and simplicity which are apt to accompany real genius, and which mere talents, or cleverness, seem to repel. My friends, Sir J. Simeon and the Baron de Schroeter, who have been seeing them several times, have, I think, a deeper appreciation of him than anyone else whom I have seen ; and, much as they like him, they like his wife not less. I can hardly say how deeply interesting she is to me. She is a woman full of soul as well as mind, and in all her affections, it seems to me that it is in the soul, and for the soul, that she loves those dear to her. She would, I have no doubt, make any imaginable sacrifice of her happiness to promote the real and interior good of her husband, and not of her happiness only, but of his also. In the same way she looks on her two beautiful children, with an affection so deeply *human* and religious, that there seems in it nothing of the alloy that so often sophisticates the most sacred ties, causing them rather to lead from God than to Him. I regard her as one of the 'few noble' whom it has been my lot to meet in life ; and with a nature so generous, and so religious a use of the high qualities God has given her, I cannot but hope

Q 2

that the happiness accorded to her after so many years of
trial, may be more and more blessed to her as the days go
by. She is a person to whom you will be greatly drawn
whenever you are near her. . . .

To wish, alas ! is one thing, and to aid is another. Every
day I am more convinced that the chief obstacle to the spread
of Catholicity is to be found in the shortcomings of Catholics
who so imperfectly correspond with the graces given to them.
. . . There is but one person in *blaming* whom we can be
sure that we are right, and that is self. I have no doubt that,
notwithstanding many efforts to the contrary, I must often,
by my own faults, positive and negative, have disedified all
with whom I associated ;—and I may have been often unconsciously the greatest obstacle to those for whose welfare I
felt an anxiety. If I had done this in your case, I can
only ask your forgiveness for an injury far greater than you
know. You are not one of those who insist, so to speak, on
being disedified, and who can see nothing fairly in the case
of a convert. On the contrary, I know that to myself your
feelings have ever been most indulgent. But in the case of
all my friends my feeling is, though in different degrees, a
painful apprehension that I may have done harm, not good,
by so little illustrating in life what Catholicism really is.
There is only one way in which we can be sure of benefitting
our friends, and that is Prayer. . . . Oh, if there were no
other reason for wishing to advance in the interior life, there
would be sufficient in the thought that we should thus be
able to pray well for those for whom we live—so far as we
live a human life.

Sorrow came to Aubrey in these years. When he had
gone to say good-bye to Sara Coleridge before leaving for
Rome in 1851, she had been unable to see him.

> ' I'm wearing awa,' Friend,
> Like snaw when it's thaw, Friend,

and I feel as if I should not be long here,' she had written to
him, and so it proved. She died in the following May, before

Aubrey had returned to England. And now in 1855, his dear mother's health was visibly declining. But the end was brightened by the return home in November of his brother Horatio, after a dangerous illness.

You who know how devoted she is to him [Aubrey writes to Miss Fenwick], and how much she has suffered on his account, can guess what his safe return, after so trying a time, must be. Such a meeting is a thing that so rises above the ordinary pleasures or interests of this life, that it is really like a vista into that higher life in which there are no more separations. Indeed among the many modes by which the human imagination endeavours (though in vain) to picture Heaven to itself, none is more natural than to think of it as the great *Reunion*—not so much because the separated reunite there, as because they and all creatures meet in God.

The following letter is written shortly after Lady de Vere's death :—

Curragh Chase, Adare: Feb. 12, 1856.

My dear Miss Fenwick,—. . . . It is indeed a very great consolation to think that these last four months, passed almost at the gates of Life and Death, were yet to her a happy time on the whole ; happy in great things, and happy in little ones too, for all little things were again given their power to please her, after once her great anxiety about my brother had passed away. Even in her last illness, and on days when her mind was wandering, her face had often a brightness and gladness about it that suggested the idea that her thoughts were refreshed at some fountain, far within, of which we knew not. Something of the same expression is now on her face, as she lies on the bed—so often a bed of suffering— sprinkled over with flowers. The last few days she had little power of conversing with the outer world,—one of the last things she said, when the wandering was but beginning, was ' Jesus my Saviour will take away my pain.' . . .

Of ourselves I will only say we have lost her who has loved us, as no one else will ever love us. She is now taken

from us ; but in our constant prayers for her she will seem to
be with us still.   God bless you.

Affectionately yours,
AUBREY DE VERE.

To Sir William Hamilton Aubrey writes a little later :—

Feb. 23, 1856.

Her mind had in her later accesses of illness, during the
last few months been frequently wandering, and it was affecting to observe how it reverted to early scenes.   She used to
address both her parents, evidently under the impression that
she was a child ; and at other times her mind was evidently
sojourning among the scenes of her early married life.   It
seemed like the instinct which leads the wounded deer back
to the forest lair in which it lay as a fawn, to die there. . .
There was something very remarkable in the devotion to
Faith and Justice which in her was united to the very utmost
gentleness of nature.   There was in her also a purity of heart,
a refinement of mind, an intensity and fidelity of affection,
an innocence, and, above all, a humility, on which the mind
dwells with delight as, day by day, her beautiful character
comes out upon the memory, with a more clearly defined
image.   The mist of daily life, and all its petty cares, seems
gradually to melt away, and that fair image to disclose
itself with a distinctness and monumental serenity, like that
which impresses itself on the features of the dead.

. . We have thus many consolations, and infinite cause
for gratitude ; but of course such a bereavement must be
very deeply felt.   I feel it at all times ; but especially at that
hour in the evening when I used to read prayers for her.   I
think the greatest pleasure I have is in reading over old
letters written to her by Lord Monteagle and other members
of her family, which bring back the whole of her innocent,
and, on the whole, happy life (though it had severe griefs) in
continuity, from girlhood to the close of her visible existence.
Sometimes it makes the whole of human life look like a

dream or a gossamer thread of dew drops dried up ere noon. At other times, every little incident which, at the moment, must have passed with little interest, seems to swell out into large dimensions, and reveal some infinite inner capacities or significance. I copy for you one prayer which formed part of her evening devotions, which she much liked, and which better than anything I could say, expresses her mind on those subjects. You will observe that it is a large and distinct confession of ' *Implicit* Faith '[1]—as such, great importance is attached to it by Roman Catholics, as respects those who either have not the means of enquiry, or have not reached *explicit* convictions on matters which we deem a part of Christianity. . . . Many persons who call themselves Anglicans do also, and I think with consistency as well as wisdom, since they admit that the Church spoken of in the Creed, and so perpetually referred to in the Holy Scriptures, is the Interpreter of Revelation, and our Guide in the Faith, whom we are bound to 'hear.' The Confession, you will observe, does not enter on the question of contending claims, nor define what or where the Church is; but it negatives Private Judgment; and thus asserts a principle of implicit, as well as explicit, belief, through which our *Faith* (if we be sincere and humble) escapes at least those *limitations* to which human *knowledge* is ever subject, when attained in the way of *discovery* : and indeed I hardly know how anyone who reads the Bible, and believes that our Blessed Lord founded a Church, can object to it, though it may not have occurred to him to use it.

The Bible which Lady de Vere read daily in her last

[1] The following is the ' Confession of Implicit Faith, suited equally to Roman Catholics, and to others, especially to sincere enquirers, or persons resolved not to fall short of any part of Revealed Truth.'

' After the Apostles' Creed.'

' All this we firmly believe ; we believe also all other doctrines which Thy Holy Church proposes to be believed, because Thou, O God, Who art the Sovereign Truth, hast promised to guide her into all Truth, and hast revealed all these things unto her. In this faith and for this faith we are resolved by Thy grace to live and die.'

illness, was a precious relic to her children, and Aubrey's sister addressed to it the following touching lines :—

To my Mother's Bible

She read thee to the last, beloved book !
Her wasted fingers 'mid thy pages strayed ;
Upon thy promises her heart was stayed ;
Upon thy letters lingered her last look,
Ere life and love those gentlest eyes forsook.
Upon those gracious words she daily fed,
And by thy light her faltering feet were led,
When loneliness her inmost being shook.
O Friend, O Saviour, O sustaining Word,
Whose conquering feet the spirit-land have trod,
Be near her where she is, Incarnate Lord !
In the mysterious silence of the tomb.
Where righteous spirits wait their final doom,
Forsake her not, O Omnipresent God !

Aubrey de Vere's loving nature had to suffer another parting which was a heavy grief to him. His mother's death was soon followed by the death of that friend of friends, Miss Fenwick,[1] who passed away in December.

Aubrey was in Rome at the time, and although the news was not unexpected, the blow was a severe one when it came.

I have not yet got used to the thought [he writes to Henry Taylor] that I shall see no more in this life one who to me too (though, of course, not in the same sense as to you) has been for so many years so much interwoven with it. She was so much not only to me, but to many others who are also much to me ; I shall ever remember her as one of the noblest and most great-hearted beings I have been permitted to know. In her peculiar characteristics of moral and imaginative elevation and generosity of nature, the person who most resembles her (of those whom I know) is my sister. I wish that she had had the privilege of knowing her, which my father and mother

---

[1] 'All hope of happiness for her in this world,' writes Henry Taylor, in his Autobiography, 'was at an end. . . . It was time she should receive elsewhere the reward of a life of love and beneficence, as nearly divine as any life upon earth that I have known or heard of, or been capable of conceiving

enjoyed, though in different degrees. They both of them appreciated her from the moment they saw her, their acquaintance beginning under her own roof near Windermere, when they met there Wordsworth, and poor Hartley Coleridge, and the Quillinans—now all gone. When one looks back on these things life seems indeed but a dream ; and to love, as well as to faith, it is the unseen things that become the realities. In some things how much she resembled Wordsworth : but then how free she was from that alloy of egotism which commonly clings to the largest masculine nature! There was another great point of difference. His was pre-eminently a happy, and, in the main, even a satisfied life. Hers, I am convinced, never was so ; certainly never from the hour I saw her first, as she rose, with her languid, reluctant form and nobly-sorrowful face, from the sofa in your back drawing-room at Blandford Square, to shake hands with your new friend. Even had she been strong all her life, though she would have had soaring hours in larger abundance, there would have remained a craving not to be satisfied. Perhaps, had she possessed the closer ties of life, she would have felt this lack but the more. Her heart was as tender as her aspirations were elevated and unremitting; and such a being in a world like this must ever be condemned (so far as the outward life goes, and even the life of the affections is part of the outward life) to 'draw nectar in a sieve.' In any case she would have felt, I think, the force of an expression of Wordsworth's which I once heard her praise—viz. the ' *defrauded* heart'; though, had her body not been the opposite of her mind, she would have had the imaginative and elemental joys of life in rare abundance. . . . Great love, great aspiration, great suffering; these are the recollections which will, perhaps, remain longest with me, as representing the earthly life of Miss Fenwick, and it seems part of the Divine design that these three should be commonly closely united.

The loss of Sara Coleridge, of his mother, and of Miss Fenwick, took from Aubrey in each case a special kind of sympathy which could not be replaced. How he strove to bear

himself in the presence of such bereavements we know from
the beautiful lines he has left us :—

> Count each affliction, whether light or grave,
> God's messenger sent down to thee.   Do thou
> With courtesy receive him : rise and bow.
> And ere his shadow pass thy threshold crave
> Permission first his heavenly feet to lave.
> Then lay before him all thou hast.   Allow
> No cloud of passion to usurp thy brow,
> Or mar thy hospitality, no wave
> Of moral tumult to obliterate
> The soul's marmoreal calmness.   Grief should be
> Like joy, majestic, equable, sedate ;
> Confirming, cleansing, raising, making free ;
> Strong to consume small troubles, to commend
> Great thoughts, grave thoughts, thoughts lasting to the end.

The exhortation of Pius IX., that he should write hymns
to Our Lady and the Saints, had dwelt in Aubrey's mind since
he left Rome ; and he devoted these years to writing the work
called 'May Carols or Ancilla Domini '—a series of poems,
some of them very beautiful, on the Christian mystery of the
Incarnation, and on devotion to Mary as the human instrument
of the birth of the God-Man.   This work, illustrated by his
favourite pictures by Giotto and Fra Angelico, gives probably
the truest picture of Aubrey's mind in his Catholic period.
The imagination is that of the ages of faith.   The intellect
runs on lines which produce and apply the reasonings of
Coleridge, Wordsworth and Newman.   There is apparent in
it the devotion of a knight-errant to the Virgin Queen, and
at the same time, a remarkable estimate of the bearing of the
position she has so long held in the minds of the faithful, on
Christian thought, in its relation especially to the rationalistic
speculations of the middle years of the nineteenth century.

In his explanatory introduction to the volume, he regards
the position of Mary in Catholicism first from the intellectual
point of view, and then from the devotional.

His main contention in the former category was, that
much of the vagueness and semi-Agnosticism of the age

arose simply from the fact that the greatness of Christianity was no longer realised. The critical powers had grown : but the faculty which adequately realised the very subject of criticism had become atrophied. Not the glorious image of religion which was present to the imagination of Fra Angelico or Giotto, but a hastily constructed lay figure, was the object of much of the nineteenth-century rationalistic criticism. The very Theism which was the basis of Christianity was misconceived. The conception of God ought to be remodelled, the critics said, to suit the moral ideas of the age. But the criticism and remodelling were executed, not on the Infinite Deity of Apostles, Fathers, and Schoolmen, but on a really anthropomorphic Deity. For the critics had apprehended no more than this in Christian tradition. The enlightened thinker would have none of the traditional, vainglorious and selfish God. But he failed to see that he was dealing with a sphere in which such criticism had little meaning. He forgot the Christian conception that union with the Infinite God should be regarded as the true end of man—that man's service of Him was the true end of human life and its happiness. The supposed antithesis between selfishness and unselfishness had no application in the Infinite God so conceived. To desire the happiness of His creatures and the fulfilment of their nature— that is to say, the unselfishness which the critics desiderated— was identical with desiring that they should serve Him faithfully—that is to say, with the selfishness of which they complained.

To minds, indeed, which had lost all realisation of the traditional greatness of the Christian doctrine, the Infinite God became either very finite or entirely indefinite. The conception of the highest, and purest, created excellence in Mary, was, the poet maintained, the best cure for this. It gave the true line of Orientation, though it avowedly fell infinitely short of the sanctity of the Creator. Selfishness and vainglory were already left far behind in the human Mary.

Produce the lines of her sanctity to Infinity, and those defects certainly would not return. Once the full beauty of this character, the perfect ideal of Christian womanhood, was understood—and as human it was within man's power of understanding—Christian worship was already lifted into an ether above the trivial criticisms of thinkers, whose acuteness was great, but whose powers of depicting or realising the religion they criticised were so inadequate. And while the thought of Mary thus helps to define the character of God's sanctity, the very infinite distance between the highest creature and the Creator, helps us also to realise the degree of the Divine sanctity.

Moreover Mary—no mere *imaginary* ideal, but conceived as existing historically, and as the historical instrument of the stupendous objective fact of the Incarnation in which Christians believe — was a standing rebuke to modern subjectivity, which, as the outcome of the denial of dogma at the Reformation, threatened to resolve Christianity into a state of the emotions, or a mere philosophy.

These profound thoughts are to be found in the course of the poet's prose introduction to his work, from which I make some extracts :—

Everywhere we find that the clear conception and familiar contemplation of the highest *Created* Greatness are the preconditions for worthy thoughts respecting that Greatness which is *Uncreated*. This is the more felt, the higher that Mystery in connection with which we contemplate Created Excellence. It cannot eclipse what is immeasurably above itself : it can assist in defining it to our intelligence, as the straight line measures the curve.

There is a true, and there is a false Theism. No one can fail to feel the distinction between the Authentic Idea of God, and an arbitrary abstraction made by Man's Intelligence, if he has always known that between Him Who is the Infinite, and her who is the highest of creatures, the interval still remains infinite—that, compared with Him Who is Absolute Being,

she who is the crown of all created excellence, remains but a
crowned Dependence, the most creaturely of all creatures,
the Handmaiden, to whose *lowliness* He had regard.

We may go farther.   The place divinely assigned to Mary
is the protection not so much of any doctrine in Religion,
however fundamental, as of Religion itself in its essence.
Mary is the guardian of all those mysteries which relate to the
Sacred Infancy : through her Holy Church keeps a perpetual
Christmas ; rejoicing in mysteries which can never lose their
objective character and historical attestation.   Through Mary
the Palpable is preserved in the Spiritual, and the Truth of
Fact holds its own against the subjective habit of the modern
mind, which, 'with error opposite to that of Narcissus,' to
quote Dante, wastes away, because it imagines that it sees
but its own face in all things, believing in no other reality.
This form of Philosophic hypochondria makes Religion
itself but a type of good things, not the living bond, by which
fallen man is bound again (*re-ligatus*) to his Creator, through
that Truth which alone is Freedom.   This is the most dangerous form of unbelief, because the most plausible.   It leaves
sacred names unchanged.   By a sort of evil transubstantia-
tion, it changes into itself the *substance* of Religion, leaving its
accidents unaltered.   The 'Species' remain to give specious-
ness to a Philosophy, whose ambition it is, not to overthrow
this or that Religion, but itself to take the place of all
Religion.

Of the gradual atrophy of our capacity for realising the
great religious ideals of olden times he writes :—

The chief intellectual dangers are often those of a gradual
character.   The human mind, insensibly shrivelling up and
dwarfing itself, reduces to pettiness its loftiest subject of
thought, without perceiving the change.

. . . . [The modern critics of Christian Theism] have never
really taken in the difference between the Creator and the
Creature, and their shortcomings have arisen, in part, from
their having never fixed their attention on a sufficiently great
exemplar of creaturely excellence.   The diversity between

different grades of being becomes most marked when we
contemplate the nobler specimens of each grade. It is easy
to confound the lower forms of vegetable with the lower forms
of animal life ; but when we rise to the higher forms of each,
their diversities are unmistakeable. . . . The highest idea of
the creature aids us to think worthily of the Creator, and
helps us in the same way as Nature helps us to conceive of
the Supernatural ; viz., on the one hand, by analogies, and on
the other, by contrasts.

Such worthy thoughts of God destroy the antithesis
between a God who loves His creatures and desires their
good, and a God who is self-centred :—

God more than creates their good. He *is* that Good : and
this He could not be, were He not the Term and End of all
things, as well as their Origin and their Life. God is all Love
and God is also His own Divine End.

This is what the modern critics fail to realise.

Their aspiration is to outsoar the anthropomorphism of the
vulgar ; their achievement is to create for themselves a God in
their own image. They say, ' *Our* God shall not resemble a
selfish and vainglorious man ' ;—and say it because their
notion of God is but Man, magnified and modified.

The Christian poet and the Christian theologian alike
speak in the following passage :—

The Church is ever ' stepping westward,' and her endless
evening does not lack its Evening Star. The remoter and
full-orbed glory of Mary shines in the eyes of the Militant
Church, beyond this vale of tears—an image of the Church
Triumphant. . . . Her mere position strengthens the Church
as with a fortified citadel ; yet her teaching is of all Teaching
the most unpolemical. It leaves a blessing even at the door
that will not open to it, but with the franker nature it leaves
the heritage of that Truth which is one with Love. It is in
the heart that it lodges Truth—that heart which it ' penetrates

without a wound,' knowing that thence it must ascend into
the higher Intellect, and diffuse itself through the being.   It
conquers the controversial spirit, that Fury of the Schools,
without a battle, by leaving for it no place : and thus Religion
remains the soft but mighty Mother of Man, and Truth retains
her placid place in a Temple which attack alone can convert
into a Fortress.

Where the Faith is associated from early days with
those unhappy contentions, which are but its accidents,
there Religion may either live on as a boast, protected
by the Institutes it protects, or it may be trampled out
as a cause of offence ; but in either case its essence is
ignored.   It gives little glory to God, and no peace to men.
It bickers on every hearth, sows the Dragon's teeth in every
field, inflames every youthful presumption, and envenoms
every sore of age.   There is no greatness which the spirit of
controversy cannot reduce to littleness.   We deal with God's
Word as we do with His Works.   Half a dozen obtrusive
white houses, scattered along a range of hills, so arrest the
eye, and force it to draw imaginary lines connecting house
with house, that in the invisible network of this luckless
geometry, all the grace and the might of mountain outlines
is lost.   So fares it with the sacred Scriptures, when favourite
texts have become the entrenched camps of amateur
Controversialists :—they may know the Bible by heart ; but
for them the Word of God exists not.   Never once can they
wander through its infinitudes with the reverent eye of the
Seer, with the simple wonder, the loving delight, the blame-
less curiosity of the child.   For the love of the Truth they
have substituted the love of *Knowledge discovered*, and the joy
of contention.

But the remedy ?   Does it lie in disparaging Doctrine ?
Certainly not ; for Revelation not setting forth a Truth
would be no Revelation.   Does it lie in substituting Love for
Truth as the soul of Christianity ?   Certainly not ; for
Christian Love is inseparable from Christian Truth.   To love
a Divine Redeemer, we must know that He *is* Divine ; and
all the Councils for successive centuries were needed but to
refute the errors that assailed that Truth.   Such warfare

must always be going on. On some far border of the Christian Empire, there will always be irruptions of new Barbarians ; and they must ever be repelled, lest they should reach hearth and home. The battle of Truth must last till its last foe is repulsed. The luminary that lights that battle-field is the Mystery of the ' Word made Flesh ' :—a sister orb reflects its light :—and to the end the prayer of the Prophet-Chief will ascend—' Sun, stand thou still upon Gibeon, and thou, Moon, in the Valley of Ajalon.' Relatively to Christian Science, Mary has a place, so inextricably woven with it throughout, that she cannot but add force to its most stringent affirmations, and a severer exactitude to its most refined definitions.

In the region of devotion De Vere regards Mary as realising the idea of Christian Womanhood—so intimately bound up with the essential genius of Christianity. For, family life built upon Christian faith and associations, and the religious life of the nun who exhibits the ideal of purity and self-denial, are both combined in the life of Mary :—

It was impossible for the married sister to remember the Sister beneath the veil, without remembering also that the home brightened with children, and the convent home on its lonely height, must alike, though in different fashions, be homes of Reverence and Worship, of Purity and of Peace. From these two homes went forth Christian Civilisation. There moved over the earth a conception of human character such as the Greek had never dreamed of. It was that of Womanhood. It had not the strut of the Pagan hero or demigod ; but it was greater than all the gods. And yet how few elements made up that greatness !—only Humility, Purity, and Love. And with how few franchises it was en-dowed ! Only with the joy of one who from childhood had panted for Divinity, as the hart for the waterbrooks, and had found Him ; and again, with the sorrow inseparable from Love in a world of sin—the Sorrow of a Heart transfixed, and from which the Sword never departed. Such was the highest Christian Idea of Womanhood. It came from Mary. It

took its place beside that Image of Man associated with the
'Ecce Homo'—the purple robe of regal dignity, and the
Head crowned with a crown of thorns.

That fair and fruitful idea which set free the intelligence
and the heart of man, raised his imagination proportionately
and created the art of the Ages of Faith. It re-revealed
beauty—no longer the Syren's smile, but the radiance on the
face of truth—the sweetness and graciousness of virtue itself.
Everywhere throughout the worlds of painting, sculpture, and
architecture, shone out that nobler beauty, severe at once
and tender, mystic yet simple, gladsome yet pathetic. It
was a spirit, but a spirit ever embodying itself in sensible
form, for the redemption of sense. Compared with classic
art, its insight was deep, and its flight was high : but it had
one fixed home, the 'Holy Family'—a limit apparently
narrow, yet found to be inexhaustible. The Holy Family
was the centre at once of things earthly and things heavenly ;
and Art, when it saw that Vision wisely desired to build
tabernacles in its light, and whispered, ' It is good for us to be
here.'

It would carry me beyond the limits prescribed by the
plan of the present work to quote a sufficient number of the
' Carols ' themselves to exhibit them as carrying out this
large design. I will content myself with selecting two, which
I take from those appointed by Cardinal Newman to be
sung at the Oratory each day in May, and copied in his own
handwriting :—

IN EPIPHANIA

A veil is on the face of truth ;
  She prophesies behind a cloud :
She ministers, in robes of ruth,
  Nocturnal rites, and disallowed.
Eleusis hints, but dares not speak ;
  The Orphic minstrelsies are dumb ;
Lost are the Sibyl's books, and weak
  Earth's olden faith in Him to come.
Rejoice, O Sion, for thy night
  Is past ; the Lord, thy Light, is born ;
The Gentiles shall behold thy light ;
  And kings walk forward in thy morn.

R

DOCENS

He willed to lack ; He willed to bear ;
   He willed by suffering to be schooled ;
He willed the chains of flesh to wear ;
   Yet from her arms the worlds He ruled.
As tapers mid the noontide glow
   With merged yet separate radiance burn,
With human taste and touch even so
   The things He knew He willed to learn.
He sat beside the lowly door ;
   His homeless eyes appeared to trace
In evening skies remembered lore
   And shadows of His Father's face.
One only knew Him, She alone
   Who nightly to His cradle crept,
And lying like the moonbeam prone,
   Worshipped her Maker as He slept.

Two letters are extant which form a fitting sequel to this account of the ' May Carols.' One shows Aubrey, not long after their publication, in correspondence with a great modern painter of religious subjects who had caught some of the spirit of the mediæval artists—Mr. Holman Hunt.

I have too long delayed [writes Mr. Hunt on September 11, 1857,] to say how much your interest in my work, and the manner in which you give evidence to the same, gratifies me. I had indeed already obtained your new book, and although I had not found leisure to study it, I had noted the poems you refer to as of peculiar value to me, as exponents of one manner of regard for the Virgin's suffering character, which I was not certain that I perfectly understood. Now that I have read these Carols you will, I trust, allow me to say how much I enjoy the poems as poetry, and how I not less admire the idea in a religious point of view of the Madonna's sacrificing at the foot of the Cross, altho' I am unable to subscribe to it as an essential article of faith. But I must not wander from the subject in hand. If I am to realise my conception of the Virgin's expression, it is my hope that my delineation of her will not offend the utmost reverence for her holiness of nature.

My choice of an actual person to paint the face from, simply arises from the fact that my powers are insufficient to work out my idea into form without having nature before me, a course that all are licensed to follow by the example of the highest authorities, Raphael for one, the unattainable beauty of whose Madonnas ought, I feel, to be excelled by a painter having so fine a face before him as that I have to guide me, were the result not depending upon the superiority of the workman that could make even the Fornarina's face suffice as a model for the most perfect embodiment of angelic sweetness and purity.

The second letter was written in 1870 to Aubrey de Vere's American friend, Miss Grace Norton, and contains a valuable addition to Aubrey's earlier analysis of the philosophy underlying the volume :—

In dealing [he writes] with Faiths of the *highest order* I am convinced that nothing can be done in the way of scientific demonstration, and that the whole problem consists in creating a *genuine apprehension* of them. They are commonly presented to us in spurious versions, and approach us in disguise—often an ugly disguise (and then we close our doors against them), sometimes, a fair, but illusory disguise, and then we turn them out of doors, as soon as we have detected them. On the other hand, if they once succeed in making their way to our apprehension, they at once take hold of us, the whole being welcoming them with an acclaim of recognition—not crying out ' This is flesh of my flesh,' but ' This is spirit of my spirit ; ' and in this sense it was, I think, that Coleridge used to say, ' Evidences of Religion ! Religion and Reason are each of them its own evidence.' This belief on my part must plead the excuse for the *unmerciful number* of my ' May Carols.' They are an attempt to bring the one great idea of the ' God-Man ' home to the apprehension, by presenting it again and again in many of its phases. One idea may unite in its pellucid simplicity, and in absolute unity, scores of ideas, which are capable of being detached from each other, like drops of water, and again of being re-united ; but which, whether in separation or in union, are equally capable of reflecting the same Heaven. I endeavoured to bring out the different ideas which compose the one idea of 'God made Man' (an idea as absolutely simple as any of its component ideas) in the hope that one or other of the number might flash into the apprehension a beam of that Truth which conquers all things to itself. But intentions are not performances ; and I fear I have so feebly done what I have aimed at doing, that only a very few very friendly readers, like yourself, will discover even that the attempt was made, or perceive that the poem had any special drift or intention. At least, however, you must accept my warm thanks for the kindness that made you tell me that my poems have been something to you. Poetry ought to help us to ' discern,' as well as to see, some of the true and fair things that engird us in the two circles, of nature, and of the supernatural ; and if it has done this in but a few instances, it has had a better success than mere Fame could give.

CHAPTER VIII

LITERARY AND POLITICAL CORRESPONDENCE

1856–1873

AUBREY DE VERE was but forty-two when his mother died. Not half of his long life was yet done. Yet it may be said that with the few years I have just reviewed of his adaptation to his new surroundings as a Catholic, the history of his life, as a narrative of incidents, comes to an end. His correspondence increases rather than diminishes in interest. But it no longer records an onward movement. Two crises in Irish politics, in which he took a share—in the sixties and in the eighties—are indeed to some extent landmarks in his history. But that is all. And the reader, in order to appreciate the remainder of his correspondence, must have before him the atmosphere and surroundings, mental and physical, in which he wrote, and which formed the setting of his life from now to the end.

The mental atmosphere is best shown in some of his own poems and letters. It was a blending of home affections, tender friendships, love of old associations, love of his country, with religious faith, now embodied for him in that form which he felt to have never lost the primitive unearthly ethos of the Gospels, and to be one with the spirit breathed in his favourite pictures by Giotto and Fra Angelico.

We have seen that the possibility of religious scepticism had crossed his mind at one moment. So, too, little as he lost, in comparison with most men, of early enthusiasms, he has left a record in some touching lines showing that even he realised some of the disenchantments of advancing life. Religious Faith alone was, in his eyes, an effective antidote to the disillusions of experience. It alone could find that secret of perpetual youth which keeps alive in later years the glamour with which the child's imagination first surrounds the earth.

> Glad childhood's dream of marvels past we rise,
> Still on our cheek the blush of sleep remaining,
> And roam the wastes of earth, our eyelids straining
> The glories of that dream to realise.
> Nor seek in vain. Stream, bird, or cloud replies
> (Echoes that mock young passion's amorous feigning)
> Fancy shines starlike forth 'mid daylight waning,
> And Hope the night bird sings 'neath shrouded skies.
> At last the charm is broken : day by day
> Drops some new veil, until the countenance bare
> Of that ice-idol, blank Reality,
> Confronts us full with cold and loveless eye.
> Then dies our heart, unless that faith we share
> Whose touch makes all things gold and gives us youth for aye.

It was this Faith ' whose touch makes all things gold and gives us youth for aye ' which shed a brightness and constant freshness over the daily unchanged routine at Curragh Chase, which was his normal life for the rest of his days. He realised in this respect the lines in his own ' May Carols,' in which he represents the undimmed youthfulness of heart associated with the devotion to the Virgin Queen :—

> Childhood and springtide never cease,
> For him thy freshness keeps from stain,
> Dew-drenched for him, like Gideon's fleece,
> The dusty paths of life remain.

In his beautiful Irish home he found all his heart desired. The past and its loved ones lived for him there, and he could dwell in the thought that they still lived in fact behind the veil. And in the summer he would visit London, and see his friends there ; going on to visit those who were most to him in England—the Taylors, the Tennysons, and a few more – and never forgetting a pilgrimage to the tombs of the beloved and revered dead.

The following letter to his sister from Ambleside in 1860 records a visit which was paid annually to the grave of Wordsworth :—

Monk Coniston, Ambleside : August 12, 1860.

My dearest Sister,—I spent most part of last Sunday at Rydal, and now send you, from the old Poet's garden and wood walks, a few flowers. . . . It is to me a holy precinct, and to have slept under his roof seems the greatest honour of my life. The house and garden are just what they always used to be, and his old servant, James, is there still.

I visited his grave also—it is at one corner of the church-yard of Grasmere—close by are his wife's, his daughter's, those of two young children, and of Hartley Coleridge and Mr. Quillinan.

Mary has just given me such a nice copy of the greater part of his works, in a single volume, such as can be carried about in one's trunk. It contains the ' Excursion,' and all his poems published before that.

I never see a touring party here without thinking of the rapture your sojourn in the land of lakes was to you when you visited it first, and giving them a ' God speed ' on your account

Affectionately yours,

AUBREY DE VERE.

The tomb of Coleridge was also a frequent, though not an annual, place of resort. The winter would see him back at Curragh Chase, happy in the family circle, but meditating there, too, on one whose memory was more to him than even that of Wordsworth or Coleridge.

Late on Christmas eve in 1860, in the library at Curragh, we find him still brooding on the thought of his father's death, fourteen years earlier :—

> To-night upon thy roof the snows are lying :
> The Christmas snows lie heavy on thy trees :
> A dying dirge that soothes the year in dying
> Swells from thy woodlands on the midnight breeze.
> Our loss is ancient : many a heart is sighing
> This night, a late one ; or by slow degrees
> Heals some old wound to God's high grace replying :

A time there was when thou wast like to these.
Where art thou? In what unimagined sphere
Liv'st thou a sojourner, or no transient guest?
By whom companioned? Access has she, near
In life thy nearest, and beloved the best?
What memory hast thou, of thy loved ones here?
Hangs the great vision o'er thy place of rest?

A letter—from which I have already quoted a few sentences—written to Hamilton in the early sixties, after an absence from home, contains perhaps the fullest expression in Aubrey's own words of the clinging love of the past which the place aroused, and its power of preserving for him that past as it were in bodily form :—

Here I am, once more, in my old home, and alone; for my eldest brother and his wife are in England. It is to me haunted ground. After a time, of course, this effect wears off; but at first, after coming here, it really seems to me a sort of enchantment. The present becomes almost nothing—a mere vapour—and the past becomes so distinct that I recognise the steps of the departed as well as their voices. The most trivial incidents rise up before me wherever I go; and in every room of the house, and every walk of the garden or woods, I see again the old gestures, expressions of face, even accidents of dress, which no one could fancy could live in memory. I allude of course to my father and mother principally, but not to them only. Very old friends, most of them long since dead, walk with them ; and the old jests are repeated, but with a strange mixture of pathos and mirth ; and my brothers and sisters (there were two younger sisters who died each at the age of fourteen) seem to me once more as in the old days of childhood or opening youth.

I suppose that many people have had this experience. To me it seems nearly the most solemn and pathetic one that life brings. With all its melancholy the preponderating feeling it includes is one of sweetness. As life goes on, and goes by, a certain tenderness, almost remorseful tenderness, seems to attach to all human relations—and even to inanimate objects. We seem to be such mere shadows—such a *help-*

lessness seems to belong to us, and our parents, and all the fleeting generations that glided on and off the stage of life, in days earlier than those we remember, that it appears an inconceivable cruelty that anyone should 'agitate the light flame of our hours' by unkindness to a neighbour, or even by want of sympathy. It seems as if everyone must have been intended to be in some sense a 'helpmate' to everyone else; and that to hurt instead of helping any of those who belong to so feeble a race—a race whose joys are so fleeting—and whose trials are so many, irrespective of those which come from a fellow-being, implies that a long madness is preying upon human society.

I am writing in the old library, and the writing-desk on which my father wrote all his poems and letters is the one my paper rests on. Among the phantoms which have been visiting me is a phantom visit from Adare. One of the party is a young Philosopher, of whom we had already heard as a scientific wonder : and now, from his discourse, we find that he is as much devoted to poetry and metaphysics as to mathematics. Then there comes the ramble in the woods, the departure, and my father's enthusiastic comments on the young Philosopher, and especially the praise bestowed on the 'transparent candour,' which made all his thoughts seem visible things.

Even those whom I never saw, but who belong to this magical past, share in the strange spectral resurrection. There is poor Francis Edgeworth. We used to talk of him and his poetry ; and as I walked about our lawn yesterday there came before me as freshly as ever his poem with the lines

> It cannot soothe me in my loneness ;
> It cannot mitigate my oneness.

Such a strange beauty belongs to the past that it seems to me as if half the value of the present is derived from the knowledge that it will one day be the past. It often happens that the moment a friend has left the room (especially at night when they separate till morning), he becomes invested with a new character ; and a softness falls on the image (that lately wore all the roughness of a jarring present) from the distant Shadowland. Of all the feelings of this sort, the strangest is that which comes to us from the recollection of our parents at an age when they were, as we then thought, getting oldish, but which, looking back on it, we see to have been Youth—the Youth we have ourselves lost in turn. To look on them thus with filial reverence, and yet with that *protective* sadness with which we regard the young and inexperienced, who are unconsciously losing what they must so often lament, is a mixture of feelings which admits of no name. It makes one realise the facts that even the parents of our parents, who seemed to us like patriarchs, had their brief day too, and were but poor gentle wrecks stranded in the sunshine when we knew them. The feeling thus inspired seems to me to help us to conceive that relenting tenderness with which the great Father must look on all His creatures, remembering that 'they are but clay,' and that with all their high hopes they have been so mysteriously 'made subject to vanity.' However, the next world is the world of realities; but here the shadows rehearse at least the great future drama. For almost all of us there must surely be some intermediate place where we are made capable of looking unblinded on the wonders of the future. To me there always seemed something so unphilosophical as to be almost incredible in the assumption that death (which is not even a sacrament) should so act as a charm or talisman, as at once to render the mass of even the good, who have hitherto been occupied mainly with the Shadowland, capable of sustaining the uncreated glories of the Beatific Vision.

Aubrey would wander through the Curragh park, his friends tell us, for hours together, never tired of its long familiar scenes. The joy and pain which nature aroused in him, with its suggestions of intense beauty in earthly things and of their brief duration, was to him an inexhaustible feeling. He returns to it again and again in his poems. We find in them the note struck by the French poet, ' O temps, suspends ton vol.' Again and again we find in different forms his favourite idea—the link which binds the first part of the letter cited above with its last paragraph—that the tantalising sense of the glory and the pathos, and yet the transitoriness, of the beauty of nature ; and of the depth and sacredness of human affections, roused by beings who pass away in a few years, can only be relieved by the belief that these things are shadows of something permanent and eternal. The flashes which come to us of a glory so much beyond the range and scale of every-day practical life remind us that the earth, with its wonderful suggestions of a 'beyond,' is indeed the 'portal' of heaven.

We can fancy that it was after drinking in the glories of a summer evening in the woods of Curragh, that he wrote the following 'evening melody :'—

> O that the pines which crown yon steep
> Their fires might ne'er surrender,
> O that yon fervid knoll might keep
> While lasts the world its splendour !
>
> Pale poplars on the breeze that lean
> And in the sunset shiver,
> O that your golden stems might screen
> For aye yon glassy river.
>
> That yon white bird on homeward wing
> Soft sliding without motion,
> And now in blue air vanishing
> Like snow-flake lost in ocean,
>
> Beyond our sight might never flee,
> Yet forward still be flying,
> And all the dying day might be
> Immortal in its dying.
>
> Pellucid thus in saintly trance,
> Thus mute in expectation,
> What waits the earth ? Deliverance ?
> Ah no ! Transfiguration.
>
> She dreams of that 'new Earth' divine
> Conceived of seed immortal,
> She sings 'not mine the holier shrine,
> Yet mine the steps and portal.'

We see Aubrey's constant delight in the beauties of his home, in such a letter as the following :—

How much I wish [he writes to Mrs. Villiers] that I could take a walk with you about these woods in this beautiful season—rather than not have your society I would even ride with you among their green alleys. What flowers can rival the beauty of woodland flowers? They are here in extraordinary abundance, because our woods are part of the immemorial forest of the country. It has often been cut down I dare say since the elk stalked under the oak branches ; but the ground has always been stoutly maintained by the ancient inhabitants (the trees) and neither crops nor cattle have ever had domination there. In every corner of the ivied rock recesses, lurk flowers whose names I do not know. The wood anemones gleam and tremble over acres together—the primroses make the banks look as if they shone by moon-light, in the forest night. In all the opens there are large spaces so covered with harebells that the ground is blue instead of green—far more blue than the blue Mediterranean which you used to look at from Nice. Then the grass walks abound in cowslips, and the rocks are minutely starred with strawberry blossoms. It is this extraordinary profusion of the spring flowers in the woods which I delight in so much.

There is an exultant joy, too, in such a stanza as this :—

O the flower of the tree is the flower for me,
That life out of life, high-hanging and free,
By the finger of God and the south wind's fan
Drawn from the broad bough, as Eve from man !
From the rank red earth it never up grew :
It was wooed from the bark in the glistening blue.

These keen joys belonging to Aubrey's poet's nature seem to have made his life ever full and rich. ' I have lived among poets a great deal,' wrote Sara Coleridge a few years earlier, ' and have known greater poets than he is ; but a more *entire* poet, one more a poet in his whole mind and temperament, I never knew or met with. He is most amiable, uniting a feminine gentleness and compassionateness with the most

perfect manliness, both negative and positive. He is all
simplicity, yet graceful, and so gracious ; sportive and jestful,
yet with a depth of seriousness in his nature ever present.
It is rather the habit of his mind to idealise *ad libitum*.
But this, if a defect, is the defect of a large and beautiful
intellect. His mind is like his face, which seems to be all
eyes and forehead ; not that it is disproportioned in size, but
that the eyes and forehead alone fix the attention and seem
to constitute the face.'

In this atmosphere, then, formed by his own temperament,
and by the home of his youth, he lived in peaceful seclusion,
and cherished and fostered the mediæval soul which lived
within him—in spite of an intellect modern, and in no way
obscurantist. He kept at a distance, not only the jarring sounds
of modern commercial life, the smoke and noise of the great
cities which represent so much of the genius of modern civilisation, but the ideals which they typify. He writes on this subject to his American friend Professor Norton, himself a student
of the Middle Ages (though not a Catholic), and in full
sympathy with Aubrey's feelings. And we see in his letter
how the Church was for him a great historical background
for his dreams, sanctioning his ideals of the past, protecting
unworldliness, reverence, obedience, in the present ; the bul-
wark against the tide of revolution which threatened in the
future, and of which Irish Fenianism cast a shadow not
without significance.

Tennyson had once proposed (Aubrey tells his friend) to
spend a winter ' alone with God,' on the rocky coast of Corn-
wall, beside the wintry sea. Something of this solitude, free
for the play of high thoughts, he invites Norton to find in the
unsophisticated retirement of the Irish country side :—

Your complaint about the mode in which the City, with
its hundred arms, keeps daily encroaching on your country
solitude, is one that would be echoed in most parts of England.

Here in this 'green' island the complaint would commonly be of the opposite character. It is one of the curious illustrations of the fact that strikes one so often, that these two islands, for some mysterious purpose linked so closely together politically, and placed so near each other geographically, are yet far more unlike each other than regions divided by oceans and continents. Whenever you cross the sea again, you must come and pay us a long visit over here. It would deeply interest you, for you are not one of those who judge by the outward senses alone, and you can see both beauty and greatness in the midst of scandals. As for the encroachments of town with its prosperous vulgarities upon the fields and ferns, this is unhappily but a type of a similar encroachment going on in our minds (by which I do not mean either *yours* or *mine*), to the great loss of the greener and lovelier precincts of them. 'The world is too much with us' even in that spiritual region; and I often think we shall have to form some religious communities of a new sort, including a 'third order,' to which any of the laity may belong. One of our rules should be that we should read the newspapers standing on our feet, by which the time commonly assigned to that opium-eating of the West would be much abridged : we should be also bound to believe exactly the opposite of whatever the 'Times' newspaper may assert on all spiritual, moral, and philosophical subjects : one half of our daily reading should consist of books written at least two centuries ago : no one should be bound to subscribe to hospitals unless he chose to do so ; but everyone should have to visit the sick poor occasionally, and even taste the cup of cold water before he gave it :—'public opinion' should be held, at least secretly, to be no Prophet, or at best not to rise beyond the dignity of a False Prophet inspired but by some deluding dream ; and virtue should have her new tripod of 'self-respect' pulled from under her, and be required to stand once more (unless she preferred to kneel) upon the ancient ways of 'our duty to God, and our duty to our neighbour.' Thus we should endeavour to live a saner life than people do at present, and to make death less like an impertinent interruption.

I am delighted to think that I shall soon see your papers

on the 'Vita Nuova.' A gust from that cold garden of seclusion, purity and peace must be very refreshing to our dusty air. The old Ghibelline with his Imperial sympathies would find himself a good deal puzzled if he had the trouble of living again, amid the contradictions of modern Italian politics. 'The Empire' was with him almost an article of faith. He thought, I believe, that God had appointed a centre of civil power as well as of spiritual jurisdiction. If he now lived, this theory would much inconvenience the sympathies which he would doubtless have also, as we all must, for Italian nationality. One thing I take to be certain, i.e. that he would rather have never drunk of the Arno again, than seen his Florence a provincial town under a semi-barbaric Piedmontese King. But what changes would he not have found ! Chivalry gone. Feudalism gone ;—the old Empire vanished in spite of

> That high Providence which did preserve
> Through Scipio the world's Empery for Rome,

but the Church still reigning among ruins—diffused through the worlds of which he had never dreamed, and amid the shocks of the old world, preserving a charmed life, and ever, like the Ark of old, lifted higher toward the summit of the mountains by the Deluge that submerges all beside. The *great* Deluge is not yet come. When it comes it will come from *below*, for the 'fountains of the great Deep' will be broken open. That day will be a bad one for Kings and States; and many an image will vanish out of the city to which public opinion now burns incense.

As time went on, it was gradually brought home to Aubrey de Vere that the wide fame to which every poet aspires was not to be his. If I read his letters aright, such disappointment as even so unselfish a nature experienced, helped to deepen his character, and to give his life consistency and strength. ' I wonder,' he once wrote to Henry Taylor, 'how people feel who write with hope. Of course one can dispense with it, if one writes in defence of what one knows or profoundly believes to be the true and the good; but I should like to know what the feeling is like.'

Again, he writes to Professor Norton :—

How pleasant must be those quiet and yet active evenings you pass in literary labours with your friends Mr. Lowell and Mr. Longfellow! I assure you your description of them made me wish very much indeed that I could form one of that circle. Literary labour, with the hope of a result, must be a very animating thing! For a great many years I have never written anything in prose or verse without the knowledge that, on account of jealousies and animosities, either political or polemical, what I wrote was in fact but a letter to some few friends, known and unknown, to be illustrated by a good deal of abuse, and recalled to my recollection by the printer's bill. I am of the unpopular side, you know, in England because I am a Catholic, and in Ireland because I am opposed to revolutionary schemes.

His devotion to the poet's craft became none the less. The appreciation of such critics as Walter Savage Landor[1] and Richard Holt Hutton, as well as of his intimates and relations, as Henry Taylor and Stephen Spring Rice, probably helped to prevent real loss of confidence as to the value of his work, and averted what J. S. Mill has called 'the disastrous feeling of "not worth while."' And failing to win the public ear, he was free from the temptation, which even a poet may undergo, to be a literary demagogue, and descend from his highest ideals in order to please the many. Penetrated with the feeling that the deepest interests of mankind lay in reviving the decaying sense of the value of Christianity —a feeling which was redoubled when he found in the

---

[1] Landor writes as follows after reading Aubrey de Vere's 'Search after Proserpine':—'Although it is almost morning, I am resolved to continue the Masque until I have read it through, for nothing (I am convinced) in the best of Greek dithyrambics was better than p. 15. It is the first time I have felt *hellenised* by a modern hand. Goethe's 'Iphigenia' is a frigid thing. There is the marble, but nowhere the Pygmaiion. Grecian daughters never complained of fathers neglecting to give them husbands. Shelley and Keats breathed the air of the Ægean—it is saturated with black frost when it blows over Germany. Had these two wonderful men lived, they would have done what it appears to me is reserved for you to do.'

Catholic Church a fixed object of loyalty—he applied himself largely to Christian themes. To Ireland also, conceived by him as essentially a nation with a spiritual mission, he devoted much of his attention. His actual poems of later life were all written in illustration of some high moral theme, or under the inspiration of Christian patriotism.

But his wider devotion to all true poetry also found an outlet in critical writings—in the 'Quarterly Review,' and elsewhere—which aimed, as did those of his friend Richard Holt Hutton, primarily at *interpreting* the special genius of the poets he selected for consideration.[1] What is often, owing to a prevalent vice, spoken of as the 'critical' faculty *par excellence*, may have been somewhat wanting in him—the faculty, I mean, of quickly detecting defects. But what Tennyson always spoke of as the highest gift of the critic, the keen eye for beauties, and for analysing and detecting aims wholly or partially achieved, which the poetic artist himself must perforce leave it to others to emphasise, he had in a very high degree. He regarded poetry as second only to religion in its function of ennobling human nature ; and he did not forget that many whom he could lead to a true appreciation of the great English bards might give no heed to his own pictures of the Catholic Church. Writing to Henry Taylor on the series of Essays he published on Spenser, Wordsworth and Shelley, he says :—

In proportion as I have failed to interest the public by my own poetry, which (besides its demerits) had, as I well knew when writing it, the disadvantage of unpopular themes

---

[1] 'I do not think' (Hutton writes to him) 'you ought to measure the chance of success of your essays by that of your poetry ; though you are a true poet, you are a poet of that quiet and refined kind that, especially writing as you do on religious subjects and in a Catholic sense, you can hardly expect a large public. Poetry to be really *popular* needs a very considerable volume of force. Yours is all qualitative. But the critical essays of a true poet on poets are always finer than any other critic can write. There is a touch and a feeling in them, which ordinary critics cannot emulate.'

S

(though themes well worthy of song, and too long neglected), I became the more desirous to benefit the cause of Poetry, if I could, by directing the attention of the young to some of the best poets we have had, and to indicate in what the higher qualities of poetry consist. An isolated essay is not sufficient to illustrate the principles I hold respecting poetry, which are very different from those now in fashion, to the serious stultification, as I conceive, of public taste, and the serious corruption, as well as enervation, of the country's moral mind.

The triple devotion to religion and to poetry, and to patriotism, was then the mainspring of his work during the remainder of his life. As he clearly recognised that popular success was denied him, the sympathy of his friends became more and more to him. The exchange of letters with his intimates was a feature in life which it is to very few in our own time. Writing once to Miss Fenwick of their common friend, Mrs. Cameron, Aubrey had thus expressed himself on this subject :—

Mrs. Cameron speaks of you with that enthusiastic and admiring love which belongs to her rich and abundant nature. With some few exceptions what starved and stunted plants affections and friendships are nowadays! The wallflower can suck a more generous nurture from the rocks of the ruin than the conventional flowers gather from the well-manured and well-protected soil of the conservatory.

Not only the close friends and connexions of his youth, but acquaintances with whom intellectual sympathy quickly formed a bond, became Aubrey's correspondents. He came in this way to be known in America, for Professor Eliot Norton and his sister were for thirty years among his most valued correspondents. They made his work known to their compatriots, and Professor Woodberry published for American readers a selection from his poems.

The friendship for Henry Taylor was, as I have already

said the deepest of his life. After their tour together in Italy in 1844, his wife wrote to Lady de Vere the following words, which speak for themselves :—

Aubrey de Vere went away with Henry, and will now return to Ireland. I wish I could give you any idea of all he has been to Henry. I could not myself have watched over him more anxiously and more tenderly, and I could not have done a quarter so much to save him from all trouble and care on our travels. Indeed Henry often and often told me that he was obliged to think as ill of his own health as he could, not to feel ashamed of seeing another devote himself so constantly to his service in little and in great things. As long as I live I shall be grateful to him.

These two men stand out before the reader of their correspondence as the very embodiment of devotion to their art—as men of letters of a type now rarely seen, combining a certain antique dignity with the simplicity of devotion to literature which often marks the gifted undergraduate or college tutor, to whom public opinion and fame are not immediately practical thoughts. Taylor had had, indeed, a considerable success in his drama 'Philip van Artevelde,' but none of his other works hit the popular taste. Tennyson had outstripped all competitors, and even Wordsworth was under eclipse before his death.[1]

Henry Taylor and Aubrey corresponded at great length, and every year the Irish poet spent some weeks with his friend. James Spedding was generally a third for part of the time. Spedding had refused an under-secretaryship, with 2,000*l.* a year, to devote himself to the study and vindication

---

[1] '*The Virgin Widow*,' writes Henry Taylor in 1850, 'has a very slow sale. . . . I imagine that Tennyson leaves little room at present in the poetical part of the public mind. Five thousand of the *In Memoriam* have been sold—of the *Prelude* less than 2,000. The *Prelude*, to be sure, is a very costly book,—but Moxon tells me that the sale of Wordsworth's other poems has fallen off. I suppose there is hardly ever more than one poet *flourishing* at a time, as there is only one Prima Donna.'

of Bacon. Taylor had also refused the Under-secretaryship for the Colonies. The trio were well matched in whole-hearted and unworldly devotion to the things of the mind. The stamp of reality, as well as of high critical acumen, was on their conversation. And one who remembers those visits notes, too, the self-respect and self-restraint which added weight and value to the views expressed by each. Not only worldliness, but even the great failing of the literary temperament, vanity, was utterly alien to Aubrey's nature. 'Nearly any man can be wounded through his vanity,' said his cousin, Lady Taylor, 'but Aubrey cannot.'

The letters exchanged between Taylor and de Vere are interesting exhibitions of the literary temperament, and some of them (which I shall cite later on) contain admirable critiques of some of our great men of letters. The mutual sympathy between the two men did for the poetry of each what the sympathy of Arthur Hallam, and of the group of his Cambridge intimates, did for Tennyson's early work, before he had won public applause—it kept alive the glow of enthusiasm which might have waned in its absence. A few specimens of the correspondence may be here given, belonging to the later fifties and the sixties :—

To Henry Taylor

April 25, 1855.

My dear Henry,—You say that my raptures and ardours partake more of intellectual and spiritual excitement than of poetic passion. Very likely they do, while they also proceed in a great measure from a peculiar state of temperament, compared with which, while they last, I should think opium-eating must be a dull thing. This, however, leaves the other question you ask unanswered ; for it is not in those higher moods that I am ever disposed to write, or even read, poetry, any more than when compassed, on the other hand, with the weariness, contradictions, and anxieties of life. The more soaring moods of the imagination are states of such pure poetry, that they seem actually to draw the mind away from any specific form of poetry, the limitations of which then become intolerable. Perhaps there may be some analogy in this respect between such *poetic* moods, and another class wholly different from them, well known in Theological science—viz. *Spiritual* Raptures (states also at once connected with, and wholly distinct from, temperament) in which all specific forms of prayer are wholly suspended in a wider sort of spiritual dilation. However this may be, it is certainly in one's middle moods, and neither in the higher nor the lower, that we are disposed toward the reading and the writing of poetry ; middle moods, I mean, without going beyond the moods poetical, which themselves, I suppose, occupy a middle position, and exercise an interpretative office, in the sphere of our total being.

When you ask what it is that my poetry *lacks*, and whether it be not *passion*, I doubt this being the true answer, though the true answer would, in that case, be probably a less flattering one. You give my poetry much more praise than I should have thought it deserved, and, on the other hand, I hardly see that this is its defect. This is no proof it may not be so, as the real fault of his verse would often be the last a poet would see. However, I will mention the reasons for answering your question in the negative.

The deficiency of passion was apparent enough to me in my first two volumes, at least when pointed out ; for in my early days of poetry I had got into an erroneous habit of looking on passion as a thing which poetry ought to be above, thus unduly putting poetry in the region, if not on the throne, of a higher power, which is really above *human* passion, though perpetually inculcating a love which is the Antitype of all human and of all natural affection. Poetry, however, is not Religion, though it has an important office relative to it, and also a double tendency—tending, as it does, at once to elevate the sensuous and to keep down the spiritual, and feed it on shadows. Poetry, then, I fully admit ought to be (inclusively) passionate. Again, I see clearly that this passion must not be a purely intellectual one, or ardour of the mind working as far as it may, apart from the rest of the being. Still less must it be a mere significance and vehemence of style, such as in Byron often passes for passion, though it is but energy—a very needful quality.

But, on the other hand, still less must poetic passion be *sensual* in its character, or sensuous, except so far as to allow to sense its proper place, as a transparent medium through which both the intellectual and the moral nature communicate with what lies behind sense. This distinction is necessary, and I fear is not sufficiently attended to. In Byron almost all the passion that is not a mere matter of *energy*, is *sensual*; and this, I think, is true in the case of many other poets who have written nothing against morals. In Thomson, for instance, the appetite for outward nature seems to me a sort of concupiscence, and reminds one of Rubens' landscapes, in which he presents you with the 'fat of the land,' mastered still by the same fallen Spirit of Art which makes his figures carnal mountains. Keats and Burns are truly impassioned poets; but I think they would not be less impassioned if divested of that material character which often, though not always, belongs to their passion. In short, poetic passion must not be confounded with anything that is predominantly material in character. This not only belongs to the dignity of poetry, but proceeds, I think, from its essence; for it is the essence of poetry that it embodies and represents the *whole* of our being, all the faculties working together under the sway of that one which pervades the rest, Imagination. What is exclusively either sensual or intellectual is so far not properly human; for in what is *properly* human the material and the spiritual are not merely united, like two metals fused together, but are blended like two elements that constitute a third. Milton's celebrated statement about poetry being 'simple, sensuous, and impassioned,' would, I think, be a very delusive one if the word 'sensuous' were not understood as meaning only *inclusively* sensuous; in which respect it stands in contrast to Science, the *aspiration* of which is *wholly* to escape sense by changing Matter into Law.

Poetry then, as belonging to the Humanities, not to Divinity, must be impassioned; but for the same reason it must be the embodiment of what is really *human* passion, and not either appetite under a veil, or intellect heating itself by exercise and conflict. Again, it must not only be *human* passion (so far as it includes passion) but human passion idealised at least to that extent to which poetry is itself an ideal art. As its delineation of nature and man is not mere copy, but imitation ; as its intellectual vision and statement are intuitive, and dispense with logical processes (except a logic of its own) ; as its poetic justice is something surer and higher than that which belongs visibly to the visible world, so its human passion must without rising above humanity, belong to our nobler humanity. It should often be such passion as might belong to unfallen humanity, and it should be always of a more elevated nature than belongs to actual life. It must not rise beyond the region of the sympathies, but it should remember that part of the office of poetry is to make peace between the sympathies and the aspirations, and prevent the gravitation of our being from remaining exclusively a downward gravitation.

To the Same

Albano, May 19, 1862.

My dear Henry,—Your new play [1] has been the greatest possible resource and interest to me during my recovery from another illness which came by way of variety, when my gastric fever had left me, viz. a very severe sore throat which my physician pronounced to be of the dyptheric genus, though not a dangerous specimen thereof. For three days your book, though it lay close by on my table, was only cheering, as indicating what lay before me, whenever I was fit to appreciate it. It has been with me a rule, ever since I was a boy, never to *read good* poetry except under the most favourable circumstances for its enjoyment. I never read it either in the midst of noise, or when liable to interruption, or when any circumstance prevents my faculties from being in as genial a condition of receptivity as belongs to them when at their best. If the poem is a reality, the poet must have had 'a vision of his own,' before he could get into the way of writing it ; and unless

[1] *St. Clement's Eve.*

the reader finds his way to the poet's point of view, and so is
able to share in his ' vision,' he can never understand the work.
And if he does not succeed in doing this at his first reading
of the poem (which of course requires docility and good will
no less than favourable outward circumstances), he generally
becomes the prey of false associations and crude theories,
and can hardly right himself afterwards. If this theory be
true, it is so much the worse for the interests of poetry; for as
the world gets busier and busier, fewer people can choose the
time, mood and circumstances under which their first reading of a new poem is to take place.

With his friend Coventry Patmore, Aubrey corresponded
in these years on their respective poetical labours ; and many
of Aubrey's letters are published in Patmore's Biography.
The following interesting letter explaining the principle on
which he had recently criticised the MS. of Patmore's
' Victories of Love,' has not hitherto seen the light :—

January 16, 1863.

. . . . A friend can advise best by simply stating what he
would do if the poem were his own, regarding his suggestions
not so much as advice, but rather as additional data laid
before the only person who is really competent to form an
authoritative judgment.

Years ago I was much struck by a sentence in one of
Leigh Hunt's prefaces—viz. that the *superfluous*, even where
all is beautiful, is yet the poet's *felo de se*. Tennyson, when
he showed me his ' In Memoriam ' in MS. used to mark with
his fingers some three or four stanzas apart from the rest, and
say, 'There! do you not see that the substance of the poem
is in these stanzas! The rest only dilute it and spoil *its
shape*.' Accordingly he would cancel them, although just as
beautiful as those he left. The fact is that it is only really
good poetry that can afford to be thus dealt with. I was
recommending Milnes once to publish a compact edition of
his best poems, when he replied that he would be too glad to
do so when possible ; but he feared that they were too nearly

on the same level to make such discrimination very practicable. As regards my own, I should be very glad if there seemed to me a much wider interval than, I can feel sure exists, in the different poems of the several vols. ;—as an indication that some of them, at least, possess more of genuine merit than I can confidently claim for them : yet as it is I have omitted one half of the only volume I have republished, and, as you know, should be glad to omit as much, or more, of the 'Search after Proserpine,' should I republish that volume. As for my poetry indeed, *it can never be forgotten* : but for a reason unflattering to a poet, viz. because nothing can be forgotten that was not once remembered, or at least known ; but if mine were to have any chance of interesting people, it would be when reduced to a condensed form.

It appears to me that single poems of length lose even more by the 'superfluous,' than volumes of short pieces by want of weeding. Wordsworth's works would, I think, gain much by the omission of at least as many small poems as would make a volume ; but far greater, as it strikes me, would be the gain to the 'Excursion' if most of the 'interstitial matter' were omitted. Indeed I believe it would be better still, if the exquisite 'Tales' and Philosophical Poems of which it chiefly consists were published in a form as separate as 'Michael' and 'Tintern Abbey.' Great and original poet as he is, even Wordsworth has much to fear from prolixity and repetition, as regards that idle prodigal Posterity, and he has already lost much. As for Coleridge, I used almost to quarrel with my dear friend Mrs. H. N. Coleridge, because she would not publish her father's volume of poems with the omission of the first hundred pages, the juvenile pieces. The statue is spoilt by the heap of rubbish at its base, and the building half hidden by the remains of what should have been regarded as mere scaffolding. Could Shelley's poems be reduced to half their collective bulk, their wonderfulness would be doubled. A Poet's less good things *betray him* : they show us how he worked. The Muse, if wise, no more admits us to her dressing-room than any other lady.

Two of the passages which I marked as better omitted

in your volume have, I think, great poetical merit, and philosophic interest, though I thought them hardly in place, and sure to be misconceived, and probably attacked : but, as for the great mass of my proposed omissions, I really believe the reason that to me so much gain would result from their omission is because I value so highly the remainder of the poems. The interval between Lady Clitheroe's letters and the higher parts of the poem seems to me great indeed : and such an interval is to me the most conclusive proof of the authentic merit of the poem in its nobler parts.

To Professor Norton Aubrey writes on his Dante studies on September 25, 1865. Norton had sent his friend two pictures of Dante, one in age, and one in youth, which he proposed to use in a work on the Mediæval Cathedrals. De Vere writes of them as follows :—

The character is *essentially* the same in the two sketches taken from the same point of view. The younger face I should have thought might have been a few years older than 20 (the age you suggest), but the older one, which is obviously a mask, not a portrait, is the same tree after it has been buffetted by the storms of life. But how deeply touching the contrast and how it recalls the Greek saying ' Whom the Gods love die young ' ! In the younger face the Soul seems to be looking out on Beatrice—or one might fancy that she had but just left him, and that he was looking along the way she had taken in her departure. The dewy morning mist that half enshrouds the 'Vita Nuova,' and half sparkles over it, rests on this face also. It is all susceptive and recipient, good influences coming to a spirit so candid and gracious, like the good Angels who came to the Patriarch when he sat at *the door* of his tent. The aged face is that of one whom the warring elements have made reserved and retired,—who has sat down ' down *in penetralibus* ' within the secret enclosure of a severe life,—a man of fixed conclusions, and who waits to the end, not without hope, but with a hope the blossoms of which have dropped from the bough, or have become petrifications. The mask corresponds well with Boccaccio's description, except that the eyes are small. But this they would have seemed in a mask taken after death, especially in old age. In old age the eyes generally sink back, as if they had seen too much that displeased them—or, as old Landor says,

> Eyes that have mirrored images too bright
> Let clouds o'ercast.

To Henry Taylor

Curragh Chase : October 30, 1868.

Your suggestions were very valuable, as they always prove. . . .

As for the rhymes, I have in half the cases you pointed out got rid of the imperfection. Where this can be done by industry, it certainly should be done. At the same time I would not insist on this perfection, because I admire the enriching effect produced by a frequent recurrence of rhyme (in the Sonnet it ought to recur *four* times) and if you insist on the rhyme being a perfect repetition of the sound, you must often either relinquish this frequency, or strain the meaning. Besides, is it certain that the necessity is not an imaginary one—a *maxim* rather than a *principle* ? When lines salute each other with that sort of 'kiss of peace' which we call rhyme, I suppose it must give them great pleasure, or they would not persevere under such difficulties ; but though the *reader* has much pleasure too in the rhyme, it seems to me that that pleasure results rather from the recurrence of a similar or very analogous sound, than of the *same* sound. What the rhyme does is to recall the *memory* of the line forgone, and thus link the different parts of a stanza into a whole. This is the reason that a rhyme ought to recur frequently, and that when, besides recurring only once, it is found only in two *consecutive* lines, the effect gives us the minimum of mental satisfaction while yet it challenges the ear in a very marked way, as in Pope's detonating 'heroic couplet,' where the lines rather exchange resonant slaps on each other's faces than any gentler form of salutation. If this theory be true, the satisfaction is more to the mind than to the ear, the musical cravings of which last are met far more by the rhythm than the rhyme. Now, the mind perfectly apprehends *analogous* sounds when not *very* like, and under their influence receives the line it is meant to remember.

Perhaps I may be only suiting my theory to my depraved practice; but I have several reasons for thinking this is not so :—1st, because identical syllables used in different senses (as 'light' and 'delight') are not rhymes, and nearly identical words, such as 'define' and 'refine' are bad rhymes; 2nd because, while I am very tolerant of imperfect rhymes when the *mind* perceives at once that the words are corresponding words, such as 'enter' and 'winter,' I rage with indignation where the words are such as 'dawn' and 'scorn,' where there is more resemblance to the ear than in the other case, but where the mind detects the resemblance to be fraudulent; 3rd, because many of our chief and so-called classical poets such as Dryden and Pope, have used these imperfect rhymes. very freely, though (unlike Wordsworth, who uses them also), they seldom made more than two lines rhyme together.

These are things in which we demand a good deal what we expect, and go a good deal by authority. I wish I could create out of nothing a strong authority on my side. I could utilise it much, by intimidating with it any 'public' that may by a smart modern miracle, become mine at a future time. Irish witnesses are said to be very strong-minded : and as we shall very soon have a 'Fair' at Stonehall (the ruined village nearest to this), I think I could easily get from ten to twenty of the stoutest pig-drivers at it to join in an affidavit that they never heard of any other theory of rhyming than the one I have now put forward; and the document, with their signatures, or their marks, might be introduced in the preface of my new volume, attested on oath. The oath would carry great weight; for everyone knows that in this land people are very scrupulous about oaths. Some time ago a thoroughly honest old woman came to Stephen as a magistrate to swear informations against another woman who had stolen her pail. In place of the usual *small* prayer-book which lay upon the table, there lay there on this occasion a large *quarto*. He pointed to it and told her to 'kiss the book'; to which she replied with indignation ' I never will swear upon that book,' and on his asking the reason of this resolution, she answered 'Because I never did ; and I never will. It is too *large* and too *dangerous*. . . . I'll leave her to God.' And so she lost her pail for ever in this world, but perhaps with hopes of finding it as big as a ship in the next, made of pure gold, and filled with the best tea.

The following letter, on the value and function of literary sympathy, was written to his cousin Charles Spring Rice, the brother of Stephen, for some years an official in the Foreign Office :—

> *To the Hon. Charles Spring Rice*
>
> November 24, 1865.

I do not think that we should differ much as regards the relation between 'Popular Sympathy' and high Art. I quite agree with you that the artist (and the poet no less) must speak what is in him in a spirit of entire independence, disdaining all the arts by which critics and public opinion are propitiated. But there is such a thing as finding what one does not seek. Painters in the old times, like the old minstrels, were unconsciously, as well as unintentionally, the interpreters of the popular sentiment ; when they spoke, the ' secrets of many hearts' were laid bare ; and the many found that the few had said for them what they wanted to have expressed. Now it is impossible, I think, but that such sympathy must have supported those to whom it was accorded. In the absence of it the artist might well have doubted his vocation. His own thoughts were, as it were, authenticated to him by the circumstance that in them others found the expression of their thoughts. The true artist is generally one who can be quiet, as well as active. The mere love of art will not always be an inducement sufficient to stimulate him. He does not know but that he may be but a dreamer ; and if so, he may enjoy his dream without taking the trouble of making more than the roughest sketch, nay, he may say, ' My eyes make pictures when they are shut' with Coleridge, and let his hand rest. It is the sympathy of others that makes him believe that his visions are those of the true seer, and that his dreams 'come from Love.' In this sense he needs not popularity in the common sense, vulgar applause or anything that pride or vanity craves, but 'Popular Sympathy.' He needs it because he is modest; if he were not, his confidence in himself would suffice for him. It is his heart that needs it. He has to address the hearts of others, and if there is no response, it is easy for him to be silent, and easy in proportion as he is without that uneasy vanity which can never be quiet. This was what I meant. The true artist is humble and has wide sympathies, therefore he needs sympathy and in this sense 'Fame is the Spur,' &c. He is also the interpreter of many hearts, therefore he needs sympathy.

To Henry Taylor

During the last ten days I have been far from well, and my Doctor, who has been with me nearly every day, has somewhat reduced me by leeches (to keep down some local inflammation) and also kept me lying down. During this inactive time I have been immensely interested with Southey's letters, given me by dear Miss Fenwick. They bring the writer so vividly before me, I can hardly think I did not know him. She used to say that one of the chief impressions his mind left on her was its swiftness. I have been much impressed by this also. How he can have learned all he knew by mere reading I cannot conceive. It puts me in mind of what Theologians called 'infused knowledge.' It is sad to me to think that he had nearly closed his career as a poet at forty-one, and that, for many years before, he had written little, till apparently a few words from Landor made him write 'Kehama' and 'Roderic.' He might have done wonders if he had carried out his plan for a series of mythological tales, and made poetry his principal object. It seems to me that what came against him chiefly as a poet was not the amount of drudgery he had to do, but rather the histories which he wrote with intense interest, and which must have drained away the Poetic Fire, and left his imagination somewhat chilled, just as his art was perfected. What a noble creature he was! I cannot tell you how sad it makes me to think of his favourite work, the 'History of Portugal,' being left unpublished. Why not get it published by subscription, if no publisher will take the risk? I would gladly subscribe 10*l.*

Opposite the couch on which I am lying in the window is the most bright-faced tree (a variegated sycamore) I have ever seen. For this characteristic I gave it, some twenty years ago, the name of ' Dofo.' Will you tell the other bearer of that name that if she leaves my two last love letters very much longer without a reply, I shall turn wholly to the tree (which with every motion of the wind seems to fling a half and half mixture of sunshine and moonshine into my face) and determine finally that ' vapid vegetable loves' are better than human friendships.

The work to which Aubrey de Vere had set himself in his writing was remarkably similar to that of the brilliant group of Frenchmen and women whose names are associated with the 'Correspondant.' Montalembert, Lacordaire, Madame Pauline Craven, and their friends were striving in France to bring home in a form persuasive to their generation the beauty of the Christianity with which the world appeared to be lightly parting. It is therefore not surprising that his perusal of Montalembert's great historical study on the ' Monks of the West' delighted him. Ireland and her early monasteries have their full share in this fascinating work, and de Vere felt that he was indeed reading the work of a fellow-labourer. Montalembert's reply to his letter of admiration reminded the Irish poet that he did not stand alone in the comparative absence of immediate popular sympathy in good work done for high ends :—

Your most kind and interesting letter of the 10th inst. [Montalembert wrote from Belgium on September 22] has afforded me the highest gratification. The book, which has absorbed all the labours of my life, ever since my public

career was prematurely closed, has met with so little acknow-
ledgment that the approbation of so competent a judge as
yourself is doubly valuable. I had hoped that the three last
volumes, being exclusively devoted to English history, would
have found more readers in England than in France. But
as yet you are the *first* and *only* person (with the exception
of our artistical friend Herbert) who seems to have taken the
trouble of reading me through, and you yourself are not an
Englishman, as you remind me in your luminous considerations on Ireland, the Celts and the Gaels.

Aubrey de Vere lived to see Montalembert's History obtain
a very wide circulation ; but such a letter, doubtless, renewed
his strong feeling as to the frequent blindness of the world to
the worth of great thoughts and of the ' things of the spirit '—to
its absorption in material interests, and in the affairs of the
hour ; to the possibilities of even absolute neglect for true and
good work, lasting long enough to damp a writer's ardour and
check his course, even if a truer estimate finally prevailed.
He has put this feeling into three stanzas :—

> Love laid down his golden head
> On his mother's knee ;
> The world runs round so fast, he said,
> None has time for me.

> Thought, a sage unhonoured, turned
> From the onrushing crew,
> Song her starry legend spurned,
> Art her glass down threw.

> Roll on, blind world, upon thy track
> Until thy wheels catch fire,
> For that is gone which comes not back
> To seller nor to buyer.

To Mrs. Craven Aubrey wrote after reading her fascinating
work, the ' Récit d'une Sœur,' in which he found all his own
feeling towards loved ones who are dead—the same habit of
living in the past and treasuring of each memory as something

sacred, the same deeply Christian view of life casting a halo round the tomb itself. Mrs. Craven thus replied to his letter :—

Paris : 73 Avenue Montaigne : March 11, 1868.

Dear Mr. de Vere,—Your letter gave me more than pleasure, it touched me deeply. Many friends, and many people whom I never knew before, have written to me about this book, but no one as you have done. Thanks also for the beautiful lines enclosed in your letter. They revived that feeling of gratitude which, in spite of all the grief I have known, ought, I know, to be uppermost in my heart and soul. You are right, indeed, to say that I am not the author of this book; that is why I can also talk simply about it, and tell you that I believe what you say about its being in one sense more useful than controversy, as it may help to show the Protestants, *without any dispute*, that they are wrong in the opinion they form of our religion, and of its action in daily life. I really think that Lord Russell mentioned it in his letter because (with that fairness of the English character which I so much love) he perceived by reading it that it was *not* true, as he had asserted, that 'Catholicism narrowed the intellect' and 'enslaved the soul.' I believe this impression has been produced on many Protestants, and I am most thankful for it. Have you seen a perfect translation which has just been published by Bentley? It was done by Miss Bowles, but under the direction of Lady Georgiana Fullerton, whose perfect knowledge of French has visibly assisted her in a marvellous way. I hope that it will now be read in England, by the many people who can't read French. I don't see that the book has lost anything in the translation. One thing, however, I regret, and I cannot understand why it was done; it is that, instead of inserting the short profession of faith (very beautifully worded, I think) which Alexandrine did read and sign (and which was also signed by the persons present at the time), Miss Bowles has inscribed the profession of faith of Pius IV. habitually read *now* by those who are received into the Church, and every point of which was of course implicitly contained in the other one, but still which

T

was *not* the document signed by them and given in the ' Récit.' In all other respects it is admirable. Now that we have a home in Paris, I hope to see you again both here and in England, where I have the greatest wish to go this year, and often again in the future, if it is the will of God. Mr. Craven unites with me in thanking you for your letter and the recollection of our ' meeting ' at Naples, which you so kindly mention. Our dear friend Montalembert is better, and hopes, as we do, that you will come over to see us here very soon, and very often.

In the meantime, dear Mr. Vere, believe me,

Ever most truly yours,

PAULINE CRAVEN.

A meeting with the author of the ' Récit d'une Sœur ' is referred to in the following letter written in the same year to his cousin Charles Spring Rice, from London, where Aubrey was enjoying one of his occasional periods of intercourse with his friends. The letter also contains very interesting references to John Henry Newman, and to Longfellow :—

July 11, 1868.

. . . . I should like much to write something serious of Newman, in the way you describe, if I could. In the meantime, I will send you a Sonnet on his most remarkable volume of poems, which I published in the ' Month,' when that volume appeared. He was pleased with the lines, and I saw that I had interpreted him aright, and as for the last line, it is expressed in such general terms, that it cannot be a stumbling block to anyone who, whether or not he sympathises with Newman's conclusions, believes that in leading forth his ' Pilgrimage Sublime ' into long forsaken worlds of Thought, that great man was destined to improve the religious condition of his country. The speciality of Newman is that, whereas men of letters are often timid men, like Erasmus, and men of speculation can generally find some superfine reason for not carrying out their principles to their natural conclusions, he has always united the heroic daring (the noble warlike element in Faith which makes it burn its ships when it has effected its landing) with the keenest intellect of the time, and, what is more extraordinary, with the most tender character and sensitive temperament.

As for his not writing as much as one could wish, I do not suppose that is connected with any suggestions from Authority. In those non-theological questions which lie on the borderland of theology, it is to be hoped that diversities of opinion will always exist, for they both witness to freedom of thought, in the genuine sphere of freedom, and also develop those faculties, and accumulate those stores through which, in the sphere of defined truth, the Church puts forth a greater and greater clearness as the ages roll by, as the world closes around her with its shadows. Between men like Newman and Manning there will always be differences as between Bossuet and Fénelon, and the curious thing is that on this occasion the Bossuet (I mean Newman) is often supposed to be the milder genius, and certainly leans least to the side of authority. But nothing that he could write would be received with other feelings than those of profound reverence —his recent letter to Dr. Pusey is the best thing that has appeared in English on the subject of the Blessed Virgin, and I do believe that his not writing more proceeds chiefly from his deep spirit of self-sacrifice, and a belief that in hearing the confessions of poor factory girls at Birmingham for hours in the day, he is making a better oblation to God than he could make by writing more. . . .

I have been seeing a great deal of Longfellow, almost always between twelve and one at night, after his return from his parties, and while he was smoking his pipe before going to bed. He is a very fine-looking man, a little like H. Taylor in face, though with not as much either of beauty or of dignity. I have taken a great liking for him. It is not saying much for him to say that he has remained wholly unaffected by the great stir which people have made about him ; but he is plainly a solidly good, upright, deep-hearted man, with a calm grave conscientious way of thinking on all subjects, and I think wide sympathies. Since the sudden and calamitous death of his wife (the Mary

Ashburton of ' Hyperion ') his hair has been grey, but his ways and bearing, though serious as well as gentle, are not depressed.   He is entirely modest, and as simple as Wordsworth himself, of whom he speaks in very becoming terms of reverence and gratitude.   I do wish I could have made him known to you and Bessie,[1] as I did to Mary, but still more that I could have made you know Mrs. Craven, as I certainly should had she but arrived a little earlier.   She is staying at Holland House, with Lady Holland, and it is certainly curious to see her among all those glittering crowds that trail their silks and satins like rainbows over the velvet gardens, on the weekly reception days.   She looks so thoughtful among the giddy, and so saintly among the worldly, while at the same time she has a native grace and dignity of manner as well as a lofty unconscious benignity that make her move like a queen among them.   I have had five or six long and interesting conversations with her.   The difficulty she tells me in preparing the ' Récit' was that of omission, for the materials were enough to make a book twice as long.   Montalembert thought it impossible the public could take an interest in anything so pure and high ; but it has already gone through seventeen editions, and the good it has done must be immense.   Even the readers of the book, she assures me, can hardly form an idea of Alexandrine, such *greatness* came to her, after her afflictions had perfected their work.   But as a sort of pellucid innocence and quiet habitual spirituality, she says that her own mother, after the many years of her life, was, if possible, even more remarkable than the young ones —a possibility which suggested itself to me more than once as I read about her.   I gave Mrs. Craven the three sonnets her book had occasioned my writing. . . . I do not think I kept a promise I made Bessie, that I would send her the two latest of those Sonnets ; I enclose them accordingly.   She must let me have them again, but is quite free to keep a copy of them if she likes to do so.

I have been going about in Society a good deal—a great contrast to my long solitude at Curragh.   At Dorchester House the other night I had a long talk with the Comte de

[1] Mrs. Charles Spring Rice.

Paris, about the Irish Church Question, on which he has written; I thought that he looked on it with a more elevated spirit, and a better discrimination between the accidents and the essence of the matter, than most of our English statesmen have done. Remoteness gives the foreigner something of the advantage that posterity will have regarding this question. He is not troubled by the petty details of the subject, whereas we too often ' cannot see the wood for the trees.'

Two other letters to the same correspondent may here be given, both belonging to the year 1868. Charles Spring Rice was suffering from a mortal illness, borne with heroic fortitude. The mysteries of life and death, ever present to his cousin, were brought before him with new vividness in their correspondence :—

Curragh Chase, Adare: April 30, 1868.

There seems to me something wonderful and mysterious in the condition of one who has been thus long lying, as you have been, at the very gates of another world. The presence of God must not only be felt in a different way, but it must exist in a different way, for one thus wrapped in a luminous cloud, and separated from all the interests of this lower material world, except only so far as those interests are rehearsals of heavenly things, and include an element of the Infinite. I always feel disposed to look with a reverence that partakes of awe upon those with whom God is thus mysteriously dealing. They seem to have advanced to some higher platform upon that mountain which human life is always ascending, if it be fulfilling its purpose —one thinks that they must hear the whispers and breathe the odours of some diviner clime ; and one fancies that even deeper down than the regions of consciousness, some celestial influence must reach them (as the souls of infants are reached by Baptismal Grace) freshening unexplored regions of their being, and preparing them for future growth. It is certain that we live at the same time in two Worlds, one Natural and one Supernatural, intermingled and yet as distinct from each other as the two spheres of Light and Sound. Of these two, most men in the strength of sensuous life realise the Natural, while they only admit the Supernatural. Exactly the converse condition must be produced when the senses meet the confutation of what seems impending dissolution, if only we can exercise at the same time, that Faith which lifts the lid of the spiritual eye.

The next letter is written from Bournemouth, at the time the residence of the Taylors:—

Belle Vue Hotel, Bournemouth : August 13, 1868.

My dear Charles,—I have been waiting to write to you until I could write to you from this place, and tell you something of those who are so dear to you. I am not an inmate of 'The Roost'[1] for various reasons (among others because, belonging to the Race Barbaric, civilisation does not suit me for more than half a day at a time), but I am with them from the middle of the day, and all the evening. I arrived the day before yesterday; the house never made a brighter or happier home than it does now.

I suppose, however perfect the individual note may be, it takes a family to sound the complete chords, a doctrine doubtless that sounds very orthodox to married ears ever listening to the harmony of diversities, and enjoying the separate contributions to such harmony from the little Cecils, little Agneses, and all the rest! It is a pity that Longfellow did not see this household. Mary invited him, as you suggested. It would have been a good specimen of England's domestic life for him to contemplate. I think England has preserved more of nobleness in her domestic life than anywhere else. It is with her as it was with the children of Israel, when the Ark of God rested under a domestic roof, and had not yet found a place in the Temple.

As for our Public Life, I must agree with you, I fear, that in it there is more of weakness and meanness than a nation can well afford in our days. At the same time, there is probably less than there was at many earlier periods.[2]

[1] The Taylors' house at Bournemouth.

[2] 'A. B. has just been taken into the Cabinet' (he writes to Professor Norton ten years earlier). 'He is the greatest scamp, as Lord Shaftesbury is the greatest

Walpole said that in his day 'every man had his price,' and thought the Highlands of Scotland had many a 'pretty gentleman,' a good proportion of whom ended their lives very honourably and religiously, in the old Irish fashion, viz. by being hanged. I suppose that in the Southern part of the Islands it was thought enough to be 'gentleman-like,' which means so 'like' that the many do not see the difference. Then as for the time of the 'Revolution,' Macaulay wrote his great Historical Novel by way of immortalising it; but even if he had succeeded in making a hero of the Dutchman who wished to die in his country's last ditch (alas that adverse Fortune should have frustrated so pious a wish), he certainly succeeded also in proving that nearly every other person concerned in that event was a traitor, not guilty of simple, but of compound perfidy, and was alternately in alliance with both parties, and betrayed both.

The statesmen of the sixteenth century were worse; and the documents brought to light by Froude and others prove in their own handwriting that Cecil, Sussex, and Queen Elizabeth herself, besides every imaginable form of perfidy, repeatedly employed assassins, at least in Ireland, to murder the chiefs they could not conquer. Probably political morality was as low in other countries. The heroic and chivalrous spirit of the Middle Ages (and even then there were hideous crimes, though probably of a more exceptional sort) was dead, and the 'Public Opinion' of modern times had not yet begun to form itself. In our day neither political vice nor political virtue attains the scale heroic. And so with Palmerston. I think you are right in saying that it is chiefly the Radicals who are indebted to him. Men who have dexterity enough to rule without principles always leave a stormy inheritance to those who succeed them. . . . I do not admire our present statesmen as much as they admire themselves. They have produced the chief dangers

---

saint, connected with the Government. Lord Palmerston till now occupied this scamp extreme himself: but now, standing between the other two, he has become the "middle-point" of comparative respectability and prudence; and I am already beginning to revere him as if he were a compound of King George the Third and Sir Robert Peel.'

of the time by not dealing righteously with Ireland, which
but a few years ago might have been easily contented, and
separated for ever from the Revolutionary side. It might
have been made the 'La Vendée' of the Empire. Now they
are divided into two classes, that of Reformers, who would
destroy the ancient Constitution they should reform and
restore, and Conservatives, who would conserve the disease
which has been eating up the country for three centuries. . . .
Good-bye, and God bless you. I need not say how delighted
I was to hear the improved account of yourself you sent
to Dofo, and that you had gone up most of the ascent of
Helvellyn. Affectionately yours,

AUBREY DE VERE.

Among the public events of the sixties, two very deeply
affected Aubrey de Vere, namely the American war, and the
Fenian movement in Ireland, which followed soon after the
termination of the war. On the former question his strong
feeling is displayed in his letters to Mr. Norton in 1863-4.
From the first he regarded the war as essentially a battle
undertaken by the North for freedom. He saw from the
first that, in Mr. John Morley's words, 'those who fought
against secession fought against slavery, and all that was
involved in that dark burden,' and he severely criticised the
aberrations of English public opinion on the subject.[1]

I subjoin a few sentences from some of the letters,
indicative of his sentiments at the time :—

October 9, 1863.

Physiologists tell us that on the retina of the eye every
object is represented upside down, but that we have grown so
'smart' by experience that we make due allowance, and
mentally set them on their legs again. I have long been
convinced that in moral, political, and theological matters our
[English] intellectual optic nerve is often subject to the same
anomaly, and that we are by no means so quick in correcting it. . . . As for English opinion on the war, Carlyle's
flippant piece of criticism is one of the saddest specimens.

[1] 'Of this immense conflict,' writes Mr. Morley, 'Mr. Gladstone, like most of
his countrymen, quite failed to take the true measure.'—*Life of Gladstone,* ii. 70.

However, the counter passage by F. D. Maurice is some compensation. Few persons rank higher in England as a philosophic writer; and his influence in the 'religious world' (as it is called) is very great. I did not know which side he took, and am glad to find he is Northern. The family of the late Dr. Arnold is strongly on the right side also, but we are sadly in a minority. Carlyle, at least, confesses that the question of slavery is the main question at issue. . . .

November 6, 1864.

On your success depends the whole hopes of a vast Continent. No matter what trials you may have to go through, at least a basis will be laid for a Christian Civilisation if, when the war is over, slavery is over too. . . . It was not to be expected by wise men that so portentous an evil could ever be got over without this tremendous expiatory struggle. I watch the events of the war from day to day with an anxiety that cannot be exceeded by that which any of you feel. . . .

February 22, 1865.

The principle of freedom has worked itself out as the true question at issue. . . . What a thing a principle is amid the confusions of men and nations! It is not so much an instrument by which men exercise power, as it is itself a power, rushing on like a storm, dragging men after it in its wake, and moulding them to its will. An Angel of Mercy, or an Angel of Wrath as the case may be; but in any case a something that can sleep long, but is very formidable when some one has wakened it. . .

On April 28, 1865, when the news of the defeat of General Lee reached him, he writes thus from Alexandria :—

I cannot help sending you just a line (by way of supplement to my long letter from Spezia) to offer you my warmest congratulations on the glorious news which has just reached us. The utter and complete defeat of General Lee—his unconditional surrender, of which a telegram this moment arrived assures us—and the capture of the rebel capital. It is indeed a magnificent termination to a war sustained with heroic constancy, and against difficulties which your enemies a thousand times over asserted to be absolutely insuperable. They would not or could not perceive that there was a great principle at your side fighting for you, and adding its strength to yours. They did not know that ' the Stars in their courses,' the whole moral order of the universe, fought against those whose triumph would have been a triumph over the glory of God and the hopes of humanity. Now then you have got a solid basis for a true Christian Civilisation, and the serpents that watched beside the cradle of a new heroic Power are strangled. A whole Continent will have expelled the poison of Paganism (for such I consider Slavery to be) from its veins and so long as that poison remained, it would have tracked all the veins of your growing greatness, and made it a curse, not a blessing to the world.

The troubles in Ireland in 1866 recalled Aubrey de Vere's attention to the subject which had absorbed him in 1848. The Fenian movement was, as Mr. McCarthy has pointed out, essentially popular. Such men as Wolfe Tone, and Lord Edward FitzGerald in 1798, or Smith O'Brien in 1848, had been leaders, with a traditional or natural ascendency. But Fenianism was entirely popular. And Jacobinism, Aubrey de Vere's *bête noire*, seemed destined to gain a formidable footing on Irish soil. Again, the American war called into existence the Irish-American soldier, and Fenian leaders in America proved henceforth an important factor in Irish disaffection.

I should like you to tell me [he writes in January 1866 to Professor Norton] what is thought in America of ' Fenianism.' Is it a mere Bubble and commercial speculation, as we often hear? Or is it a Reality? In Ireland its character is wholly *Jacobinical*. It wholly repudiates those sentiments of devotion and loyalty that characterised the great historical struggles of Ireland, previous to the eighteenth century, and, in a large measure, the struggle for Catholic Emancipation. It has as much of Communism as of irreligion about it; it is as strongly disliked by the farming class, as it is denounced by the Catholic Clergy. It gains a great many recruits, I hear, among the poorer class, and among the loose young men in the towns, and I fear will do much harm if it lasts, being equally out of sympathy with the old Catholic instincts of Gaelic Ireland, and with those purely *Constitutional* exertions by which alone Ireland can get what is still lacking to her.

The first declaration of hostilities came in 1865, when the Fenian leaders in America openly announced their intention of raising an army in Ireland to fight for Irish independence. More than a year of agitation followed, and in March 1867 a very futile attempt at an insurrection was made. In the same year came the endeavour to blow up the Clerkenwell prison, in order to rescue the Fenian prisoners therein detained. Both enterprises were ludicrously unskilful in their execution. The insurrection was fully known to the Government beforehand. The explosion might easily have killed the Fenian prisoners, and could not have liberated them, and as it turned out, did kill a few innocent bystanders. But the whole episode drew serious and general attention once more to Irish grievances and disaffection.

Aubrey de Vere looked on with that keen sympathy for Irish wrongs which he had shown in 1848. But now, more than ever, his ideal of Catholic Ireland was utterly inconsistent with sympathy for any revolutionary movement. He desired a loyal Catholic priesthood, and a Government which should attach the people to itself by fair treatment. The symptoms of Fenian sympathy among the priests jarred with this cherished ideal, and he wrote his grateful thanks to Bishop Moriarty of Kerry, who early in 1866 spoke out strongly to his clergy on the subject.[1]

[1] The text of the letter is as follows :—

February 12, 1866.

My dear Lord,—I cannot thank you sufficiently for sending me your Pastoral. It speaks out loudly and plainly the great truth so needed in our land, that Loyalty is an imperative *Christian* duty. What I value in it especially is that it does not base this duty on the good of Society but on the Christian Law. It is only when thus brought home to the conscience by the power of Religion that

But, while deprecating disloyalty, de Vere did feel strongly the wrongs of his Catholic countrymen. He wrote urging Gladstone to take the opportunity of the newly born realisation on the part of England of the national sense of wrong in Ireland, by remedying one crying grievance—the establishment of the Irish Protestant Church. De Vere urged that its funds should be redistributed for religious purposes, but with regard for the principle of equality, and endowing the Catholic, equally with the Protestant Church. He received from Gladstone a general assurance of agreement with his views; [1] but for the moment he was very uncertain as to the course which the Prime Minister would take. He had already noted the uncertainty of Gladstone's movements, and in the course of his correspondence on the subject, we find a very able psychological study of that statesman's mind. He writes as follows to Charles Spring Rice in the first stage of the Fenian agitation :—

Ireland, Old Church : October 27, 1865.

I suppose that we shall have some furious political storms soon, after such a long period of artificial peace. First will

admonitions to the discharge of the duties that belong to subjects have a chance of affecting the minds of men whose passions urge them in an opposite direction. Protestantism was at the first a religious Revolt, and however propped up by prescription, must ever remain but a chronic Anarchy—but Catholicism is so essentially founded on Faith, and therefore on obedience, that I have never been able to understand how anyone can be a real Catholic, understanding and loving his religion, who is not a thorough Loyalist, both as regards his Church and the State.

I hope also that those of our own Clergy who have allowed themselves to omit the inculcation of loyalty (as needful a thing as the other Virtues) as part of a Christian's duty, will learn how unambiguous is the law of the Church on this great matter.

I earnestly hope you will publish your Pastoral at once, as a Pamphlet, and send it to our more eminent public men. They should see that one who so emphatically declares the duty of Loyalty sees also how profoundly the present religious inequality that prevails in Ireland must be felt by the most loyal as a wrong. Ever most faithfully yours,   (Signed) AUBREY DE VERE.

[1] 'My views of the Irish Church as an Establishment,' Gladstone wrote, 'are probably not far from yours, and I hear with satisfaction of your labours, and of anything that may tend to an adequate preparation of the public mind for the future.'

come Lord Russell's attempt, and after its failure, Gladstone's. What he will do who can say ? . . . [His is] a nature as erratic as disinterested—he has only to rub his eyes and see what he pleases.

The opposite faculty, which sees not what is plain, is at least as dangerous. It is enjoyed by those who, because a few hundred crazy Fenians are not formidable, see nothing formidable in the circumstance that the great bulk of the Irish people (utterly averse as they are to Jacobin Principles) continue notwithstanding, century after century, disaffected, and who see no connection between winning their affections and putting an end to disaffection. As for me, hating revolution and democracy as I do, there is much that I see ' looming in the distance ' which makes me wish that some statesman would arise who could take advantage of the only part of the Empire that retains loyal instincts, and put an end to that which separates them from loyal objects ; but bad workmen always complain of their tools, and empirical statesmen will not see that while the present unequal Ecclesiastical Settlement is maintained, the black banner of the Tudors still floats over Ireland ; and that the very loyal instincts thus insulted are the hidden root of what is called disloyalty. . . . The principle of equality might still be established without destroying what exists—by levelling up, not levelling down—but in a few years more the opportunity will be lost. . . .

Lord Grey did prepare, in 1866, a scheme of concurrent endowment, practically on the lines suggested by Aubrey de Vere, with whom he corresponded on the subject at some length. But Lord Russell declined to accept it. Moreover the Irish Hierarchy were not favourable to it.

In the event, Gladstone made up his mind that only by joining hands with the Radicals who were in favour of the secularisation of Church property could his scheme of disestablishment be carried. To Aubrey de Vere's great regret, a step was taken in the direction of alienation of Church property from religious purposes. In his opinion, Lord Grey's scheme might have been accepted by the Catholic Clergy at the outset, but its chilly reception in many quarters, convinced them that it was only from the advocates of secularisation that they had anything substantial to hope. De Vere's letters on the subject (addressed to his cousin Charles Spring Rice), though expressing his strong regret, are also remarkable for the sympathetic analysis of the movement of Gladstone's mind towards a conclusion which was so unwelcome to him.

I do not doubt Gladstone's conscientiousness [he writes on April 13, 1868]; but I regard him as in great error. But he has had great temptation. A statesman wishes not only that Right should be done, but that his party should have the honour of doing it ; and Gladstone finds his party reduced to nothingness without the aid of the 'advanced Liberals.' I suspect also that as an English High Churchman he thinks State-Control so fatal to Religion, that if Liberty were won by the loss of all Endowments, he would think the Church a gainer.

A month later he deals with the subject at some length :—

Curragh Chase : May 18, 1868.

I would have answered your letter by return of post had it been less interesting. I have expected every day to have time to do so, *at length*; but, at all events, I must not put off telling you how much pleased I was at getting your most friendly and affectionate invitation. It is, however, only in the Spirit, not the letter, that I can profit by it. I am not generally staying long in London, and when I am there I have to be in and out at such unseasonable hours, and in short to live such a vagabond life, that it does not do for me to be in a respectable house ! I wish I could manage it, and that all the more because it would be like those dear old times in Brook Street, and those fair days earlier still in Blandford Square, when we were under one roof in London, and when even at that grumpy time of the day—breakfast (the wrong of having to get up still rankling in the mind, and all the impending trouble of the day winking at one maliciously), still we never quarrelled. But I hope to be in London in about a fortnight, and though I must get into my old lodging, which is conveniently near my Pagan Club and Popish Chapel, and where one may live a lawless life without remorse, I am sure we shall see a great deal of each other. The world goes rushing on at such a rate that I suppose its wheels must soon catch fire—which doubtless makes the generation of the 'not fast' cling all the more to old friends and old times.

I have no doubt that we agree in principle respecting this great question, which has at last turned up for settlement, much more than we can differ as to points of detail. The line that Gladstone has taken is very unlike that one which I urged on him last year, and which I have done what I could to recommend, not only as a non-revolutionary plan, but as the only plan that can long maintain the principle of Religious Endowments, and a National Confession of Christianity, either in Ireland or England; but still, I do not think that the change of opinion he has undergone is any index of want of sincerity. The clue to Gladstone's career is the very peculiar character of his mind. It approaches to genius more than any other mind that moves in the political sphere, but it has to work in a region in which genius is subject to all the aberrations of genius, and can but occasionally enjoy its inspirations. It is not a political mind, it is a scholastic mind; and had he had the luck to live in the thirteenth century, he would have ruled some fair province of Theology, with some logical Sceptre of Iron encrusted with gems. Living in the nineteenth century, he has to be a politician, and he has not either the shrewd knowledge of men or the 'practical judgment' respecting things (a faculty seldom associated with the logical, except in men of first-rate genius) which are all in all in politics. Clarendon said of old that of all educated men, the Clergy made the worst politicians. . . . They know more of politics than statesmen often know of Theology, and have often a keen appreciation of its fundamental principles; but principles are one thing and the application of them

quite another. Delicate distinctions which in Theology are
all-important become in politics sometimes what is called
'visionary,' and sometimes what looks 'disingenuous.' Gladstone shares with Theologians not only this too great subtlety
of intelligence, but also the impassioned ardour that often
goes along with it. If he shows ardour to a degree that
mocks at danger, now that he finds himself at the popular
side, remember that he showed just as much in his vain
endeavour to protect Christian marriage from the Divorce
Law, and also in denouncing the 'Ecclesiastical Titles Act,'
when it pleased a great nation to go mad for a season, and
when even cool heads thought that those who opposed its madness would never get returned to Parliament again ! Gladstone
said to me once, that he would die happy if he had done his
country the immense service of settling this greatest of all
questions that remain to be settled.

I have no doubt, then, that his aims on the subject have
been from the first conscientious, and that to them he feels a
sort of devotion which would shrink from no sacrifice. But
the Purity that one finds in the Life Political is the Working
Purity, not the Vestal Purity. It has to work with others,
and pray to be forgiven not only 'in this one thing' but in a
good many. Gladstone knows that, now that the great
political Rope-dancer is gone, the reign of 'address' and
'banter' is over, and that parties have to form themselves
anew, and that on principles—the principles that divided
them in old time being worked out. Statesmen wish not
only that great things should be done for their country, but
should be done by their party. Now, without Mr. Bright and
his allies, the Liberal Party, if it could exist, could carry
no great measure. Even Bright himself, I fancy, finds the
same 'pressure from without' brought to bear on him. You
will remember that the other night those Scotch Voluntaries
(the Sons of John Knox and the East Wind) were very near
upsetting their coach by declaring that not a penny of
Ireland's Church Property should go to the Catholic Religion
or to Catholic Education, or even to the support of Maynooth,
and that not only Gladstone, but even Bright had to give
battle to their allies.

That Gladstone preferred the solution of concurrent endowment he expressly told de Vere. But theological animosities proved too strong and too universal—coming, de Vere notes, even from the Broad Church Protestants, who, as being 'innocent of all Theology,' might be expected to be as 'free from Theological animosities as an oyster is secure from gout in his toes.' Thus the choice really lay 'between Protestant ascendency in Ireland, and Secularisation.

Gladstone [Aubrey continues] prefers the latter—and why should one doubt his probity in this? I do not think it suggests any serious doubts, either as to his political or religious sincerity. In politics he has a passionate hatred of all that seems to him injustice—witness his fierce invectives against the old Government of Naples, and the temporal dominion of the Pope as he understood it. Now, he knows that twenty years ago all the Liberals in England maintained with Macaulay and Arnold that all the civilised world could show nothing more absurdly unjust, and nothing more unwise and unchristian, than the religious supremacy of a small and modern minority, in the midst of an ancient Catholic nation like Ireland. He knows that since then England has gone all lengths with the 'Liberal' and even 'Revolutionary' side in every country except Ireland and Poland. He knows that Ireland has become educated, and must become rich, and that a second Ireland has been created in America, and will be created in Australia, both of which will always share the discontents of the old Ireland. . . . He knows that the whole European Order is breaking up; that England must have serious storms before her, that there is no security either for her maritime or her commercial superiority over other nations, and that yet she has to defend against them 'an Empire on which the sun never sets.' Is it wonderful that under these circumstances he should care more for getting rid of a huge flaw that gapes at the very centre of that Empire, and that, in case of foreign war, would make Ireland the chief difficulty of England—than for maintaining that paradox and anachronism which Elizabeth never would have created

U

in Ireland had she not fancied that Ireland, like England would allow her to 'tune all its pulpits,' and would adopt her Faith?

As to his religious sincerity there is surely no reason for doubt. He cannot but say as a High Churchman (and not a Bishop) ' I cannot sympathise with the degradation of an ancient Church in Ireland, and the religious ascendency of 700,000 Protestants, not a hundred of whom believe in what we Anglicans call the ' Visible Church.' . . . Doubtless he thinks that, as an Establishment, the Church of England is enormously endangered and discredited by being bound up with another Establishment, existing under opposite circumstances, and the very *reductio ad absurdum* of the Establishment principle. But doubtless also what he would say is ' The Church of England must be free.' . . . I think he would say that if the English Establishment can be preserved consistently with the freedom of the Church of England this should be done, and can only be done by removing the Irish incubus—but that in both countries the chief thing to look to is the freedom of Religion, on which depends sincerity of conviction and vitality of Faith

Aubrey de Vere visited Rome in 1870 while the Vatican Council was sitting. The occasion was calculated to stir his deepest feelings. Rome had long been to him the key to a true philosophy of the history of Christendom, the normal centre of the principle of authority and order in social life. As early as 1840 he had written a poem on St. Peter's Chair at Rome, in which, though he had not yet joined the Catholic Church, the ideal philosophy of society inspired by mediæval Christendom—an organic spiritual polity, with Rome as its centre—had been suggested.

In more recent years he had been watching with painful interest the gradual destruction of the Papal kingdom, which he valued, not for itself, but as indispensable in this imperfect material world for the independence and freedom of the spiritual power of the Papacy. Year by year he marked its stages by sonnets, collected later on under the title of 'St. Peter's Chains.'

He had written as follows to a friend in the earlier days of the Sardinian attack in 1862—and the letter is still instructive reading, although its forecast shows his never-failing sanguineness, which could not but encounter disappointments :—

The Sardinian King . . . . is an usurper of many kingdoms ; but the usurpation which I can least forgive him is that of the name *Honest man*—king. Neither he nor Napoleon are gentlemen, and therefore they cannot act like such.

'So then,' you will say, 'you are for returning to Despotism in Italy?' Not at all. I am earnestly for a free Italy. If Austria can be *honestly* induced to give up Venetia I shall be delighted, and I shall hope to see *all foreign* influence excluded from Italian affairs. I also earnestly wish to see the component parts of Italy internally free and progressive. This, however, can only be realised in the form of an Italian Confederation, in which the various States shall retain their ancient distinctness, and each shall have the form of government which suits best the character of its race, and its progress in civilisation. To this better state the present may be a stepping-stone, and when Victor Emmanuel is cast aside as a broken instrument, it may turn out that Providence has used his ambition as an instrument of good. He and Cavour I regard as traitors to the cause of Liberty, because they have separated that cause from the kindred cause of Religion by their attacks on the Church, and from that of good morals by their recent violations of the Laws of Nations. If right may not be violated for the interests of Religion (as of course it may not) neither may it be violated in the name of Liberty, without a double treason.

And now for the Pope. . . . Without any fault on the part of the Popes, the Congress of Vienna, in 1815, damaged the moral position of the Holy See in Italy, by establishing Austrian influence all over Italy, and thereby establishing

despotism.   The Popes, as heads of the Guelphic Party,
have always represented both popular institutions in Italy,
and independence of the foreigner.   From 1815 to the accession of Pius IX. the opposite course was forced upon them.
The result was that religion was left chiefly to the grey-
heads, while genius and hope, the young and the aspiring,
gravitated to the side of irreligion, which for the moment
seemed that of freedom.   The present break-up will restore
the balance ; and religion will resume her natural place, just
while an upstart Government loses its borrowed plumes.   If
an Austrian intervention had restored the Pope, his moral
prestige would not have returned.   The wheel must be
allowed to go round all the way, and the heart of Italy will
come back with a remorseful love to the first asserter of
Italian Freedom.   There is cause for much indignation, but
for no alarm, at all that is going on in the Papal States.
Popes have been again and again turned out and have always
come back.   The *temporal* authority of the Pope has no
Divine Promise, yet even *it* is the most long lived of political
authorities.   Like the spiritual power, it is the Burning Bush,
ever in conflagration, yet never consumed.   It is not fixed,
like the Apostolic Supremacy of St. Peter's See ; but it seems
to be the *shadow* of that immovable substance, cast upon the
revolving sphere of transient and temporal things, there
abiding, but abiding ever in unrest, ever trembling and never
passing away.   The temporal authority of the Popes is the
most insecure of temporal dominions, relatively to any short
period, and the most secure relatively to the lapse of ages.
I can see many reasons why Providence should have made
this temporal dominion a permanent accident of the Papal
authority, and also made it always insecure.   Far from adding
to the dignity of the Spiritual Power, it is rather a Body of
Humiliation in which that power suffers, and never has it been
more the mark for ' barbaric javelins ' and the ' arrows of the
proud ' than of late centuries.

I am not, however, one of those Catholics who believe
that the Pope would be *permanently* better without it.
Living in the world, not living a monastic life, the Pope
must have some status and the kingly status seems the

most decorous and natural one for him; moreover if not a king he would be a subject, and kings . . . would be always reproaching him with being under foreign influence. It is however only as his *ordinary* state that temporal dominion seems useful to him ; and occasional violations of it seem always to do good in the long run, the exiled or martyred Popes having always been the greatest ones, while very prosperous Popes, like Leo X., have often preceded revolts or periods of corruption. As regards the Church, then, I have no fears. Italian Liberty, on the other hand, I regard as in extreme jeopardy, though of that, too, I am far from despairing.

In 1866 Aubrey's historical imagination was again aroused by the war between Prussia and the Austrian Empire—the surviving relic of the Holy Roman Empire. The Temporal Power of the Papacy, and the heir to the ancient German Empire, still symbols, however faint, of the ideals of Leo and Charlemagne, seemed both to be passing away together.

Aubrey looked on with deep regret, but yet with a sense of resignation to the inevitable. ' The old order changes, giving place to new.' And, in writing to Professor Norton on the subject on July 18, 1866, he makes the best of the situation, looking at the more attractive aspect of the modern spirit of liberty which was taking the place of the Catholic exclusiveness of mediæval days :—

A mighty historical Empire [he writes] seems to be dying —Austria—the shadow at least of the German Empire of the Middle Ages in which the old Roman Empire lived on a ' posthumous life.' In place of this, it seems as though the world were to see a Northern Teutonic Empire embodying the spirit of Frederick the Great, and Goethe and Dr. Luther. (I always call the last Dr. because I am not intimate with him !) Lest you should think this proceeds from Catholic prejudices, I must tell you that the Catholic Church generally flourishes more under Protestant than under Catholic Kings, from being more free and poor, and let more alone.

Poor Austria! she had already let go her last hold of
Italy ; and as Wordsworth says,

> Men must grieve when even the shade
> Of that which once was great is passed away.

When Aubrey reached Rome in 1870, he witnessed the
counter-stroke of the Papacy, in response to the blows struck
at the surviving shadows of the Christendom of Charlemagne.
As the last vestige of its old status seemed to be passing away,
the Holy See was on the eve of defining its position as infallible
exponent of Christian dogma, meeting modern rebellion
against its authority by an assertion of its claims on the
faithful remnant of Catholics ; impressing on them de
Maistre's programme for the nineteenth century, that ' the
same blood should circulate in the veins of the whole Catholic
world.'

On the vexed question of the proposed definition of
Papal Infallibility Aubrey had an open mind. He never
had any sympathy with the violence of such of its prot-
agonists as M. Louis Veuillot ; he had less with the school
of Friedrich. Both of the extreme parties violated the laws
of charity, but the extreme liberals added an offence against
reverence for authority. The personalities indulged in by
both were abhorrent to Aubrey. Indeed, the jarring note of
controversy and personal recrimination was so distasteful to
him, that he leant rather more towards the 'definitionist'
side than did such friends of his as Mrs. Craven, and Montalembert. For it was on the side of the 'left' that acri-
monious personalities, in his experience, predominated. The
same tendency was also promoted by his sense of the un-
fairness of English public opinion, alike on the question of the
expiring Temporal Power of the Pope, and on the Ecumenical
Council itself. If Catholics debated the question before
the definition was made, they were accused by the newspapers of 'disunion' ; if they urged the duty of submission,

once it should have been passed, they were charged with servility. Such injustice towards those whom he most loved and respected aroused the spirit of deep uncritical reverence which was always natural to him. He wrote as follows to Charles Spring Rice :—

Hôtel de la Minerve, Rome : March 16, 1870.

I have often been near writing to you, but waited in hopes of being able to send you more news. Every day one hears quantities of things which have a deep significance, and interest one down in the depths of one's being ; but the net result in the way of news is small. The Council will, I have no doubt, leave vast and most useful results behind it ; but a body of nearly eight hundred Bishops moves slowly. In society there is a good deal of excitement on the subject of the Definition relative to Infallibility, and it is curious to see with what vehemence the matter is discussed by those whose ordinary attitude of mind is the opposite of controversial. This is all right, of course, as the present is the time of discussion ; in the meantime many charges of 'disunion' are directed against those persons who when (discussion having passed away, and Definition taken its place) they are as tranquil as they are now sometimes excited, will have the opposite charges levelled against them, those of servile submission, stagnation, &c. In lay society I am sorry to see that there are sometimes personalities, and a tone of exaggeration which I never observe among the Bishops. They seem to me almost always grave, reverent, and charitable in speaking of those from whom they differ. This is doubtless because, being called on to judge in these arduous matters, the graces needful for the formation of a sound judgment are abundantly given to them—a boon not to be expected by those who are not called to the same high functions.

Three months later Charles Spring Rice, to whom this letter was written, passed away. Death visited at almost the same time another equally beloved household. For Henry

Taylor lost his son.   Aubrey's feelings at the time are indicated in the following letter to Miss Grace Norton :—

Athenæum Club, Pall Mall, London : July 27, 1870.

My dear Miss Grace Norton,—I am so much obliged to
you for your most pleasant and friendly letter.   It reached
me at one of those periods when cheering accounts of one's
friends are more than usually valuable.   I had been passing
some time at Bournemouth with my friends the Henry Taylors,
and their house, you will easily believe, is now a very sad one.
The son they are deploring was an object of great pride to
them, as well as of unbounded love ; and many years of his
boyhood had been an almost constant battle with death.
They are all deeply cast down ; but the eldest sister seems to
me the one the most so.   He had been her companion, in a
special sense, from their childhood ; and I am not easy about
her health, for she looks very delicate.   I have hopes of being
allowed soon to take her over with me to Ireland, where she
would be at her cousin's, Lord Monteagle's, on the banks of
the Shannon, and in the society of young people whom she
is fond of.   The change of scene might do her good.   I will
not fail to give to her parents the kind assurance of sympathy which you send them on behalf of all your circle.   They
were speaking more than once of the enjoyment they had
had in your brother's society, and their hope that they would
see him again.   While with them I received the sad news of
the death of my cousin, Charles Spring Rice, Lady Taylor's
brother, which carried me off to Folkestone, where I passed
several days.   He had fought for three years with a painful and
almost hopeless malady ; and it was indeed time for him to
be at rest.   He was not only contented to die, but had been
contented to suffer, often saying that no pain could be too
much while it purified us, and made us fitter for God.   He
was Assistant Under-Secretary in the Foreign Office, and one
would not have thought that Diplomatic life was the school
for piety.   These are the things which remind us how difficult
it is to say that mere circumstance is either propitious or
unpropitious to our spiritual development.   All seems to
depend on what is *within*, ' the buon cuor,' as the Italians

say. It is a wonderful thing to see the mixture of anguish and of gratitude to God in his widow. When her time of consolation comes, it cannot but be the right consolation, and it can hardly fail to be a very great one.

Well—all is not sorrow even in this world—and your letter tells me of much happiness, and of that sort of happiness which, in some respects at least, is the best that earth can give, because it leaves no wound behind, and causes no anxiety while it lasts—the happiness that comes from nature's grace and goodness—from shady trees, and horizons fair and far, and delicious weather, and those beautiful clouds which have been drifting over your Italian home. These are, indeed, as you describe them, matters for daily and hourly thanksgiving, as well as for still and profound enjoyment. And how much more should we enjoy them if only one could be more grateful for them! The Visible World was certainly not endowed with its marvellous beauty for nothing. It was intended in all its successive processes to encompass us with a series of ministrations, adumbrating at least, if not revealing, all that lies beyond the Veil—all of which visible things can be but emblems, and instruments. Just as in reading a *first-rate* poet we feel that there is meaning beneath meaning, that that which lies on the surface is probably of the least worth, and that which lies deepest is probably beyond our feeble ken ; so it seems to me with nature. In proportion as we discern her beauty, we feel that it is a shadow of some higher beauty that we can but guess at. To understand it, even as far as it can be made intelligible to us, nature must have an interpreter that is beyond nature.

The effort that those old Greeks made to find such an interpreter in their mythological pantheism seems to me one of the most extraordinary efforts of combined imagination and intellect. And yet one says of it, as of antique sculpture, ' but how *hard-hearted* all this sweetness is ; and how morally *superficial* is all this intellectual significance!' It leaves the real problem untouched. It dares not look reality in the face. It ignores all that it fears to face, and fancies it can make the end less sad because it can enwreath the Sarcophagus with a choir of laughing marble nymphs. People seem to me very imperfectly to perceive how completely *Christian* Symbolism (the only other key, so to speak, for the interpretation of nature) rests upon the opposite idea from that of Pagan Pantheism—viz. on that of the Incarnation. It was to illustrate the Incarnation in this point of view that I wrote the *Descriptive* poems among my 'May Carols,' as the rest of them were written to show (so far as a theme so mystic admits of poetic illustration) that the whole cycle of Christian Doctrine and Devotion finds its centre in the single great verity insisted on by St. John, 'The Word was made Flesh and dwelt among us.' The Idea of the 'God-man' resumed all; and every year has convinced me more deeply that millions of those who accept that Idea *in terms*, have never the least grasped it, and that very few of those who do not accept it have ever comprehended it—or rather have ever apprehended it; for of course the human mind does not affect to comprehend in its fulness, more than that petty lore which it creates for itself. . . .

I sent a poem in the beginning of this month to the 'Atlantic Monthly.' If they publish it, you will perhaps read one more 'Irish Legend.' But such poems are but a poor return for a poem such as that Photograph from Fra Angelico. There can be nothing higher in art; and most truly grateful to you was I for it. How many who would rail against the 'coronation of the Blessed Virgin' might still exult in this delineation, interpreting it after their own fashion, as the crowning of Humanity or that triumph when Humanity ceases to be 'subject to Vanity for a time,' and puts on her Immortality? Will you also give my best wishes to your sister for the second and smaller photograph from that sublime work? The first copy I had lent to Lady Taylor, because she and her daughters had admired it so much. The sorrow embodied in that work is the 'true Sorrow,' just as the joy embodied in the Photograph you sent me is 'the true joy,' and it is thus that in Christian art alone, Humanity finds its meaning and finds a voice.

Pray give your sister-in-law my best thanks for her letter and give my most affectionate remembrances to all your circle.

Ever most sincerely yours,

AUBREY DE VERE.

I wish we could have a few walks at Siena like that at Florence. I wonder whether you recognised the quotation from Dante in that passage in my Preface to 'May Carols' in which I speak of that 'Error opposite to that of Narcissus,' under which the modern intelligence is disposed to see only a reflection of its own dreams in all things, and thus to count as 'subjective' only, the truths that are most authentic and independent of our own creative and brooding imaginations. I once illustrated the subject thus when discussing modern 'Rationalism' with Alfred Tennyson, and found that Dante's prophetic image struck him.

It was under the influence of his visit to Rome in 1870 that Aubrey set to work on his return on his 'Irish Legends,' the second instalment ('Inisfail' being the first) of his illustration of what he regarded as the place of the Irish race in the providential scheme. 'To different nations,' he wrote, 'different vocations are assigned by Providence; to one an imperial vocation, to another a commercial one; to Greece an artistic one, to Ireland, as to Israel, a spiritual one.' Ireland alone among northern nations had remained part of the spiritual polity of which Rome was the centre; it had thereby proved (he held) the thoroughness with which it had assimilated the genius of Christianity. The appearance of this poem was the occasion of an interesting letter to Taylor :—

Torquay : July 25, 1872.

Now for the 'Legends.' . . . I am convinced that at least they furnish a noble *theme* for Poetry, . . . Odd as it may sound, I think I was assisted by reading Homer's Odyssey in Worsley's beautiful translation; for, though nothing can be more unlike than the Pagan and the Christian themes, still the old Homeric *way of seeing things* helped to take one out of modern associations. What a divine Poem we should have had if that grand old Father of Bards, who was ever seeing the Human so intensely, and yet seeing the Divine, or, at least, the Supernatural behind it, could but have had a great Christian theme instead of a Pagan one. It is wonderful, and to modern poets a great reproach, I think, how much of true religious sentiment, despite the aberrations of pagan fancy, Homer combined with his profound appreciation of the Humanities, and with that perfect spontaneity which belonged to his imagination. He lived on singularly easy terms with his gods ; but in him familiarity did not breed contempt. It seems impossible to suppose that it is only a false religion that is capable of blending thus with poetry, without interfering with its deep humanities, and its keen vivacities. It must surely be the fault of the modern poets that in their attempts at religious Poetry the element of Poetry was commonly left out, while the Religion was often represented only by those parts of Theology which do not admit of being poetically exhibited. Dante was an entire success, and Milton, though I cannot but think he often failed egregiously, met with a splendid success, quite frequently enough to show that when he failed, the fault was not in his religious theme, but in his treating it sometimes as a controversialist, sometimes as a Schoolman, not as a Poet and a Humanist. Æschylus wrote the grandest of religious Mysteries, his ' Prometheus,' as well as the most tragic of human tales, his ' Agamemnon '—while Euripides, whose tragedies had in them least of the religious, had also least of human passion, aiming more at the sententious and the didactic. I never could see why, if poetry may be philosophical, its Philosophy may not be the Christian Philosophy which, when rightly understood, is surely the most vital of philosophies, and the most in sympathy with things natural, though it descends from the region of the Supernatural.

In my ' May Carols ' I endeavoured to set forth the Christian Religion in a philosophical form, through a series of poems illustrating the cardinal doctrine of the Incarnation, in the various phases which it presents to the *Individual Intelligence*. The aim of the ' Legends ' is the exact converse. Its endeavour is to illustrate Christianity as a Power energising in human society, and transforming it from the animal to, or at least towards, the spiritual. For this end no theme would have answered which did not present the strongest traits of natural affections and human sympathies, as well as show the influence of a Divine Religion upon these. Accordingly, there is more of human nature, I believe, in this poem than in my previous poems, and if there had been twice as much of religion in it as there is, I do not see why that need have presented any obstacle to a representation of human nature far more various and vivid than I have been able to give. It seems to me that those who like the poem like it chiefly for its delineation of character, especially St. Patrick's character.

In 1874 Aubrey de Vere made his first attempt at drama, the subject being Alexander the Great. He was not sanguine as to its success—'there is even less chance for a Drama by me, than for any other form of composition. Most likely it will turn out to be my latest failure' (he wrote to Taylor). 'But if so it is all the better that it should be off my hands as soon as may be; for my parental sensibilities are like those of the *animals*; and once a book is launched, and ought to "do for itself" I care much less about it than when it remains a beautiful chicken hidden in an egg, or even a tender blind puppy.'

Its success, however, was sufficient to encourage him to follow it up by his 'St. Thomas of Canterbury' two years later. The two poems were intended as a dramatic contrast, as the author has explained in his 'Recollections.'[1]

There was a certain didactic strain in the dramas, and they were designed to minister to that large philosophy of history of which I have already spoken. Aubrey de Vere boldly affirmed that on these great subjects in which the interests of religion were concerned, English public opinion was hopelessly at fault. 'In them,' he wrote to a friend, 'England is simply what Rome is in commerce and manu-factures. Verily there is a diversity of gifts in this world.'

People do not, as a rule, like being 'instructed' on such

[1] See *Recollections*, p. 366.

subjects, or finding their cherished preconceptions assailed. In the ordinary course of things his 'St. Thomas' would probably have received little notice; but a very unusual man, Richard Holt Hutton, was at that time a power in English criticism. Hutton was deeply attracted by the ethical side of Catholicism, and his strong sense of justice was offended by what he considered the unappreciative attitude of the public, thirty years ago, towards the Roman Catholic point of view. His writing in the 'Spectator' had been largely instrumental in gaining that hearing for Newman's 'Apologia' which made it an undoubted triumph. He wrote a very appreciative review of the new drama, to which Aubrey refers in the following letter to Taylor :—

Athenæum Club, Pall Mall, S.W. : July 6, 1876.

. . . . Your being so much pleased with the critique in the 'Spectator' (certainly a most friendly and useful one), only proves what I knew before—viz. that you are much more interested in the success of what I write than I am myself. Though I am by no means indifferent on that subject, and indeed could not afford to be indifferent so long as I have heavy printers' bills to pay. . . . The first thing Tennyson said to me when we met was, 'So I hear you have taken "Becket" out of my hands.' I told him that, my work being now done, the sooner he wrote a better one the better; but that I did not want the poetic mind of England to be in the first instance preoccupied by a drama setting forth what I regard as the national prejudice on the subject, as contrasted with deeper and larger principles. We have many indications now that the public takes abundant interest in Ecclesiastical subjects, when treated from its own point of view. It is well that, once in a way, it should see them treated from a different point of view.

I have not yet heard many opinions about the book ; Emly thinks it my best work. Patmore thinks very differently, as you will see from his letter. Pray return it. On the whole, I expect it to do less well than 'Alexander,' but even in that case I think it would have been worth while writing the book, if only as a new sort of drama, and as a vindication of principles, on very important subjects, deeply affecting human happiness, and on which the judgment generally prevailing is for the most part neither deep nor impartial.

Aubrey's interest in the work of others is shown in his correspondence with Miss Thompson,[1] some of which I have been allowed to see. ' I am glad,' he writes in one letter, 'that you mean to pay the Tennysons another visit. . . . He could give you many a useful hint as to Poetry considered as an art. Italy will, I trust, be propitious to your poetry. You must throw your heart into it, and be constant to it, without being anxious about it.'

The following letter to the same correspondent refers to a translation undertaken by her at his desire :—

Derwent Island : September 12, 1876.

My dear Miss Thompson,—I am very much obliged to you for finding time to write to me amid the Orange-groves of the South, and not less obliged to you for so kindly undertaking the translation I was so anxious to see done by you. The safest address to which you can send them is ' Athenæum Club, Pall Mall, London,' which *always* finds me.

Translation is a difficult thing, but it is also a fascinating one to those who have the gift. Only poets can translate poetry, and then only if diction and versatility rank high among their gifts. Shelley and Coleridge are, I think, our best poetical translators ; and if the former had fulfilled his intention of translating Æschylus, he could perhaps have given us the *sublimest* volume in the language, and disciplined his own genius, both in the best and speediest way to perfect his own powers for original compositions of *solid* greatness. Solidity was what his genius lacked, and this it lacked because it had never learned self-control. Wordsworth told me that he had translated above a score of Michael Angelo's sonnets, though he had only thought three of them perfect enough for publication.

[1] Now Mrs. Wilfrid Meynell, the well-known poet and essayist.

I have been very much touched by the thought of the French nun [of whom you tell me] producing, in her holy seclusion, and without a thought of fame, poems on the highest of subjects, and remarkable at once for elevation of thought, and artistic grace of proportion. . . . Another part of the poem has been sent to me which I dare say you will also like to read, so I forward it. I believe that in all there will be five or six parts.

I envy you in Italy, and, as I see, in a part of Italy which you have old associations with. I hope that Italian skies may be equally auspicious to your art and to your sister's.[1] With kindest remembrances to her, and to your father and mother, believe me,

Yours very sincerely,
AUBREY DE VERE.

Two interesting letters from John Henry Newman to de Vere belong to the years I have been dealing with in this chapter.

Aubrey de Vere became in these years more closely acquainted with the great Oratorian who had long been his most revered master in religious thought. The occasion was the formation of the Catholic University of Ireland, in the 'fifties.' De Vere, after some hesitation, accepted the position of Professor of English Literature, and a remarkable lecture delivered in that capacity, on 'Literature in its Social Aspects,' is to be found among his published Essays. The sympathy between the two men was very close. The student of Newman will note the similarity up to a certain point of the lines of thought to be found in Aubrey's letters of 1842, and the philosophy underlying the 'University Sermons,' and the 'Essay on Development'—both of them published at a later date. Direct influence, no doubt, strengthened this similarity of view in later years, though the Irish poet never had any share in the extraordinary dramatic sympathy with a critical and even with a sceptical

---

[1] Lady Butler, painter of the 'Roll Call.'

standpoint which was so marked a characteristic of Newman's writing.

When Newman wrote ' Callista ' he placed on its title-page the beautiful lines on ' Reality,' which Aubrey de Vere had recently published in his volume,—' The Infant Bridal and other Poems,'—lines which bring out clearly one quality which they shared in common, namely that intimate sense of communion with God which is denied to ordinary men, and is the special privilege of the saints and mystics. Let the lines be here set down :—

> Love thy God and love Him only,
> And thy breast will ne'er be lonely.
> In that one great Spirit meet
> All things mighty, grave and sweet :
> Vainly strives the soul to mingle
> With a being of its kind ;
> Vainly hearts with hearts are twined ;
> For the deepest still is single.
> An impalpable resistance
> Keeps like natures still at distance ;
> Mortal, love the Holy One
> Or dwell for aye alone.

Aubrey de Vere always hoped that Newman would follow up ' Callista ' by another tale on the ultimate victory of Christianity in the Roman Empire—a subject to both of them so significant, and in some ways so suitable to a time when English Catholics stood to our great empire in a somewhat similar relation to that of the early Christians to Rome. But the thorough mastery of the period which Newman felt to be needed, in order to make the moral of such a tale something higher than an *ex parte* argument, deterred him from writing it.

' If a tale such as you mention came into my head,' he wrote in 1863, ' I would certainly write it, but it is not likely to do so. It requires a great deal of reading. The subject of the struggle of the Roman Empire with Christianity is one which has long interested me more than any other subject.

x

I should like to have given twenty years to it. Now, it is very unlikely that I should ever give six months.'

Newman was indeed, in the early sixties, despondent about himself and his work, and shrank from writing. His efforts at Dublin had failed. His subsequent attempt to edit the ' Rambler ' and bring Catholic thought in England to a point at which it could fully assimilate the results of contemporary science and research, had been put an end to by an episcopal admonition. The theological views prevalent at that time— and more rigidly enforced than in the early years of the century, when the Catholic revival had welcomed the original genius of Moehler and Döllinger—were a great trial to him, and he hesitated in his old age to risk incurring the charge of unorthodoxy, with the possible further risk that his influence might be lessened by such a charge, and that some of the good he had already done, in raising the standard of theological thought, might be undone.

The ' Apologia ' was written as an inevitable act of self-defence in 1864, and shortly after its appearance, Newman wrote as follows to Aubrey de Vere, in answer to an exhortation that he should publish more on these great subjects :—

The Oratory, Birmingham : July 6, 1864.

My dear de Vere,—Your letter was most acceptable and pleasant ; thank you, too, for your beautiful little book.

As to myself, I have had a great trial, and am very wearied—but I trust that on the whole I have done my work —though, of course, being done so hurriedly, it might have been done better.

As to my writing anything on subjects of the day, recollect the Duke of Wellington's saying, that a great country cannot have a little war—nor can a great subject in theology. To touch on a subject is to be crude and misleading ; it is to incur nearly all the censures which the Church uses of books, the ' erroneous,' ' next to heresy,' ' ill-sounding,' ' scandalous,' and 'temerarious.' Already, as it is, I hear murmurs about my book, which may give me trouble. This is the main cause I cannot write—I have no wish, at my age, to be involved in controversy, and to spend my strength in self-defence. I think it very hard that I may not write under the antecedent concession that I am a fallible mortal, but that every turn of expression is to be turned into a dogmatic enunciation. Those who thus wish me to talk with the tongues not of men but ' of angels,' had better themselves have a little ' charity.' I say this, even supposing I am wrong—but I am not conscious I am, and see what loss of time it is to prove *after all* that I am right.

Ever yours most sincerely in Christ,
JOHN H. NEWMAN,
of the Oratory.

The 'Apologia,' however, did in the event prove to be a turning point in Newman's influence. Its enthusiastic reception by the English public, and the share of many English Catholics, including the episcopate, in that enthusiasm, reassured its author's sensitive mind. Six years later he published the ' Grammar of Assent.'

Another letter to Aubrey gives an interesting account of the genesis of that work :—

The Oratory : August 31, 1870.

My dear Aubrey de Vere,—It is a great pleasure to hear your commendations of two publications of mine. As to my Essay on Assent it is on a subject which has teazed me for these twenty or thirty years. I felt I had something to say upon it, yet, whenever I attempted, the sight I saw vanished, plunged into a thicket, curled itself up like a hedgehog, or changed colours like a chameleon. I have a succession of commencements, perhaps a dozen, each different from the other, and in a different year, which came to nothing. At last, four years ago, when I was up at Glion over the Lake of Geneva, a thought came into my head as the clue, the ' Open Sesame,' of the whole subject, and I at once wrote it down, and I pursued it about the Lake of Lucerne. Then when I

X 2

came home I began in earnest, and have slowly got through it.

Now you must not think, in consequence of my thus speaking, that I am sure myself that I have done any great thing—for I have felt very little confidence in it—though words like yours, and you are not the only person who has used such, are a very great encouragement to me—but I could not help feeling that I had something to give out whatever its worth, and I felt haunted with a sort of responsibility, and almost a weight on my conscience, if I did not speak it, and yet I could not. So that it is the greatest possible relief at length to have got it off my mind—as if I heard the words 'he has done what he could.' And, while I say this, I really am not taking for granted that your favourable criticism is the true one—and I recollect that what a man thinks his best work is often his worst. But then I think, too, that sometimes a man's failures do more good to the world or to his cause than his best successes—and then I feel as if I could die happier now that I have no Essay on Assent to write, and I think I shall never write another work, meaning by work a something which is an anxiety and a labour. 'Man goeth forth to his work and to his labours until the evening' and my evening is surely come—though not my night.

Ever yours affectionately,
JOHN H. NEWMAN.

Moments come in the story of every deep feeling of love or friendship, when something makes us realise and reflect on what has been so much to us. In 1873 Sir Henry Taylor, who was now over seventy years old, was preparing his Autobiography, and calling back his letters to Aubrey de Vere for this purpose. The past was ever something magical to Aubrey, it came upon him with new vividness as he read their early correspondence. The exchange of letters on the occasion is very touching. Aubrey had, a few years earlier, begun the process of arranging his own correspondence, and described

the feelings which this task had brought, and I preface the
letter of 1873 by an earlier one :—

Curragh Chase: March 3, 1868.

Weeding among old letters does indeed make us feel
that the Past is full of ghosts ; but ghosts differ in their
classes as much as the other spirits, black, white and grey ;
and the ghost which you sent me in the form of a recollection of 1844 is indeed a 'spirit of noonday.' Everything that belongs to old days wears for me a magical
brightness, and a colouring like that of mountains a little
before sunrise. You see I do not say a 'little after sunset.'
On the contrary, although there is a melancholy about the
past, still the best scenes it presents to our memory somehow
seem to me presented even more to one's hope. They are
less records of what was, than pledges of what may be, and
therefore must be, in that far future that alone makes either
present or past intelligible. One knows, looking back on
them, that somehow they were not all that they seem to have
been, or rather that, though they were all, and more than all,
yet they were not either felt aright or understood aright at
the moment. To-day I can smell the sea odours mixed with
those of the rich vegetation along the Riviera, and see how
that radiant land and divine climate brightened up my fellow-
travellers ; to-day I can take my stand with you under the
huge arch of the old Roman bridge at Narni, and observe how
intensely you appreciated Italian scenery, and how thoroughly
you approved of mountains that knew how to keep their
distance ; but still one knows that an actual present always
has its 'fly in the compôte of spices.' I remember my
vexation at Alice's getting ill, as the carriage wound up the
steep hill of Perugia, and the strange touch of grief I felt at
observing for the first time what looked like a *solid* tress of
grey in your hair as you stood before me at church in Naples.
Consequently, I think it best to conclude that those old
times, compared with which later times seem so beggarly,
were chiefly to be valued as omens of some excursion we shall
make 'among the Palms of Paradise,' if ever we have the luck
to get there.

Aubrey de Vere to Sir Henry Taylor

Curragh Chase, Adare : November 18, 1873.

Your letter has given me a strange day—one with an indescribable mixture of sadness and sweetness; for it has sent me looking over your old letters, and in them retracing more than half my life.   The sad thought is : 'Can such tracts of happiness, indeed, lie behind one?' with the question : 'Did one, indeed, while passing through such golden regions, fail so much to value them at their full worth?'

The thought is one which has often come to me, but which, 'as the sweet years insensibly go by,' recurs more often, and with more power, viz. that nothing of good which has been vouchsafed to us has been given in vain, and that all good things would have been worse than vain if they were not intended to remain with us for ever (if we do not mar our destinies), even in the most advanced stage of our future being—to remain with us—glorified, no doubt, or they could not coexist with that Beatific Vision which constitutes Heaven ; but in and under the glory, revealing to us a reality greater than that which they presented to us on earth, because more essential and less accidental.

Sir Henry Taylor to Aubrey de Vere

No. 66, Eaton Square, S.W. : November 24, 1873.

My dear Aubrey,—In the last year or two I have had many such days as you describe, for many have been passed amongst old letters.   But though there has been some sweetness in them, the sadness has been in much larger measure. Most of the writers have been long dead, but I hardly think that their letters, with all the lost love that they represented (so far as love is lost by death), were so depressing to me as those which represented ardours that are dead and gone, though the objects, or subjects, of them are still living.   We must hope that there is a resurrection for the loves that are buried alive.   The credit you give me for constancy I can take, in a sense.   It is the coldness, rather than the inconstancy of the affections that I have to complain of in myself.

And it is a great comfort and consolation to me that in your case, what may fail in me through age or death, will be made up by the youthful warmth of my girls' affections. For I think there is no one they are more fond of than they are of you.

Ever yours affectionately,
HENRY TAYLOR.

Aubrey de Vere to Lady Taylor

Curragh Chase, Adare : December 1, 1873.

That fragment of your letter to Miss Fenwick was, indeed, a voice out of that vast and lonely region—the realm of things that were, and of things departed. These things make one very sad. They would not do so if that strange thing, Human Life, were only lived aright. Its flowers would then only fade to take their place in those precious vases :—

Where sweets compacted lie.

I do believe that, if life's sorrows were only its *inevitable* sorrows, the voices from the past would be an eternal harmony in our ears—a lullaby when we need one—at other times an inspiring march, helping us on the upward way to that land where all good things await all who worthily enjoyed them. . . . We see, alas, these things, and all things so *superficially*. We understand so slightly the great end for which Friendships are sent out on their mission, and the large degree in which things, apparently small, frustrate that end. These small things are forgotten ; yet who can say how they live on in their consequences—at least in their negative consequences—intercepting good that might otherwise have been ? The only consolation is found in a great truth, beautifully expressed, I remember, in Manzoni's 'Promessi Sposi,' which we read together in those old days of travel. It is to this effect—that, however devious may be our track, as we wander through the labyrinth of life, Providence has provided things so wonderfully that, *at every step* of it, there branch forth two side-paths, one of which leads us back to the great Way.

CHAPTER IX

ENGLISH AGNOSTICISM AND IRISH JACOBINISM

1874–1886

MY own first meeting with Aubrey de Vere came in the year 1874, or 1875. It is stamped on my memory by an amusing incident which occurred on the same day. Aubrey de Vere was at Farringford, enjoying the daily society of his dear friends the Tennysons, and of Mrs. Cameron, who lived at Freshwater Bay. Cardinal Vaughan, then Bishop of Salford, was staying with my father and mother at Weston Manor, and Aubrey de Vere came to tea with us one afternoon, in company with Tennyson and Mrs. Cameron, to meet his old friend. Mrs. Cameron was at that time photographing various persons, to represent the characters in the 'Idylls,' and I had heard her grumble at not being satisfied with her attempts at a representation of Lancelot—face, figure, age, or expression, was wrong in every candidate. As Mrs. Cameron and Tennyson entered the drawing-room together, Bishop Vaughan was standing in the glow of the winter fire, looking, as he ever did, the most knightly of priests, and Mrs. Cameron stood for a moment transfixed, as Aubrey de Vere himself had done twenty years earlier in Rome. Then she cried out, pointing to him : 'Alfred, I have found Sir Lancelot.' Tennyson's bad sight prevented him from seeing at whom she was pointing, and he replied, in loud and deep tones: 'I want a face that is well worn with human passion.' The Bishop smiled and blushed, and the general laughter could not be suppressed. Tennyson and he were made acquainted, and their meeting, after this somewhat unpromising beginning, proved a great success.[1]

Aubrey de Vere stayed, I think, talking to Dr. Vaughan after the others had left, and I went into our chapel to play the organ. A little later on I looked down from the organ gallery, and saw his slim form in one of the benches rapt in devotion. I joined him and spoke to him, and he begged me to play again the Andante from Beethoven's 'Kreutzer Sonata,' which I had just finished. We walked to Farringford together afterwards, talking of many things of common interest, and arranged to meet again.

I met him from time to time in London a few years later. We were both friends of R. H. Hutton, and were often his guests for breakfast or dinner, at the Devonshire Club. The dinners were large gatherings including political notabilities —Mr. Gladstone and Mr. Forster I remember there on more than one occasion—and, welcome though he was, Aubrey de Vere did not show in the presence of large numbers his most characteristic gifts. But at the breakfasts—consisting of three or four at most—it was otherwise. I remember feeling from the first that Aubrey de Vere and Hutton were well matched in their absolute simplicity, and the conversation between them was memorable. Hutton was the more powerful, more critical, more pungent, with more mental angles and prejudices. But de Vere shed a moral sunshine over the company. There was a grace in his thought and expression which Hutton lacked, and his hopeful enthusiasm, and determination to see the best side of everyone and everything were to me very refreshing. Both were equally remarkable for an earnestness, and a

---

[1] The story is told of the Cardinal's first meeting with another great man, which was equally amusing. On this occasion the humour of the situation arose not from his being unknown, but unknowing. He was introduced to Millais at the Manchester Exhibition, and quite failed to catch his name. The drift of the conversation showed that he was a painter, but no more. 'When I began to paint,' said Millais, 'I could only get five pounds for a portrait.' 'Indeed,' replied Vaughan, with the utmost sympathy, 'I trust you are doing better *now*.'

simplicity and reality of thought, of which a larger experience of life has since made me realise the rarity. There was also a delightful, though limited, sense of humour apparent in Aubrey's conversation. I well remember the joy he gave to Hutton and myself by his account of Wordsworth's praise of his wife. After enumerating her many virtues, the Bard of Rydal went on slowly, gravely, and emphatically, 'And it was, perhaps, her greatest quality that she never molested me in my affection for other women.' De Vere's broad smile (he told us) was not lost on the poet, who continued seriously, and almost combatively, ' If she *had*, Mr. de Vere, let me tell you, it would have been in the highest degree offensive to me.'[1]

Equally characteristic of his humour, and moreover of his power of administering a rebuke on occasion, was another story—which, however, I did not hear at Hutton's table. Aubrey de Vere was walking, in Rome, with an acquaintance of ' anti-popish ' sentiments, who rather ostentatiously spoke of the patrons of each church without the prefix ' Saint,' as ' Ignatius ' or ' Philip ' or ' Clement.' This was most distasteful to Aubrey, but he stood it for a time. At last he stopped, took off his hat, and bowed low to his companion. ' Why do you do that ? ' the latter asked. ' I want to show my profound respect for one who is on such familiar terms with the saints,' was the answer.

De Vere and Hutton admired each other intensely. I recollect two successive breakfasts : after the first, de Vere had to leave early, and Hutton said to me when he had gone, ' What a wonderful man that is ; what simplicity and purity of character ! I wish I were more like him.' On the next occasion they were breakfasting with me at the old St. George's Club, in Savile Row, and Hutton left early. ' What

---

[1] Aubrey de Vere was careful to add that the ' other women ' were in reality not youthful beauties, but such friends as Miss Fenwick, and one or two of her contemporaries who were admirers of Wordsworth's muse.

a wonderful man!' exclaimed de Vere. 'How unworldly and single-hearted! *How I wish I could be like him!*'

Aubrey's friend William Monsell, my father's old school-fellow at Winchester, who was now Lord Emly, was another link between us, and I sometimes met Aubrey de Vere at Tervoe, and often at Lord Emly's rooms in John Street The vigour, keenness, and large-hearted geniality of our host brought into relief de Vere's very distinct characteristics,—his gentleness and fastidious refinement. In 1887 we formed a dining club, of which Lord Emly was president, and I was secretary, for the purpose of discussing the Irish problem, then of such interest to all Catholics. Among our members were, besides Aubrey de Vere, Colonel (now Sir John) Ross of Bladensburg, the late Lord Petre, and Mr. Woulfe Flanagan. I remember Colonel Saunderson being one evening among our guests. In this way, and at our own home at Hampstead, a few years later, I not unfrequently saw Aubrey de Vere. I remember that he used at once—after perhaps a year's interval since we had last met—to begin some old topic of interest, as though our former conversation had been broken off only half an hour previously.

I used also sometimes to go and talk to him at the Athenæum, where year after year he appeared at the end of July, when the fashionable world was leaving London, and I well remember the tall, refined, rather aristocratic figure, dressed in a velveteen coat, descending the wide staircase. He talked much to me as he did to others of the friends and scenes of his early life, and of his favourite poets. His memory for poetry was extraordinary; but in this as in much else, he struck one as only just falling short of a gift which would have been marvellous—for he was rarely quite word-perfect.

In 1884 we spent a week together with the Arundells of Wardour, at Wardour Castle. This brought out an aspect of his tastes with which I had not previously come in

contact. He revelled in the old documents and records of
family history preserved there. 'This is my ideal,' he said to me.
'A beautiful place, full of the historic records of an ancient
house, and with nothing of "smartness" or excessive wealth
or display, which brings nearly always a touch of vulgarity.'

He himself on this occasion was certainly innocent of
display and excessive smartness, being dressed, most of the
day, in an overcoat.

Indeed, as to appearances he was not observant, and his
coats and umbrellas were often old friends. But he was
particular in avoiding any social solecism in the matter of
dress, if he did give his mind to the subject. When his
nephew, Robert Vere O'Brien, was married to Miss Arnold
Forster, he was in some doubt as to the colour of the tie
which would befit the occasion. He brought two in his
pocket, and was detected behind a pillar in St. Peter's, Eaton
Square, putting on the right one, after he had secured the
desired information.

He never seemed to me to change during the whole time of
our acquaintance—from the later seventies, when our London
meetings first became frequent, to 1898, when I last saw him
at Adare, at the house of our friend, Dean Flanagan.

Religious philosophy was a favourite topic of his conversation, but in a form in which it was ever picturesque, and
deeply interesting. He had when I knew him reached the
phase which was especially interesting to Hutton and myself,
when theological controversy between the Churches interested
him less than of old, and the great question—Is England, is
Europe going to give up Christianity as a dream or a legend,
and lose the beliefs, but for which, Christian ideals and the
Christian life cannot very long continue to exist? was an
absorbing thought with him.

This change is also apparent in his correspondence with
Henry Taylor, and it led to a renewal of religious sympathy
between them. The friendly controversies, which had followed

Aubrey's change of communion, were now succeeded by letters in which the friends were closely agreed, in deprecation of the developments of the agnostic view of life which was steadily gaining adherents in England. In the seventies the scientific agnosticism of Huxley and Tyndall was to the front. It was affecting the Universities and the English world of thought. The publication of John Stuart Mill's Autobiography, while revealing the noble moral character of the writer, for the moment impressed the world chiefly as presenting a frank and outspoken avowal of a godless view of life, as being the best that the critical reason can attain to. To many minds, especially among the more intellectual, the general trend of thought appeared to be tending towards the rejection of Christianity, and of the definite Theism of which Christianity had so long been the guardian. A very eminent man of science said to a friend at this time, ' The era of Christianity is now over. Its theology is in exactly the same position as was the pagan mythology in the days of Augustus.' A certain credulous optimism, a semi-conscious faith in the human mind, as holding a course of unmixed advance to truer knowledge on all subjects, as it was unquestionably attaining to an exacter scientific knowledge of the phenomenal world, lay at the root of the credence widely given to this view of the situation. The march of science dazzled the average mind, and inclined men to ascribe a similar progressiveness to all departments of human acquirement—to artistic and religious perception as well.

Aubrey de Vere, on the other hand, had ever demurred to this unmixed optimism. He held, as we have already seen in his account of the 'May Carols,' that there was a positive religious insight in the Middle Ages, which the modern world was losing. Just as in art, architecture, or literature, a later age may lose the purer standard of appreciation of an earlier, so in religion. We see religious insight gained and lost in the story of individual lives. There is no law of unmixed advance for it in persons or in races. It varies in different ages. And it varies in different men. Human consciousness (he recognised) was limited : and an age, like an individual, might pay for absorption in one subject, by losing its powers of deeper insight in another. Thus he held that it was the part of a wise man to cling to the religious ideals of the ages of faith, and to point out the failures of the age of science in such matters. The St. Bernards and St. Bonaventures witnessed to truths as essential to a complete view of life as those proclaimed by the Huxleys and Tyndalls. Aubrey ever maintained that a certain grasp and insight dependent on the thorough assimilation of Christian ethical ideals, were being more and more lost by society in the nineteenth century, that science, instead of being utilised to correct the theological setting in which the relations of man with God have been expressed in a prescientific age, was being allowed to extend its province unnaturally, and to expel, both from the attention and from the appreciation of men, the highest truths of religion.

The heroes of his youth, Coleridge and Wordsworth, together with the hero of his later life, John Henry Newman, had been witnesses to the ideals which were being forgotten. Theological liberalism as exhibited in such a book as ' Natural Religion,' on the other hand (a book which he read with special interest), played into the hands of the dangerous tendency which was gradually permeating society. So avowedly did the works of Shelley. So to some extent did the teaching of Carlyle, in spite of the quasi-religious energy with which he combated certain excesses of modern radicalism.

The following letters illustrate Aubrey's attitude on these subjects. He writes to Lady Taylor in sadness, after a perusal of Mill's Autobiography in 1873, and passes from Mill to Mill's friend, Comte. Comte expressed, with French clearness and definiteness, the very tendency which de Vere considered so disastrous and so unphilosophical—to get rid of the mysterious 'beyond,' because it could not be proved by an empirical philosophy. The religious feelings could not be got rid of, yet an arbitrary theory of knowledge was allowed to dissociate them from the mysterious transcendental object, to the reality of which they have ever been a standing witness, and on which they have for so many centuries been exercised. The famous saying of the French philosopher was literally realised. God did not exist, therefore He had to be invented—and the Grand Être, Humanity, was proclaimed. That this procedure issued in an absurdity —feelings corresponding with something far greater than self, being applied to a god which self had fashioned—was not surprising. The wheel had 'come full circle.' Men made their own god, and the creed of science issued in a new idolatry. He expresses the result as follows :—

The Comtists, who affirm that it is only in its childhood that Humanity thinks of the things *Above,* and in its crude youth that it speculates on the things *Within,* discovering later that the only interesting things belong to the sphere of things *Around* - viz. material and social philosophy—have managed to tack on a quasi-Religion, in connection with this materialism. 'You should worship,' they say 'the Grand Être—i.e. man—not the Individual but the Abstract Race, for of God you know nothing—not even His existence.' That is, they combine Atheism with Idolatry (the ignoring of a God, and the conscious worship of a creature), and both with the adoration of that which they know to be a Thought, not an Existence. And this is what the boastful Nineteenth Century takes for a Philosophy.

In a letter to Professor Norton, dated January 24, 1874, we see Aubrey returning to the thoughts he had gained from his beloved Wordsworth, as the true antidote to the destructive religious philosophy of the Mills, and the Comtes :—

Who was that Recluse? Probably Wordsworth himself —one of the Wordsworths that might have been, had not the

Phantom been exorcised in time by another Wordsworth watching from a higher eminence, and seeing all things in a clearer light. In each of us there are so many men that might have been—each of whom would have had his own career, and after that his own Eternity! This is one of those thoughts which most press upon us that great truth—the existence of an over-ruling Providence, superseding neither the laws of Nature nor the freedom of the soul, but yet shaping all things for good—i.e. good to 'men of good will.' Even the Pagan world seems to have never lost sight of this grand idea, which, you will remember, is put forward in the 'Excursion' as the reply to the question 'Who will show us any good?' I allude to the passage in the beginning of 'Despondency Corrected,'—' One Adequate Support,' &c.

I used to wonder why in that passage, and elsewhere in this great philosophic poem, Wordsworth had not made a more distinct confession of Christianity. It may have been that in his earlier life a sort of modesty disinclined him from speaking as plainly on this high matter as he did when age had given him authority ; or perhaps he would have said that that 'assured belief' in Providence, which he affirmed the need of, could not fail to close with the belief in the great Deliverer and Saviour Who, having created man, became man, as the only *final* and complete means of redeeming him from Evil. I think I once remarked to you that the idea of the Incarnation is the idea of a Providence 'capitalised,' and at the same time raised to the Infinite. It is not only as easy, but far easier, to believe that God gives His charities in gold than in coppers, and that He led us to the Throne *also*, than that He merely extends a hand to help us as often as we trip among the pebbles on our earthly path. Reading that memorable passage in the 'Excursion' again, I find that it includes a distinct assertion of Faith, Hope, and Charity, as the means of Communion with God, and ends with the recognition of God as the All-Holy Judge, as well as the Universal Father. If Wordsworth wrote this without, at the moment, observing that he was making the Christian Confession amid the factory wheels of the Nineteenth Century, just as St. Paul had made it amid the din of the Philosophers at Athens, it is all the clearer proof that a genuine Theism is but the first rehearsal of Christianity. Theism means that humanity is lifting up its hands, at least, if not yet receiving the Crown.

Another token to me of the same truth is the mode in which the recent writers against Christianity, unlike most of those in the last century, declare war equally against Theism. The latest specimen of this is John Mill's Autobiography, in which, towards the close of his life, he makes the statement (which he seems to think too obvious to need proof) that the existence of evil in the world proves the non-existence of a Supreme Being at once infinitely Good and infinitely Powerful—having been brought up to believe that Christianity is the most noxious of all false religions; while the only ground to take against it is the impossibility of accepting Theism itself! It is very sad to me to observe the progress which this mode of thinking (or rather un-thinking) has made since the days when Tennyson's 'In Memoriam,' even while canonising 'Honest Doubt,' sang its 'Strong Son of God, Immortal Love.' In place of this sort of thing we have now another Arnold, who informs the world that what used to be worshipped as God is 'the tendency of all things to Righteousness.' Civilisation and Progress are what we are now told to believe in. Our teachers fail to tell us what effect the 'Civitas Dei' had in building up Civilisation, when the attempt of the Pagan world had ended in a corruption which needed the inundation of the 'Barbarians' to wash it away Nor do they remember that the very idea of 'Progress' had not shone on the world till it shone as a pale reflex from the Christian idea of the Church Triumphant, i.e. of a humanity not only progressive but glorified.

In September 1877, he writes to Taylor, after a visit to the places associated with the two great witnesses to spiritual truth in these latter days, the Edgbaston Oratory, and the Lake Country. He conversed with the living Newman, and meditated on the dead Wordsworth :—

Monk Coniston, Ambleside : Sept. 12, 1877.

I passed a night as usual at the Birmingham Oratory. Dr. Newman, who, by the way, particularly enquired after you,

Y

of whom he doubtless hears through Lord Blachford and the
Dean of St. Paul's, seemed in excellent health and spirits.
As usual he is busy, and has lately brought out two more
vols. of reprints, of which he made me a present. Mr.
Copeland, the *Anglican* Clergyman who has lately re-edited the
eight vols. of Dr. Newman's 'Parish Sermons,' was staying
there, and I was very glad to meet him again, and had met
him at Oxford, the time that I tarried there before joining you
in Blandford Square. He spoke with immense enthusiasm of
Dr. Newman, and said his writings would do more than anything else he could see to withstand the flood of unbelief
which, in his opinion, is advancing with such frightful swiftness
over England, and tearing up whatever has not roots, or that
is not built upon the rock beneath the sands.

I came here on Monday, having passed Sunday in going
over those haunts about Windermere, with which my Father
was familiar during his residence among them, with his tutor
in boyhood, and about which I often heard him speak before
I saw the land of lakes. I visited once more the grave of
Wordsworth, and various places about Rydal and Grasmere
to which he had taken me—and it seemed as if I could still
hear his voice beneath that of the pine-groves—almost as
continuous. What a work he did for the age! His influence
could even find a way through some cleft in the rock, to the
poor dried-up heart of John Mill, and leave there some dews
of healing; and doubtless those who have ever felt that
influence will be slower than their neighbours to rush to the
'Hog wash' (to borrow Carlyle's expression) spread before
them by the modern materialistic philosophers, who have
invented for themselves the new name 'agnostic.'

In 1878 Aubrey paid a visit to Ruskin at Coniston, in the
course of his annual pilgrimage to the Lakes. His impressions,
given in a letter to Professor Norton, of December 8, 1878, are
interesting both in themselves, and in their bearing on the
religious questions referred to in the letters just cited.

To Professor Norton

Coniston : December 8, 1878.

I am particularly pleased to write to you from this spot, and to write to-day, because it is close to our friend Ruskin's residence, and I have been seeing him here this day, as well as at his own home a few days ago.   You will be glad to have an account of him from one who sees him with a ' fresh eye ' ; and I can send you a very good one.   He seems to me very much as when I saw him last year.   They tell me he does not walk as far, and that he is sooner fatigued with head-work than he used to be ; but of this one sees nothing during a visit of a few hours.   He speaks on the same subjects as of old, with the same animation, and the same admirable felicity of diction as well as charm of imagination.   He was speaking of you with the greatest affection—also on Art, and Literature, as well as on various topics philosophical and social.   His remarks were always most suggestive and interesting, though in some cases too much influenced, as it appeared to me, by what might be called Carlyle's declamatory way of thinking. In spite of all Carlyle's originality, force and heartiness, as well as his captivating art as a Prose-Poet, I cannot but think that, in chasing *Truth*, his vehemence makes him constantly over-run and trample down the object of his pursuit ; and that many of his admirers have, through their sympathy with him, been defrauded of much, at least as valuable as aught that they have got from him.   Though Wordsworth's line ' We live by Admiration, Love, and Hope,' is one of the best ever written ; and Pope's lines

Nought to admire is all the art I know,
To make men happy and to keep them so,

are certainly among the worst, I cannot but believe that, if Ruskin had not in some matters been carried out of his natural course by an exaggerated admiration for Carlyle, he would before now have reached a happier goal.   I trust, however, that he will one day reach it.   He is a man who for me has quite a peculiar interest—he has such high aspirations, and warm sympathies and friendly confidings (things much

better than even his great abilities) and his trials have been
so many and so sad! These last are, however, to me an
additional pledge that he is watched over by that Providence
which shapes our ends, 'rough-hew them as we may'; and a
vivid, realising Faith which, as Wordsworth affirms (in his
'Despondency Corrected'), is the one only support under the
trials of life. I hope you admire that Book of the 'Excursion'
as much as I do. It seems to me far the finest piece of Moral
and Religious Philosophy ever put into poetry, and also the
noblest assertion of Theism—which in his later life the great
Bard saw completely to involve Christianity, implicitly if not
explicitly. A poem of his later life, little known, and called
'The Primrose on the Rock,' strikes me as invaluable, as the
connecting link between his religious convictions at the earlier
and later periods of his life. You would admire it much.

I rejoiced in all you said about that lovely pleasure ground
of the world, Italy, and your recent Renaissance studies.
Certainly that period was, for good and evil, a wonderful
period. On the one side a period of progress—on the other,
one of 'counter-revolution,' the old pagan spirit endeavouring
to force itself back into the Body from which it had been
exorcised, not without tearing the victim severely, so many
centuries before. Our own century is at once a development
of that Renaissance, and also a partial Renaissance of a
very different sort—a Mediæval Renaissance—of which our
friend Ruskin's favourite, *Scott*, was a chief leader. As
the centuries roll on, I suppose that each of these Renaissances
will recur—perhaps a dozen times each—mixing up in
different proportions the more durable elements of both
periods, with other elements of which we as yet little dream.
Here, for instance, comes Modern Science on the field with its
huge promises—promises which I doubt not will be more
than fulfilled—but on one condition only, viz. that the sons
of science should learn to revere (as Bacon did) a Power yet
greater, whom many of them think it a merit to insult.

The same line of thought is continued in a letter to the
same correspondent later, in connection with Norton's work
on the Mediæval Cathedrals :—

Feb. 1, 1881.

While each of these wonderful Monuments reminds us of what man can do when all his noblest intellectual faculties, political aspirations and spiritual yearnings are jointly embodied, under the guidance of the greatest thing man knows, Religion, it is remarkable that they all, at the same time, witness sadly to that great truth, viz. that, though 'to will is with us,' yet to do that which we willed is beyond us. Great as Siena Cathedral is, it is nothing to what it aspired to be. 'Half the prayer was granted,' as old Homer says. The Cathedral of Bologna was to have been far longer than St. Peter's is! Long years ago, Henry Taylor felt this sadly one night, as we stood under the stunted towers of the Cologne Cathedral. I tried to console him by suggesting that it was better that man's aspirations should go beyond his powers of execution, than that we should execute splendidly what was not worth attempting. Flaxman's remark on Canova was 'that man's hand is too great for his head.' If we have again as great an age as the Thirteenth Century with all its limitations was, that must prove an age greater yet; and doubtless we may be on the way to it—in which case we shall have nobler buildings than the world then erected, for there will be nobler things demanding expression. At present a nation's chief organ for expression is of course the Press—which, in spite of its higher aptitudes, has a special and lamentable facility in the expression of all that is not worth expressing.

The monastic life always remained to him a standing witness to the possibility of preserving the religious ideals of the thirteenth century, and we see in the following letter the feelings which a visit to a convent aroused in him :—

To the Hon. Mrs. Charles Spring Rice

Old Church: April 19, 1881.

Dearest Bessie,—Thank you very much for sending me Gem's [1] letter, which I return. It helps one to realise the daily

_____

[1] Miss G. Marshall, the sister of Mrs. Charles Spring Rice.

life that goes on around her; and to realise what is so bright,
and peaceful and good is a pleasure indeed, and something
more than a pleasure. The outward world seems to grow
more restless every day—more bustling, and more tumultuous
about things of no real importance; and by contrast the
convent life seems sometimes the only life fit for people in
their senses; or rather it would be so were it not for the
many monks and nuns 'in the world' who are the salt that
keeps that world from wholly corrupting its ways. I went a
few days ago to see a Convent of 'the Perpetual Adoration'
near Limerick, which is the more interesting because it has
grown up, like the order of the 'Little Sisters of the Poor,' in
a manner apparently accidental and unplanned, out of a little
Association of poor women who, though they could not
forsake their several employments, agreed to say the same
prayers at the same time. They seem very holy and happy.

This is of course an anxious time to my sister, as her son
is in South Africa, and we are daily expecting news. She is,
however, of a calm serene temper, and I hope will soon have
good news. Love to all. God bless you.

Affectionately yours,
AUBREY DE VERE.

The late Lord Coleridge sent to Aubrey de Vere, in these
years, a volume, privately printed, of personal records in
prose and verse. Aubrey found, in the sacredness of human
ties therein revealed, a further contribution to his philosophy
of religion :—

Curragh Chase, Adare : May 19, 1879.

My dear Coleridge,—. . . In reading the records which
you have brought together, I have seemed to myself to find
the image of a life enriched from so many sources of good,
that he who has lived it can never look back upon it (whatever its trials) without gratitude, and without also a grave
happiness, mingled with the saddest recollections it may
bequeath. It seems the image of a life which could hardly
have been except in England, and the England of this nineteenth century, the heir of many centuries of culture and of
freedom.

To me there is often a deep, though latent, biographical interest in poetry, and I have often regretted that poems were not arranged in the historical order of their composition, while myself endeavouring to make out that order as I might, and thus see the image of a life looking forth through the mist, and revealing itself the more because it did not profess to do so. Your life has included three lives—the life of letters, the public life, and the domestic life—and you at least are not among those who have to lament

I have lost the race I never ran.

I have now read all of those poems which have a biographical interest, and shall soon have read all the others ; in the meantime I find that I have marked in the table of contents, as having especially pleased me on a first reading, the following, viz. : 'To a little Child,' 'She walked along the Way of Life Alone,' 'Evening Hymn' (p. 138) 'Sursum Corda,' and the last paragraph of 'Rhoda,' which brought vividly before me the lovely scenery I enjoyed a few years ago with Henry Taylor, at Blachford. But far before all these poems I place the one entitled 'Extremus Labor.' To me that poem seems quite one of the most beautiful elegiac poems in our language. My brother, whom you may have known when he was in Parliament, exclaimed, when he had finished his perusal of it yesterday : 'This is not only a poem of extraordinary beauty and pathos, but it is a most finished work of art, and both in metre and diction is far better than what is given to us by most of our professed poets now living.' I cannot express my own opinion of it better than in his words; and I cannot but hope you will one day allow this poem to be published. I rejoice in the thought of the pleasure it would have given to my dear friend, your aunt Sara Coleridge. She would have thought with me that real good might be done by that poem if known. *Thus* to illustrate the affections is to prove that they were made for immortality, and that all the more because they cost us so much. Among the 'evidences of Christianity' I would place poems which show what great things the Human Ties are when they bloom from the stock of what Wordsworth calls

'Christianised humanity.' To have seen her by whom such a poem was inspired must ever remain a real gratification to me. It helps me to understand those noble drawings which you showed me the morning I breakfasted with you. Pray remember me to your daughter, and tell her I have not forgotten the enjoyment I derived from her beautiful music, and believe me

Most sincerely yours,
AUBREY DE VERE.

In June 1881 the positions of Carlyle and Irving respectively, in reference to the movements of religious thought in the nineteenth century, are compared and contrasted in an interesting letter to Henry Taylor :—

12 Leinster Street, Dublin : June 6, 1881.

My dear Henry,—. . . What you have recorded of Wordsworth and Coleridge from your recollections and your Autobiography will do more than avert the mischief which Carlyle's disparaging tone might have otherwise done to their memories ; and I greatly rejoice in the tribute you have paid to Mrs. Wordsworth. She deserved it.

Great allowance is due to Carlyle's harsh judgments when one remembers that dyspepsia, of which he gives such a touching description ;—but I think his sadness, increasing as it did with years, proceeded yet more from the utter inadequacy which any religious views adopted by one who has discarded Christian Faith must ever have. . . . Carlyle was deep-hearted—though not by any means, as his votaries fancy, deep-minded.

Once when I said something of this sort to Carlyle, he answered by boasting of the sense of strength, deliverance &c. which came over him when, after his long struggles of doubt, he had finally discarded Revealed Religion. I answered that I did not recognise the two states thus compared, as, in reality, the state of Belief and that of Unbelief— that long before what he called his deliverance, Faith was with him apparently but a mast blown overboard, but which a ship half capsized continued to drag at its side—and that when the last stroke of the axe had cut away that mast, the ship 'righted.' The most painful thing to me, by far, about Carlyle was the mode in which (with all his constant and fierce assertion of the claims of truth, and doubtless his theoretic devotion to truth), he seemed to be always and recklessly over-running and down-trampling both the springing field and the harvest field of the very highest truth. . . .

As Faith, of course, presupposes Humility, this apparent Pride used to give me the painful feeling that, in a happier and wiser moral condition, even if he had remained a sceptic, he would not have gone beyond doubt, and that even if he did not attain to Faith, he would at least have preserved enough of the philosophic temper to admit that the Spiritual Faculty of Faith on which, from the first, all Christendom has based man's power of holding commerce with the Spiritual Truth, might exist, as a great Reality—though in some persons, or under certain circumstances, very inadequately developed—and that with it might also exist a whole world of high intelligence, to be recognised only through that highest faculty working conjointly with the next highest, viz. Reason. To this suggestion he would only reply by stormy declamation, and by degrees I grew to think or hope that what looked like a grievous moral deficiency might be but a structural intellectual defect—that if his thought on those high themes was but intellectual declamation, this might be because he could think in no other way ; that intellectual self-possession was with him inconsistent with any energetic thought ; and that he was obliged to lash himself into a rage before he could get his mental powers to work. If this was the case, [the world mistook] for a philosopher one on whom it might safely have lavished its applause as a ' prose-poet.' *That*, I think he was, more than any other man of late times, and he turned to a rare gift his lack of the 'accomplishment of verse.' But if ever his ' gnarled and unwedgeable ' prose should be translated into a good style, like Addison's, the band of votaries will discover that in their Philosopher there was no Philosophy at all.

In that case, they will doubtless only ' move him into the

second chair '—that of Prophet. Once when he was denouncing, in a very rude way, things that I regarded as sacred, I answered, 'Mr. Carlyle, many persons regard you as a Prophet; and I do not dispute the title, on condition that it is borne in mind that in the old Hebrew days Prophets were classed in two categories—the True Prophets and the False Prophets.' He took the remark with perfect good humour. At a later time he rode over to see me when I was staying alone at Ladon House (you were living in London), and immediately began, 'I hear you are thinking of becoming a Roman Catholic. Now I give you a warning. You were born free : do not put yourself into that prison.' I answered, 'But you know I am already a Christian, and I have often heard you say that Catholicism, little as you like it, is the only form of Christianity that has any coherency, solidity, or power about it.' 'That is quite true,' he replied, 'but Protestantism is a much better thing, for all that, for Protestantism has its face turned in the right direction.' I answered, 'I have long since cast my lot with Christianity, and I grow daily to see more plainly that Catholicism is the permanent form of Christianity, and likewise that the objections brought against both, however plausible, are equally fallacious, and, for the most part, are substantially the same.'

Carlyle's immense success will never be understood, I think, till he is criticised simply as a prose-poet of the 'philosophic school of Poetry,' just as Scott, in his novels, was a great prose-poet of the narrative school. Great as was Scott's success, it would have been twice as great only that he had never formed, what is indispensable for poetry, whether metrical or in prose, viz. a powerful style. I doubt whether Scott had enough of passion about him to have succeeded in such an attempt. Carlyle had there the advantage over him. Like Burns, he had the *perfervidum Scotorum ingenium*, and the educated and uneducated peasant broke his way alike, and early, into a style full of power and free from the conventional. The other merits of style he knew and cared little about ; and he had demerits without number, borrowed from his German reading, I suppose, which, however, only added pungency to his peculiar form of prose poetry, giving an apparent depth (which was quite illusory) to his writings, flattering young readers with the notions that they understood what was too hard for their elders, and imparting to what he wrote a something characteristic, physiognomic, and grimly exciting, like that which was imparted to his discourse by the flashing eye, the reddening cheek, and the vigorous and musical Scotch brogue. When Scott (in most respects so unlike him) was gone, prose poetry was a field in which he walked without a compeer,—for 'poetical prose' is another thing altogether. Had he been capable of writing poetry in metre, he would have been distanced by rivals greater than himself.

I should think that Edward Irving, who doubtless had also the *perfervidum ingenium*, must no less have possessed a great dash of fragmentary genius about him; and he must have had much of what is higher still; or Coleridge could not have thought he discerned in him 'more of the Pauline spirit' than in any other modern man. Carlyle, I think, wholly mistook their relative positions, when he looked down with something like a good-humoured contempt on the aberrations of the old friend whom he still held dear. . . . Carlyle probably thought that flattered vanity had led Irving into at least intellectual insincerity. But it has been well remarked that a very deep and strong sincerity was evinced in Irving by the mere circumstance that he never himself spoke in the 'Unknown Tongues.' Most of the enthusiasts who thus spoke probably believed that the Inspiration had fallen on them, because they wished it to fall on them. No one wished for it more ardently than Irving; yet he never thought that he possessed the gift, although the illusion would have been most natural to one of his vivid imagination, and strong excitabilities. . . . The Irvingites whom I met have seemed to me men with a singular appreciation of high ideas, while at the same time unable even to take an interest in the authenticity of those ideas. To the question 'But are they facts?' they seem contented with the answer, 'They eminently deserve to be such, and your questions sound very captious.' Irving demanded facts as well as ideas, just because he had great intellectual sincerity, and if his fancy, tired of 'wandering o'er the world,' 'ran its bark ashore,' it was because he mistook fictions for facts. I think we are bound in candour to admit that this does not condemn him either morally or intellectually, up to the measure of the world's estimate. . . . Those who were confident that the 'Tongues' could not be a reality, as well as that they probably were not, had no more reason for their confidence than he had for his converse confidence, and belonged chiefly to that crowd which escapes credulity, not by being above it, but by being below it. In short, Irving made a great mistake, but not one that Carlyle had any right to impute either to vanity, or want of intellect, if he had had previously reason to regard him as a great-hearted and able man. Both Carlyle and Irving had been brought up in Calvinism, i.e. in a religion which combined, in a stunted and truncated form, some of the highest doctrines of Christianity, with heresies scarcely compatible with an authentic Theism.

The 'John-Knoxious' System satisfied neither of them. Carlyle extricated himself from it, apparently by discarding the good as well as the evil that belonged to it ; Irving's was an attempt, even if a blind one, to reach a something greater without being unfaithful to the truths once his. Carlyle prospers, and is applauded even by the world which he scorns and insults. He turns into a Philosophy that belief which the Savage is content to accept on instinct, viz. that Might is Right; and an age of progress admires him. Irving dies early—before he has time to learn the lessons which his experience might have taught him, and sift the chaff from the wheat ; and he is regarded with contempt, or supercilious compassion, by a world for the spiritual behoof of which he laboured to the end with zeal, though erring zeal.

A letter, amounting almost to an Essay, on Shelley was written to Henry Taylor in the following year. The letter was occasioned by an article on Shelley contributed to the 'Edinburgh Review,' by Mr. Henry Reeve. Aubrey views Shelley as the embodiment of the modern, anti-Christian movement, yet as something quasi-angelic—his pride and genius, attaining to the outcome of anti-Christian principles with the rapidity with which the high-bred racehorse reaches his appointed goal. Yet he recognises the beauty of a nature the general movement of which was determined by an underlying temper of mind which frustrated its promise. From this letter I make the following extracts :—

Curragh Chase, Adare: Dec. 12, 1882.

I was very glad to get the October number of the ' Edinboro'' which you sent me ; and I have already read the articles on ' Shelley and Mary ' and on ' Natural Religion,' both of which I was anxious to see. In the year 1833, when my sister made acquaintance with Wordsworth, they spoke of Shelley, and when she referred to some high traits of character indicated by Shelley's poetry, Wordsworth answered : ' Doubtless he was a man with beautiful dispositions ; but dispositions are one thing and character is another.' H. Reeve's article contains quite enough to show that Shelley abounded, not only in beautiful but in noble dispositions : but his character had (I think) two great natural defects. The first of these was want of robustness, for it was too much cast in a feminine mould. This impaired his genius very much, taking from it solidity, and self-possession, throwing his thoughts too much on wires, and making the emotional part of his nature proportionately too large in quantity, and too hysterical in quality. But one sees plainly that the years were making him less of a visionary and more of a man ; and whatever he lacked of robust strength was made up to him, for practical purposes, though not poetic, by the extraordinary degree in which he possessed another sort of strength, one that belongs to the Irish more than the English temperament—that of elasticity. Nothing could keep him down long.

Shelley's chief defect, however, seems to have been a lack of reverence quite extraordinary in a man of his genius—for high genius seems to be commonly as quick as mere vulgar talent is slow, in recognising the greatness of the things above us. It was so even before the full greatness of those things had been revealed to us, as far as we can bear such revelation. Plato always writes with reverence : Diogenes, who 'trampled on the pride of Plato with *greater pride*,' preferred living in a tub to living in a palace, but his whole life was a strut. There is an insolence of audacity in some passages of Shelley, on religious subjects, which admits only of two interpretations, so far as I can see—viz. something in his original cerebral organisation, doubtless augmented by circumstances that hindered proper development in some part of it . . . or else pride in quite an extraordinary degree, such as Byron, with all his sins and follies, probably was not guilty of, his prominent defect having been a much less formidable one, viz. vanity, from which Shelley, who was singularly modest, though also singularly devoid of humility, seems to have been exempt, as he was from everything coarse or unrefined. Which of these solutions is the true one we can never know; but there seems to me no abstract improbability in the former. . . .

I never can make out whether Shelley was a Fallen Angel still fierce with the pride that caused that fall, or an Angel in duresse struggling with sad limitations. Something angelic there certainly was about him, something that I recognised from the first day that I read his poetry, and of which I never see the slightest trace in his imitators, and never saw a trace of in Byron during my boyhood's day of Byronic delusion, though I fancied there was a good deal of the Titan about him. This angelic quality, limited and deflected as it is in Shelley, manifests itself to me, not only in the emotional parts of his poetry, but in its intellectual processes. There is a marvellous intuitive power about its intelligence, a most subtle, and wholly consistent discernment, and following up, of principles, which many readers have missed, because they took it for granted that errors such as his were incompatible with such gifts—which is to forget that in the region of things spiritual, and, to a large degree, of things moral, all errors are compatible with all degrees of intelligence, if you presuppose the absence of humility, and of the veneration which generates humility. His intelligence had also a keen logic about it : this gift of logic has been denied to him by some critics because his conclusions are often so wild and injudicious. But the logical faculty far from being one with judgment, seldom, when largely developed, co-exists with judgment, whose processes are of a practical, not syllogistic, order ; and when a man's premises are wild, he will reach wild conclusions with a speed (like a racehorse's) proportioned to his strength and breed. I observe that nearly everything now said by the ' wild ' writers on politics, ethics, or religion, were contained implicitly in Shelley's principles, and put forward with infinitely more power by him—for which reason they make a prophet of a youth half-inspired, and yet wholly ignorant of that highest knowledge which is most needful to man. This is not consistent with the notion that Shelley's was an incoherent mind. I observe also that one of his characteristic gifts was good sense, which he always exercised for a friend, with skill, even as regards matters of business, but which he seldom exercised for himself. This gift he had interdicted himself from the use of, in connection with the highest matters of spiritual moment, by that one act of moral insanity committed in his boyhood, by which he trampled Belief underfoot. . . .

While so frequently assailing, not this or that religious doctrine, but religion itself, which he mistook for a moral tyranny, and while denouncing the connecting link between man and all religion, viz. Faith, which he mistook for weakness, Shelley could, notwithstanding, never have passed out of the region of religious things and thoughts, and turned to other matters. A religion, strong in its divine truth, or a quasi-religion splendid with illusive beauty, though at heart essentially irreligious, was to him a necessity, for neither material things, nor human affections sufficed to him ; and in frivolous matters, or worldly interests he had no concern. He mused as habitually as the most religious man on some great Deliverance for the human race ; but in his scheme the Deliverer was to be, not a God-man, but a Man-god, not a Redeemer descending to earth in compassionate humiliation, but a Titan fighting his way upwards, and hurling mountains against the Heavenly seats. ' Prometheus Unbound ' is thus the Shelleyan Gospel, and throughout it we find ideas at once exactly parallel with Christian, and exactly their opposite.

The victory announced by Shelley is to be that of science, and fearless revolt against all authority, and all in Religion that implies veneration. . . .

The two schemes of thought are opposite, but both are coherent ; and the erroneous scheme was not the illogical babble of a visionary, but the challenge of the false prophet of song.   As the one scheme had to denounce impiety, unbelief, pride, impenitence, so the other had to brand Religion as superstition and tyranny, belief as credulity and weakness, humility as cowardice and insincerity, and to leave no place for penitence.   All this Shelley clearly and openly proclaimed : what he had not apparently even a glimpse of, was the real character and the immeasurable grandeur of a scheme of thought dealing with all those elements included in his own scheme, but dealing with them in an opposite manner, and subjecting them to other and higher truths than those which he had cognisance of.

Shelley's views on these subjects, as well as on political, were anticipations of the views now put forward by the most admired Rationalistic writers, without the tenth part of the power and beauty with which he clothed them, and in an equivocal language which he never would have deigned to use, and which makes them ten times more formidable.   By nothing has this been more brought home to me than by the admirable review of ' Natural Religion ' in the same number of the ' Edinburgh ' which reviews ' Shelley and Mary.'

. . . . What is this new Religion which is to supersede the present Christianity without doing it any injury, while leaving man a mind without light, or a heart without hope, or a life without guidance ; and which is to remain fully entitled to the august titles of Theism and Christianity ?

It consists of three distinct but blended elements, three constituent schemes of thought [the Religion of Nature, the Religion of Beauty, and the Religion of Humanity].   Each of these three was launched into the modern world sixty years ago by Shelley, and illustrated with a splendour and persuasiveness no other modern writer can approach : but it was not passed off as a Religion, because Shelley, being a coherent thinker (though one who started from false premises), knew well that it was not a Religion either new or old, but the denial and repudiation of all Religion, and the substitution for it of something which he deemed to be better, because, while it taught men to admire everything, it admonished them also to worship nothing.

These three Religions of the Future, the author of 'Natural Religion' says, are to constitute the future great Religion which has cast off the 'Supernatural,' which has renounced all *Dogma* (a word that means just the same as *Doctrine*) and the moral system of which is to be so vague that, though it cannot tolerate the 'worldling,' or men who have not fine sensibilities, yet it has ample room for those who regard 'the pruderies of virtue as the greatest hindrance' of real virtue, and who consider that we have not yet a large enough inductive basis, as the Edinburgh Reviewer says, 'to construct any moral system.' . . .

It seems quite a heartrending thing that, after eighteen centuries of Christianity, persons who claim the name of Christian believe that 'Christianity' is a thing which may *mean* all the doctrines of the Creed, and need not include belief in a God (for a God, not Personal, can be no more a God than the law of gravitation is God), nor the belief in an immortal Soul. There seems something appalling in the thought that the question should be made to rest on such considerations as whether mankind could, or could not, retain certain *elevated and poetic emotions* when they had discarded their God, and their Redeemer. It is as if God had no rights in the matter, or as if man, after professing for centuries to serve God, need have no respect for God's rights, and had only to ask whether he (man) could not get the imaginative excitements he was used to at a cheaper rate, and warm his hands contentedly before the embers of a dying fire, though the sun had been blotted out of heaven. How the heart of man must have been shrinking up into microscopical littleness to render such an appeal to his intellect possible. If there is no God, say our new prophets, remember that the Material Universe is a grand substitute for one. If there has never been a Saviour content yourself with the thought that there is a saving charm in

z

flowers, art, poetry, and benevolence. You are where you were. This seems to me the worst sign of the times we have yet had, and the worst omen for the future. H. Reeve has earned our gratitude for the manly protest the 'Edinburgh Review' has made against it.

Again in 1884 we have the record, in a letter to Henry Taylor, of a pilgrimage to two shrines—one of a dead and one of a living prophet :—

Monk Coniston : October 8, 1884.

I have passed two days at Lord Coleridge's, immensely enjoying the haunts of Coleridge, the Poet, in his youth, and much admiring the noble house, built on the site of the old residence, and preserving the best part of it, while, among the other additions, is that of a library, seventy feet long. Opposite my window, and within a stone throw of it, is the grand College Church, which I looked at for at least an hour before I went to bed, as it shone in the moonlight. Coleridge had two of his sons, with their wives and children, with him, while his sister lives close by in what they call the Manor House. . . . I found Cardinal Newman well in health, and as clear as ever in mind, but not strong. He made very friendly enquiries about you. The present political state of the country distresses him much ; and his sympathies seem strongly with the House of Lords, and opposed to all revolutionary courses.

The 'eighties,' saw the renewal of the Irish question in an acute form. The Parnell Movement, Gladstone's Land Bill of 1881, the Phœnix Park murders, the labours of the Land League, 'boycotting' and the 'plan of campaign,' the Nationalism of the Irish priests, the Papal interference—these were all the further developments of the Jacobinical tendency which had exercised Aubrey's attention in the 'sixties.' We find throughout his letters the same principles as in the earlier ones—his sympathy with his countrymen, his opposition to all that savoured of Jacobinism, and to all concession wrung by agitation. He preached to the clergy the duty of loyalty. He urged on the Government the question of university education for Catholics. He opposed the secularistic principle in education, as he had in the case of the Irish Church, and urged that, at all events, those who preferred it should be allowed to benefit by State endowments, without being compelled to accept a secularistic training which they disapproved.

He had felt throughout, like many other Irishmen, that the refusal to legislate in accordance with the requirements of the population, where the Irish claim was so obviously just, was the first stage in the inevitable sequence, oppression, retaliation, panic, undue concession.

' I always said,' he writes to a friend, ' that if Statesmen continued to resist just demands, like that for a Catholic University Education, and wise concessions, such as Glebes and Parochial Houses for the Catholic Priests, they would end in making nearly unlimited concessions to demands which, far from averting " Repeal," will tend to bring it about.'

On the general situation, at the beginning of 1881, he writes as follows to a friend :—

January 14, 1881.

Things remain in a state in this country which, if allowed to last much longer, must eventuate in the rapid *Jacobinising* of a people till lately perhaps the most Catholic in Europe ; a catastrophe which I have long looked upon as among the possibilities, and as a thing far worse than the restoration of the Penal Laws would be. All parties have been deeply in fault ; the agitators for their knavery, the people for their foolishness, the Government for allowing sedition free scope, and the Priests for joining the Meetings and sanctioning Jacobinism. You will find in to-morrow's ' Tablet ' a letter on this subject written by me, and signed ' Catholicus.' It is written for the Priests, though it hardly names them, in the hope of getting them to avail themselves of that last chance of retrieving the past offered to them by the ' New Departure,' afforded by the Government's late declaration of its policy.

They may use that opportunity for breaking with the Tenant League, and endeavouring to separate the Farmer Class from it. Otherwise they must go on with a Jabobin Movement till it turns on them and devours them. . . .

To his cousin, Edward Calvert, he writes on January 31 :—

A secular Priest once told old Lord Monteagle that the Parish Clergy disliked the intrusion of the Monks for reasons like those which made an Anglican Clergyman dislike the Methodist Preacher. As among the English Clergy there is a 'two-bottle orthodoxy,' so in Ireland there is a ' two-tumbler orthodoxy,' which is *faithful* in the carrying out of a *low* standard, but which looks on the introduction of a high standard as disparaging to itself. While the Seculars of this Diocese have commonly gone with the Tenant League movement, the Limerick Redemptorists speak of it with horror, and say that wherever they hold their Missions they find it is demoralising and decatholicising the people. What Mr. O'Conor says as to the danger of Mr. Parnell's movement producing disunion between the Priests and the people is profoundly and alarmingly true. It is partly to shun this danger that the Priests have been attending the Jacobinical meetings, and blessing the banners of injustice and wrong. Of course the danger is only thus deferred to be aggravated later. If they wait till a rising takes place, and then shrink back, the people will cry out 'You joined us because you were afraid for your dues, and you desert us because you fear for your lives.' One of the Priests near this, who constantly denounced the Tenant League to me as destroying the character of the Irish people, has just taken the chair at one of their meetings—of course from cowardice.

Writing to Henry Taylor he comments on Mr. Forster's appointment as Chief Secretary :—

Limerick : May 21, 1880.

. . . I have a very high opinion of Forster. In his conduct of the English Education question he showed a very remarkable independence, and devotion to principles in resisting the bigotry of the Secularists, who wanted to create an exclusive ascendency in favour of non-religious Education. He insisted on establishing fair play between the two sorts of education, and letting the people make their choice. They generally preferred religious Education, and the 'Liberal' Secularists, who were more popular than the People (as some have been described as '*plus Catholique que le Pape*') were immensely displeased at their having been allowed a choice, and Forster's seat was in serious danger. I believe he has come to Ireland, though fully entitled to a much higher place in the Government, simply in the hopes of doing good, and also that he is more likely to do good there than anybody else ; though not unlikely to make concessions to the agitators on the Land question, which I should rather not see made. I have been entirely opposed to nearly the whole of the demands made by the Irish Agitators in my time, except those that relate to University Education. To have settled that question long since in a manner consistent with the desires and conscientious convictions of the immense majority of Irish parents, who approve of religious education for the same reasons as induce most English parents to prefer it, would have been in the highest sense conservative policy, and would have detached from the agitators their most influential, though not most numerous, supporters. . . .

I am glad Una went to see old Carlyle, and I am sure it was a pleasure to him. I did not know that Southey had lent him a helping hand when he wanted one. Many instances, such as those of Landor and Elliot, prove that his strong political opinions did not prevent his having friendly relations with those who wholly differed from him. Dowden's little book shows that, though Southey's political judgments were often erroneous (I dislike the word 'narrow,' because it is so commonly used in a rhetorical if not tricky way), yet a great many of them were what are now called 'enlightened,' and have by degrees been acted on to a very large extent. I am sorry that a brief letter against the Atheists and Materialists of the day, which appeared a year ago in the papers with Carlyle's signature, was not written by him. I think that such a protest with his name, against a philosophy to which he might well have applied an epithet he was fond of in old times, viz. 'hog's wash,' might have been more useful than elaborate arguments to some persons. It is a great thing to help people to trust their higher *instincts*.

The attitude of the majority of Irish Bishops came upon him as a great disappointment. He writes thus to Mr. John O'Hagan :—

Curragh Chase, Adare : February, 1881.

The recent Resolutions of the Bishops at Maynooth were a painful surprise to me. I had hoped that they must have seen by this time that their flocks needed serious moral guidance, unless the sheep were to be allowed to be changed by that political Circe, Mr. Parnell, into a 'herd of swine' and induced to run violently down 'a steep place into the sea.' The 'Resolutions' said not a word about Duties, but spoke strongly about Rights, respecting which the people seem for some time to have been sufficiently awake. They complimented the people likewise on their justice and generosity ; which will be cited doubtless by the Tenant Leaguers as a compliment to them : since it is their proceedings which have filled the ears of the world. I console myself, however, by the hope that the Bishops may be only reserving their advice in order to give it with more effect a little later. If it is much longer deferred it will come too late ; and the result will be the Jacobinising of the Irish Race at both sides of the Atlantic. . . .

Miss Edgeworth once admonished Lord Monteagle, then a young man, to be on his guard as to the use of any language which might stir up in the Irish nature a certain element which it has in common with the French, adding, that, though a gentle and devout people, they might, under circumstances, be very rapidly hurried on to excesses like those of the French Revolution. In the Irish there are two characters ; and principles like those lately enunciated would soon elicit the lower, and smother the higher.

As regards, not the methods for seeking Land Reforms, but the nature of the Reforms to be sought, I cannot feel sure how far we should be of one mind; but then *that* is a wholly and entirely different question. I am for Lord Dufferin's suggestion, respecting a measure very large, but gradual in its operation, and just to all parties, for the creation of a Peasant Proprietary. If half Ireland came by degrees into the hands of Peasant Proprietors I should see in this nothing but benefit to all classes; but the operation should be gradual as well as just, or it would prove the ruin of many among those raised to a position for which they had not yet acquired the proper aptitudes. I should also be in favour of a great Court of *Appeal*, not Initiation, accessible to all on the cheapest terms, and to which *all* alleged wrongs, rising out of the Land Tenure relations, might be referred. A court of *Appeal*, not of *Initiation*, would, in my opinion, provide for *exceptions*, without making 'free contracts' cease to be the general rule. Thus, the authority of parents is the rule; but cases of cruelty are dealt with as exceptional. . . .

You well know the views I take of Anglo-Irish History, during *the whole* of the previous period. As regards the future, it seems to me plain (1) that 'different parts of Ireland have to be dealt with in very different ways; and (2) that throughout Ireland we need two things, viz. a *permanent* basis of sound principles applicable to a normal state of things, and also *temporary* measures to meet what is abnormal in our present condition.

His impressions on the first draft of Gladstone's Land Bill are given in a letter to Henry Taylor :—

Curragh Chase, Adare : April 13, 1881.

. . . . That Bill is a marvellous piece of dexterity in the way in which it at once maintains, at least verbally, and speculatively also, the principle of ' Freedom of Contract,' and yet provides for so many exceptional interferences with it as to bestow upon the tenant the practical effects of the three principles (the 3 F's) they contend for, without directly conceding those principles themselves. But it remains to be seen whether the *dexterous* maintenance of a sound principle will produce the same results as a simple and unequivocal maintenance of it would have produced. His land measure of 1870 by no means conceded (as I think I proved last year in a letter to the 'Times') the principle that the Tenant has a 'co-Proprietorship' in the land. But it did concede a right which might easily be confounded with the right not conceded, and the result has been the creation of demands founded on a principle claimed as conceded in 1870—demands which he now defers to, but which will not be the last demands. Mr. Gladstone does not perceive the practical effect of such legislation, because in him the logical faculty is predominant, not the judgment. His is a thirteenth-century Scholastic mind, which has thrown itself on the political sphere because he lives in the nineteenth century. This is, I think, the reason that so many of his political acts, while perfectly conscientious, have been a surprise to friend and foe alike, like the Knight's move at Chess. Probably, however, after the Irish Agitation has been so long allowed to go ahead, it will be considered necessary to pass his measure. Its working will depend much on the course subsequently taken, as to the putting down, or not putting down, sedition in Ireland. The Irish are like children—easily ruled unless you give them their head.

To Miss Harriett Calvert

Curragh Chase: March 2, 1882.

The deplorable misconduct of two successive Governments, in allowing the Land League to take its way, has demoralised the people; and they by this time hold, probably with entire sincerity, the Socialistic and Jacobinical principles put forward by the agitators, including two of the Bishops. With the exception of these two, the Roman Catholic Clergy have behaved much less ill than last year, and not only, I think, because the Land Meetings have been put down at last, but because they had become seriously alarmed by the irreligious as well as seditious spirit growing up everywhere. Of course, as the people still keep the Faith, we may hope that they will return to the moral and social principles that follow from it; but this will not be unless they are ruled with a strong hand;

and every day one sees more plainly that Gladstone is a Radical at heart, and has audacity enough for any course which the necessities of Radicalism may require.

In May came the Phœnix Park tragedy, which confirmed Aubrey's worst fears as to the spirit of Jacobinism which was getting hold of a section of his countrymen. He wrote as follows to Miss Arnold Forster, whom he had known in the days of Mr. Forster's Chief-Secretaryship, and who afterwards married his nephew Robert Vere O'Brien :—

Curragh Chase : May 9, 1882.

My dear Miss Forster,—I cannot help adding a few words to my letter of yesterday, to tell you how deeply grieved I am at the affliction into which this terrible tragedy in Dublin has, I am sure, thrown you and yours. I met Mr. Burke one day at your house, and was so much struck by him that I much hoped that we should meet again. No one could see him without saying to himself 'that is *a good man.*' You were doubtless very intimate with him, and with his poor sister, of whom I heard so interesting an account. It is she, not her brother, who is now to be pitied.

You were probably also intimate with Lord and Lady F. Cavendish ; and here, again, it is the survivor and the bereaved one who is to be pitied. I met her at dinner at Mr. Denison's, one day last year, and was much impressed by a sort of sweet nobleness that I observed in her.

I fear that this dreadful occurrence (when I first heard the rumour, I thought it must be either unfounded or at least much exaggerated) will have been a great shock to your mother, and to all of your family—perhaps as great as could have come to you without a connection with one of your own family.

The political result of this crime must be deeply adverse, and may be fatal, to the detestable cause it was intended to support.

Believe me, most sincerely yours,
AUBREY DE VERE.

The following criticism on Gladstone's mind and policy was written to Taylor two months later :—

July 24, 1882.

I do not think that even those who regard Gladstone as a man of high genius and lofty aspirations ought, on that account, to repose any considerable *faith* in the solidity of his political judgment, and accept for that reason what they would otherwise condemn. The character of his intellect is, I have always thought, scholastic, not political. . . .

Moreover, he has a ductility which, even when he does not change his principles, makes him apply them in different, and even opposite, ways at different times. His mind swings round as it seems to me in a manner marvellously sympathetic with the movements of his will, which last is very much moulded by circumstance, imperious and audacious as it is in action amid all his changes. Whatever opinion he takes up he at once fortifies by all the resources of a most versatile intelligence, and advocates with an impassioned dialectical skill, and with a confidence wholly out of proportion to the grounds on which it rests—a confidence which by his admirers, as well as others, is regarded as an intense sincerity, and which gives him the strength that comes from sincerity when men less singularly constituted would have to struggle with the weakness that comes of instability. I recognise in him the 'various talents,' but not the 'single mind,' which your poem attributes to Southey. He seems to me to have, moreover, a marvellous habit of self-deception, which is not incompatible with a fitful spirit of self-sacrifice. I think thus that he is rather a man to give a partial admiration to, than to rest any considerable faith upon. There are brilliant streaks of genius in his mental structure, I admit ; but I cannot regard him as, in a high sense, a man of genius—otherwise in his numberless speeches and essays there must have been a greater number of passages rendered capable of reaching posterity, either by depth of wisdom or strength of expression. He seems to me to be singularly destitute of that insight into principle which belongs to high genius. . . .

He seems again to me to be without that instinctive know-

ledge of human nature which belongs to high genius. Thus
he evidently thought that a pacification of Ireland through the
efforts of Parnell, when liberated, and of others, imprisoned
because 'steeped to their lips in treason,' would have the same
effect as a pacification by the victory of Law over Lawlessness.
... Such a pacification as he proposed would have done harm,
not good. Another quality that belongs to high genius is
'The Inspiration of Common Sense.' Gladstone seems to me
to have far less of this form of inspiration than the mere average
man has. At one moment he tells the Irish people that every
eviction is 'a sentence of death,' at another, he tells landlords that he can do nothing for them if they do not assert
their rights—that is, evict those who openly profess the
'repudiation of rent' principle; in a day or two he forgets
what he has said, and when in a year or two he finds that the
Irish Land Leaguers, engaged in what we call murders, and
they call a guerilla war, have not forgotten his words, he
fancies that the mischief is done only because they have put an
ingenious interpretation upon those words. He allows a scarcely
masked rebellion to go on for a year and a half, and then
imagines that he can restore order by concessions so enormous
that all Ireland attributes them to fear alone, and yet not large
enough to satisfy a Jacobin appetite. He believes in 'Freedom
of Contract,' but believes also that he can legislate in opposition to that great *Law* of the world Economic, with no more
serious consequences than would follow from casting aside
some trite old maxim. There is to be a great flood of words,
and out of it is to arise 'a new created World.'

He is at this moment granting imperial money to pay the
arrears of Irish Tenants who had refused to pay their rent,
in most cases, because forbidden to do so by a 'Manifesto'
against such payment, issued by the Land League, and carried
into practical effect by a body of outrage-mongers who stand
to that Land League simply in the relation in which the
Executive always stands to the Legislature. He does not
see that this is the triumph of the Land-Leaguers, who may
now fairly say that they are not only putting a large slice of
the Irish Landlord's property, but that of the English tax-
payer also, into the pocket of the Irish Tenant, whose merit

is his faith in the promise of men that openly said in Parliament that they had substituted the 'unwritten Law of the Land League for the Law of the Land.' Their followers will naturally say : 'If after two singularly prosperous seasons, we have imposed this tax upon England, who shall resist our claim when the next bad season comes, and we cannot pay rent?' Those who have paid will say : 'We have imperilled our lives by keeping our engagements, in spite of the Boycotters, to see those who made "the Queen's Writ cease to run" (as the Judges complained) rewarded by having a great part of their arrears cancelled, and half of the rest paid by the Government?' Now, in carrying this Arrears Bill, Gladstone is a true logician; for it is in strict sequence with his Land Act of last year, founded on the discovery of the 'Co-Proprietor' principle, and the undiscovering of the Free Contract principle—they are parts of a whole; and those who swallowed the horse can swallow his tail. But 'Common Sense' would have told Mr. Gladstone what it tells every Irish Proprietor, and every Irish peasant, respecting the consequences of such legislation.

Mr. Gladstone has more of genius than Mr. Disraeli, and more of generous aspiration, but, as regards Statesmanship, the Democrat who became a Tory, but never quite knew whether he preferred to improve Toryism or to 'improve it off the face of God's earth,' had much in common with the Tory who has become a Radical, while all his religious sympathies must continue to be with authority and antiquity. Neither of them ever really belonged to the party of which fortune by way of a practical joke made him the head —the party he has 'educated' alike out of its principles and traditions. . . . I never was either a Whig or Tory, in a party sense, and held their doctrines only so far as those doctrines were held in common by both, but I respected both of England's great historical parties, and I think it an anomaly that they should both be destroyed by the heads they had so unfelicitously set upon bodies of another type, for the profit of men, whose aspiration is to change 'an old and haughty nation proud in arms' into a little America. Of this I am certain, viz. what is done in Ireland will be done in England, later but ere long, unless England comes to regard the separation of the two countries, and her own consequent degradation to the rank of a third-rate power, as the lesser evil of the two.

As for the difficulties of an alternative course, I admit that difficulties there were, occasioned by the preceding Tory Government not having put down with a strong hand the illegal meetings which the Irish had been holding for many months; but a little firmness, blended with timely remedial measures, would have removed those difficulties. In place of losing a year, Gladstone should have, in 1880, passed a measure to enlarge the ' Bright Clauses,' and render easier the gradual creation of peasant proprietors, by helping farmers who had laid by money, and thus proved that they were exceptional men, to buy their farms. This would have rendered property more secure, by widening the base of the Pyramid, and have helped the landlord class far more than any empirical tinkering of the Land Tenure can do. . . .

But the primary duty of an Executive is to execute the existing law; and to allow of its being superseded by the ' Unwritten Law,' for any purpose, was as completely ' doing evil that good might come,' as any of the Land League proceedings.

I return you both your own letter to Lord Grey, and his to you. The view I have expressed will show you how strongly I go along with nearly all that he has said. He takes his stand *super antiquas vias.* No others, I am sure, are solid ; and a spirited charge into an Irish bog is one of the last enterprises likely to end profitably. Adieu at last.

Aubrey wrote a pamphlet on the situation, copies of which he sent to Cardinal Newman, now in his eighty-fifth year, and to Matthew Arnold. The replies of both are interesting :—

February 6, 1885.

My dear Aubrey de Vcre,—I am a very bad person to ask for an opinion on a political question. I was painfully struck with your concluding pages, but they went beyond politics. The truth is that since 1832 I have no political views at all. I then thought what called itself the Reform Bill was a revolution—indeed Lord John so called it—and what you now truly call a Revolution is that same old Act which was then by violence and blood-and-gutter articles in the [press] effected, though it has taken fifty years and more perhaps, to carry it out.

You will say that patriots should make the best of things, but that is the duty of politicians. They have done so, and to have staved it off for fifty years is no bad work; but *I* could as easily command a force in the Soudan, as give an opinion how to meet the Radical party. I think your Pamphlet a very good one, but I am ignorant of the elements of the question. I did not know what 'Proportional representation' meant, or 'Single member districts' till your Pamphlet told me; what I have felt all along most keenly since I went to Ireland is that, if a revolution was in progress in England, much more, alas, was it making its way in Ireland.

Yours affectionately,
JOHN H. Card. NEWMAN.

Athenæum Club, Pall Mall : February 10, 1885.

My dear Aubrey de Vere,—I have read your pamphlet with interest, and others too will read it with interest; but if you look at what I have said about Ireland in the last number of the 'Nineteenth Century,' you will see I do not believe in government of Ireland by the 'Loyalists.' The 'Loyalists' have had their chance, and they have missed it; I see no solution now but self-government for Ireland, imperial matters being reserved.

I do not believe the landed class will retain power even in Scotland and England, nor do I wish them to retain power, for their virtue, as a political force, is used up. But it is in Ireland that this class will first disappear. Ten thousand perils and difficulties beset the future of Ireland, and of England's relations with her; but the remedy for them is to be found, I think, in courses not yet tried—hardly even suggested.

Most truly yours,
MATTHEW ARNOLD.

A fitting pendant to the preceding letters is the following, to Henry Taylor, when Gladstone's ultimate direction on Irish affairs was becoming unmistakeable :—

Curragh Chase, Adare, Ireland : February 4, 1886.

. . . I suppose there is no doubt that Gladstone is now to be regarded as a Home Ruler? Will he be able to take the bulk of his Whig friends with him on the ground that he is 'the Grand Old Man,' an accident which seems to me to have resulted chiefly from some of his Whig Colleagues having changed into 'Grand Old Women,' and loved him 'not wisely but too well.'

Did you foresee that Gladstone would go as far as he has lately done? Did anyone?

Before he actually proposes a measure of Home Rule, I think he will wait a little, partly to keep as many of the Whigs with him as possible, till the country has got used to him in his new character, but chiefly to prepare for his Home Rule Measure by creating a necessity for it, and then appealing to that necessity, a thing which he has already done several times. The way to create this necessity would be to create first 'an elective Executive' for Ireland, under the name of 'local Self-Government' or 'County Courts.' Such an 'Executive' would of course be practically a Legislature without the responsibilities of an avowed Legislature. He could then say to Parliament 'Having already conceded the *reality*, why fight about the *name* of a Dublin Parliament?'

A year after the excitements incident to the Home Rule campaign had subsided, Aubrey de Vere published (in 1887) a volume of 'Legends and Records of the Church and Empire,' followed a little later by 'Medieval Records and Sonnets.' Many of the poems in both volumes had been published before. But they were now grouped anew and supplemented in each case by other poems, giving a unity to each volume. To both groups he prefixed an explanatory analysis of his theme. Those inexhaustible subjects, the

gradual permeation of Christian ideals and beliefs throughout
the civilisation of the Western nations, and the subsequent
partial realisation of a Christian pólity, are dwelt on in these
introductions.

In the first he traces the infusion of Hebrew Theism into
Roman civilisation ; its development in the doctrines of the
Trinity and Incarnation—the former deepening man's sense
of its mystery, the latter bringing it closer to his heart and
intelligence. To the Hebrew and Roman element was added
the Greek element in the theology of the Alexandrian school.

Later on this equipment of the Church was taken over by
a new blend of races, which brought new blood and energy
to the task of welding the triple forces of Christianity—the
Hebrew, the Roman, and the Greek—into a polity recalling
the name and prestige of the ancient Empire.

The profound interest of that period [he writes] proceeds
mainly from the varying relations in which the old Roman
Empire and the barbaric races stood to each other. The
eventual union of the southern with the northern races
resulted in the Holy Roman Empire of Charlemagne. The
memory of the earlier empire had not only survived, but
impressed the barbaric races themselves with an awe which
they could never shake off. Those who had not feared to
storm the walls of Rome scarcely dared to look up at its
monuments. Their chiefs were less proud of their triumphs
than of some titular decoration received from an emperor of
the East, whose power did not extend beyond his palace. . . .
In spite of their wrongs at the hands of Rome, they felt that
the Roman Empire was a thing too great to die. In Gaul,
and especially along the borders of the Rhine, rose many a
stately city, built by old Roman Coloni, which proved that the
Roman civilisation and the barbaric races were not incapable
of coalescing. In proportion as the latter became Christian, a
disposition grew among them to regard a universal realm under
an Emperor as the completed condition of humanity ; for
such a spiritual realm was presented to them in the Church,

and such a spiritual head in the successor of St. Peter. A civil, seemed to them the complement of an ecclesiastical, unity, as centuries later, it seemed to St. Bernard and Dante.

Still more were those who had once lived under the protection of the Empire reminded of their loss, while successively harried by the aggression of rival barbaric chiefs. They recalled to memory that wonderful 'Pax Romana' which had given rest to the world for two centuries after Augustus, the prosperity which that peace had produced, and the security ensured by the Roman Law to all who were willing to worship the 'Dea Roma.' Could not such an Empire be restored under Christian conditions?

The second volume—dealing with the period after the Holy Roman Empire was an accomplished fact—had its lesson for our own times. He returns in it to his favourite thought, that the grasp of, or appreciation of, high moral ideas could be lost by an age just as artistic, or literary taste may become depraved. With no tendency whatever to question the material, and in some respects mental, progress of the race, he never forgot the very trite truth that intellectual capacity is not goodness. True, to admire a noble standard is not to act up to it. But to cease to admire it is to make its attainment impossible. And it was in this region of lowering of ideals that, as we have already seen, he almost unreservedly disparaged our own times in comparison with the 'ages of faith.' His aim like that of Chateaubriand in the 'Génie du Christianisme' was to awaken his readers to the debt we owe to Christianity, both in what we possess and take for granted, without recognising its original source, and in what we have ceased to appreciate and lost through callousness. The introduction is in this instance a remarkably characteristic indication of the thoughts of the poet :—

The greatest of man's losses [he writes] is that which he incurs from his deplorable power of growing callous to that which for centuries the humblest could appreciate. The

A A

descendants of those who built our cathedrals could see nothing in Gothic architecture ; and there was a time when Dante and Shakespeare scarcely survived except as names. We still make our boast of Columbus and Copernicus ; but we sometimes forget that these were mediæval men, and men specially imbued with the mediæval spirit. They were the two great gates between the world of the Middle Ages and our own world of more extended knowledge and individual freedom. . . .

The Middle Ages still survive among us more than we know, in their instincts of honour and affection ; what was most special to them is therefore more perceived by us when we compare them with earlier times which held in them but a faint promise of better things. They were eminently Christian ages ; and this characteristic may perhaps not unfitly be indicated in poetry, since its mood is the indicative mood rather than the imperative, and since it prefers to suggest rather than to dispute. Christian *ideas*, as distinguished from Christian law and the details of doctrine, were far more alien from Pagan ideas in the days of old Christendom than they are among the modern nations. Many of them would have had no meaning for the Pagan intelligence, and would have been repulsive to Pagan sympathies.

Life to the earnest mediæval Christian was both a lighthearted and a very serious thing. It found a type in the vigil. The Believer watched and waited for a future, both far off and near him—a future which moulded his present. That future rendered hope to him a great necessity and a great duty, as well as a constant support. It was the Pagan philosopher's boast that he made the best of the present, and ignored the uncertain future. To him that future was a nightmare. But to ignore the future is to renounce hope, and without hope life can be, at best, but a good-humoured despair. The Pagan too commonly regarded life as a superficial thing because he was superficial himself ; and Greek art was, except when at its highest, often at once epicurean and hard-hearted. To live was to the Pagan to glide swiftly over an ice-plain which might at any moment break, if a weight were stayed upon it long. The tomb was an opprobrium to be disguised with gay sculptures; and the dead body a scandal, to be burnt. To the mediæval mind life was a deep thing. To it the Divine was ever glancing forth from things which to the 'mind of the sense' seemed but trifles. To deal kindly with a leper was to clothe and feed a God. To scandalise one of Christ's 'little ones' might be to forfeit a deathless inheritance.

Yet to the mediæval man life was a light-hearted thing also. It was so because as regards spiritual matters his heart was at rest; because carefulness in them left a narrower place for worldly care; because no seriousness was squandered on trifles; because mortification averted satiety. A true poet tells us of 'the men of old' that :—

> They went about their gravest deeds
> Like noble boys at play.

To that characteristic of the Middle Ages we owe largely those exquisite delineations of youth, so full of loveliness and of gladsomeness, which charm us in the pictures of the early masters. At that time youthfulness often survived in old age, which was not then regarded as life's inevitable frustration and joy's confutation, but rather as the rest of a quiet hope (like the Church's feast named 'Expectatio'), beside the gates of perpetual youth.

In the pictures of saints there is also doubtless often a profound sadness, but it was a noble sadness, not a merely negative one, that of cowardice or exhaustion, such as in old times caused the term 'miserable,' like our word 'wretch,' to be a term of reproach. Earth was then regarded as an exile, not a 'Patria.' To the Christian the great things were the Invisible things: but from this it followed that the Christian 'moved about in worlds not realised' by the senses, that they might be the better realised by the soul. Such worlds must have been phantom worlds but for those three angels of man's life, Faith, Hope, and Charity, which moved among them and irradiated them. Paganism and Christianity had each of them its Beatitudes; but they were different Beatitudes : the Pagan's aspired only to a 'mens sana in corpore sano'; the Christian's were those of the Spirit— sorrow here, but a Comforter, and hereafter the Vision of God.

But it was not on heaven alone that the mediæval mind was set. 'The Meek shall inherit the earth' because the most heavenly minded can best appreciate it.

'We live by admiration, hope, and love,' and in those qualities the nobler of the mediæval men were especially rich. It was their happy gift to look on all things with a child-like gaze of wonder, not with the spectacled eyes of the 'minute philosopher.' To this much in their character contributed. It was imaginative not critical. It 'delightedly believed' much that many modern men unreasonably disbelieve. It cared more to admire than to be admired. With much of a childish instability, and something of that strange and heedless cruelty, sometimes to be found in children, it united a child-like simplicity. It loved to wonder, and was not afraid of proving mistaken. Stormy passions swept over it, and great crimes alternated with heroic deeds; but it was comparatively free from a more insidious snare than the passions—that of self-love. It possessed eminently also another merit, the charm of which the Greek poets heartily appreciated, that of Unconsciousness, and thus escaped many weaknesses which belong to more conventional ages. Unselfishness was a marked characteristic of that time, and the spirit of self-sacrifice. It was then more common to be devoted to a fellow-creature or a noble cause. Hence the degree in which loyalty flourished, living like a soul in other virtues, the comparatively small temptation to self-assertion or self-applause, and the great reverence then felt for those humble virtues—obedience and fidelity. Then, as now, pride was to be found, but it was more often the pride of ancestral worth, than that of wealth or intellect, or that surly and ignoble pride which sees in the 'hierarchy of society' only a war against independence, as if a measureless dead level were more beautiful or more healthy than a country diversified by hill and plain. The Middle Ages were cheerful ages; and if their great Italian representative, Dante, was the most spiritual of poets, Chaucer, their English representative, was the most mirthful and human-hearted.

Walter L. Colls, Photo

Aubrey de Vere (Ætat. 87)
From an oil painting by Elinor M. Monsell.

CHAPTER X

LAST YEARS

1886–1902

NEARLY all the letters which I have, belonging to Aubrey de Vere's last years, are either marked by his tender and romantic feeling for the past, or are devoted to religious problems. The long friendship with Henry Taylor took its place in 1886 among the sacred memories, for his friend went in that year to join Coleridge, Wordsworth, Sara Coleridge, and Aubrey's own father and mother. His friendship with Mrs. Villiers, which had never been quite the same since his change of religious communion, regained something of its old intimacy for the years that remained to her. Henry Taylor's death brought a touching exchange of letters between them.

This renewal of intimacy may here be prefaced by another letter, written three years earlier—largely a Christian exposition of the theme 'De Senectute':—

Aubrey de Vere to the Hon. Mrs. Edward Villiers

Curragh Chase, Adare : October 26, 1883.

My dearest Mrs. Edward,—I am so much obliged to you for your letter—the pleasantest one I have had from you for many years. Our friendship began in 1843, and has therefore lasted forty years. If you have any reason for being grateful to me for having been constant during that time, I have surely still more reason for being grateful to you. In the latter thirty years I have made many new friends ; but, as I think you are aware, it is to my old friends that I am always most attached. There is a most touching, indeed exquisite

poem by Charles Lamb on the subject of early friends.
Make Lytton *read* you that poem; and if Lamb's works are
not in the house, make him get them at once, for the sake of
that poem. It is called, I think, 'The Old Familiar Faces.'

Alas! I know how many of your oldest and nearest
friends, those of that nearness which makes our kinsfolk seem
a part of ourselves, you have lost lately. These are incomparably the greatest sorrows of human life, but they are also
those which admit of incomparably the greatest consolation—
the hope of meeting again in a world which has no separations,
and which (better far) is no longer clouded by sin. I suppose
that here below we have but a glimpse of what even human
ties, not to speak of heavenly ties, would be, in a world in
which Love was not blunted, and diluted to a small part of its
natural power, by that ever-clinging plague of *Self-Love*. All
our enjoyments depend, almost wholly, on the vividness of
our corresponding sensibilities. What music is to one without an ear, and a landscape to one with no eye for beauty—
such the human ties are to those in whom *Self* is so strong
that all others, however near, seem to them comparatively at
a distance. In a higher world this mist of Self-Love will be
removed, and those whom we recognise beyond it will draw
near to us, like objects seen at sunset in the pellucid climates
of the South. They will be changed in themselves as
gloriously as they are changed to us, for they will have lost
their obscuring imperfections, and thus shine out, each the
pure Ideal of some special type of excellence. Their
individuality will be not diminished by the change, but
immeasurably intensified. What was *accidental* will have
vanished, while the essential is glorified; and we shall say
'Now, for the first time, I see you as you are.'

We may well believe that the least of the human affections
in a sinless world will far exceed the greatest here below ;—
and yet of course the human part of Heaven can be as
nothing compared with the Beatific Vision, and the Creature's
fruition of his Creator. Surely if we think so little of these
things it must be because, here on earth, we are habitually
bound and drowned in sense and the animal life. The bodily
appetites are dangers at least without a mask ; the real tyranny

of our material tabernacle is that perpetual weight with which
it oppresses the spirit, and dulls and blunts all spiritual appre-
hensions. One sees at once from the tone of mind evidenced
in St. Paul's Epistles what these last *may* be—what a perpetual Pentecost *may* be kept up in a human heart, and what
a perpetual delight and thanksgiving human life may then
be, even here on the earth, and all the more when we fall into
'divers Tribulations.' It was simply that he had acquired
that finer ear for the celestial harmonies which a few among
us have for ordinary music, and an eye for the far-off Celestial
Glories exceeding ours in power, as much as the great eye of
a telescope exceeds the unaided eye of the astronomer who
has sense enough to use that aid. Miss Fenwick might well
say in advanced life 'Heaven grows so rich to me.' I trust
she has long since discovered that its wealth was as much
beyond what one can even imagine on earth, as a gold mine
is beyond the buttercup a child fancies to be a treasure. To
her the Land of Purification must have been largely anticipated
by that land of trial and pain which she trod on earth but
which, I cannot doubt, she used so as to let it do the great
and blessed work of the Intermediate State—abolishing
self-love, and making the human will wholly one with the
Divine Will. That singleness of will and absolute absence
of mixture in our motives is the real meaning of *Purity*, and
all other purity is but a poor rehearsal of it. Till it is
perfected within us, doubtless even the Beatific Vision if it
were glowing all around us would be to us but what the
Vision of the Heaven and Earth can be to the blind mole.

If it is the weight of the body and the vanities of the
world which hide from us the great spiritual truths, which
we know, and which are as rich in beauty as in truth, surely
we should be grateful that before the earthly discipline is
over, there comes to us that gracious twilight time of age in
which vanities confess themselves to be but vanities, and
the body to be but a prison, and the Light Divine makes
way to our Faith through each new chink in the walls of our
earthly dwelling. It has come to both of us. It has indeed
its drawbacks ; every season of life has them ; but it has notwithstanding a grandeur, and a beneficence about it (could

we but see them aright) which belong to it in a supreme
degree. It forces disinterestedness upon us, for no earthly
advantages continue to be worth having ; the earthly lights
grow dim that the stars may reappear. You remember
Leolf's Soliloquy on the seashore in ' Edwin the Fair,' and
those noble lines about the reversal of earthly hope being

> an argument to Hope
> That she was licensed to the heart of Man
> For other than for earthly contemplations,
> In that observatory domiciled
> For survey of the stars.

There is also a magnificent passage in Wordsworth's
' Excursion' in which he affirms that the common expression
' The *vale* of years' ought to have been 'the *eminence* of
years.' Perhaps the 'vale' may be under the 'eminence;'
and perhaps if we were but on 'speaking terms' with our
Guardian Angel he might lift us from the lower to the higher.

That copy of verses you came on was mine. You did not
much like them when I gave them to you, I think in 1849,
except the line,

> For oft the wedded is a widow too,

and I never heard any one else allude to them. I had been
thinking of Ireland, and I had just seen you in the black garb
of widowhood. Ireland is at present in a very sad state from
which Providence will probably lift her, after she has done
penance. There are nations more plausible, but not less
guilty, though in other ways, who do no penance because
Providence says, ' Why should I afflict them any more?
They will not repent.' Under the weedy surface, however,
there is in Ireland much rich soil ; and amid all the din and
tumult there is a real and living Faith surviving in most of
the peasant homes, but especially the humblest. Many of
the priests did as wrong in attending the Land League
meetings (under severe pressure) as statesmen did in
recognising so long, as legal, meetings which they at last had
to suppress as illegal, no less than immoral. The present
demoralisation is the inevitable consequence of the Saturnalia,
licensed for nearly three years by those who shirked the first
duty of an executive, the maintenance of law and order.

But a hand at once strong, just and beneficent, may yet, with the help of Ireland's strong and real religious Faith (of which outsiders hear little, though they hear much of Irish crimes, the disgrace of that Faith) restore all. All parties have much to answer for. The agitators, the statesmen, and a large section of the priests, have *most*, and the parties chiefly blamed (viz. the proprietors and the *poor* people) have *least*.

And now I must say good-bye, and God bless you. Give my love to all your children who may be near you, or to whom you write, and tell Lytton I hope he is preparing to give us more poetry. He has had large experiences of life since he gave us his latest volume, and every new field of life ought to turn up a fresh crop for a poet.

Affectionately yours,
AUBREY DE VERE.

Curragh Chase, Adare: April 8, 1886.

My dear Mrs. Edward,—I knew that you would be one of those who would most feel the death of dear Henry Taylor; and with that feeling I directed an envelope to you several days ago, though I have not been able to fill it till to-day, when I have your affectionate and sympathetic letter to thank you for. He was, as I believe you know, by many degrees the chief friend that I have ever had; and the thought that in this world I can never see again that noble and beautiful face (in later years so venerable as well as so beautiful) is to me a very grievous one. I shall probably be at Bournemouth every year, as long as I retain vigour, even if those bereft ones should fix their abode elsewhere, that I may walk in the woodways, where we used to walk together, and sit on the seats under the pines, on which he used to sit, each year more frequently, when wearied or heated. But it is a great consolation that he should have escaped, what I used so much to fear for him, viz. a long and perhaps painful decline, with depressed spirits, and all that sad helplessness which belongs to prolonged illness in advanced age.

I think that his was the most manly, upright, just and generous nature which I have ever known—so unalloyed by

selfishness, and so entirely free from that morbid sensitiveness
which is said to belong especially to men of letters, and the
root of which is to be found in self-love and vanity. From
these last two evils he was more entirely free than that truly
great man, Wordsworth, who in moral strength and sincerity
resembled him. As regards Religion (to reply to a part of
your letter) what God requires of each of us is that we should
do *our best*, and that best differs very much according to the
circumstances in which we are placed, and under which we
have been brought up. In his early days, as you know,
circumstances were very much against him. You know also
that in his mature life he took—unlike many of his associates
in youth—the happy resolution to make Christianity the Law
of his Life ; and that he *kept that resolution faithfully to the
end*, during years in which Unbelief, even its most extreme
forms, is everywhere around men, even as the air they breathe.
To remain true to Faith he had long believed that it was
necessary, and therefore a duty, in his particular case to
mortify the speculative intellect,' an expression he often
used in speaking to me. It was a view of duty which I
could not but strongly respect, although it was at variance
with his prosecuting further enquiries, which I could not
otherwise but have much wished that he should prosecute,
since in my own case they had led me *from*, not into great
spiritual dangers, and given me what, with advancing years,
I have more and more regarded as the one great Blessing of
my life. That his course in this matter proceeded from a
real sense of duty, not from inferior motives, was shown by
his faithfulness to what God had given him of Divine Truth,
by his consistency, and deep seriousness, and by the ever-
widening charity which is itself the development of a living
and growing Faith. The duties of different persons are
often different. He was *not* one of those who have stood
still, or who have but wavered backward and forward in
spiritual things. He did not remain where he was. He
made a great advance, at a great crisis of his life. He had
courage to break with the past, and place himself in a new
spiritual world, the associations of which must, at first, have
been sometimes strange to him. Nor can I doubt that he

often prayed to God to give him whatever additional light or knowledge was needful for him, but could not in other ways be safely sought by him.

This prayer, made constantly and sincerely, seems to me practically the *sum of religious duty* with very many now. Very many must have great fears lest controversial enquiry might not rather shake their belief in the great Truths already theirs than add to their knowledge of Revealed Truth. But they know that *Prayer*, for all the light and knowledge God sees to be good for us, can never lead us into any danger, and must deepen the knowledge we already possess, whether or not it presents additional truths to our Faith. . . . If we use aright the truth known to us; and if we constantly make this prayer to God for all that knowledge of His Will and Way, which He wishes us to have; and if we do this with a single-hearted resolution to allow nothing in our will to be at war with the Divine Will, either abiding where we stand, or making an advance, according as He teaches us, then we shall have *done what we can.* God requires no more of us; but He requires thus much. Where that is faithfully done, I do not see why any Christian should have anxieties for other Christians, though dear to him as himself, except such anxieties as every Christian ought to have respecting himself, lest he should not have used aright whatever gifts were confided to him, whether gifts of knowledge or other gifts.

You see I have complied with your wish that I should speak frankly to you on this subject.

It must be a great consolation to you to reflect on the great addition which was made to the happiness of him whom we have lost—but only lost for a time—by his friendship with your husband and yourself. It was true and faithful as he was himself; and perhaps the most beautiful, certainly the most pathetic, lovely, and characteristic of his poems, remains its monument. His friendship with your husband must have seriously affected him for good; perhaps next to that with Southey, and with dear Miss Fenwick, who was so tenderly devoted to him, and so generously devoted. I often think of her in connection with him—may they be together now, and forever, in that world, in which friendships that have been pure and sound are gloriously renewed—where all affections are made perfect in the charity of God, and where self-love has no part. Thank you very much for transcribing that touching and beautiful passage from the letter of his wife. She was a devoted wife ; and the thought of all the happiness he had in her, must be to her the greatest of consolation, next to that divine hope of endless reunion, which is the supreme consolation. To me he was the most constant of friends, as well as the one most helpful for good. I often wonder how I came to have so much of his friendship, being so unworthy of it. That sense of our unworthiness seems to me the great alloy in connection with our friendships, and especially with those which have been the closest. All those who were dear to him will become more to me than before, for his sake. . . .

Ever your affectionate old friend,

AUBREY DE VERE.

The following letters to myself refer to two poems—'St. Peter's Chains,' and the 'Death of Corpernicus.' They were on subjects on which we largely shared the same feelings and views, although I could not at the age of thirty-two attain to the sanguineness of temperament which he preserved at seventy-four. I greatly prized, too, the sympathy he showed towards my own work, undertaken, as much of it was, to promote the same ends as his, and the encouragement which the veteran writer extended to one who had yet to learn his craft.

'St. Peter's Chains' was a series of sonnets on the Roman question. They expressed his view, which deepened every year, that the Church in communion with the Apostolic See could alone ultimately guard Christianity from the agnostic tendency of modern free thought. Hence he considered that in the long run, Papal independence would mean freedom for religion ; and religion must be free in order to be the effective safeguard of social order. The downfall of Papal independence would also mean the final destruction of the Christendom which had so long represented corporate faith in Christianity. He greeted with approval Montalembert's saying, that the spiritual and temporal authority must be combined in Rome, that they may safely be separated elsewhere. At the same time he was careful to dissociate himself from the 'impossible crusade,' simply to give back to the Pope the old 'States of the Church,' to restore exactly the *status quo* before 1870. True independence must be won for the Papacy, but in such a form and by such means as are best suited to new conditions. His great desire was to arouse public opinion from apathy on the subject, to a sense that modern anarchy and socialism would eventually triumph, if the Papacy, the great historic guardian of the principles of order and authority, did finally lose its effective freedom. At all events, the victory of the anti-clerical fanatics, who treated the freedom of religion as unimportant, would mean the victory of a principle of anarchy.

Heathfield Lodge, Bournemouth : August 23, 1888.

Dear Ward,—I wish much that I could profit by your renewed invitation, and meet my old friend the Bishop of Salford [1] under your friendly roof ; but I only stay here till Tuesday next ; and my engagements during that time would not allow of my being away for a day.

Pray tell the Bishop of Salford that I hope he received my volume 'St. Peter's Chains.' It is an attempt to attract the attention of Catholics to an enormous and most dangerous scandal and opprobrium, which can only be arrested by the creation of a sounder 'Public Opinion,' or rather Christian Philosophy, than now prevails in lands nominally Christian and even Catholic. If Catholics remain apathetic on that subject, they cannot expect that Protestants will rise again even to such an appreciation of it as they possessed twenty years ago. The Pope in his Allocution has sent a challenge abroad over Christendom, and it ought to meet a response from thoughtful men—a challenge that has nothing to do with

---

[1] Afterwards Cardinal Vaughan.

that imposssible 'Crusade' which used to be preached up some years ago.

With kind remembrances to your wife,

Yours very sincerely,

AUBREY DE VERE

Again, he wrote to me a little later :—

To me the question seems to be nothing less than the substitution of an antichristian civilisation, for that great Christian civilisation reared up from the days of Constantine, and pre-eminently from those of Charlemagne, under which the great monarchical institutions of Europe grew up, together with those relations of Church and State essential to the freedom of each, and in the absence of which, Society has nothing to look to except an endless succession of those two deplorable alternatives, viz. anarchies, under the name of Republics, and Imperial Despotisms. . . .

My aspiration was to induce thoughtful persons, such as eventually form Public Opinion, if not to the adoption, at least to the serious consideration of this Philosophy. . . . If the plague is not stayed, the Italian monarchy will probably be the first to fall, a thing I should regret as much as any Italian patriot.

A letter on the same subject to our common friend Baron Frederick von Hügel [1] further explains his position :—

Monk Coniston, Ambleside : September 5, 1888.

My dear Frederick von Hügel,—I must not lose a post in sending you my hearty thanks for your most pleasant and interesting letter ; and assuring you that it is all the pleasanter and more interesting to me, because it makes mention both of what you are in sympathy with, and what you are not in sympathy with in my recent volume. Relatively to the last, I may as well mention that the difference between us may be practically less than you might suppose. An Italian *Con-*

---

[1] The eldest son of the late Baron von Hügel, the friend of Metternich, and for some years Austrian Minister in Tuscany.

federation was I think the true Italian *Ideal* ; but a complete Italian *Unification*, excluding only Rome and the Campagna, which should have been left in the Pope's hands, under a European Guarantee, would, as I have said in my Preface, have been all that the interests of Religion and of Civilisation, would in my opinion have required. The Popes should perhaps never have had more, probably the Pope would be quite satisfied with such an arrangement, and would willingly consent that the Romans should retain all the benefits of Italian citizenship in things civil, military and political, and also all the Laws of Italy, excepting only any that may be opposed to Religion. Such an arrangement, considering that the Romans alone would be exempt from conscription, and a grinding taxation, could hardly leave them a grievance. The complaint would come from the Mazzinians and Jacobins, who have often avowed that it is not the Temporal only, but much more the Spiritual Power of the Church, which they hate, regarding it, and Christianity itself, as the main obstacles to their Ideal, viz. a socialistic Republic in Italy and *everywhere else*. They dragged the Italian Revolution out of its natural course ; and will, I am convinced, destroy the Italian monarchy and the permanent independence of Italy, if peace is not made soon between Church and State. I agree with you in wishing much that Catholics were allowed to vote at Elections. I believe that if there were now a Cavour among Italian Statesmen he would show the courage Bismarck has shown, and cancel what was criminal and blundering in the past, in spite of all outcries, sneers and imputations. But it is not the greater danger, but the nearer danger, that the statesmen of our day think about. I am wholly against *foreign* interference. I look but to 'Public Opinion.' . . .

Very sincerely yours,
AUBREY DE VERE.

I have been passing a fortnight at Bournemouth to see Sir Henry Taylor's family, and have since then been at Clevedon, where I visited the Church 'by that broad water of the West' where Tennyson's early friend, Arthur Hallam, lies buried, and saw the Tablet referred to in Tennyson's wonderful poem,

'When on my bed the moonlight falls,' [1] quite among the finest in 'In Memoriam.' There, too, I visited Coleridge's Cottage, to which he took his bride, and where he wrote his exquisite 'Æolian Harp' and several other poems. On my way here, I passed a night at the Birmingham Oratory, as I do every year, and found Cardinal Newman well and cheerful, and with a smile as sweet as ever, if not more so. In a few days more I shall say my annual 'De profundis' over Wordsworth's grave.

The 'Death of Copernicus,' published by Aubrey de Vere in the 'Contemporary Review' in 1889, was an attempt to foreshadow that blending of science with Christian faith which he regarded as the one hope for the future of civilisation; the cause of each being promoted in such a spirit as not to interfere with the other; science not insisting on urging hypotheses crudely, rudely, in a form aggressive to religion, and disturbing to the faith of many; faith being dissociated from undue conservatism and rigidity in theology. Copernicus, whose work 'De Revolutionibus Orbium,' had the sanction of Paul III., is represented in the poem as hesitating whether to destroy his MS. because it might be unsettling to the minds of believers at that time, or to publish it as a contribution to knowledge—to the ultimate synthesis between religion and science. The poem touched on a line of thought with which I had already attempted to deal, and I had written to him expressing my interest and sympathy.

Curragh Chase, Adare, Ireland : October 17, 1889.

My dear Wilfrid Ward,—Accept my best thanks for the great kindness of writing me that most interesting letter respecting my poem 'The Death of Copernicus.' I should have thanked you for it earlier, only that I have long been a wanderer, and on my return found an accumulation of business waiting my attention.

[1] *In Memoriam*, lxviii.

It struck me that to delineate the picture of a Christian Philosopher when so many who call themselves philosophers are turning their backs on Christianity, and endeavouring to kick down the ladder by which they mounted, might be of use ; and several letters which I have received (one from the Dean of St. Paul's) seem to corroborate that impression. Of those letters yours is the most interesting, and most indicates that the poem has been read with attention, as well as a friendly spirit and true understanding of it.

I quite intended, as you remark, to express a strong sympathy with the principle of ' Development' not only in Theology, but in the practical applications of Christianity to Social Life ; and I anticipate, that statesmen, when next on the point of despair, from the tendency of Poor Laws to Socialism, and the destruction both of industry and property, will find the world unexpectedly saved by the creation of a new religious order, more wonderful than any of the preceding active orders, which will solve that all but insoluble problem, through the joint action of a Divine motive with corporate action, and of the wisdom of the heart with science and experience. All national histories will have to be re-written from the 'standpoint' of the Sacred historians, but with all the added lights derived from political experience and social Science.

I quite agree with you that many of the apparent discrepancies between the Mind of the Church, and what may be called the Mind of Science, result from the fact that we are really very imperfectly acquainted with either of those two minds. Each extends a hand stored with truths, but each chooses to lift but a finger at a time ; and this partial knowledge of truths seen separately, and not in their wholeness and unity, while it has given rise to heresies in Theology and puzzles in Science, must have also the effect of making Theology and Science sometimes at variance apparently when they are in accord, or when one of the two is silent. Macaulay says, with more depth than commonly belongs to him, that Science has made no discovery as regards the Supernatural from the time of Solon to our own, and never can make one.

I have not yet seen your book about your father ; but

from what I have heard of it I am most anxious to read it ; and I will turn, when I see it, at once to the chapter on Galileo.

I have strong hopes that you will be able to walk in the footsteps of your father in all these high questions, and show like him how much may be done in Philosophic Theology by a Catholic layman who is loyal at once to truth and to the Church. If you should find anything erroneous or ill-expressed in that poem of mine, pray point out the passage to me.

With kindest remembrances to your wife, believe me,

Very sincerely yours,

AUBREY DE VERE.

The following letter is especially interesting from its reference to ' Lux Mundi ' and to the problem, to which the case of Abbé Loisy has since given fresh prominence, presented by modern Biblical criticism. Aubrey de Vere quickly descried the reverent tone in ' Lux Mundi,' and the attempt of the writers to achieve what he had in his mind, in the poem on the ' Death of Copernicus '—the task of keeping pace with contemporary thought and criticism, yet in so reverent a spirit as not to endanger that Christian faith which ultimately rests largely on that impalpable quality, a ' tone of mind.' ' Essays and Reviews ' had distressed him as rationalistic in tone. In ' Lux Mundi ' he found intellectual positions somewhat similar, but urged in an opposite spirit—a contribution to the great synthesis of the future, and not a disruptive aggression of science on theology. Contrasting the present Bishop of Worcester's essay on ' Inspiration ' with its treatment in ' Essays and Reviews,' he had written to me a little earlier ' Their spirit was rationalistic, his is ecclesiastical. He sees that the Church and the Bible are mutually supplemental.'

He still felt, however, as we have seen that he had felt, as early as 1849, that the function of the living Church which had to adjust Christian theology to the results of modern Biblical science, could never be efficiently performed, save by a Church which was organically one. Thus, he regarded much of 'Lux Mundi' as illustrating, in strict logic, the claims of the Catholic and Roman Church, however little this might be contemplated by its writers. On this subject, and on some documents which Cardinal Manning had lent me, concerning the Vatican Council, he wrote the following letter :—

Curragh Chase, Adare : October 9, 1891.

My dear Ward,—I wish indeed that I could have a good talk with you on the subjects you refer to. I could not accept Lady Leslie's kind invitation ;[1] and our house here is so crammed that I could not ask you to pass a few days here ; but if you should be going soon to Tervoe,[2] and let me know beforehand, I will gladly meet you there.

My sojourn at Rome [during the Vatican Council] brought constantly before me how utterly impossible (humanly speaking) it would have been for the Church to have done its work, if it had not had a central See, endowed with great power as well as dignity. Passions ran so high there that, practically all would on that supposition have been confusion, and the result of all the deliberations 'nil,' except the scattering broadcast the seed of subsequent confusions and animosities all over Christendom. Yet it was not by anything like tyranny or overbearing authority in the party of the Pope that this calamity was averted. The excitement seemed to me much the most violent on the side of the opposition, probably because those ranged at that side foreboded defeat. Some of them seemed to me to have practically forgotten that the Pope had anything more than a precedency of dignity, and even that, on condition of his making himself a nobody. He had praised in some published words, a work on Papal Infallibility, conveying his thanks to an author who had sent him the volume. I heard that act stigmatised as a gross infringement of the freedom of the Council, and as violating the impartiality needed from the Pope. What would the objectors have thought of Pope Leo's letter at the Council of Chalcedon, and the response of the Bishops, 'Peter hath spoken through Leo'? Mrs. Craven told me, years after

[1] I was staying with Aubrey de Vere's cousin Sir John Leslie at Glasslough, Co. Monaghan.   [2] The house of Lord Emly, near Limerick.

the Council, that she had come to see that the opposition
Bishops had made a serious mistake in the part they then
played. I need not say how glad I should be to see the
documents respecting the Council of which you speak.

Will you remember me very kindly to Sir John and Lady
Leslie and their family ; and ask Miss Emily Leslie if she is
staying with them, whether she could lend me ' Lux Mundi '
(if she has a copy of that book) and also lend me again Dr.
Liddon's Sermons on that subject which I returned to her at
her London address. They would assist me in completing
that Essay which I mentioned to you. I should much wish to
know how far the views of ' Lux Mundi ' are shared by the
High Church body. Do you know? If they are largely
shared that school must be getting on the road to Rome.
While such views were held only by members of the ' Broad '
School, that meant little. They can obviously be only held
safely in a Church that is Infallible and also visibly One.
I hope, however, that their comparative safety in the Catholic
Church will not tempt Catholics to advance otherwise than
with careful *deliberation* along that road, for their very sense
of security, combined with the attraction of novelty even to
the staidest mind, might lead them to conclusions which they
would see needed at least some modification, and which, in
the meantime, might endanger Protestants of a rash temper,
while they also repelled Protestants of the conservative order.
*My sympathies are with the men of progress as regards this
matter* ; but I should think that a gradual progress would
prove safer than a rapid one. Yours very sincerely,

                                    AUBREY DE VERE.

I suppose you know Coleridge's tract on Biblical inspiration, entitled ' Confessions of an Enquiring Mind.'

He treated some of the subjects referred to in this letter
soon afterwards in a very interesting Essay, published in a
volume entitled ' Religious Problems of the Nineteenth
Century,' which he dedicated to myself.

Browning died in 1889, Newman in 1890; Tennyson

three years afterwards. Richard Hutton passed away in 1897. As friend after friend was taken, Aubrey seemed to live more and more in the past, and to concentrate his thoughts ever more on what he felt to be the one substantial source of future hope. He continued his yearly pilgrimage to the haunts and graves of Wordsworth and Coleridge. Bournemouth was added as another shrine after Henry Taylor's death. And after 1890 the yearly visit to Cardinal Newman at the Oratory was exchanged for a yearly visit to his grave at Rednall.

When Browning died, Aubrey wrote to me, expressing pleasure at the general recognition of his greatness, and added the following estimate of him. ' He was a true-hearted man and poet, and a great thinker in verse.'

The death of R. H. Hutton in 1897 aroused in him, I think, a deeper feeling. He had often spoken to me of Hutton as a quite unique individuality, alike in his simple, devoted, and absolutely unworldly character, and in his massive and somewhat mystical intellect. Aubrey regarded him as a potent factor in the English world of thought, keeping before it, through his writings in the ' Spectator,' an absolutely sincere and unworldly standard of criticism. He held that mere men of the world, though they could not but respect Hutton, quite failed to understand him. Like a vital force which eludes the analysis of chemist and dissecter, while it is the most essential factor in making the human tissue, the true secret of his influence on the world lay in something beyond what it could perceive or explain This feeling appears in the following letter :—

Low Wood Hotel, Windermere : September 6, 1897.

My dear Wilfrid Ward,—I must send you at least a few lines of most cordial thanks for your letter, and especially for the latter part of it, in which you speak with so much insight and so much judgment of our dear friend Hutton. I go entirely along with you in all that you say of him, and do

not think that you overrate him in the least. He was indeed
a rare being, and one of those in whom the world, however
much it may see, will miss what is perhaps still higher than
what it admires.

I went out to see him at Twickenham, four or five times
during the six weeks I passed in London this summer; and
was very fortunate; for they were all of them spoken of by
his devoted niece as good days for him; days on which
there was less bodily suffering than on most days, and no
mental wanderings. I cannot but think that his high
religious fortitude and submission indicate that he must have
been living under a *very high grace from God*, and therefore
his Catholic friends may safely regard him as one belonging
to the soul of the Church. His change from Unitarianism to
a belief in the doctrines of the Trinity and the Incarnation
was surely a greater change than is made by Anglicans in
becoming Catholics.

If only the letters [of Hutton] of which Dr. Martineau
spoke to you should be published it will be a great benefit to
religion. . . .

   With kind regards to your wife,
       Yours very sincerely,
         AUBREY DE VERE.

I saw him for the last time at Adare in the following
summer—erect and alert, but with memory somewhat impaired. More vivid is my recollection of some time spent
with him in 1893 at Tervoe. The day before I left was the
eightieth birthday of our host, Lord Emly. In the evening
we sat together in the drawing-room, which had assumed a
striking appearance, from the recent importation of the
beautiful Empire furniture from Lady Emly's château at
St. Jean de Luz. Dr. Healy, Bishop of Clonfert (now Archbishop of Tuam) and Father Flanagan, of Adare, were of the
party. Aubrey de Vere and Bishop Healy told us wild and
romantic stories from Irish history and folk-lore, until past
midnight. The picture remains most vivid to me, and I may
be forgiven for recalling its trivial details—the listeners, Lord

Emly, with genial smile, taking ever and anon a pinch of snuff, and Father Flanagan, holding up his glass of whisky and water to the light, his face beaming with quick intelligence and Irish humour : the narrators, the Bishop with strongly marked Irish physiognomy, the glow of imagination in his eye, as with full voice and animation, he told the legendary lore handed down among the people from father to son through the centuries; Aubrey de Vere, refined, dreamy, animated, too, telling the old stories which had inspired his ' Inisfail,' and his ' Legends of St. Patrick.'

I have some letters to other correspondents written during the same years as these to myself—from 1889 onwards. And I have been favoured by friends and relations with recollections of him belonging to the same period. Both the letters and the reminiscences give a picture of the evening of his life, passed in religious peace, full of tender memories of old days, of devotion to the interests of the Church and his country, of sympathy for those he loved, of the desire to make them share, as far as possible, in the beliefs and hopes which were so much to himself, yet ever choosing, with the tact of the heart, those thoughts which he knew to be within the store of each friend to whom he wrote. It was truly a gracious sunset, after a long summer's day, as he moved onwards

> In kindly curves, with gentlest fall,
> By quiet fields, a slowly dying power,
> To that last deep where we and thou are still

In 1887 Aubrey's niece, Mrs. Monsell (a daughter of Mrs. Robert O'Brien) came to live at Curragh Chase with her children, and I am indebted to her for some recollections of his daily life during the ten years which ensued :—[1]

Though seventy-four years old he showed as yet no sign of old age. His complexion was fresh, his step elastic. Our

[1] The recollections are written from notes taken in conversation.

feeling after a few weeks of daily intercourse came to be that he was veritably a 'saint.' During the first months of our residence he used frequently to take me out for long walks, speaking of my husband who had been taken from me, and suggesting beautiful thoughts for my consolation. Religion seemed to be everything to him, and he said to me ' Theology is more to me even than poetry.' But when I asked why he had never become a priest, he said most decisively that he had never had any vocation whatever for the priesthood.

His daily life was very regular. He breakfasted at 9.30. Afterwards he went for a short walk, and the picture of him pacing up and down the terrace outside the house, in his velvet coat, sniffing in the spring air, is still very vivid to me. He also wore a skull cap, made by Mrs. Watts, after the pattern of her husband's skull caps, and whenever he paid them a visit, they would give him a fresh one. After his walk he went to the library, in which his father before him used to write and read, where he passed the rest of the morning. After luncheon he again went to the library, until the day began to decline; then he would go for a walk. If walking alone, he would at times be so abstracted that he did not recognise his friends as they passed him. But he often walked with a companion. Then he would take the keenest interest in every tree and shrub, every walk and flower bed in the park. Each spring he used to look out daily for the first appearance of the variegated sycamore, and when it came would say, pointing to it with delight, ' There is the great lamp.' He could not bear the disappearance of the trees, which he remembered all his life, and there was an old larch tree, which was long supported by the most unsightly props, which he erected year after year, to keep it from falling.

The park was for him full of memories of his father and mother. He loved the flicker of the evening sun through the beech trees in the 'sunset walk' which his mother had made. The voices of the crows always made him recall his father's saying ' It is like water running fast across shingles.' He was extremely active, and would at times in the course of his walk climb up really steep hills in the park.

In the evening he would play backgammon, or listen to

music. But not unfrequently he would propose to read poetry to us, asking, 'Shall it be a Wordsworth night, or a Coleridge night or a Tennyson night?' He threw his whole heart into the reading, and I have known him unable to sleep afterwards from excitement.

He became very fond of my children, but this love for children was, I think, an acquired taste. When I was away, they would dine with him. Then he would tell them stories. 'Shall the story be heroic, comic, or tragic?' he would ask. Or he would read Tennyson's 'Oriana,' or the 'May Queen.'

He loved pretty things around him, and always had flowers in his room. And he was sensitively fastidious in some things. Ugly things were a real trial, and a bad smell was intolerable to him. He could not bear binding engagements, and if he went for an expedition, did not at all like being asked at what time he would return.

But he was extremely patient with those who did not respect his fastidiousness, and was self-reproachful if his patience had failed him. We wanted to put a pretty paper in his little bedroom, to replace the very ugly one which had been there for years. 'No,' he replied, 'I allowed myself to be so much annoyed with the ugliness of the present paper when Vere first put it up, that I will atone for my ill temper by keeping it.'

A young soldier, a connection of his, was staying with us, and began to whistle in the drawing-room in the evening. This was a great violation of Uncle Aubrey's canons of good manners. Yet he loved the exuberance of young life, and it was amusing to watch the struggle in him. He did not *say* anything to the youth, but whispered to me, 'Surely this is not good manners.' And when the whistling recommenced he gave a very conspicuous start. 'I hope, at all events, he *saw* me start,' he remarked afterwards.

I remember his patience when a young artist talked of Raphael 'painting in castor oil,' and disparaged him in a way which shocked my uncle's deepest prejudices. He listened in silence, and said to me afterwards, 'The nurses say of a young fat child "It is good to have something to grow out of"; that young man will grow out of those views.'

He was amusingly distressed at being unable to make
friends with dogs, and quite resentful at their want of logic.
'I treat them with kindness and even profound respect,' he
said, 'but I see I bore them. Yet some of their favourite
masters often beat them.'

We all knew how much to him was his religious life, and
it was the source of the great patience which I have seen him
show, under acts of inconsiderateness from others which most
men would have resented. Daily we saw him walking up
and down reading the Psalms from his mother's Bible, or
reciting the Breviary. Once a month he was visited by
Father Flanagan from Adare, who stayed the night, and gave
him Holy Communion in the morning. But he was most
scrupulous, in his intercourse with my children, not to say one
word which could tend to proselytise. He regarded it as a
matter of honour and conscience, to respect the religion of
their parents, in which they had been brought up.

I was always urging him to write his Recollections; and
had he done so in the early years of our life together at
Curragh, they would have been far fresher and more brilliant
than they were as they appeared. But he had always other
tasks, which he regarded as worth more than anything relating
to himself or his own life. And he waited until age had at
least somewhat impaired the elasticity of his mind.

But, though he would not write, he was ever speaking of
the past. The recollections of his parents especially, and of
all he felt that he owed to them, were never-ending. And as
he left far behind him the average life assigned to man on
earth, preserving still so much of the keenness and freshness
of youth, I could not but recall the words, 'Honour thy
father and thy mother, that thy days may be long in the land.'

He long continued to pay his annual visit to Rydal in
these years, and nearly always passed some time with his
cousins the Spring Rices at Old Church, near Ullswater.
Miss Agnes Spring Rice tells me of the intense happiness he
always derived from the old associations of the Lake country.

The days are passed : memory remains—
Memory whose joys exceed her pains

were the lines he wrote in the Old Church visitors' book in his eightieth year. He would take long walks showing his cousins his favourite haunts, discoursing of Wordsworth, and quoting poetry—though never his own poetry. A favourite spot was the waterfall, Aira Force, near Ullswater, which Wordsworth had loved : but the lines Aubrey used yearly to recite there were ·not Wordsworth's but Coleridge's— beginning :—

> Unperishing youth,
> Thou leapest from forth
> The cell of thy hidden nativity.

His happy serenity was disturbed by any want of appreciation of his favourite scenes : and after a drive over Kirkstone Pass on the coach, during which a fellow-traveller would talk instead of silently admiring the view, it was some time before Aubrey could recover his composure. He relieved his feelings by writing in the Old Church visitors' book :—

> The old silent seer Numa used to say
> 'The Muses are not nine but ten.' This day
> We lack the tenth. He named her 'Tacita.'

Sayings of his at Old Church are remembered. 'A self-made man who never forgets his maker,' was his description of a certain purse-proud *nouveau riche*. He approved of Wordsworth's criticism of Scott's poetic descriptions of scenery. 'Nature does not permit an inventory to be made of her charms.' Though nearly always sympathetic, and ready to see the good in every thinker and writer, he could be fierce where he really disapproved. 'How did that dreadful book get here?' he asked of a volume of poems which he regarded as immoral in tendency. 'I should like to *burn* that book.'

The following letters were addressed to Miss Norton, the sister of his friend Professor Eliot Norton :—

Curragh Chase, Adare, Ireland : June 14, 1889.

My dear Miss Norton,—It was indeed most kind of you to spare me a little of your time on that Easter Sunday, and write me that letter which I read with so much interest. It put me most pleasantly in mind of old days, both in Italy and England, and both pleasantly and mournfully of your sister, whom I always think of when I think of you, and that is very often. I wish we could have a few more walks again like those we had of old, and also that those walks could be with you in *this place*, which you have not seen, but which I must have spoken of to you, and which you would think very lovely. It has a mingled brightness and stillness about it, like that which one sees resting on monastic faces, such as those which you used to admire in Old Italian pictures, and which are to be found still in many a convent. Surrey's 'soote season' is with us still; and I sometimes wish it could remain with us for ever; but it is better that that permanence should be deferred until we can enjoy it side by side with those we have loved and lost—for the present. One of them is John Field, whom I always remember with such affection. If you know his widow's address, would you send it to me, as I should like to write to her?

Yesterday evening my widowed niece, Ellie Monsell, who lives here with her children, was reading to me some of Carlyle's letters in your brother's last two volumes. They interested me much. In several of them his tone seemed to me much more religious than it was in his later years. In that matter I should fear that his extraordinary enthusiasm for Goethe must have been injurious to him. No wonder that the Calvinistic traditions he inherited from John Knox did not keep their hold of him; but I wish that when he came to the separation of the roads, he had not taken the wrong turn—the downward one. . . . To me Carlyle always seemed a man with much heart—an ardent and courageous one—united with a singularly vivid imagination and perceptive power. But surely his admirers often mistake the matter, when they take him for a great thinker. He could not be that, for he had not the faculty of thinking with self-possession. .. Wordsworth tells in the 'Excursion' that we should not speak of the 'vale of years,' but of the '*Eminence*' of years. It seemed to me that as poor Carlyle grew older he got deeper and deeper down into a forest, lion-haunted, and black with trees. Much of his gloom doubtless came from his temperament, but how much of it would not have been spared to him had he but clung fast to Faith, that Faith which is one with Hope, no less than with Charity—not that Earthly Hope of which the type is a sail ; but that Heavenly Hope, the symbol of which has ever been the anchor, at rest because it has gone down into the depth of things.

As I approach the close of earthly life, every year makes me feel more, that the one great source both of happiness and of peace, in our declining years was intended to be *Authentic Christianity*, as distinguished from the imitations of it set up by men who fancy that they make it more easy of acceptance by cutting it down, and divesting it of those high mysteries which alone give it power and reality—mysteries which no authentic Religion could ever have been without, when propounded to our limited faculties, and none of them really more mysterious than the very first principles of Theism or of Morals. This belief has been just now vividly recalled to me by a little book which I have only just finished my perusal of, and which, while my enthusiasm about it is fresh, I will ask your kind acceptance of. The last chapter of it, the XIIth, is that which has struck me the most—so pray *begin* by reading that one if you have time to read the book. It seems to me a philosophy so sound and deep, like that of Newman, that one marvels how such writings as Renan's could ever have been mistaken for philosophical. Perhaps I should tire you if I went on with one of those topics which are so apt to run away with one's pen. So I will only beg of you to give my affectionate remembrances to your brother and his two children whom I have met, and believe me,

Ever most sincerely yours,

AUBREY DE VERE.

I hope you will get a copy of my ' Legends of St. Patrick ' which I sent you lately.

Curragh Chase, Adare, Ireland : 1891.

I know what heavy losses you have sustained, and deeply lamented them ; and in the last few years I have myself lost my only sister, Sir Henry Taylor, and (on the first day of this year) his widow, my cousin. Your brother met her as well as her husband at Bournemouth. They were quite enthusiastic about him, and often spoke of him, and I am sure he will regret her departure as well as his. On the other hand, I have had the pleasure of becoming acquainted with one of your brother's sons and two of his daughters, to whom you must give my kindest remembrances.

Then, among others who, though less near to me, were very dear, is Cardinal Newman, to whom I used to pay a visit every year on my way to Wordsworth's country, and his quiet grave among the old yew trees of Grasmere's churchyard. The outburst of enthusiastic admiration for Newman on the part of writers from every school of English thought was very cheering to those who remembered how entirely he had been misunderstood, and misrepresented for many years after his submission to that Church which had converted the English race to the Christian Faith. In the last November No. of 'Scribner's Magazine' I published a Sonnet, expressing a hope that those who now praise Newman so eloquently will also read his works, especially those of his maturer days.

The condition of Ireland seems somewhat more hopeful now that the Parnellites are divided into two warring parties and that the scales seem to be falling from the eyes of many in England, over whom a 'mist of imbecility' seems to have been resting for some years. As for myself, I am well, thank God, and much cheered by the circumstance that my elder brother has forsaken his hermitage, and come to live here with me and our niece, who has been living here with her four children since her widowhood.

Athenæum Club: August 10, 1891.

I have sent to you through our friend Mr. Woodberry a copy of my brother's Translations from Horace : but in memory of old times you must allow me also to send you a volume of my own, 'The Search after Proserpine,' some of the poems in which you read probably when I sent them to your brother, though others will, I dare say, be new to you.

I hope they may remind you of our pleasant walks and talks—pleasant indeed though too few—in Oxford, among the green lanes of old England, and near beautiful Florence. None of those Recollections will dwell with me more faithfully than that of our 'all-golden afternoon' on that lovely little river, and amid the stately courts and grand gardens of Hampton Court. I hope we shall also meet on the banks of Windermere, and visit Wordsworth's grave together. I wish that he and Newman (England's two greatest men of late times) could have been buried near to each other. If you know before the eighteenth when you go to the land of Lakes, would you send me a few lines telling me, addressing to ' Post Office, Bournemouth ' ? After that time my address will be ' Monk Coniston, Ambleside.'

St. John's Cottage, Clevedon: August 18, 1891.

Just a line both to thank you for your letter of the 14th and to tell you that to ensure your getting a room that looks out on the lake at ' Low Wood Hotel, Ambleside,' you should write a letter that will reach Mrs. Logan, Proprietress of the ' Low Wood Hotel,' at least three or four days beforehand, saying that you want such a room, otherwise you will have little chance of getting one.

I have just returned from visiting ' Coleridge's Cottage,' where he dwelt during the first few months of his marriage, and wrote one his loveliest poems, ' The Æolian Harp.' The view from the hill above it is wonderfully like his description of it in another of his poems. The ' unendangered Myrtle ' has been sadly reduced by a recent storm : but it still lives and will sprout again ; and I enclose a spray of jessamine, probably a descendant of the one he described. You can place it before that poem in your copy of his poems.

In a short time more I hope we shall stand before the grave of Wordsworth. Those two great poets will thus be associated together in your recollections, as they were for so many years in the bond of a great and early friendship.

We—that is, Sir Henry Taylor's daughters and I—have been seeing a great deal of your friend Woodberry, to whom they took a great liking, at Bournemouth. We brought him to see many relics of Shelley at his daughter-in-law's, which interested him much.

That poem of mine to which you refer ('The sunset river') was one of those published in the 'Atlantic Monthly,' and I heard that Longfellow was much pleased with it. Afterwards it was included in my poem 'Inisfail,' now out of print, but to be reprinted. The poem about 'Spring's Chalice' is one of the series entitled 'May Carols.'

Curragh Chase, Adare : September 26, 1891.

This period of your stay in England is now, I think, very nearly exhausted, and I must send you a few words of farewell. Come back to us again next year if you can, that so those among your old friends who have already left behind them man's allotted 'threescore years and ten,' may see you again, and not unreasonably hope to do so. We will go once more to Wordsworth's grave, and again read his poetry on that grassy seat fronting the 'Aerial Rock' whose 'solitary brow' his fancy crowned with 'votive towers.'

To the widow of his old friend and Tennyson's,—'old Brooks,' Aubrey writes in the following year :—

Athenæum Club, Pall Mall, London : August 8, 1892.

My dear Mrs. Brookfield,—I cannot tell you how much pleasure your friendly little letter has given me. It shows me that you, like myself, remember old days and old friends. For my dearest friends are my old friends : to me they never grow old : they may be 'out of sight,' but they are never 'out of mind.' I wonder how many years ago it was that dear Stephen Rice one Sunday morning, soon after Church took me to your house, to introduce me to you and your husband ; he was so much interested by his conversation with you, that he wholly forgot to introduce me to either of you until, after the lapse of some ten minutes, I reminded him of his omission. I have been reading old letters again lately, and in those of Alice Taylor I find constant references to you, especially when those letters came from the abode of the Ashburtons. You know that she had a most enthusiastic friendship for you; though many in her place would, on the contrary, have had a jealousy.

We used sometimes to talk of religious matters and Rome. That is a theme too large to enter on here ; so I will only tell you that, as the years go by, I have regarded my submission to the Church as the one great blessing for which I have more reason to be grateful than for all the others put together. On the other hand, I regard as the one serious misfortune of my life that I was not a Catholic from my early youth. If I had been one, my life would have been worth ten times as much to myself and others.

Thank you for telling me of my dear old friend Kate Perry. I wish I had known that she was in town. She is one of those whom I most associate with the pleasant days of old. Will you give her my love ? Since her health has been infirm, she has had a place in my prayers morning and evening. To think of her is to think of Miss Fenwick, the Henry Taylors, and many besides.

Adieu, and God bless you, my dear friend. I think I called on you every year that I visited London ; but somehow there seemed a fate against my finding you at home.

Ever your affectionate old friend,

AUBREY DE VERE.

To-morrow I go for about ten days or a fortnight to Bournemouth, to be near the Taylors.

To an old friend who had lost her only sister and constant companion, he writes thus three years later :—

Curragh Chase : May 30, 1895.

Were our wills but perfectly united with the Divine Will, of course the Divine Consolation would come to us at once. Perhaps when that Consolation is deferred, for it is never denied, this is because God wishes that we should be able to offer to Him that *highest* tribute of our devotion which we offer, when in the midst of a distress not yet relieved, we still say ' Thy Will be done,' in a blind Faith.   These are perhaps the times in which the swiftest growth is made by us, though we do not feel it, during which we descend to the deepest depths of the Divine Love, and after which we ascend most swiftly to its heights.   The greatest saints, we know, have often resembled their Saviour in His sacred *Dereliction* as well as in so much beside, and have borne well a trial much sharper than they were called to bear later, in their death.

. . . God bless you, my dear old friend, and all of us in all our trials, and especially in the last great trial, just before the endless joy.

Curragh Chase, Adare : December 23, 1895.

This is only a line to say ' May all the blessings of this holy season be with you.'   We cannot always *feel* that blessings are blessings, but we can always know it, and act on that knowledge, clinging to God all the more closely as the tempest howls around us.   It is in our saddest, and most comfortless times, I believe, that we are making the *greatest progress.*   The Angel of God is moving on before us, and we are clinging to his skirts ; what we think the tempest is really but the speed of his onward movement.   A friend of mine wrote to me not long since about my drama of St. Thomas of Canterbury, and said that the most valuable thought in it was the one expressed in certain lines describing the Saint when his trials were at their highest, and his consolations at their lowest.   I will copy and enclose them.

That God gives comfort to those who wait patiently and trustingly, ' clinging to Him as the limpet to the rock,' he was ever insisting.   And the comfort is the sweeter for the trial.   Years earlier he had written to his sister after a time of sorrow : ' I can very well understand what you say.   There is no calm like that after a storm, no sweetness so piercing and full as that which the heart can receive when it has been prepared for it by sorrow.   It is like the odour of a garden when the evening sun comes out after a day of rain.'

There were new friends in these years as well as old with whom he corresponded. Miss Mary Anderson (now Madame Navarro) has given a graphic page of her Recollections to Aubrey de Vere, whom she came to know through their common friendship with Tennyson, a few years before the great bard's death. Miss Anderson tells of their walks on Hampstead Heath, when Aubrey would pour forth his recollections of Wordsworth, and of Sir Henry Taylor.

We visited the National Gallery together several times [she continues]. He liked to select some of our favourite pictures and ask 'What does this figure say to you? What do you think the artist wished to show in this or that one?' Of the wonderful creations of Angelico, Perugino, Botticelli, Raphael, he had always something stimulating to say. He did not look at their work from a painter's point of view. The drawing, the way those mystic colours glorify the canvas, meant less to him than what the Old Masters said to the highest and best in his soul and mind. Aubrey de Vere's friends call him the Orb, and are wont to say that his feet alone touch the earth, the rest of him being already in heaven. . . . Though old in years, the peace of his spiritual life has left his face unfurrowed. His colour is fresh, red and white, his eyes young, clear and blue; and his smile that of a child. All this youthfulness contrasts curiously with his grey hair and tall thin stooping body. One of his great charms to me is his carelessness of externals. I remember driving with him through the Park during the season. I was in my smartest gown and bonnet. We were in a victoria. He held up a gamp-like umbrella to keep the sunlight from his eyes. Years had turned its cotton blackness into green, and one of its ribs had fallen in from the decay of age. But he clung to it as he clings to his friends, whether in sickness or health, riches or poverty.

'I am glad,' writes Aubrey himself to Miss Anderson, after one long visit to the beloved Peruginos and Fra Angelicos, 'that we saw these pictures of the Saints together once more. . . . I think we agreed that if, when in doubt, we rested our eyes on their faces, either remembered, or actually before us, those faces would sometimes give us better counsel than our own logical processes.'

When Miss Anderson's book of Recollections was published his letter to her—in his eighty-third year—was characteristic :

The Athenæum Club, Pall Mall, London : July 25, 1896.

My dear Friend,—I am so much afraid of missing you again this year that I must write you a line to beg of you, in case anything should bring you to London before the middle of August, to let me know (as it is impossible for me to go to Worcester) whether there is any place here where I should have a chance of finding you at any particular hour you might name.

I have been reading your book of youthful recollections with very great interest and delight. In the case of those friends to whom I am much attached, there is a strange fascination in all that belongs to an earlier period of their being than that at which we first met. I like to see, though more dimly in that earlier time, the beautiful later time which existed latently in that earlier time, and practically formed it. The courage which you showed in all your later life, and without which you never would have known either its joys or its sorrows, and anxieties, was shown early in that ride which you took on the wild horse, without bridle or saddle : it seemed to make you much more known to me than you had been before.

I liked also very much to see again, but through your eyes, not my own, or rather through your eyes as well as my own, so many of those who have been so much to me. I recognise them so well, while I see more in them than I saw before. One of your best and pleasantest sketches is that of Cardinal Newman ; and it gives a part of his manifold nature little known and well worth knowing. His love of

that child shows that in one respect celibacy *cost him much.*
Tennyson also *lives* on your page. Excellent also is the
sketch of Gladstone in p. 190. Your preference of Tennyson's
reading to what you have heard on the stage is strongly
confirmed by my own experience. Charles Kean's readings
aloud of Shakespeare, during a few visits which he paid us at
my father's house were the most vivid intellectual and
imaginative delight I have ever known. When I afterwards
saw him play the part of King Lear, on the stage, it was a
grievous disappointment to me. The refinement and pathos
were gone. It was to a great degree but rant—a sacrifice
offered up to the remote Upper Gallery.

I was greatly touched by what you said of the nuns at
that Ursuline Convent after the lapse of twenty-nine years.
You felt yourself changed. The old nuns seemed hardly older
than before. Time has to be civil in his dealings with those
whose lives are, even while they are on earth, nearly in eternity.

The sketches of Houghton and Longfellow are excellent ;
and what you say about Shakespeare at Stratford-on-Avon
touched me very much. I wish you could have given us
Wordsworth, and Henry Taylor also. What you said of
myself gave me much pleasure, because it showed how strong
must be your friendship, to see so much where there was so
little to be seen ; and because it reminded me of those
pleasant and dear days at Hampstead ; but whenever I read
such kind things of myself I am tempted to say, ' What
then ? Have I been a *hypocrite,* too, all my life besides my
other vices ? ' I have followed all the chances and changes of
your life ; its trials, as well as its brave joys, with deep
sympathy in your book, and my predominant feeling was a
hope that all you have yet known of life was but a shadowy
prelude of all the joy yet reserved for you, both in this
life and in a better one. Come again to your friends at
Hampstead, who speak of you with such affection, and let
us pay another visit to the dear old saints at the National
Gallery, and let your husband be of the party.

With kindest remembrances to him,

Your affectionate friend,

AUBREY DE VERE.

Aubrey de Vere published in the following year (1897) his own Recollections, which he describes to a friend as 'an attempt to share my youth also with some of those with whom I have shared some of the pleasantest days in these my later years.' On this work Mr. Edmund Gosse has an interesting comment in the course of the following reminiscences of its author, written immediately after his death, which he has kindly placed at my disposal :—

Aubrey de Vere's appearance at about the age of eighty-three is very vivid in my recollection. He entered the room swiftly and gracefully, the front of his body thrown a little forward, as is frequently the case with tall and active old men. His countenance bore a singular resemblance to the portraits of Wordsworth, although the type was softer and less vigorous. His forehead, which sloped a little, and was very high and domed, was much observed in the open air from a trick he had of tilting his tall hat back. . . . There was something extraordinarily delicate and elevated in his address. He was, in fact, conversation made visible. I never knew a more persistent speaker. If he broke bread with one, the progress of the meal would be interrupted and delayed from the very first by his talk, which was softly, gently unbroken, like a fountain falling on mosses. On one occasion when we sat together in a garden, in the summer, Mr. de Vere talked with no other interruption than brief pauses for reflection, for three hours, in itself a prodigious feat for an old man of eighty-four, and without the smallest sign of fatigue.

In spite of the fact that he occasionally used what are called 'strong expressions'—with a little playful affectation, I used to think, of the man of the world—Mr. Aubrey de Vere had an ecclesiastical air like that of some highly culti-vated, imaginative old *abbé*. He possessed a sort of distin-guished innocence, a maidenly vivacious brightness, very charming and surprising. He once remarked to me that the feminine characteristics of Newman were always recurring to his memory, that, as he looked back to the early Oxford days, he continually had the impression in Newman of 'a kind of

virginal remoteness mingled with extremely tender grace.'
When he said this, I could not help feeling that, although
there was no 'remoteness' about Mr. de Vere, there was
something of the same feminine grace.

The principal, perhaps the only, sign of extreme old age
which the poet presented until lately, was the weakness of
his voice. This must have been, I think, very melodious, but
already when I knew him first, it had become so faint as to be
sometimes scarcely audible, particularly in company. It was
therefore very pleasant to be alone with him, especially in the
open air, when he seemed to speak with particular freedom
and ease. The astonishing fulness of his memory made his
conversation marvellous and delightful. He not merely
passed, with complete comprehension of the relative distance,
from events of 1820 to events of to-day, but his verbal
memory was astounding. He garnished his recollections of
Wordsworth, Rogers, Landor, or Sir Henry Taylor with
copious and repeated quotation from their poetry. Indeed,
he once assured me that, of certain favourite poets—in
particular Wordsworth, Shelley and Keats—he still retained, at the age of eighty-four, 'substantially the bulk of
their writings.' He said that his principal occupation had
been and still was, in his solitary walks, or by the fire, to
repeat, silently or aloud, pages after pages of poetry. His
memory of the great writers was, he believed, so exact that,
in these exercises, he had the illusion that he was reading
from the printed book.

The friends of Mr. Aubrey de Vere were so well versed
in the stores of his memory, that they anticipated an immense
pleasure from his Reminiscences, which he published in 1897.
This was a charming book, in many ways, but it was in some
degree a disappointment. It was in no sense what we hoped
it would be, an autobiography; it recalled a variety of incidents and places which had interested the writer, but it told
but little of what had moved him most. The inherent delicacy
and shyness of the author spoiled the effect. 'Self,' he said,
'is a dangerous personage to let into one's book'; but unfortunately without it, an autobiography is 'Hamlet' with the
part of the Prince of Denmark omitted. There is so much in

Aubrey de Vere's 'Recollections' which is delightful, but those who enjoyed his conversation, miss in the published book a great deal that they recall as particularly original and delightful. I once asked Mr. de Vere, who, among all the great souls he had known, had impressed him the most? He said instantly, 'Wordsworth and Newman; they are the two for whom my love has been most like idolatry.' There were precious pages about Newman in the 'Recollections,' but the great disappointment of that book was the comparative absence of any salient notes about Wordsworth. I think Mr. de Vere felt the subject almost too sacred for annotation, and yet in personal talk he was always ready to return to it. His loyalty to Wordsworth was a passion.

Many notes one had taken down of Mr. de Vere's conversations were rendered nugatory by the publication of his book. Some, however, have still their value. He toned down in publication the impression of his seeing Newman for the first time in 1838, and his spoken words, which I noted in 1896, are much more striking. I had asked him to tell me how the future Cardinal struck him. He was silent for a moment, and then replied, with a light in his blue eyes :— 'The emotion of seeing him for the first time was one of the greatest in my life. I shall never forget his appearance, I had been waiting some time, and then the door opened and Newman, in cap and gown, entered very swiftly and quietly, with a kind of balance of the figure, like a very great lady sweeping into the room. That was my first impression; the second was of a high-bred young monk of the Middle Ages, whose asceticism cannot quite conceal his distinguished elegance.' Another unpublished impression of Oxford deserves to be recorded. Mr. de Vere went to hear Newman preach his famous sermon on 'Unreal Words.' He was a little late, and as he took a remote seat he thought with annoyance that he would not hear any thing. But he heard every syllable; Newman's voice was musical but very low, yet every word told. Mr. de Vere observed to himself on this occasion that it seemed as though Newman's *thought* was so clear that it was impossible not to perceive the impression of it. You seemed less to be hearing him speak than think. Innumerable links, such as these, with the past, are broken by the death of a most beloved and venerated man.

The very keen interest taken in his poetry by a group of American friends, with whom his correspondence now became frequent, was evidently a great pleasure to Aubrey de Vere in his last years. Many private letters and able reviews in the American papers, showing very high and discriminating appreciation of its purpose and merits, reached him during the last decade of his life. 'This encourages me to hope,' he writes to an American admirer in 1895, 'that my verse may yet do more of good than I should have thought likely.'

To my poetry your article certainly did full justice, and more than justice [he writes to the same correspondent], but that I believe is a fault which poets easily forgive. Praise to a poet little known is a serious encouragement, when it is directed to qualities which are those he *wished* his poetry to possess, and endeavoured to impart while he could not guess how far he had succeeded in that endeavour. When Words-worth and Coleridge in youth published a volume in common, the former intended to illustrate *Nature* chiefly in her humanities, as he always did, and Coleridge, to illustrate the *Supernatural* in the form of the *Marvellous*, i.e. as it is illustrated in 'The Ancient Mariner,' 'Christabel,' &c. My aspiration had something in common with both those aspirations, and more perhaps apart from both. My aim, in most of my poetry, was chiefly to illustrate, not *Nature*, but the *Supernatural* in the form of Supernatural Truth, and the Supernaturalised affections, that is to say those affections that have their root in a Supernaturalised humanity—not so much a humanity *unfallen* as a humanity *redeemed*. I wished also to illustrate that humanity in its relations with our *fallen* humanity by recording the conversion of two very different Nations, viz. Ireland and England, and also to record some of the conflicts of Nature and Grace as well as their harmonies during the two chief periods of the world,

viz. that from the Fall of the Roman Empire to the time of
Charlemagne, and subsequently through the great Medieval
period to the beginning of the modern time still in its rude
boyhood, but destined to resume all that preceded it, in
common with progressive Science and Freedom which will
prove gifts or curses according as they subject themselves to
Christian truth and love, or revolt against these.   Such at least
was the *Scheme* of my poetry, in case it had interested people
enough to render its completion a thing practicable.   Some
poet one day will probably execute this Ideal (the Christian
Ideal) better than I could have done and at a fitter time.

The following reminiscences by Miss Helen Grace Smith,
sister of Mr. Walter George Smith of Philadelphia, a member
of the University of Pennsylvania, and at one time President
of the American Historical Society, belong to the year
1897 :—

It was a summer afternoon in London, and we were
finishing our luncheon in the quiet gloom of our little
dining-room which served for drawing-room as well, and
which was only half brightened by the red geraniums in the
windows, when Mr. de Vere's card was brought to us.

We had made no picture of him in our mind, and we
were surprised and wholly delighted when he entered the
room.   A tall slender figure, unbent by age, he brought an
atmosphere of genial light and gladness with him.

We are very apt to associate sadness with age, or at least
a look of settled gravity and habitual care.   In the presence
of Aubrey de Vere, there is the vigorous freshness of morning;
or else his is one of those rare evenings of life, when the sky
is lighted to the very zenith with the glow of the sunset.
His eyes are clear and bright, kindling, as he speaks, with
rare enthusiasm; he has a keen sense of humour, the gift
of all Irishmen, and at the same time a calm dignified
presence. . . .

We talked of Wordsworth, and Mr. de Vere told us many
anecdotes of the great poet, to whose grave he had but lately
made his annual pilgrimage. . . .

Of Tennyson he spoke with intense admiration, and told us that, after evenings spent in intercourse with that poet, he would go home to his rooms, through the London streets, unconscious of the sights and sounds about him. Tennyson read aloud to him the manuscript of the famous ' In Memoriam,' and as the poet's voice would drop at the end of the lines, making the sound almost inaudible, his hearer read with him, looking over his shoulder, and saw the poet's tears roll down his face, so great was his emotion.

Mr. de Vere quoted some verses of the poem with slow, sonorous intonation, and read us besides some of his own father's sonnets.

He talked of Coleridge and Southey, and the Brownings ; with the latter he had been closely associated in Italy.

Of Robert Browning he has written with marvellously discriminating power in the Sonnet which begins : 'Shakespeare's old oak, gnarled and unwedgeable.' And of Mrs. Browning he spoke in terms almost affectionate. . . .

He spoke with admiration of Mrs. Augustus Craven, the charming Pauline de la Ferronnays, whom he had known, and whose memoir by Mrs. Bishop had just appeared. We talked of the great City of London, and Mr. de Vere reminded us of the Temple Church, which we had not yet seen, where the stone Crusaders lie in stately calm on the pavement, and the pale English sunlight is warmed into red and golden glories by the pictured windows above them. He told us of the tomb of his ancestors, the 'fighting Veres, in Westminster Abbey.' We bade adieu to the dear old man, who in a few hours had made so profound an impression upon us ; but we were happy enough to see him again, for the next day he came with some sprays of blooming lavender, which he presented with a quaint gallantry to my sister and to me, keeping one piece for his own buttonhole.

That night he dined with us, a stately figure in his velvet coat, and with that gentle courtesy of manner, which seems also to have passed away with much else that belonged to a former time.

We talked chiefly of his poetry, especially that wonderful

poem, 'The Higher Purgatory,' which was inspired by Saint Catharine of Genoa ; and of which Mr. de Vere, in a recent letter to me writes thus : ' My poem, " The Higher Purgatory," was an attempt to extend the benignant and consoling influence of St. Catharine of Genoa's great work on the " Holy Souls," one that seems to me to draw our departed ones nearer to us, and make the thought of them more soothing, and therefore more frequent.'

Our parting that night was to be the last, for we were leaving London the next day, and indeed in a few weeks would be returning to America, so that with the hope of meeting him again was mingled the fear that, at his great age, this hope was slight. Should we not see him again, ours is a lovely remembrance of the gentle poet, in his serene age, looking out on the world with undimmed vision, keeping the generous impulse of youth, joined to the certain wisdom of maturity, with a faith that in its entire simplicity is like the inexpressible faith of a child, pure, radiant, calm, a jewel kept inviolate by reverent hands.

As he stood at the door, for a final adieu, he turned his clear gaze on us, and said, ' When you go back to America write to me, and if I am not here when you return to England, pray for me.'

During the four years that yet remained to Aubrey de Vere, he preserved almost to the end a keenness and enthusiasm which are best attested by his letters. When he was tired his memory would sometimes fail him in conversation, but with pen in hand the old vigour returned. His thoughts still went constantly back to the beautiful Lake country, to Wordsworth, to Miss Fenwick, to Southey and the Coleridges.

The two following letters are to Miss Norton :—

Curragh Chase, Adare : March 3, 1897.

I think of you very often, my dear friend, and rejoice to be able to think of you now in conjunction with thoughts of Wordsworth's Land, and of that lovely region of which he was

the great Prophet and Priest, and which I have visited every
year, or almost every year, since his death.   How much I wish
that your brother had been with us that year, when we visited
it together.   It is rich to me in associations—including those
connected with my Father.

We have had a pleasant time of it here this year, and
indeed all the ten years since my widowed niece, Mrs.
Monsell, and her children, have made this house their home.
My elder brother, who lives himself in a cottage upon Foynes,
an island fifteen miles off in the Shannon, lent this house to her.
. . . They have enjoyed the beautiful scenery we have here,
and a good deal of exquisite poetry, which I have half read
and half recited, to them evening after evening ; and I have
enjoyed not less their music, their pleasant ways, and their
constant cheerfulness.   I hope you will some day make their
acquaintance.

Your brother wrote me such a beautiful letter a short
time ago, for which I was very grateful.

Curragh Chase, Adare : January 1898.

It was indeed most kind of you to send me that very
pretty and interesting Kalendar of the Year as marked by
the birds of America ; a present as pleasant as that of the
'very seasonable Kalendar designed to be used by manie
lovers of Master William Shakespeare,' of whom I need not
assure you that I am one of the most zealous and dutiful.
There is only one thing which I cannot forgive him, and that
is his dying at fifty-three, and passing the last three years of
his life without writing.

I must not forget to tell you that there is one of the birds
in that pretty Kalendar which I looked on with particular
pleasure.   It is there called 'The Blue Bird,' and is there
associated with the month of March.   Doubtless it is the
bird referred to by Tennyson in one of the loveliest poems of
'In Memoriam' as 'The sea-blue bird of March'; and in his
son's Memoirs of the Poet, the name of the bird is given.
I quite agree with you in your high praise of birds.   The
other animals are not to be compared with them.   If there
were no birds among us the earth would be a poorer thing,

and Heaven would be much farther off. One would hardly
think it a degradation to be changed into a nightingale or a
lark. The last of these things is what you call it, 'The truest
symbol of true Life.' Wordsworth and Shelley have each
written a poem on the lark; and, unlike as they are, each
stands among the highest poems of their respective Poets.

And now adieu, and God bless you both. May all the
blessings of this New Year be with you both.

How I wish we were to meet this year at Windermere,
and stand together beside Wordsworth's grave!

The appearance of Tennyson's Life revived many dear
memories, and there is something of the fire of earlier days
in the following letter to Mr. Gosse :—

Curragh Chase, Adare : March 14, 1898.

My dear Mr. Gosse,—Thank you very much for sending
me the 'North American Review' with your critique on the
Biography of Alfred Tennyson. (I always like to speak of
him with his two names, which, from old habit, sound to me
like a single one.) I have read it with great pleasure, both
from its ability and eloquence, and also because you have
spoken of the poet throughout with the full courage of your
opinions. There was a time when to 'damn with faint praise,
assent with civil leer,' was the most that he received from the
more influential critics, and was more than was given by
many of them to Wordsworth, Coleridge, Shelley, or Keats.

As well as I remember, Old Christopher North was the
first Editor (except Leigh Hunt) who plucked up heart of
grace and 'wrote all like a man,' and so forced the public at
last to read Wordsworth. He said so often and so loudly to
the world what St. Augustine had said to the Pagan world,
'So read the things that you may *deserve to understand them,*'
that at last a large part of that world did come to understand
that the greatest of the *philosophic* poets was even then
living in their midst. Alfred Tennyson's poetry came to be
understood very much earlier, because his College friends
had taken up his poetry with the generous passion of youth
and confessed boldly the Faith that was in them.

But even to our own time Alfred Tennyson has grown to
be better and better understood, and his son's brave book
about him will advance that good work ; for which cause I
rejoice in the additional impulse which will be given, especially
in America, by your criticism. Your article includes many
remarks of great value which I had not seen elsewhere, much
as has been written of him of late. Among these is the
paragraph about the 'Hidalgo of the Imagination.' Another,
of a very different sort, carries with it much practical significance, namely the passage in which you remark on the
amount of incomparable poetry which might have been lost
to the world, if Peel had not had courage to save A. T. from
worldly cares by a pension given him *before* his fame had
become at all an established matter.

I must not end without tendering you my best thanks for
the terms in which you spoke of my remarks on this great
poet in his Son's book. It will help to serve my poor
endeavour to aid a great poet's work to serve his country.
Wordsworth and Tennyson seem to me the only English
poets who have done more than half as much as it was
given to them to do in poetry. I am glad you praised the
correspondence between the Queen and the Poet. It is
admirable on both sides—so simple and dignified and sincere.

Believe me, dear Mr. Gosse,

Yours very sincerely,

AUBREY DE VERE.

On the death of Mrs. Forster, whom he had known in
early life as Miss Arnold, the aunt, and mother by adoption of Mrs. Robert Vere O'Brien, he writes thus to his
nephew :—

Curragh Chase : November 1, 1899.

I do not wish to write to Florence lest she should put
herself to the painful task of answering a letter on a subject so
distressing ; but I should like you to tell her, though indeed it
is hardly necessary, how truly I am grieved at the great trial
through which she is now passing.

It was before her Mother was married, and I think as

early as 1845, that I first became acquainted with her in that beautiful mountain land to which she always continued to be much devoted; and I shall never forget what a bright and beaming creature she then was. I have often seen her since then, though not so often as I should have wished to have done; for she was one but to look upon whom was to strengthen one's belief in all that is good and true—one whom we associate with worlds that are all goodness and peace. I cannot help associating her with Miss Fenwick, who used to speak of her with great tenderness, as well as of her Mother. I know what a loss this must be to both her daughters; and to Francie[1] that loss must be the more grievous because they were always together. Will you tell her, with my love, how deeply I sympathise with her in her sorrow? I hope I may soon hear that the health of both sisters holds up, and that Francie may soon be with you in Ireland.

Aubrey de Vere to Walter George Smith

Curragh Chase, Adare, Ireland : January 10, 1897 (My birthday).

Coleridge has a beautiful line in his translations of the 'Piccolomini,' viz: 'The fair humanities of Old Religion,' and among these 'humanities' we may surely place the 'Christmas Greetings,' which have survived so many kindly usages of the same sort that once were, and have now either died or (worse still) frozen into 'The compliments of the Season.' I was greatly pleased at receiving yours, and those of your sisters, and I did not think them at all *too late ;* for as several of the Church Festivals have their 'Octave' so the chief mysteries of the Faith carry a glory around their heads that sends their light in a wide circle, like the halo round the head of a pictured Saint; and so I send my 'Many Happy Xmasses' and 'Many Happy New Years' to you and yours. The great Child-Festival of the year, in which the Holy 'Innocents' have so justly their part, and in which our Lady's Month of May is often celebrated in defiance of the snows, is practically with us—still with us and fresh as ever, though the

---

[1] Miss Arnold Forster.

more secular feast of the New Year has already got a touch of Time's dirty fingers about its own.

In the middle ages, Christmas had its Boy-Bishop, who walked at the head of the Cathedral Procession, with a mitre on his head, and a Bishop's Staff in his hand, and in Rome, I dare say, you have seen a boy preaching on Christmas Day.

In 1898 he made his pilgrimage to the tombs of Words worth and Newman for the last time. Henceforth he did not leave Ireland. Mr. Walter Smith visited him at Curragh Chase in the autumn :—

Curragh Chase, Adare, Co. of Limerick : October 22, 1898.

My dear Walter Smith,—Your letter has been a great pleasure to me, and all the more so because it holds out a hope that we shall have a sight of you here, and when this much has been accomplished, I trust you will find it possible to make your visit one that counts not by hours, but by days.

My nephew, Major O'Brien, and his wife, with whom I am now on a visit here, desire me to tell you this from them, for they have now passed into possession here, which is a better arrangement than that this should take place after their old Uncles have passed away. You will find them most genial people, and it is most pleasant to see him, after fighting during many years for his country, now finishing many goodly works left unfinished by his Grandfather, while he is still young enough to enjoy such toils.

Pray let us hear from you how soon you will be able to come and see those old woods before their Autumn glories have waned from them. In the main they belong to the 'Forest Primeval' of Ireland. We always speak of them with respect, and never think of blaming them for having sheltered the wild hordes who marched out of their fastnesses among the Galtee Mountains one night, and burned one of the Desmond fortresses, which the 'gentle' English Poet, Edmund Spenser had selected for his residence. In that fire it is said that the Poet's infant child perished, and also the latter half of the 'Fairie Queen.' But the wild Irish objected

D D

that some 600,000 acres of Desmond property had been confiscated a short time before, and that in Queen Elizabeth's days such a residence could not have been a healthful residence for an Englishman, however poetical. My nephew desires me to tell you that there is a railway train from Limerick to Adare, which is but four miles from this place, and that he will send a waggonet to meet the Limerick train to Adare on your arrival there, if you let us know by what train you reach Adare.

Yours very sincerely,

AUBREY DE VERE.

To Walter George Smith

Curragh Chase, Adare, Co. of Limerick : March 1899.

I have spent a great part of this morning reading your letter, which it brought to me, and musing on one whom I have never seen, but whose image rose up before me with a vividness which made her seem like a memory. Your letter gives a portrait of your mother, which is deeply touching to me, for hers must have been of the same *type* of character as my mother's, and they must have died at nearly the same age. The printed account of her also is deeply interesting. Hers was evidently one of those lives which give the only real answer to that pathetic question, now so often asked, viz. 'Is life worth living?' I have endeavoured to answer it in one of my late sonnets, but it is best answered by that sort of answer, given by a brief biography. It has then often a completeness which comes in a great part from its brevity. Yesterday you had heard but the name, and to-day you have a total life before you, a life lived aright, and therefore not lived in vain. Her life has its unity, because it was evidently the life of Faith, and that Faith is now represented by her children, who will be remembered among those who helped to advance it over the huge new world, in the day of its difficulty and distress, when many despised it.

I read with great pleasure the paper in the ' Irish Monthly,' that paper in which I have so large a part, and had hoped to have written to thank [your sister] before now for the kindness which made her write it. Pray tell her so with kindest remembrances to her and her sisters. You must bring them all three over here again soon, that I may show them these old woods of ours in their best season, and make them all hear my Æolian Harp, and read them my favourites among Coleridge's Poems.

To Miss Arnold Forster

Curragh Chase, Adare, Ireland : 1900 : St. Patrick's Feast.

The days have gone by, and each day I expected to write to you in order to tell you how grateful to you I have been for the very great enjoyment I have derived from your beautiful book, ' Studies in Church Dedications ;' but each day the writing was suspended by additional reading, or by reading again what I had read before, perhaps more than once—such as your account of the death of St. Columba. It was chiefly my reading that stood in the way of my writing ; and now that I have come to the writing, I find that a very few words will suffice as well as a much [longer letter] to tell you what I most wished to say, viz. that I think you have written a book of great spiritual value, and one for which your country will thank you the more heartily in proportion as her heart grows larger and wiser. All those years which were spent upon that labour of love must have been very happy years, notwithstanding the severity of the task imposed upon you by the labour of love.

Yesterday evening as I read the 'Conclusion' (vol. ii.) I could not help thinking that when you have had a good long rest, it may be your happy lot yourself to supply the biographies you speak of as omitted, such as the Fathers of the Desert . . . and some of Irish Missionaries on the Continent. In one respect there is nothing like Ecclesiastical History for impressing the consecrated imagination at once with the idea of sanctity and of the multitudinous. The Saints often seem to throng, as the angel-hosts do. So of course do the sinners. But if history told us only of the sinner hosts, and if there were no counter Ecclesiastical history to tell us of the saintly multitudes also, we should

D D 2

have to fly from history, so dreadful would the spectacle often become to us. Perhaps there may have been times and races, when among Christians, the majority may have belonged to the saintly type, however bad the exceptions may have proved. No doubt there were sad inconsistencies even in the holiest periods and places ; but the passionate admiration which once existed for Saints (such as still exists for genius) seems to show that there was a time when the human heart was 'in the right place,' and when man's sympathies were swayed by a heavenly gravitation, more than by an earthly one ; and the degree in which your book makes us feel that great truth as well as admit it, is to me a great part of its charm.

I hope you will be in this house while I am here that I may have an opportunity of pointing out to you at least a few of the many passages in your book which I have marked with pencil crosses, that we may discuss at least some of the numerous inferences which they suggested to me or may yet suggest as I read. Not a few of these are in the chapters which relate to our three chief Irish Patron Saints, St. Patrick, St. Bridget and St. Columba. It was a great pleasure to me to find that, in dealing with those three great Gaelic Saints, you had had quite a special success. All three of them had moved the sympathies of the English people in a pre-eminent degree, perhaps owing in a large part to the degree in which diversities of character, as well as resemblances, often move common sympathies between races—a sign, let us hope, that one day there may exist a bond of union between the two countries as strong as the antagonism which has too long existed. They may one day pledge their healths mutually one to the other at the Holy Well of Patterdale, as they doubtless did at many a Holy Well in both the Islands of old : and build with the common labour a church in many a spot to which . . . as we learn from your book they may assign the name of 'Pardon,' as so many names such as 'Grace' and 'Charity' were also assigned, until the Land itself had put on the aspect of an illuminated missal.

The post will be so soon going out, that I must not put

off till another day sending on this letter. Your book has innumerable merits besides the few I have named, if I had time to name them, but one of these seems to me its style, which is thoroughly good, and especially suited to its matter. I am so glad that she who probably watched the progress of your noble enterprise with an interest which only a mother can feel, lived to see its completion. It must have been, I think, the greatest gratification of her later life, as the loss which her departure occasioned you was probably the greatest sorrow which you have known. I rejoice to have seen her again that last time. . . .

To Miss Helen Smith

Curragh Chase, Adare, Ireland : September 25, 1900.

I am very grateful to you for the letter which you wrote to me on the 29th of August last, from Waterhead Hotel, Ambleside, the same day that you had knelt at the grave of Wordsworth and said a ' De Profundis ' for him, though not the first time that you had done both these things. I should have known where you had written, if only from the pictured hotel paper on which you had written ; and this is not an inappropriate day for me to answer your letter, for last night when some friends who have been staying here for some time, and have just now left us, had asked me to read them some poetry before they bade us adieu, I read them Wordsworth's ' Yarrow ' Poems among others, and ended with his great ode, the greatest of modern times, that of ' Intimations of Immortality from Recollections, &c.' I hope you will take many an opportunity of reading both that 'ode and his ' Laodamia.' They seem to me his two grandest poems, and whenever I have responded to the same challenge, I read the same poems aloud. I shall again hope that we have been in sympathy, and that you too have read those two wonderful poems to listeners worthy of them.

Most heartily do I congratulate you on having been travelling lately in Egypt, the Holy Land, and Greece. I, on the contrary, have not been able to make my usual pilgrimage, either to Grasmere or to Windermere. This was, in part, because I did not feel strong enough to pay them my usual visit.

Thank you for giving a thought to me when you were passing the Irish coast. I wish we could have met you again in England once more, or in Ireland, as I had the good fortune to meet others of your family in our Irish home.

This, alas, was not to be, but you say most truly that we must hope that we shall meet once more *somewhere* on Earth, and if not, then at least, later in Heaven. In the meantime, we are constantly reminded how unlike to Heaven is this earth with all its sad ways. Only this morning, a letter from South Africa from A. B., has brought us the sad news that he has just lost one finger of his left hand, in a battle with the Boers.

It was a happy coincidence that in this, the last year but one of his life, when Aubrey could no longer pay his visit to the land of Wordsworth, a book was sent to him, written by one who was almost his own contemporary, and dealing with the very scenes and persons that were so dear to him. Mr. Ellis Yarnall's work on 'Wordsworth and the Coleridges' is referred to with delight in most of Aubrey's letters of the year 1900.

He writes thus to its author :—

April 25, 1900.

Dear Mr. Ellis Yarnall,—My good friend Walter George Smith did me no small office of friendship when he made me a present of a most interesting book of yours which gave me many days of delightful reading. I read as slowly as I could, for I was in no hurry to get to the end of it ; for it was like associating once more in pleasant familiarity with many of those who had added a greater brightness to what, in any case, must have been the brightest days of my life. It is true that the greatest of all the great men named in your book— S. T. C.—I never had the good fortune to meet, but his daughter Sara Coleridge was one of my chief friends, as well as one of the most wonderful women I have ever known ; and her brothers I knew well. But, if I never met Coleridge,

I saw a great deal of Wordsworth, whom I have always regarded as the chief poet of modern days; though I did not dispute the truth of his statement, when standing beside him, close to his own lake of Rydal, I heard him say : 'If Coleridge had but gone on writing poetry for ten years more' (practically he ceased to do so at twenty six) 'he must have become the chief of all the modern poets.'

I remember well the friendly expressions which you used respecting me, in the letter to which you refer in connection with Sara Coleridge, by which I was much gratified. She was certainly the most wonderful woman I have ever known, but it was not to her intellectual faculties, chiefly, that the term 'wonderful' would ever have been applied, so much more wonderful would her moral and spiritual being have appeared by comparison. It was extraordinary how much of her Father there must have been in her. One cannot help thinking that if their two lives had been more closely drawn together, so that she had been able to have lived with him in entire sympathy, as well as affection, he might have been able to accomplish that great work in its fulness which was the great object of his desire.

The moment I had read what you had written about W. E. Forster I wrote to some of his relatives, telling them what ample justice you had done to him ; but they had doubtless learned this before, and derived from it a very real gratification.

I have lately been reading again that beautiful book on English Literature by Professor Reed, which was so much appreciated by Wordsworth, and the influence of which in America must have enabled Wordsworth's poetry to do so great a work in the way of *spiritualising* the American as well as the English mind. That was more and more Wordsworth's end in writing. I remember his once saying to me, 'When I was young I thought much of being remembered ; now that I am old and must soon embark upon the great Ocean of Eternity I do not ask how many are those who stand upon the shore ; and can still keep my little pinnace in sight. My hope is only that so long as my poetry *is* read, its moral influence may prove a salutary one.' . . .

Messrs. Macmillan published a new edition of my poetry in six volumes a short time ago. I should like to send you a copy of some among them, or among my essays if you have not got them already : perhaps you would let me know as to this : though at my age one does not expect either one's verse or prose to be much read either in America or England.

Believe me, yours very sincerely,

AUBREY DE VERE.

The last letter I have from him is one to a niece, dated Christmas Day 1901—less than a month before his death. A few repetitions (which I have omitted) betray failing memory, but the drift is clear :—

I owe you both so much for all you have been to my dear brother during his long and severe illness. I am most truly obliged to you for the two portraits [of yourselves], which will always be so precious to me during whatever period, long or short, I have yet to live. . . .

God bless you both, and give you both cause to rejoice in the good which you are ever doing for others, and do come here, to this old place, as soon as you can. . . .

Many happy Christmases to you all, and especially to Stephen.

The end may be told in a few words. He was in his usual health up to January 12, 1902, two days after his eighty-eighth birthday. On that day he went to Mass at Adare in an open carriage. He caught a chill, and became seriously ill on Tuesday the 14th. Even in his wanderings he was constantly praying for his friends, 'holy and saint like,' writes his niece, Mrs. de Vere, 'in his death as in his life.' Mrs. de Vere's stepmother, Mrs. George Wynne, was near him constantly. His old friend Dean Flanagan came from Adare to see him, and Father Fitzgerald gave him the last sacraments, and was often with him to the end. He remained unconscious, hovering between life and death for a few days. On the bookshelves around him stood the works of his favourite poets, the books on theology which had been there ever since his father had given them to him as a boy and future clergyman, the books which he had added when the Catholic religion became his absorbing interest in middle life—such as Abbé Ratisbonne's 'St. Bernard' and the 'Lives of the Irish Saints.' From the walls looked down on him the pictures of his 'master,' Samuel Taylor Coleridge, of old friends who had preceded him into the Spirit-world—James Spedding, Alfred Tennyson, Stephen Spring Rice—and of his own mother.

On the 21st at 7.30 in the morning, and quite peacefully at last, his gentle spirit made that passage of which he had so often spoken and written—from the land of Dreams to the land of Realities.

> Who mourns ?   Flow on, delicious breeze !
>   Who mourns though youth and strength go by?
> Fresh leaves invest the vernal trees,
>   Fresh airs will drown my latest sigh :
> This frame is but a part outworn
>   Of earth's great whole, that lifts more high
> A tempest-freshened brow each morn
>   To meet pure beams and azure sky.
>
> Thou world-renewing breath, sweep on,
>   And waft earth's sweetness o'er the wave !
> That earth will circle round the sun
>   When God takes back the life He gave !
> To each his turn !   Even now I feel
>   The feet of children press my grave,
> And one deep whisper o'er it steal—
>   'The soul is His Who died to save.' [1]

[1] 'A Song of Age.'   Aubrey de Vere's *Poetical Works*, vol. iii. 382. Kegan Paul, 1884.

APPENDIX

AUBREY DE VERE'S PHILOSOPHY OF FAITH

FROM two letters to Sara Coleridge written in 1850, and afterwards expanded and published as Essays, I make (in conclusion) some extracts as completing the outline of the philosophy of faith which de Vere elaborated at this time. In them he attempts further to explain his view of the Church, not as offering an alternative position on disputed points of theology, but as preserving for her members the normal means of practical certainty as to the reality of the supernatural world—even as to Theism itself—supplementing and fixing the spiritual intuitions of the individual, by the revelation of Christ and the meditations of the Saints, which form the collective wisdom of Christianity, stored within the living and abiding Church. Religion like science has (he maintains) its own *organum investigandi* ; and it is found in the participation of the individual by faith in this collective wisdom of the Church :—

A method (he writes) that belongs to one department of thought will not answer for another. Experiment will not suffice where syllogisms are required nor deduction only where induction is needed.

Intuitions will teach us nothing in political economy, though much in mathematics. The fine arts have a method of a more imaginative order. Theology, or the science of supernatural and revealed truths, must likewise possess a method of its own. . . .

Ascertain whether, if in scientific matters our liberty of thought is not interfered with by the impossibility of contesting primary axioms, and could receive no vindication from our throwing off the yoke of the multiplication table, the sphere of supernatural truth may not include a provision through which we can exercise religious faith, and attain a certain knowledge, not only without abdicating our faculties, but as the only means of really using them? As there are acts which we can only do individually, so there are others which we can only do collectively, and in our national capacity. May there not be truths also, which we can discover separately and, yet again, other realms of truth which the human race can only conquer and retain through that collective unity which is called the Church.

Latitudinarianism is practically the comment which time passes on the experiment of private judgment. . . .

Nevertheless the individual mind has its important functions in developing and correcting the collective mind :—

Thomas Aquinas was confessedly a thinker as well as Luther or Calvin, but the *method* which he pursued gave him as data the authentic and authoritative conclusions of the whole Christian world up to his time, and imparted to him thus, beside his own mind, another mind as large as that of Christendom. The supplemental use of this larger mind no more involved the suppression of the individual mind, than the use of the telescope involves the loss of one's eyesight.

This brings us to a yet more momentous consideration. The belief in this collective mind of Christendom, which supersedes, not individual intellectual exertion but private judgment—that is, merely *isolated* exertion—was no theory invented in later times for the guidance of theological inquirers, but was involved in the very idea of the Christian Church.

And while faith in the corporate growing Church thus involves the acceptance of the collective wisdom of many and of the most gifted seers, private judgment must fail, because one ordinary Christian cannot possibly be equal to doing the work of generations of Saints and thinkers. ' Private judgment, therefore ' (he writes) ' bequeaths less than it inherited, and its patrimony daily wastes like the prodigal's.'

And further, it is only the keen edge given by faith, as distinct from private judgment which can maintain that attitude of mind which marks off keen devotional assent of religion from the balancing and wavering attitude of the mere philosopher :—

The clear-sighted see plainly enough, that the question at stake is, not contending versions of Christianity, or even Christianity itself, but Religion, as distinguished from philosophy, and Theism itself as a *Religion*.

The isolated private judgment, in proportion as it really energises dwarfs religion or renders it uncertain :—

It reduces the Church to the littleness of the individual, instead of imparting to the individual the stature and the faith of the whole mystic body. . . . Once more, even though reason were indeed infallible, the isolated individual must be capable of misusing it ; as when a man makes some fatal mistake in casting up a sum in arithmetic. In taking self alone as a ground of spiritual knowledge, and as our sole guide to God, man, as it were, creates his own creator. The higher we soar the more we need humility. For this reason the intuitions of faith are allowed to remain obscure on earth, though certain ; and docility, as well as spiritual discernment, belongs to Faith.

The principle of private judgment intercepts, by the interposition of a fallible medium, the direct communication between God and the spiritual mind of man. . . . The rule of private judgment divests faith likewise of its vitality, and its power, by chilling the ardour of strong minds. In such minds the freezing sense of insecurity produced by the impossibility of discriminating between faith and imaginative illusions, will reduce the religious sentiment to a low and sordid tone, mistaken for the 'golden mean.' Enthusiasm will, in such circumstances, commonly be the attribute only of the light and injudicious ; and as such it will do as much harm as good, for in religion, as in all things, no substitute can be found for good sense. A community which cannot eliminate doubt from its theological creed has its vulnerable point, and feels it. Heroic virtue it half fears as a peril or a temptation. It has admitted the formula of nature into the region of supernatural truth, and substituted 'Per-adventure' for 'Amen.' It becomes at once reduced and trans-posed ; and its very truths lose their substance while they retain their name.

In point of fact, there is of course much true religion, much that is more than mere philosophy, outside the Church, but this is because, while professing 'private judgment,' many in all communions are really acting on the principle of faith :—

So far from the religion of those who belong to Bodies that affirm private judgment having been really based on that principle, it has practically been based on that of authority, so far as it has been a life and not a battle-cry, though of a most imperfect authority. In all the sects the successive generations have followed more the tradition of their forefathers, and the authority of their ministers than any real conclusions of their own minds, on Divine matters beyond the reach of men without learning. 'Private Judgment' remains, indeed, answerable for many of the heart-burnings, sometimes denounced under the name of 'The Plague of Controversy;' but in the sects themselves the more beneficent influences of Religion worked up unperceived from the ground of authority. The more respectable sects retained the Primary Creeds which expressed the Authoritative Judgment of the Church.

Through realisation of the heights ascended by faith, we distinguish docility from credulity, and identify rationalism with narrow self-sufficiency :—

Docility is an initiative form of Divine Faith. Through it we come to Christ as little children ; and in the Christian, the child lives ever on in the man. The Martyrs did not lack spiritual discernment ; yet none were more remarkable for docility and the spirit of submission. It was Arius, and the other heretics, who ridiculed their humility as superstition.

The will as well as the mind is the seat of faith. To the latter discernment belongs, to the former submission ; accordingly that only is heresy which includes by act or omission the sin of the will : and conversely a belief that does not include the submission of the will is unprofitable, even when it chances to be sound. The authority of the Church is the organ through which Divine Grace, shed abroad in the heart, trains man in the habit of submission. Obedience is not a principle merely, to be learned by precept, but a habit to be taught by providential circumstance and Divine institutions. It is thus that our moral being, in its own inferior sphere, is shaped and moulded not by precept only, but by circumstance, such as the claims of the civil power, parental rule, social traditions, the weakness of childhood, the limitations of knowledge, the need of joint action, and therefore of subordination.

The knowledge which comes from on high includes properties distinct from those that address the intelligence, as light possesses other qualities, chemical, magnetic, and vital, beside those that address the eyes. Such knowledge is therefore capable of constituting an instrument of living communication between the Creator and the creature. . . . It elevates and exercises all the virtues. Coming from the heights, it sounds the depths, and therefore presupposes submission, not assertion, in the act of recipiency. It carries God with it in every ray. He it is who exists in those beams, and in each of them, sacramented in light. This is the knowledge capable of expanding into the Beatific Vision as the optic nerve into the retina of the eye. Such is the reward reserved for faith, and the obedience included in faith.

Opinion, on the other hand, has no such latent property; for nature, when unaided, or when, for the aids God has given, the aids man has chosen have been substituted, includes no principle through which man is capable of conversing with spiritual realities. Its 'little systems have their day,' and amuse us while here below ; but they cease where mere human forms of perception cease. The world has played with them till it is tired of its plaything ; it is now sick of their petty restraints and peevish inconstancy. It suspects the existence of a world mightier than itself, deeper, loftier, more lasting—the supernatural world.

The place for private judgment, or merely human faith, is man's total world, except that one spot which is too sacred for it, and where Heaven meets Earth. . . . Are we robbed of our own because one spot is kept inviolate for the descending feet of those Powers from above who visit our earthly life ?

In the passages just cited the neophyte pursued a definite line of thought, which is as interesting now as when he worked it out. So far as he confined himself to the realisation in Rome, of Coleridge's idea of a Catholic Church, as the guardian of faith in the unseen, in contrast with the wavering private judgment of the individual, he was on strong ground. But a good deal more was mixed up with his treatment which has less interest and permanent value. That a Christian's faith in the unseen world involves an attitude of humble docility, the individual yielding himself to the guidance of the Divine revelation and of the spiritual intuitions of Christ and the saints which are embodied in a Church, acquiring a confidence and edge from this share in the higher wisdom which ratifies, fixes, and develops the weaker individual perceptions, humble trust thus passing into an insight and strength which are denied to self-sufficiency,—this was a thought of great power and significance. But the further questions which such friends as R. H. Hutton, and James Spedding raised, and which occupy many of us now, did not fully take their place in Aubrey's mind—namely, how to combine this attitude of faith, which gives triumphant certainty as to Christianity as a whole, with such exercises of criticism in detail as are needed to eliminate superstition or mere credulity. The Church, it is true, had preserved as in one continuous organism the revelation of Christ, and the Christian *ethos* of the Saints. Protestant individualism had dissipated this inheritance, and was the loser. But the conservative tradition in Catholicism which had brought this about had inevitably preserved tares as well as wheat. And Aubrey often writes as though the attitude of docile receptivity he advocates should involve the uncritical reception of all that has been handed down. Although, however, he was so urgent as to the primary thought which filled him, and which was little understood at that time, that he gave comparatively little attention to this important question of the correction of inherited traditions and speculations which sometimes blended contemporary superstition and passing intellectual fashions with spiritual truth, he admits in general terms, as we have seen, the function of the individual reason in correcting and supplementing the reason of the Christendom of the past; and we have seen that his sympathies were enlisted by the Biblical critics who some years later took up the work of Richard Simon in the Catholic Church.

His mind was too open for it to be otherwise ; but nevertheless he dreaded precipitation, and his sense was so strong that the chief danger of the time was a loss of a real appreciation of Christian Ideals, that in any temporary conflict between the immediate interests of living Christian faith as a whole, and the immediate interests of scientific criticism, his sympathies were overwhelmingly on the side of the former. In this respect he resembled his later master Cardinal Newman ; but he had less appreciation, I think, than the Cardinal of the urgency of the Biblical problem. He was less alive to the necessity of a recognised school of Christian Biblical criticism which should command the respect at once of Catholic thinkers, and of fair-minded experts in all communions, for the safeguarding in the long run, of faith itself in minds more critical and less ideally spiritual than his own.

INDEX

PRINTED BY
SPOTTISWOODE AND CO. LTD., NEW-STREET SQUARE
LONDON

THE LIFE AND TIMES

OF

CARDINAL WISEMAN

BY

WILFRID WARD,

AUTHOR OF 'WILLIAM GEORGE WARD AND THE OXFORD MOVEMENT,'
'WILLIAM GEORGE WARD AND THE CATHOLIC REVIVAL,'
'PROBLEMS AND PERSONS,' ETC.

GUARDIAN.—'All that Mr. Wilfrid Ward touches turns into gold. . . . The book never loses its interest or its grace. It carries the reader on from movement to movement, and controversy to controversy, with unfailing vigour and dash. . . . Mr. Ward has thought his subject out as well as written about it. His book is stamped with the individuality of its author, and bears the impress of his gifted mind on every page.'

ACADEMY.—'These ample volumes are rich in humour and in the charming accidents of humanity, rich in valuable historic retrospect, filled with good matter, and written with an excellent art.'

SIR M. E. GRANT DUFF, in the *BANFFSHIRE JOURNAL.*—'Mr. Wilfrid Ward is surpassed by no one amongst Catholics whose language is English in philosophical, literary, and historical power. . . . If he wrote in French he would not be considered at all presumptuous if he hoped for an early place amongst the Forty of the *Académie Française.*'

PALL MALL GAZETTE.—'As to the general merits of Mr. Ward's work there cannot be more than one opinion. . . . It is admirably written, for the most part, in a clear intelligible style. . . . He has, too, an impartial pen. . . . Moreover, Mr. Ward has a saving sense of humour. . . . He both appreciates and tells a good story admirably.'

DAILY CHRONICLE.—'Mr. Ward's work is a monument of judicial fairness. . . . There are features in the present biography that guarantee its permanent value as a contribution to the ecclesiastical history of our age. Briefly, it is the work of a scholar and a gentleman; its style is easy and readable; and there are evidences throughout of careful study and accurate statement. . . . Mr. Ward is to be congratulated on an admirable piece of work, and we cannot wish him better than that he should continue his labours in the same field.'

TABLET.—'We can best sum up our impressions of this long-expected book by putting on record our deliberate and confident belief that it will some day take its place among the classical biographies of the language. But, as its title suggests, it is much more than a simple biography. Mr. Ward has been at great pains to get the atmosphere and proper perspective of his picture, and to enable his readers to understand the moral and social and intellectual conditions under which the work of the great Cardinal was done.'

LONGMANS, GREEN, AND CO.,
London, New York, and Bombay.